# SYSTEM STRUCTURE IN DATA, PROGRAMS, AND COMPUTERS

**Prentice-Hall**
**Series in Automatic Computation**
***George Forsythe, editor***

ARBIB, *Theories of Abstract Automata*
BATES AND DOUGLAS, *Programming Language/One*
BAUMANN, FELICIANO, BAUER, AND SAMELSON, *Introduction to ALGOL*
BLUMENTHAL, *Management Information Systems*
BOBROW AND SCHWARTZ, *editors, Computers and the Policy-Making Community: Applications to International Relations*
BOWLES, *editor, Computers in Humanistic Research*
CESCHINO AND KUNTZMANN, *Numerical Solution of Initial Value Problems*
CRESS, DIRKSEN, AND GRAHAM, *FORTRAN IV with WATFOR*
DANIEL, *Theory and Methods for the Approximate Minimization of Functionals*
DESMONDE, *Computers and Their Uses*
EVANS, WALLACE, AND SUTHERLAND, *Simulation Using Digital Computers*
FIKE, *Computer Evaluation of Mathematical Functions*
FIKE, *PL/1 for Scientific Programmers*
FORSYTHE AND MOLER, *Computer Solution of Linear Algebraic Systems*
GAUTHIER AND PONTO, *Designing Systems Programs*
GOLDEN, *FORTRAN IV: Programming and Computing*
GOLDEN AND LEICHUS, *IBM 360: Programing and Computing*
GORDON, *System Simulation*
GREENSPAN, *Lectures on the Numerical Solution of Linear, Singular and Nonlinear Differential Equations*
GRISWOLD, POAGE, AND POLONSKY, *The SNOBOL4 Programming Language*
HARTMANIS AND STEARNS, *Algebraic Structure Theory of Sequential Machines*
HULL, *Introduction to Computing*
HUSSON, *Microprogramming: Principles and Practices*
JOHNSON, *System Structure in Data, Programs, and Computers*
KIVIAT, VILLANUEVA, AND MARKOWITZ, *The SIMSCRIPT II Programming Language*
LOUDEN, *Programming the IBM 1130 and 1800*
MARTIN, *Design of Real-Time Computer Systems*
MARTIN, *Programming Real-Time Computer Systems*
MARTIN, *Telecommunications and the Computer*
MARTIN, *Teleprocessing Network Organization*
MARTIN AND NORMAN, *The Computerized Society*
MATHISON AND WALKER, *Computers and Telecommunications: Issues in Public Policy*
MCKEEMAN, ET AL., *A Compiler Generator*
MINSKY, *Computation: Finite and Infinite Machines*
MOORE, *Interval Analysis*
PYLYSHYN, *Perspectives on the Computer Revolution*
PRISKER AND KIVIAT, *Simulation with GASP II: A FORTRAN Based Simulation Language*
SAMMET, *Programming Languages: History and Fundamentals*
SNYDER, *Chebyshev Methods in Numerical Approximation*
STERLING AND POLLACK, *Introduction to Statistical Data Processing*
STROUD AND SECREST, *Gaussian Quadrature Formulas*
TAVISS, *The Computer Impact*
TRAUB, *Iterative Methods for the Solution of Equations*
VARGA, *Matrix Iterative Analysis*
VAZSONYI, *Problem Solving by Digital Computers with PL/1 Programming*
WILKINSON, *Rounding Errors in Algebraic Processes*

# SYSTEM STRUCTURE IN DATA, PROGRAMS, AND COMPUTERS

Lyle R. Johnson

*IBM World Trade Corporation*
*Management Science Services Staff*

Prentice-Hall, Inc.

*Englewood Cliffs, New Jersey*

Current printing (last digit):
10 9 8 7 6 5 4 3 2 1

13-880336-6
Library of Congress Catalog Card No. 75-109107

Printed in the United States of America

PRENTICE-HALL INTERNATIONAL, INC., *London*
PRENTICE-HALL OF AUSTRALIA, PTY. LTD., *Sydney*
PRENTICE-HALL OF CANADA, LTD., *Toronto*
PRENTICE-HALL OF INDIA PRIVATE LIMITED., *New Delhi*
PRENTICE-HALL OF JAPAN, INC., *Tokyo*

*To my parents*

# PREFACE

*Data system* is used here to designate the artifact that consists of a digital computer, a control program, and an accessible library of programs and data. Such a system is at the intersection of many technical ideas. Taken one by one, these ideas are not especially elusive; the more challenging problem is to see how they fit together. My goal in this book is to provide a compact introduction to data system technology for the reader who is at least as interested in a coherent perspective as in the ideas themselves.

In twenty years, we have seen an evolution from the digital computer to the computer system to the combined hardware and software system to the data system. The undergraduate curriculum for computer science now includes intermediate courses in data structures, programming languages, computer organization, systems programming, and switching theory. The details of computers and data processing are groomed in a vast literature. As a result of these developments, it has become increasingly difficult for one to maintain a rounded appreciation of the system as a whole. Most professionals in the computer industry follow specialized vocations that lead them away from systematic consideration of the data system as a whole; few have time to enjoy the benefits of a curriculum approach. In addressing my book to interested members of this audience, I have aimed at crispness in style and frugality in detail.

The book may also be useful as collateral reading for courses in computer science, engineering, or programming. Under the instructor's guidance, a system overview can stimulate discussion, encourage generalization, testify to the breadth of systems technology, and demonstrate that technology has consequences.

In view of the objectives of the book, little use is made of mathematics and even the occasional uses do not go beyond simple algebraic equations. Needless to say, since the field of computers and data processing has borrowed many of its words and usages (e.g., the use of symbols) from mathematics, semblances of mathematics must appear rather frequently. For the sake of brevity, the history of data systems is not treated systematically. However, two overtures are made to history. First, whenever illustrative detail is introduced for the sake of concreteness, an attempt is made to place the detail in historical perspective. At several junctures, I have quoted at length from sources of historical interest. Second, a bibliography of about 240 references is chronologically organized in the Appendix. This bibliography has two purpooses, the obvious one being to cite explicit references in full and the other being to give a rough indication of the order in which ideas have emerged. To serve the latter purpose, which I personally regard as decisive for anyone who is trying to grasp the outlines of a technology, I have listed more references than I have cited in the text. For the most part, it is the original or early mention of an idea, not subsequent embellishment, that is emphasized. Inasmuch as the list is a workaday tool developed to meet practical needs in technical editing and technology monitoring, concessions are made to convenience and articles in well-known journals take preference over documents involving other sources.

The design of a data system involves trade-offs among things as diverse as computers, programs, data organizations, and languages. In trying to envision a book-length treatment that would highlight relationships, my thought was to start with a few unencumbered abstractions, subordinate system detail, examine simple cases, and go on to synthesize with the aid of the abstractions. The most useful starting point I have been able to find is the tree diagram, a construct familiar in the data-system literature as an aid to exposition. Also, at a great distance from informal usage, the tree has a niche in mathematics as a special case of a formal graph. Since neither usage has dealt seriously with the problem of classifying data aggregates, the tree diagram is introduced in Chapter 1 in a form that can easily be used to illuminate the organization of data as well as of languages, programs, and computers.

If the conventional notion of a library is generalized to include procedures, one comes to see the data system as an energized library. This viewpoint dispenses with the awkward distinction between numerical and nonnumerical processing, dramatizes the rudimentary character of the contemporary data system, and brings the technologies of searching, resource-allocating, and task-sequencing activities to the fore. It is the speed of the data system as a calculator that tends to impress the casual observer, but one needs some grasp of technology to appreciate why a data system can be relatively slow in responding to a search-invoking query. Typically, one needs an even surer grasp of technology to rationalize the response times of a given system for two different queries (or two systems for a given query).

Convinced of the importance of search, I felt obligated to explain the antecedent of search, viz., data organization. However, the more I looked at data organization, the more I was troubled by the problem of explaining that a data aggregate represents two entirely different kinds of information: first, the data themselves and, second, the organization of the aggregate. Before

I was through, I found it necessary to devote four chapters to search: structure in data (Chapter 2), structure representation (Chapter 3), table searching (Chapter 4) and table sorting (Chapter 5). By contrast with the relatively familiar topics that appear later in the book, the material covered in these four chapters will seem alien to many readers. In large part, this is symptomatic of the state of the art. The traditional exposure to computer engineering or programming has always been content with incomplete empirical treatments of data organization. In the iceberg of data-sytem technology, one might say, data organization was long suppressed below the water line. Although this tradition will not suffice in an examination of the iceberg itself, some readers may want to cover Chapters 6–11 before they turn to the rather abstract, analytical treatment that I found necessary to encompass the subjects of Chapters 2–5.

To enumerate systematically, Chapter 1 defines *structure* in terms of an abstract tree diagram; Chapter 2 employs this definition of structure in classifying data aggregates; Chapter 3 treats methods of representing structure; and Chapters 4 and 5 discuss methods of searching and sorting tables in the context of structure. Chapter 6 introduces the notion of a program and discusses program structure. Chapter 7, which treats of task mechanization, is a conventional "building-block" discussion of the digital computer. By the end of Chapter 7, the groundwork has been laid for discussion of the three functions that dictate much of the complexity of data systems: task sequencing (Chapter 8), program translation (Chapter 9), and table management (Chapter 10). Chapter 11 is a summary that outlines the salient properties of one contemporary data system and discusses technological trade-offs that bear upon the design of a system.

A nuisance for anyone who attempts a unified treatment of the data system, surely, is that the words one would like to use have already acquired restrictive technical meanings. In fact, a given word may have acquired several different meanings at various times and in various contexts. For example, engineers and programmers may use the same word with different connotations. On the other hand, one may find three or four different terms being used for the same concept. Ultimately the author must make decisions—and some of his decisions are likely to seem atrocious to at least some readers. In general, my objective is economy in word counts and lengths, the sort of rule a business analyst invokes in flipchart presentations to executives. I have introduced new terms in a few instances where the needs seem greatest. In an attempt to avoid haggling over words in mainstream discussions, I have elected to indicate the sources of terminology in the commentaries at chapter endings.

I am grateful to Mr. A.D. Falkoff and Mr. J.H. Pomerene for comments at an early stage of manuscript development and to Dr. H.M. Gladney, Dr. R.A. Myers, and Mr. J.L. Lawrence for remarks at a relatively late stage. I am also indebted to my wife; her questions induced me to clarify many passages. Finally, I wish to express my appreciation to the IBM Corporation for the services of its Research Library, for secretarial help in the iterative preparation of the manuscript, and in particular to Mr. J.C. Logue for the timely encouragement and support needed to bring the project to fruition.

Lyle R. Johnson

Thornwood, New York

# CONTENTS

# SYSTEM STRUCTURE IN DATA, PROGRAMS, AND COMPUTERS

*Chapter 1*

# THE TREE DIAGRAM

Let a complex that consists of a library of stored data and programs, a digital computer, and a control program be termed a *data system.* Such systems play an increasingly important role in satisfying the data processing requirements of modern societies. The data system is a technical artifact, which is to say that nontechnical definitions do not go far towards explaining the system or bringing the properties and functions of the system into perspective. Before one can comprehend and appreciate the data system, one needs to assimilate the central ideas that have gone into the development of data systems. As it happens, these ideas do not fall neatly into traditional categories; one can be sure that one or more technologies are emerging, but one should not rely heavily on their putative jurisdictions.

This book is an introduction to data system technology. One practical objective of the book is brevity. To this end, the emphasis is on basic principles. The line between hardware and software is lightly drawn, and specialized terminologies are either pruned or subordinated to concepts derived from consideration of abstract structure. Moreover, the chapter organization eschews the luxuries of a tour through diverse related disciplines; instead, it immediately plunges the reader into the bare abstractions of the tree diagram. These abstractions are gradually fleshed out and supplemented in subsequent chapters; the whole presentation builds toward a concrete example of the data system in the concluding chapter. The reader who is more interested in data systems than in data system technology may want to start by scanning some of the latter chapters for data system color.

Since a data system is a general-purpose tool for data processing, it is fruitless to attempt a catalog of all possible applications. It is possible to classify data structures, on the other hand, and such a classification serves two purposes: it (1) provides a framework for classifying applications and (2) leads to rationales for many of the functions now provided by control programs and programming languages. Chapters 2–5 place a heavy emphasis on data organization. Chapters 6–11, which are more concerned with processing, go on to motivate the kinds of complex operations now provided by digital computers and control programs.

It could be misleading to attempt an examination of data system technology without founding the discussion on a reasonably general definition of structure. The purpose of this initial chapter is to lend utility to the term *structure* by defining it explicitly. To this end, the notion of a tree diagram is formalized, four important classes of tree diagrams are characterized, and methods of identifying vertices are discussed.

## 1.1 Introductory Definitions

The construction of Fig. 1.1 is an example of a *tree diagram.* A vertex in a tree diagram is referred to as a *point*. The number of points in a tree diagram is the *moment* of the diagram. The tree diagram of Fig. 1.1 is of moment 20.

An arrow that connects two tree-diagram points is called an *arc*. The number of arrowheads incident to a point must equal either 0 or 1. A point with no incoming arc is a *root point*. The number of its root points is the *radix* of a tree diagram. The diagram in Fig. 1.1 is of radix 3.

The number of arcs that emanate from a given point is the *degree* of the point. A point of degree 0 is a *leaf point*. The number of its leaf points is the *weight* of a tree diagram; the diagram of Fig. 1.1 is of weight 12. As shown

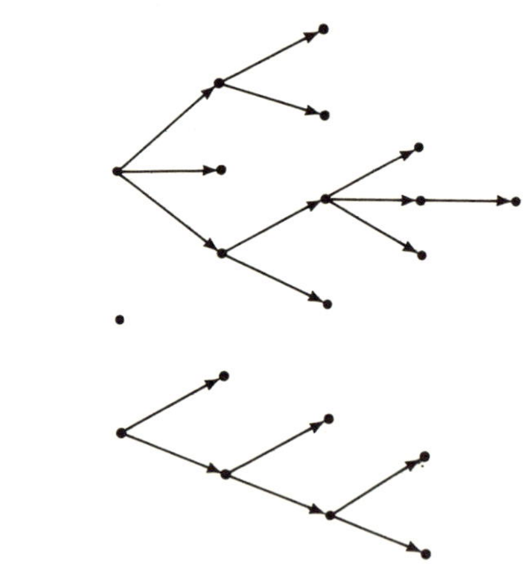


**Fig. 1.1** A tree diagram of moment 20, weight 12, radix 3, and height 5.

in this figure, it is possible for a point to qualify both as a root point and a leaf point.

Points are marshaled into columns called *levels*. For the sake of uniformity, we insist that root points appear on the leftmost level, that all arcs point from left to right, and that any two points connected by an arc appear on adjacent levels. The number of levels in a tree diagram is the *height* of the diagram. Unless otherwise stated, levels are numbered $1, 2, \ldots, h$, where $h$ denotes height. In discussing tree diagrams, the letters $h$, $r$, $t$, and $w$ will be favored in denoting height, radix, moment, and weight, respectively. For the tree diagram of Fig. 1.1, $h = 5$, $r = 3$, $t = 20$, and $w = 12$.

From a point of degree $d$ on level $k$ there emanate $d$ arcs to points on level $k + 1$. We may view the level-$k$ point as a *parent point* and, in the same context, the $d$ sibling points on level $k + 1$ as a *point family*. Although the root points of a tree diagram have no parent point, it is useful to define them as an additional point family. The tree diagram of Fig. 1.1 contains nine point families, as indicated in Fig. 1.2 (now that directionality is established, the arrowheads will be omitted from arcs). The number of member points in a point family is the *dimension* of the family.

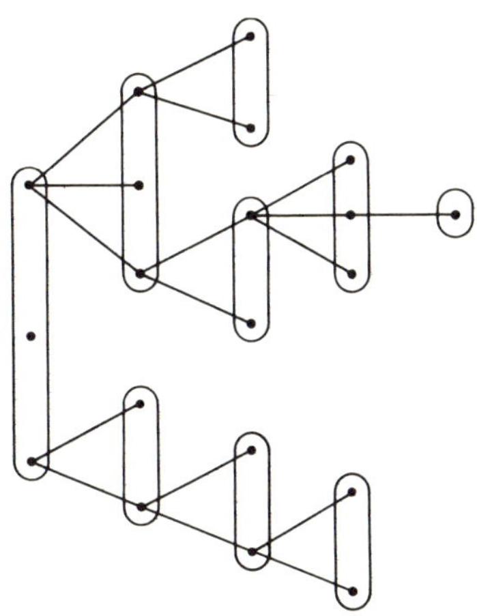

**Fig. 1.2** A delineation of point families.

The number of points in a level is termed the *count* of the level. Scanning from left to right in Fig. 1.1, the levels are seen to be of counts 3, 5, 6, 5, and 1. Obviously, the moment of a tree diagram is equal to the sum of its level counts. Moreover, because the count of level $k + 1$ is exactly the sum of degrees from level $k$, it follows for any tree diagram that its moment equals its radix plus the sum, say $s$, of its point degrees. That is,

$$t = r + s \tag{1.1}$$

In the tree diagram of Fig. 1.1, for example, $r$ is 3, $s$ is 17, and $t$ is 20.

If points on the first $p$ successive levels of a tree diagram are connected, the $p$ points and their $p - 1$ intervening arcs are said to constitute a *path diagram* of *length p*. (Any root point, of itself, is considered a path diagram of length 1.) Its level-1 and level-$p$ points are the *initial* and *terminal* points, respectively, of a path diagram of length $p$. Inasmuch as each point in a tree diagram is the terminal point of exactly one path diagram, there are $t$ path diagrams in a tree diagram of moment $t$, and the most convenient way of identifying a path diagram is to identify its terminal point. A path diagram is *maximal* if its length equals tree-diagram height. Outlined in Fig. 1.3 are a path diagram of length 2 and a maximal path diagram of length 5. As defined here, every path diagram starts from a root point.

A given point, say point $x$, is said to be *reachable from* every point in the path diagram terminating in $x$. (Because $x$ is a point in this path diagram, $x$ is considered reachable from itself.) Moreover, looking out toward the leaf points, the set of all points reachable from $x$ is said to constitute the *subtree diagram* of $x$. Because $x$ serves as the root point of the subtree diagram, subtree diagrams are necessarily of radix 1. A subtree diagram of moment 3 is shown by delineation in Fig. 1.3.

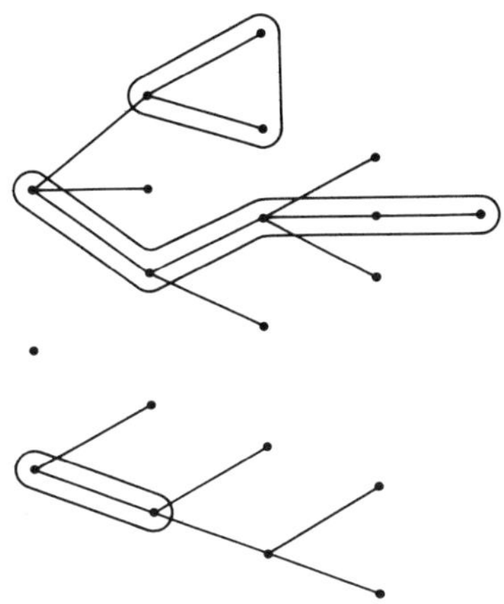

**Fig. 1.3** Examples (from top to bottom) of a subtree diagram of moment 3, a maximal path diagram of length 5, and a path diagram of length 2.

Because each point in a tree diagram is the root point of one and only one subtree diagram, there are $t$ subtree diagrams in a tree diagram of moment $t$. Clearly, to identify a point in a tree diagram is at once to identify three entities: a path diagram, a subtree diagram, and the point itself. If the level of the identified point is known, the length of the corresponding path diagram is also known (it is equal to the level index).

Note that if point $x$ is a leaf point, it still possesses a subtree diagram (of

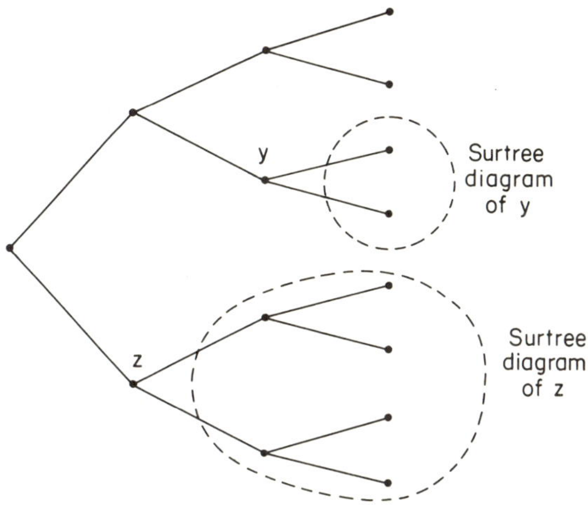


**Fig. 1.4** Examples of surtree diagrams.

moment 1). For the case in which $x$ is not a leaf point, it is useful to define a *surtree diagram* of $x$ that excludes $x$ itself but is otherwise identical to the subtree diagram of $x$. If point $x$ is of degree $d$, its surtree diagram contains $d$ root points. The surtree diagrams of points $y$ and $z$ are outlined in the tree diagram of Fig. 1.4.

The number of points in a subtree diagram is the moment of the subtree diagram. Likewise, the number of leaf points in a subtree diagram is the weight of the subtree diagram. In the tree diagram of Fig. 1.5, each point is accompanied by the weight of its subtree diagram.

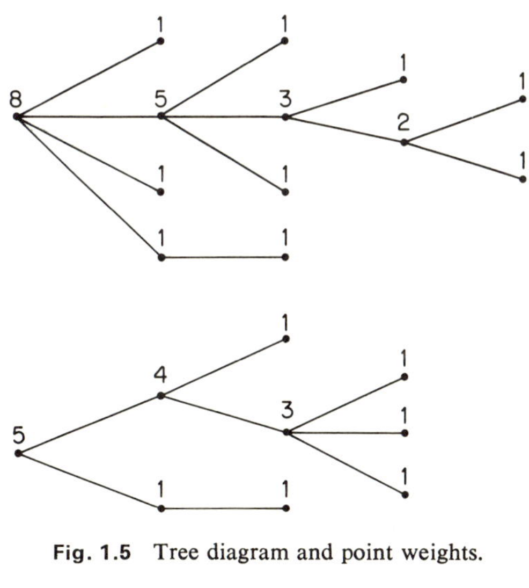

**Fig. 1.5** Tree diagram and point weights.

Its pattern of points and arcs will be referred to as the *structure* of a tree diagram. Two tree diagrams with the same structures are said to be *identical*. As we go on, it will be shown that the structures embraced by finite tree diagrams are general enough to illuminate most of the organizational facets of data systems.

## 1.2 Distinctive Classes of Tree Diagrams

Section 1.1 established a tree-diagram notation involving five symbols:

| | | | | | |
|---|---|---|---|---|---|
| $h$ | height | $s$ | degree sum | $w$ | weight |
| $r$ | radix | $t$ | moment | | |

From here on, these symbols and their meanings are assumed to be familiar to the reader.

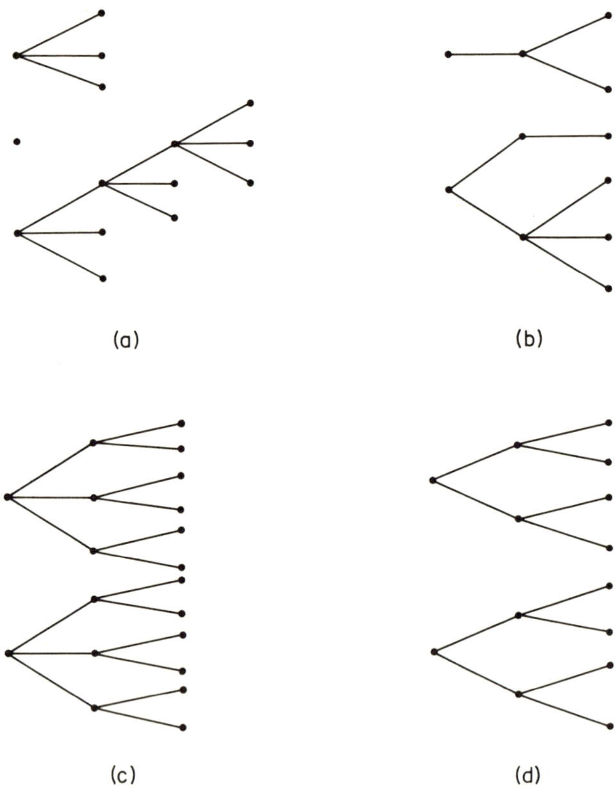

**Fig. 1.6** Examples of $r$-way, uniform, base $r$, and radix $r$ structure: (a) three-way; (b) uniform; (c) base (2, 3, 2); (d) base 2, height 3.

The tree diagrams of most interest in system analysis have special structures. Worthy of note are four special classes:

$r$-way structure

Uniform structure

Base-$\boldsymbol{r}$ structure

Base-$r$, height-$h$ structure

In an $r$-way tree diagram, all point families are of dimension $r$. In a uniform tree diagram, all leaf points appear on the uppermost level. In a base-$\boldsymbol{r}$ tree diagram, the families of each level are identical in dimension, but the dimensions may vary from level to level. The boldface, italic $\boldsymbol{r}$ denotes a sequence of $h$ integers, one integer per level, such that each integer of the sequence prescribes the family dimension for the corresponding level. A base-$r$, height-$h$ diagram is both $r$-way and uniform; moreover, it is the special case of base-$\boldsymbol{r}$ structure in which all of the integers in $\boldsymbol{r}$ are identical. Examples of the four classes appear in Fig. 1.6, where (a) shows a three-way tree diagram of height 4, (b) a uniform tree diagram of height 3, (c) a base-(2, 3, 2) diagram, and (d) a base-2 diagram of height 3.

**$r$-way structure.** In any tree diagram of one level, there is only one family. As a result, $w = t = r$ and $s = 0$. Given an $r$-way diagram of one level, and assuming that we are to construct an $r$-way diagram of greater height by appending one family per step, we see that each step will append $r$ new leaf points and cancel one existing leaf point. At each step, therefore, $s$ is increased by $r$ and $w$ by $r - 1$. Hence, the number of steps is given by $s/r$ and we can write

$$w = r + \frac{s}{r}(r - 1).$$

Solving for $s$, we obtain

$$s = \frac{r}{r-1}(w - r). \tag{1.2}$$

Substituting (1.1) into (1.2) and simplifying, we have

$$t = \frac{r}{r-1}(w - 1). \tag{1.3}$$

If the number of leaf points in an $r$-way tree diagram is known, the moment is easily calculated from (1.3).

Rearranging (1.3), we obtain an equation for $w$ as a function of $r$ and $t$:

$$w = 1 + \left(\frac{r-1}{r}\right)t. \tag{1.4}$$

Hence, given the moment of an $r$-way tree diagram, one can readily calculate the weight. Also, from (1.3), we can write

$$f = \frac{t}{r} = \frac{w - 1}{r - 1}, \tag{1.5}$$

where $f$ denotes the number of families in the diagram.

A tree diagram is *almost r-way* if every point family is of dimension $r$ with the exception of one point family, which may be of dimension $r^*$, where $2 \leq r^* \leq r$. Let $w^*$ be the weight of an almost $r$-way tree diagram. In most applications of this structure, the objective is to construct an almost $r$-way diagram starting with a set of leaf points; in other words, $w^*$ is given but the dimension $r^*$ of the smallest family is an unknown. It can be verified, using (1.1) and (1.5), that

$$r^* = 2 + \text{remainder}\left(\frac{w^* - 2}{r - 1}\right) \quad \text{for } r \geq 2,\ w^* \geq 2. \tag{1.6}$$

Hence, to obtain $r^*$, we add 2 to the remainder obtained in dividing $(w^* - 2)$ by $(r - 1)$. If $r^*$ equals $r$, the diagram is properly $r$-way.

**Base structure.** In a base-$r$ tree diagram of height $h$, the weight is a power of $r$. Specifically,

$$w = r^h \quad \text{for } h > 0. \tag{1.7}$$

To obtain equations for the degree sum and moment of a base-$r$ diagram, sub stitute (1.7) in (1.2) and (1.3), whereupon

$$s = \frac{r}{r - 1}(r^h - r) \quad \text{for } r > 1 \tag{1.8}$$

and

$$t = \frac{r}{r - 1}(r^h - 1) \quad \text{for } r > 1. \tag{1.9}$$

For example, if $r = 10$ and $h = 3$, then $t = 10(1000 - 1)/9 = 1110$.

A level-by-level summation of powers of $r$ provides an alternative for obtaining the moment. That is, for a base-$r$ diagram of height $h$,

$$t = r^1 + r^2 + \cdots + r^h = \sum_{i=1}^{h} r^i. \tag{1.10}$$

In the case of the base-**r** structure, the equations for $w$, $s$, and $t$ are necessarily more elaborate. Let $b_i$ denote the dimension of each level-$i$ family and $c_i$ the count of level $i$. Then

$$c_i = b_1 \times b_2 \times \cdots \times b_i = \prod_{j=1}^{i} b_j. \tag{1.11}$$

Since $c_h$ is the weight $w$ that we seek,

$$w = \prod_{j=1}^{h} b_j \tag{1.12}$$

Using (1.11) and the line of reasoning used in (1.10), the moment is obtained as a sum of products. That is,

$$t = c_1 + c_2 + \cdots + c_h = \sum_{i=1}^{h} c_i = \sum_{i=1}^{h} \prod_{j=1}^{i} b_j. \tag{1.13}$$

Perhaps the easiest way to obtain $s$ is to find $t$ by (1.13) and then apply (1.1), which permits us to write $s = t - r$.

If (1.13) appears forbidding as an equation, it is simplicity itself when seen in the context of an actual base-$\boldsymbol{r}$ tree diagram. For example, given a base-(2, 3, 4) diagram,

$$c_1 = 2$$
$$c_2 = 2 \times 3 = 6$$
$$c_3 = 2 \times 3 \times 4 = 24;$$

hence $t = 2 + 6 + 24 = 32$. Moreover, $w = c_3 = 24$ and $s = 32 - 2 = 30$.

**Uniform structure.** Because the families in a uniform tree diagram are permitted to have haphazard dimensions, (1.1) holds but systematic relations of the kind in (1.2)–(1.13) do not apply. The advantages in recognizing uniform structure will become evident later.

## 1.3 Point Identification

As a graphic means of portraying structure, the tree diagram is highly congenial to mental processes. For storing and communicating structure, however, the tree diagram can be far from convenient. How could one represent a tree diagram in a telegram? Before structure can be transmitted via keyboards, it must be represented in the form of text. Methods of naming points and designating arcs are essential to textual representations.

Figure 1.7 illustrates a method of naming called *indexing*. This method assigns each point a distinct name, an *index tag*. Consecutive integers are assigned to the points of each family, the order of assignment being from exhibit top to bottom. Root points are indexed initially. Except that each point takes the index tag of its parent as a prefix tag, families on subsequent levels are indexed in the manner of root points. If we delineate prefix tags by commas, the tag of a level-$k$ point consists of a sequence of $k$ integers. As stressed in Sec. 1.1, any tag that identifies a point also identifies a path diagram and a subtree diagram.

Although the index origin can take any integral value, the choices of most significance are 0 and 1. The former is particularly useful where tags are likely to become variables in algebraic equations. The latter choice is more congenial in exposition because it is consistent with the habitual notions of ordinality

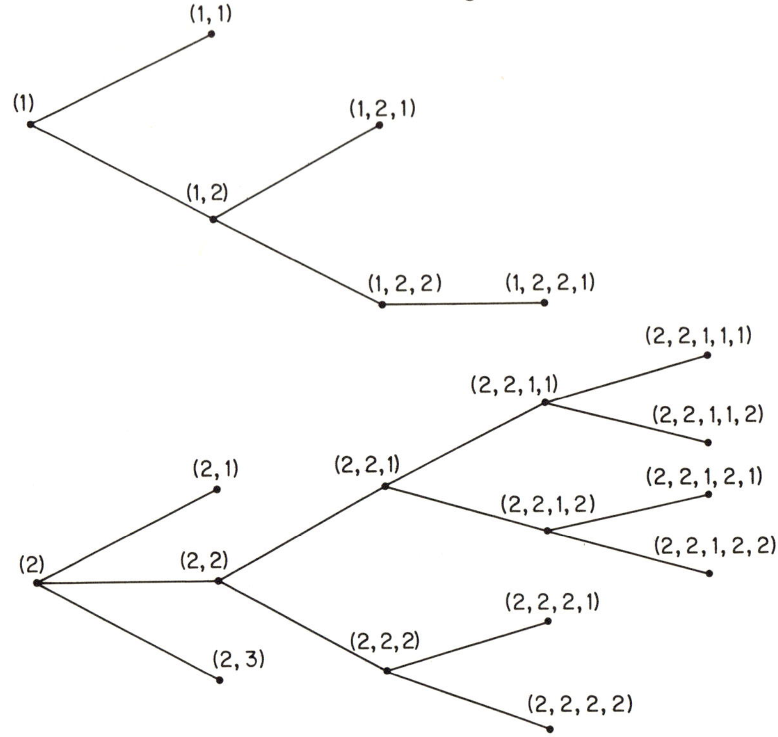


**Fig. 1.7** Tree diagram and 1-origin index tags.

(level 1 of a tree diagram is the first level, for example). Where the origin is unspecified, we shall assume that indexing starts with 1.

Because each tag provided by indexing is tantamount to a set of instructions for reaching the named point, a set of index tags for a tree diagram is an explicit representation of the diagram, and the diagram is easily reconstructed from the set. Each tag corresponds to a point; the number of integers in the tag indicate the level of the point; and the integers themselves tell which points are to be connected as a path diagram. Except in the case of a one-level tree diagram, a full set of tags is somewhat redundant: Leaf-point tags suffice because all other tags are implicit in them.

In $k$-origin indexing, the points within each family are distinguished from one another by a sequence of the form $k, k + 1, k + 2, \ldots$. In other words, for any family of dimension $d$, a sequence of $d$ consecutive integers is employed as a naming alphabet. Figure 1.8 illustrates a second method of point naming. In this method, which we term *integer dubbing*, the naming alphabet need not consist of consecutive integers—although every integer in the sequence must exceed each of its predecessors in the sequence. In dubbing, moreover, every family of a tree diagram may have a different naming alphabet. The full name of a point is called a *dub tag*.

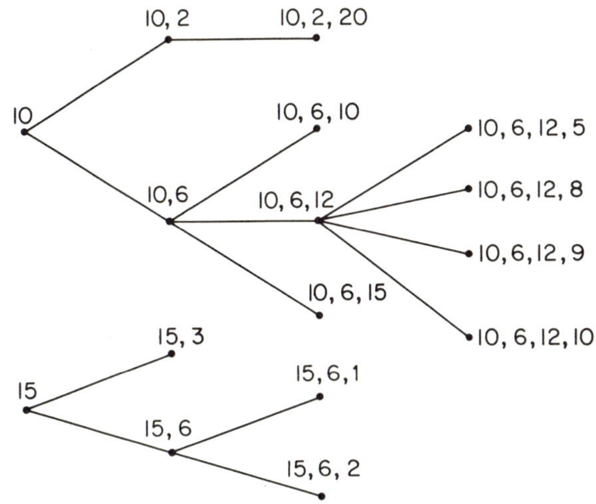


**Fig. 1.8** Tree diagram and illustrative dub tags.

Because dubbing yields distinctive tags and preserves within-family order, a tree diagram can be reconstructed from a set of dub tags as well as from a set of index tags. But indexing and dubbing differ in that index tags have a *distance* property not possessed by dub tags. Each component of an index tag yields information concerning position within a family, whereas the corresponding components of a dub tag do not. As a result, indexing is superior to dubbing in contexts where it is desirable either to generate or interpret tags with a minimum of information. Given the index tag of one point, the index tags of neighbor points can readily be produced. Because numerical analysis specializes in algorithms that move systematically about in regular structures, generating tags enroute, mathematicians prefer indexing as a method of point identification.

It should be stressed that mathematics limits itself, for the most part, to structures that are timeless. Where structures are static, an established relationship between names and points can persist. On the other hand, consider an indexed structure in which leaf points can be deleted or inserted in an arbitrary manner. If the uppermost point in a leaf family is deleted, all of the remaining points in the family must be reindexed. Had the structure been dubbed, renaming would typically be unnecessary. In a world with a static population, human beings could conceivably be named by index tags. But in a world of birth and death, names with some of the properties of dub tags are more appropriate.

Although we have introduced dubbing in the context of integer naming alphabets, dubbing is typically employed with less restrictive naming alphabets. The generalization to mnemonic tags is discussed in Sec. 1.4.

## 1.4 Alphameric Tags

For a character set the designers of digital systems ordinarily turn to the keyboards of conventional business machines. An *alphameric* character set includes the decimal digits, the English letters (often uppercase only), and a subset of punctuation marks and special symbols. Give or take a few special symbols, a minimal set might include the following 48 characters:

$$\begin{array}{cccccccccccc} 0 & 1 & 2 & 3 & 4 & 5 & 6 & 7 & 8 & 9 & A & B \\ C & D & E & F & G & H & I & J & K & L & M & N \\ O & P & Q & R & S & T & U & V & W & X & Y & Z \\ , & ; & . & - & + & = & \& & \% & \$ & / & @ & \# \end{array} \tag{1.14}$$

One useful character not shown in (1.14) is the *null character*, some explicit symbol for *blank* that is nonprinting in the normal mode of operation. For our purposes the null character can be represented by a tiny circle $\circ$.

The term *set* implies an unordered collection. As a first step toward structure, a system designer may rank the characters in some desired order and thereby define a *collating sequence*. The null character is usually assigned the lowest rank. Although the digits are usually consecutive in the sequence, and the letters as well, the relative placement of digits, letters, and special symbols has been something of a designer's choice. The trend is toward a larger set recommended by the American Standards Association.

If $m$ and $n$ denote decimal digits, we can write.

$$\begin{aligned} m &< n \\ m &= n \\ m &> n \end{aligned} \tag{1.15}$$

with assurance that one and only one of the three relations holds true for given values of $m$ and $n$. However, if variables $b$ and $c$ denote characters in an alphameric alphabet, we cannot write relations for $b$ and $c$ that are analogous to those for $m$ and $n$. In the context of a given collating sequence, however, we can define a function that yields the rank of a character—and we can compare the ranks as in (1.15). That is, we can write

$$\begin{aligned} \text{rank } (b) &< \text{rank } (c) \\ \text{rank } (b) &= \text{rank } (c) \\ \text{rank } (b) &> \text{rank } (c) \end{aligned} \tag{1.16}$$

with the usual assurance that one and only one of the relations is true.

Since a comparison of the ranks of two characters is a commonplace operation in data processing, it is inconvenient to be overly meticulous about the distinction between (1.15) and (1.16). We therefore follow an established practice and speak of "comparing characters" when we mean "comparing the ranks of characters."

Because of the laws of arithmetic, (1.15) generalizes for integers. For example, no problem arises if $m$ takes the value 8 and $n$ the value 761. To reduce the task of matching integers to a series of digit-by-digit comparisons, the shorter digit is padded on the left with zeros, and digit-by-digit comparisons proceed from left to right until (1) a mismatch is characterized or (2) the integers are determined equal. A subtraction operation, followed by a test for zero, plus, or minus difference, achieves the same result.

An integer is a digit string. The general alphameric counterpart to an integer is called a *character string*. Two strings can be matched, using character-by-character comparisons, with much the same discipline employed for integers. However, if the strings contain unequal numbers of characters, it is customary to employ a lexical convention and pad the shorter string by appending null characters on the right. For example, to match ADDITION and ADD, the strings become

$b$: ADDITION

$c$: ADD ○○○○○

whereupon a series of left-to-right comparisons will serve for strings as effectively as for integers. The example

$m$: 0 0 8

$n$: 7 6 1

shows the contrasting format for integers. In data processing practice, padding conventions are usually optional and character-set restrictions may require that the null character be simulated by an available character of low rank.

Since every standard collating sequence incorporates the sequence A, B, C, . . . , Z, strings are best exemplified with this sequence. The sequence

FOUR, ONE, THREE, TWO (1.17)

is an example of a sorted sequence of strings. This sequence can be obtained from ONE, TWO, THREE, FOUR by matching and moving strings. (Sorting methods deserve an extended treatment, which appears as Chapter 5.) To say that a sequence is sorted is to imply that a collating sequence governs the arrangement of strings in the sequence.

The concepts of collating sequence, string, and sorted string sequence open the way for a discussion of alphameric dubbing. The numerical example of dubbing given in Sec. 1.3 provided a direct contrast between dubbing (Fig. 1.8) and indexing (Fig. 1.7). But dubbing admits of strings as readily as of integers, and strings have the potential advantage of being mnemonic. Figure 1.9 provides an example of a tree diagram with alphameric dub tags. The sorted sequence

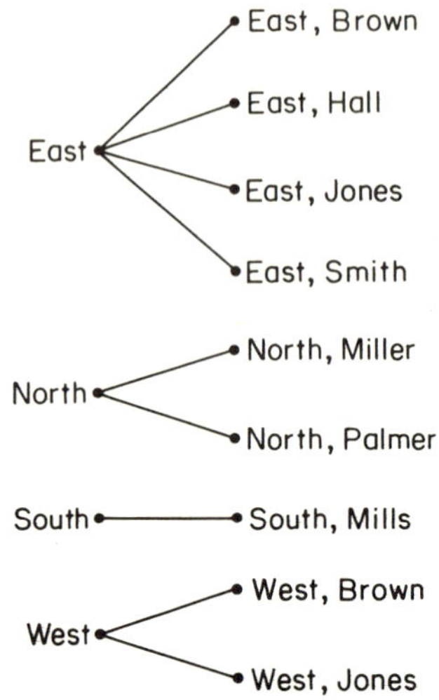


**Fig. 1.9** Example of alphameric dub tags.

$$\text{EAST, NORTH, SOUTH, WEST} \tag{1.18}$$

distinguishes among root points and the four sorted sequences

$$\begin{array}{l} \text{BROWN, HALL, JONES, SMITH} \\ \text{MILLER, PALMER} \\ \text{MILLS} \\ \text{BROWN, JONES} \end{array} \tag{1.19}$$

distinguish among members of the four families on level 2.

The structure of the tree diagram in Fig. 1.9 can be captured in a rectangular table of nine rows and two columns; each row in the table contains the tag of one leaf point and the rows are in leaf-point order:

$$\begin{bmatrix} \text{EAST} & \text{BROWN} \\ \text{EAST} & \text{HALL} \\ \text{EAST} & \text{JONES} \\ \text{EAST} & \text{SMITH} \\ \text{NORTH} & \text{MILLER} \\ \text{NORTH} & \text{PALMER} \\ \text{SOUTH} & \text{MILLS} \\ \text{WEST} & \text{BROWN} \\ \text{WEST} & \text{JONES} \end{bmatrix}. \tag{1.20}$$

As it stands, the table of (1.20) preserves within it the sequences in (1.18) and (1.19), for if perchance the rows of (1.20) become disordered, (1.20) can be restored by sorting row strings. Since dubbing and indexing both preserve structure, their relative advantages and disadvantages must depend on the context in which they are used. As stated earlier, indexing is congenial to systematic analyses of a static structure. On the other hand, dubbing suggests itself for volatile structures in which the tag is more invariant than its position. English words, abbreviations, and other mnemonic devices can be used to make dub tags congenial to the human mind.

As methods of identifying points, indexing and dubbing assume a given collating sequence and thereby embody a tree diagram within a corresponding set of tags. The tree diagram is manifested when the tags are sorted. Before leaving the subject, we shall remark upon a less efficient method of point identification.

The tree diagram of Fig. 1.10 is related to the diagram of Fig. 1.9 in the sense that families have been rearranged. Again, the structure of the tree diagram can be captured in a table of nine rows and two columns:

$$\begin{bmatrix} \text{EAST} & \text{SMITH} \\ \text{EAST} & \text{BROWN} \\ \text{EAST} & \text{JONES} \\ \text{EAST} & \text{HALL} \\ \text{SOUTH} & \text{MILLS} \\ \text{WEST} & \text{JONES} \\ \text{WEST} & \text{BROWN} \\ \text{NORTH} & \text{MILLER} \\ \text{NORTH} & \text{PALMER} \end{bmatrix}. \tag{1.21}$$

However, if the rows of (1.21) get out of order, there is no way to recapture the original order without access to the sequence

$$(\text{EAST, SOUTH, WEST, NORTH}), \tag{1.22}$$

which distinguishes among root points, and the sequences

$$\begin{array}{l} (\text{SMITH, BROWN, JONES, HALL}) \\ (\text{MILLS}) \\ (\text{JONES, BROWN}) \\ (\text{MILLER, PALMER}), \end{array} \tag{1.23}$$

which distinguish among members of the four families on level 2.

A process that determines the position of an element in a sequence of elements will be called *ranking*. Consider the tag (WEST, BROWN). If (1.22) is

*Chapter 2*

# STRUCTURE IN DATA

Data processing deals with organized aggregates of data. Because analysts in different fields of inquiry go about organizing data in their own traditional ways, following differing motivations and employing specialized terminologies, a general framework that brings the various techniques into one perspective is desirable. The tree diagrams of Chapter 1 offer such a framework.

After the notion of a data aggregate has been suitably defined, various types of aggregates are identified and discussed. The analysis starts with the simplest cases of data organization and proceeds step by step to the more complicated cases.

## 2.1 Point Specification

A tree diagram with index or dub tags is an abstract representation of a classification system. As a consequence, a tree diagram can systematize a collection of data if we establish a correspondence between each datum in the collection and a point in the diagram. A point in one-to-one correspondence with a datum is said to be *specified* by the datum. To depict specification, the point is replaced by a circle and the corresponding datum is written inside the circle. The point tag may be written outside the circle.

Consider a tree diagram of moment $t$ and weight $w$, that is, with $t$ points and $w$ leaf points. The tree diagram becomes a *structurand* (an abbreviation of "structured operand") after all leaf points have been specified. Although every leaf point in a structurand must be a circle, no stipulation is made regarding other points—none, some, or all of them may be circles. A structurand of exactly $w$ circles will be called a *trim*; leaf points and only leaf points are specified in a trim. At the other extreme, a structurand of $t$ circles is a *tree*; all points are specified in a tree. A general structurand, a trim, and a tree are illustrated in Fig. 2.1.

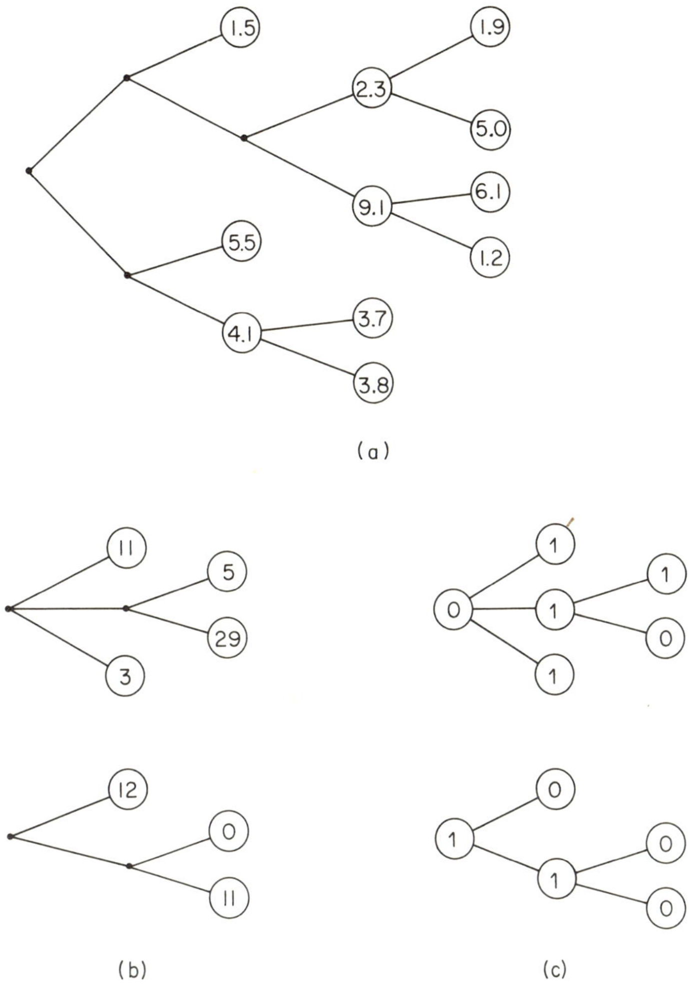


**Fig. 2.1** Examples of a structurand (a), a trim (b), and a tree (c).

Two structurands with identical structures and extents of specification are said to be *compatible*. If $A$ and $B$ denote compatible structurands, and if $A$ and $B$ are indexed, the two sets of index tags are identical; moreover, each distinct index tag is associated with a pair of circles (one in $A$, one in $B$) or a similar pair of points. To put it another way, two structurands are incompatible if any circle in one corresponds to an unspecified point in the other.

An encircled datum in a structurand is called a *node*. A node that specifies a leaf point may be termed a *leaf*; a node that specifies a root point may be termed a *root*. In discussing a tree, we may speak of a *path*, the sequence of nodes along a path diagram; a path is a sequence of nodes that starts with a root and terminates on a node. We may also refer to a *level* (the nodes at a level), a *family* (the nodes of a point family), a *subtree* (the nodes of a subtree diagram), and a *surtree* (the nodes of a surtree diagram). In speaking of a trim, on the other hand, we avoid the term *path* and speak of a level or family only where all of the level or family is known to consist entirely of leaves. But one can refer confidently to the *subtrim* or *surtrim* of any point.

If $B$ denotes a structurand, and if $R$ denotes the set of values eligible as nodes of $B$, then structurand $B$ is said to be of *range* $R$. For discussion purposes, a fourfold classification of range usually suffices:

| | |
|---|---|
| *Logical* | 0 and 1 are admitted in $R$ |
| *Integral* | all integers are admitted |
| *Numerical* | rationals (ratios of integers) are admitted |
| *Arbitrary* | character strings are admitted. |

In Fig. 2.1, the general structurand is a numerical structurand, the trim is an integral trim, and the tree is a logical tree.

The term *arbitrary range* is too inclusive to be characterized precisely. In one application, a datum may be a keyboard character, a telephone "number," a part "number," a mailing address, or the like. In another context, a datum may consist of a unit of text, examples being words, sentences, messages, characters, lines, or pages. In fact, character sets and string lengths are design parameters; as such, they take on a usefully restricted meaning only in a practical context. Moreover, in some highly specialized applications, the range is generalized to permit nodes to consist of drawings, photographs, or the like.

Inherent in every structurand is a tree diagram. All of the structural distinctions made in Sec. 1.2 can be turned to advantage in characterizing trees and trims. Thus we can refer to $r$-way trees or trims, uniform trees or trims, base trees or trims, and $r$-way uniform trees or trims. Such characterizations help to bring a structurand into analytical perspective. The first questions usually concern structure, extent of specification, and range:

1. Is the structurand a trim? a tree?
2. Is the structure $r$-way? uniform? base-$r$?
3. Is the range logical? integral? numerical? arbitrary?

After these questions are answered, additional properties can begin to take on significance.

Three classes of structurands are sufficiently ubiquitous and useful in exposition to deserve special nomenclature and notation. The names themselves can suggest the answers to questions 1 and 2, and by suitable conventions, notation can imply the answer to 3. Sections 2.2–2.4 treat these three structurands: the scalar, vector, and matrix.

## 2.2 Scalars

A structurand defined of moment 1 will be referred to as a *scalar*. A scalar is the ultimate in structural simplicity. Let the lowercase, italic letters $a, b, \ldots, y, z$, denote scalar variables, the notational convention commonly followed in algebra. However, the scalars under discussion here are permitted arbitrary ranges, a proviso that is alien to algebra.

Using notation to suggest ranges, we shall favor the following usage:

| | |
|---|---|
| $a, b, c$ | arbitrary range |
| $i, j, k, l, m, n, p$ | integral range |
| $u, v$ | logical range |
| $x, y$ | numerical range |

As in Chapter 1, the letters $h$, $r$, $s$, $t$, and $w$ will be reserved for tree-diagram parameters. This leaves a few letters that can be assigned a range at time of use.

A set of 26 symbols that suffices for most expositional purposes can be entirely inadequate for a typical data-processing application. The problem is usually solved by one or both of two expedients. The first assigns names consisting of several characters—such as SUMA, SUMB, SUMC, RATE, WGHT, etc.—usually choosing mnemonic strings to bolster the human memory. The second expedient marshals scalars into tables in meaningful ways, an artifice that reduces the need for names because cells in a table can be identified by supplementing the table name with indexing.

## 2.3 Vectors

Again borrowing from algebra, a structurand defined of one level will be called a *vector*. A sequence of either the form

$$\boldsymbol{a} = (\boldsymbol{a}_1, \boldsymbol{a}_2, \cdots, \boldsymbol{a}_n)$$

or the optional form

$$\boldsymbol{a} = \begin{pmatrix} \boldsymbol{a}_1 \\ \boldsymbol{a}_2 \\ \vdots \\ \boldsymbol{a}_n \end{pmatrix}$$

is a vector of *dimension n*. In either format, the vector is enclosed by parentheses. It is customary to refer to node $\boldsymbol{a}_i$ as the *i*th *component* of vector $\boldsymbol{a}$. In a vector written horizontally, components are delineated by commas. For our purposes, no distinction is to be made between the vertical and horizontal representations of a vector; the choice is solely a matter of convenience.

Vectors will be denoted by the boldface, lowercase, italic letters $\boldsymbol{a}, \boldsymbol{b}, \boldsymbol{c}, \ldots, \boldsymbol{z}$; moreover, the scalar conventions regarding ranges will be emulated. Vectors with invariant meanings will be denoted by lowercase, boldface Greek letters. The example that follows uses the Greek iota.

Let $\boldsymbol{\iota}(n)$ denote a vector of the first positive integers, such that $\boldsymbol{\iota}(n) = (1, 2, \ldots, n)$. Hence $\boldsymbol{\iota}(4) = (1, 2, 3, 4)$ and $\boldsymbol{\iota}(1) = (1)$. The utility of this notation is extended if the vector can start with any positive or negative integer, say $k$. For this, let

$$\boldsymbol{\iota}^k(n) = (k, k + 1, k + 2, \cdots, k + n - 1). \tag{2.1}$$

Hence $\boldsymbol{\iota}^3(5) = (3, 4, 5, 6, 7)$ and $\boldsymbol{\iota}^0(4) = (0, 1, 2, 3)$. The vector $\boldsymbol{\iota}^k(n)$ is called a *k-origin interval vector of dimension n*. When $k$ is omitted, $k = 1$ is assumed. The vector of dimension zero, a useful fiction called the *null vector*, has a representation in $\boldsymbol{\iota}(0)$.

The components in a vector of dimension $n$ are conventionally identified by a subscript index that runs through a $k$-origin interval vector of dimension $n$. Hence, if $\boldsymbol{x}$ is a vector of five components, we have

$$(\boldsymbol{x}_1, \boldsymbol{x}_2, \boldsymbol{x}_3, \boldsymbol{x}_4, \boldsymbol{x}_5) \text{ if } k = 1$$

and

$$(\boldsymbol{x}_0, \boldsymbol{x}_1, \boldsymbol{x}_2, \boldsymbol{x}_3, \boldsymbol{x}_4) \text{ if } k = 0.$$

In the absence of an explicitly stated origin, $k = 1$ is assumed.

Two compatible vectors, say $\boldsymbol{a}$ and $\boldsymbol{b}$, are said to be *identical* if $\boldsymbol{a}_i = \boldsymbol{b}_i$ for each value of their common index $i$. The vectors (17, 12, 0) and (17, 12, 0) are identical; the vectors (17, 12, 0) and (17, 0, 12) are not.

A subsequence of $m$ consecutive components in a vector of dimension $n$ may be referred to as an *infix* of the vector. For example, the vector (6, 5, 3) is one possible infix of the vector (2, 1, 6, 5, 3, 8). The restriction on $m$ is that $1 \leq m \leq n$. An infix of vector $\boldsymbol{c}$ that contains the first component in $\boldsymbol{c}$ is a *prefix* of $\boldsymbol{c}$; likewise, an infix of $\boldsymbol{c}$ that contains the last component of $\boldsymbol{c}$ is a *suffix* of $\boldsymbol{c}$. Hence, (2, 1) and (5, 3, 8) qualify as a prefix and a suffix of (2, 1, 6, 5, 3, 8).

Let $\boldsymbol{d}$ be any vector. If unequal to all of the remaining components of $\boldsymbol{d}$, a component of $\boldsymbol{d}$ is *distinct in* $\boldsymbol{d}$. A vector that consists entirely of distinct components will be termed an *alphabet*. Every interval vector is an alphabet. The vectors (17, 12, 0) and (A, B, C, D) are alphabets, as is (D, C, A, B). The vector (cat, dog, fox) of dimension 3 is an alphabet. Although few writers define *alphabet* with this much generality, many require it to mean more than A, B, C, . . . , Y, Z. The ensuing state of ambiguity argues for the general definition. As used here, an alphabet is an ordered set of character strings.

**Ranking.** Consider an alphabet $\boldsymbol{b}$ with index $i$ and a scalar $c$. The $\boldsymbol{b}$ *rank* *of* $c$, defined as the value of $i$ for which $\boldsymbol{b}_i = c$, will be indicated by the expression $\boldsymbol{b}\ \iota\ c$. (If $c$ does not occur in $\boldsymbol{b}$, then $\boldsymbol{b}\ \iota\ c$ yields a null.) Here are some examples:

$$(1, 2, 3, 4)\ \iota\ 3 = 3$$
$$(9, 5, 6, 2)\ \iota\ 5 = 2$$
$$(\mathrm{A, B, C, D})\ \iota\ C = 3$$
$$(\mathrm{B, A, X, C})\ \iota\ A = 2$$
$$(\text{charlie, baker, able})\ \iota\ \text{baker} = 2$$
$$(1, 2, 3, 4)\ \iota\ 5 = \circ\,.$$

To generalize the operation in a very useful way, replace the scalar $c$ by a vector $\boldsymbol{c}$ and let the result be a vector $\boldsymbol{m}$ that is compatible with $\boldsymbol{c}$. For example,

$$(1, 2, 3, 4)\ \iota\ (1, 2, 4) = (1, 2, 4)$$
$$(9, 5, 6, 2)\ \iota\ (9, 5, 6, 2) = (1, 2, 3, 4)$$
$$(\mathrm{A, B, C, D})\ \iota\ (\mathrm{B, A, D}) = (2, 1, 4)$$
$$(\mathrm{D, C, B, A})\ \iota\ (\mathrm{B, A, D}) = (3, 4, 1)$$
$$(\mathrm{B, A, D})\ \iota\ (\mathrm{A, B, C, D}) = (2, 1, \circ, 3)$$
$$(\mathrm{A, B, C, D})\ \iota\ (\mathrm{A, B, C, D}) = (1, 2, 3, 4)\,.$$

Notice that whenever an alphabet is ranked in itself, the result is an interval vector. In a sense, then, every alphabet is an interval vector in disguise—a disguise that can be stripped away by ranking operations.

**Mapping.** To supplement the ranking operation, consider a *mapping operation* $\boldsymbol{m} \int \boldsymbol{b}$ that produces a vector $\boldsymbol{c}$ with the property that $\boldsymbol{c}_i = \boldsymbol{b}_{\boldsymbol{m}_i}$. (If $\boldsymbol{m}_i$ is outside the indexing range of $\boldsymbol{b}$, then $\boldsymbol{c}_i$ is defined as null.) Examples:

$$(1, 2, 3, 4) \int (\mathrm{A, B, C, D}) = (\mathrm{A, B, C, D})$$
$$(4, 3, 2, 1) \int (\mathrm{A, B, C, D}) = (\mathrm{D, C, B, A})$$
$$(2, 3, 4, 4, 3, 2) \int (\mathrm{A, B, C, D, E}) = (\mathrm{B, C, D, D, C, B})$$
$$(2, 3, 4, 2, 3, 4) \int (\mathrm{D, B, C, A}) = (\mathrm{B, C, A, B, C, A})$$
$$(2, 3, 4, 3, 2, 1) \int (\mathrm{A, F, C, D}) = (\mathrm{F, C, D, C, F, A})\,.$$

The integral vector $\boldsymbol{m}$ is called a *mapping vector*. Clearly, given an alphabet $\boldsymbol{b}$ and a suitable mapping vector $\boldsymbol{m}$, a mapping operation can generate any possible vector of range $\boldsymbol{b}$. Note that a result vector is always compatible with the given mapping vector $\boldsymbol{m}$.

The $n$ factorial (written $n!$) arrangements of $n$ consecutive integers starting with $k$ are called the *k-origin permutation vectors* of dimension $n$. The six permutation vectors for (1, 2, 3) are

$$\begin{array}{l}(1, 2, 3)\\(1, 3, 2)\\(2, 1, 3)\\(2, 3, 1)\\(3, 1, 2)\\(3, 2, 1)\,.\end{array} \tag{2.2}$$

One of the permutation vectors is the interval vector itself; such a vector is therefore sometimes referred to as an *identity permutation vector.* (In discussions of permutation vectors, $k$ is assumed to be equal to 1 unless otherwise specified.)

As defined here, the ranking and mapping operations $\boldsymbol{b}\ \iota\ \boldsymbol{c}$ and $\boldsymbol{m} \int \boldsymbol{b}$ assume that $\boldsymbol{b}$ is an alphabet, that $\boldsymbol{c}$ is of range $\boldsymbol{b}$, and that $\boldsymbol{m}$ is of range $\boldsymbol{\iota}(n)$, where $n$ is the dimension of $\boldsymbol{b}$. Moreover, one-origin indexing is assumed. There are useful ways of relaxing these restrictions, but they are not particularly germane to this discussion. We mention one parenthetically.

A suitable permutation vector $\boldsymbol{p}$, compatible with $\boldsymbol{d}$, provides an explicit means of indicating a desired rearrangement of a vector $\boldsymbol{d}$. The desired vector is the result of the mapping operation $\boldsymbol{p} \int \boldsymbol{d}$. For example, if $\boldsymbol{d}$ is an arbitrary vector and it is desired to form a vector $\boldsymbol{c}$ that contains the components of $\boldsymbol{d}$ in ascending collating-sequence order, for a suitable $\boldsymbol{p}$ we can write $\boldsymbol{c} = \boldsymbol{p} \int \boldsymbol{d}$. If $\boldsymbol{d}$ contains some identical components, it is advantageous to insist that identical components retain in $\boldsymbol{c}$ the same relative order they had in $\boldsymbol{d}$. In practice, the components will be associated with other data, and the preservation of relative rank may be important in the inert data.

The problem of generating the required permutation vector, while highly significant, is too involved to cover at this point. In commercial data processing, where vectors of very large dimensions are often encountered, sorting takes on a good deal of economic importance. Sorting procedures are discussed at length in Chapter 5.

**Compression.** Let $\boldsymbol{b}$ denote any vector and $\boldsymbol{u}$ a compatible logical vector, and consider a compression operation $\boldsymbol{u}/\boldsymbol{b}$ that obtains a result vector from $\boldsymbol{b}$ by suppressing $\boldsymbol{b}_i$ wherever $\boldsymbol{u}_i = 0$. Components in the result vector preserve the relative order they had in $\boldsymbol{b}$. Here are four examples:

$$\begin{aligned}(0, 1, 0, 1, 0)/(1, 2, 3, 4, 5) &= (2, 4)\\(1, 0, 1, 0, 1)/(1, 2, 3, 4, 5) &= (1, 3, 5)\\(1, 1, 0, 1)/(\mathrm{B, A, C, D}) &= (\mathrm{B, A, D})\\(0, 1, 0, 1)/(1, 0, 1, 0) &= (0, 0)\,.\end{aligned}$$

The dimension of the result vector equals the sum of all components in the vector $\boldsymbol{u}$. If $\boldsymbol{u}$ consists of 0's only, the result is a vector of dimension zero, which can be represented by $\boldsymbol{\iota}(0)$.

Apparently on the premise that vectors cannot be of arbitrary range, some authors use the term *sequence* for nonnumeric trees of one level and *vector* for the numerical counterparts. The effect of this is to subordinate a primary category, structure, to a secondary category, range.

## 2.4 Matrices

A row-column display of data will be called a *matrix*, another term from algebra. Here is an integral matrix, say $\boldsymbol{R}$, of three rows and four columns.

$$\boldsymbol{R} = \begin{bmatrix} 12 & 0 & 10 & 15 \\ 16 & 6 & 31 & -4 \\ 9 & 28 & 33 & 4 \end{bmatrix}. \tag{2.3}$$

The boldface, italic capitals $\boldsymbol{A}, \boldsymbol{B}, \ldots, \boldsymbol{Z}$ will be reserved for denoting matrices. If $m$ denotes the number of rows in matrix $\boldsymbol{B}$ and $n$ the number of columns, it it customary to say that $\boldsymbol{B}$ is an $m \times n$ matrix. The matrix of (2.3) is a $3 \times 4$ matrix.

Let $i$ denote row number and $j$ denote column number in a matrix $\boldsymbol{B}$. Then let $\boldsymbol{B}^i$ denote the $i$th row, $\boldsymbol{B}_j$ the $j$th column, and $\boldsymbol{B}^i_j$ the $(i, j)$th element of $\boldsymbol{B}$. From (2.3), for example,

$$\boldsymbol{R}^2 = (16, 6, 31, -4) \qquad \text{and} \qquad \boldsymbol{R}_3 = \begin{pmatrix} 10 \\ 31 \\ 33 \end{pmatrix}.$$

Moreover, $\boldsymbol{R}^1_1 = 12$, $\boldsymbol{R}^1_2 = 0$, etc. Although this notation for denoting rows, columns, and elements is not widely used in algebra, it is easy to read and therefore useful in documenting procedures.

The numerical matrix and vector are well known from matrix algebra, a highly developed mathematical discipline of no direct relevance to a discussion of system structure. In mundane dress, on the other hand, the matrix is an ordinary two-way table, a means of communication that nicely combines row-column structure and the plane geometry of a sheet of paper. As a structurand, moreover, the indexed matrix is a convenient representation of an indexed base-$\boldsymbol{r}$ trim of height 2. For example, the matrix of (2.3) is shown as a base trim in Fig. 2.2(a). Each row in the matrix is a family of leaves in the trim, and each row corresponds to one root point. Note that a $3 \times 4$ matrix corresponds to a base-(3, 4) trim.

The leaf tags are of the form $i, j$, where $i$ is a row index and $j$ a column index. To show how the indexing pattern may be altered, let $A$ be an $n \times m$ matrix such that $A_i^j = B_j^i$ for every element of $B$. In algebra, $A$ is the *transpose* of $B$. The transpose of (2.3) is

$$\begin{bmatrix} 12 & 16 & 9 \\ 0 & 6 & 28 \\ 10 & 31 & 33 \\ 15 & -4 & 4 \end{bmatrix}. \tag{2.4}$$

The matrix of (2.4) corresponds to the trim of Fig. 2.2(b).

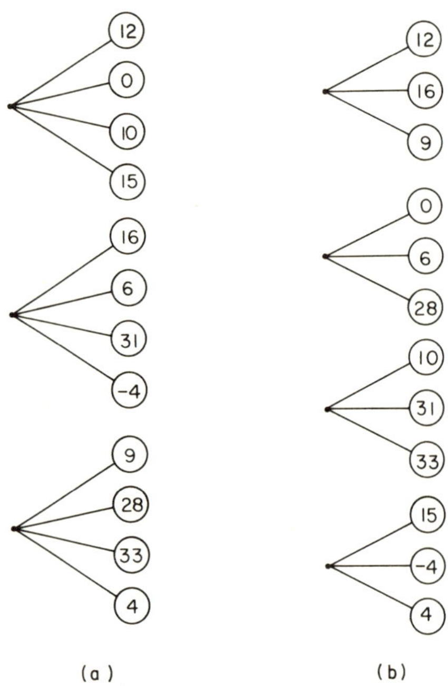


**Fig. 2.2** Representations of a matrix and its transpose: (a) matrix shown as a trim; (b) transpose shown as a trim.

Precisely because the importance of numerical matrices in mathematical computation is so widely recognized, it needs to be stressed that matrix structure has other, more significant, implications for digital systems. A row-column structure excels at combining modest complexity with representational convenience; moreover, it transforms easily and understandably into vector structure. Because vectors are especially congenial to a digital system, matrices are ultimately stored as one long vector. More significantly, trees, and trims of more than two levels, are given representations that employ matrix or vector structure. Representation is further discussed in Chapter 3.

## 2.5 Arrays

Base trims, i.e., trims with base-$\mathbf{r}$ structures, are better known as *arrays*. Nomenclature differs regarding height, so that a base trim of height $h$ may be variously referred to as an $h$-way, $h$-dimensional, or $h$-level array. For our purposes, the convenient compromise is to let *array* and *h-level array* refer to generic classes of base trims and to speak of *base-*$\mathbf{r}$ *trim* whenever the structural information in $\mathbf{r}$ is relevant. The height-2 array is a matrix, of course, and the height-1 array a vector.

Figure 2.3(a) exhibits an integral base-(3, 2, 4) trim in which leaves, reading downward, have the values 1, 2, . . . , 24. Since we are going to consider a procedure that rearranges leaves, these values will serve to highlight the original order of the leaves.

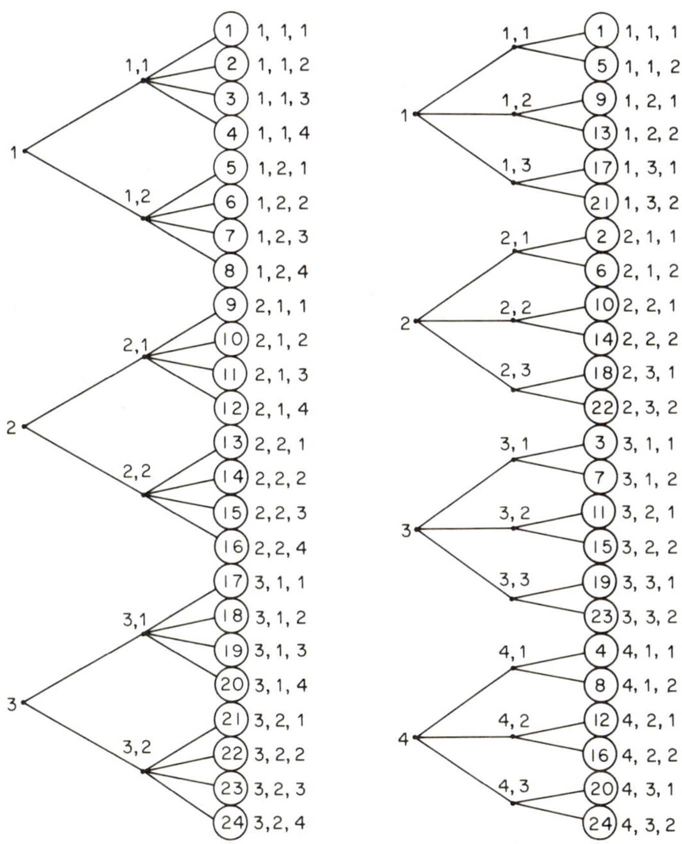


**Fig. 2.3** Two indexed base trims with identical sets of leaves: (a) base-(3, 2, 4) trim; (b) base-(4, 3, 2) trim obtained by rearranging (a).

If the index tags of the leaves are viewed as a 24 × 3 matrix and columns are subjected to a (3, 1, 2) permutation (so that column 3 becomes column 1, column 1 becomes column 2, and column 2 becomes column 3), then the matrix of (2.5) is obtained. When rows of (2.5) are sorted, we obtain (2.6).

$$\begin{bmatrix} 1 & 1 & 1 \\ 2 & 1 & 1 \\ 3 & 1 & 1 \\ 4 & 1 & 1 \\ 1 & 1 & 2 \\ 2 & 1 & 2 \\ 3 & 1 & 2 \\ 4 & 1 & 2 \\ 1 & 2 & 1 \\ 2 & 2 & 1 \\ 3 & 2 & 1 \\ 4 & 2 & 1 \\ 1 & 2 & 2 \\ 2 & 2 & 2 \\ 3 & 2 & 2 \\ 4 & 2 & 2 \\ 1 & 3 & 1 \\ 2 & 3 & 1 \\ 3 & 3 & 1 \\ 4 & 3 & 1 \\ 1 & 3 & 2 \\ 2 & 3 & 2 \\ 3 & 3 & 2 \\ 4 & 3 & 2 \end{bmatrix} \qquad (2.5) \qquad \begin{bmatrix} 1 & 1 & 1 \\ 1 & 1 & 2 \\ 1 & 2 & 1 \\ 1 & 2 & 2 \\ 1 & 3 & 1 \\ 1 & 3 & 2 \\ 2 & 1 & 1 \\ 2 & 1 & 2 \\ 2 & 2 & 1 \\ 2 & 2 & 2 \\ 2 & 3 & 1 \\ 2 & 3 & 2 \\ 3 & 1 & 1 \\ 3 & 1 & 2 \\ 3 & 2 & 1 \\ 3 & 2 & 2 \\ 3 & 3 & 1 \\ 3 & 3 & 2 \\ 4 & 1 & 1 \\ 4 & 1 & 2 \\ 4 & 2 & 1 \\ 4 & 2 & 2 \\ 4 & 3 & 1 \\ 4 & 3 & 2 \end{bmatrix} \qquad (2.6)$$

Assuming that leaves move with tags, the base-(4, 3, 2) trim of Fig. 2.3(b) is obtained.

Because there are six ways to permute the columns of a three-column matrix, four additional base trims can be similarly generated from the trim of Fig. 2.3(a). The six permutations and resultant structures are:

| *Array* | *Permutation* | *Structure* | *Example* | |
|---|---|---|---|---|
| I | (1, 2, 3) | Base-(3, 2, 4) | Fig. 2.3(a) | |
| II | (1, 3, 2) | Base-(3, 4, 2) | | |
| III | (2, 1, 3) | Base-(2, 3, 4) | | |
| IV | (2, 3, 1) | Base-(2, 4, 3) | Fig. 2.4(b) | (2.7) |
| V | (3, 1, 2) | Base-(4, 3, 2) | Fig. 2.3(b) | |
| VI | (3, 2, 1) | Base-(4, 2, 3) | | |

Each case leads to a different arrangement of leaves and to a properly indexed array. Arrays II–VI are said to be *transposes* of array I.

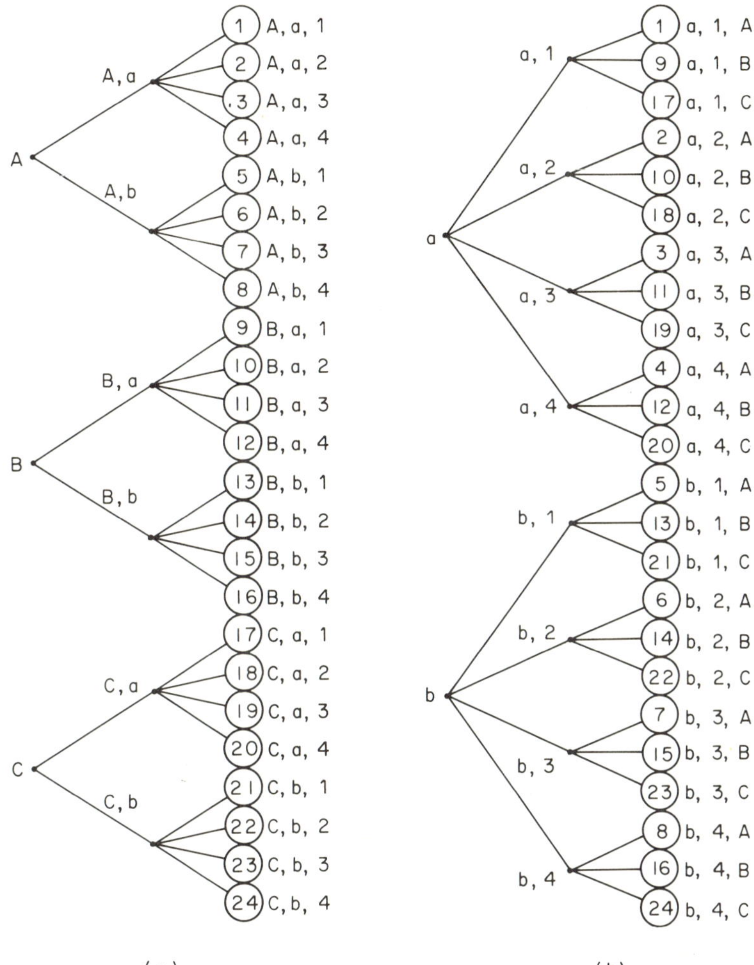


**Fig. 2.4** Two dubbed base trims with identical sets of leaves: (a) base-(3, 2, 4) trim; (b) base-(2, 4, 3) trim obtained by rearranging (a).

Figure 2.4(a) is identical to Fig. 2.3(a) except that for demonstration purposes the tagging alphabet (1, 2, 3) is encoded as (A, B, C) at level 1 and (1, 2) is encoded as (a, b) at level 2. The base-(2, 4, 3) trim of Fig. 2.4(b) corresponds to case IV of (2.7). It is to be noted that the tagging alphabets of the levels move positions in accordance with the same (2, 3, 1) permutation that governs column interchanges in the leaf tags; that is, (a, b) moves to level 1, (1, 2, 3, 4) to level 2, and (A, B, C) to level 3 in rearranging Fig. 2.4(a) to obtain Fig. 2.4(b).

Any process that starts with a trim and fills it out as a tree is said to *close* the trim. Although the three different trims in Figs. 2.3–2.4 are alike in the "data" sense, their differing leaf arrangements can have implications for processing convenience and cost. For example, consider the task of closing the trim of Fig. 2.4(a) by specifying each point as the sum of the leaves in its subtrim. With the aid of two accumulators, one per level to be specified, a serial pass over the leaves provides all needed information, as may be seen by stepping through the accumulator readings:

| *Point Specified* | | *Level-1 Accumulator* | *Point Specified* | | *Level-2 Accumulator* | *Leaf Entered* |
|---|---|---|---|---|---|---|
| | | | | | 1 | 1 |
| | | | | | 3 | 2 |
| | | | | | 6 | 3 |
| | | 10 | A, a | ← | 10 (clear) | 4 |
| | | | | | 5 | 5 |
| | | | | | 11 | 6 |
| | | | | | 18 | 7 |
| A | ← | 36 (clear) | A, b | ← | 26 (clear) | 8 |
| | | | | | 9 | 9 |
| | | | | | 19 | 10 |
| | | | | | 30 | 11 |
| | | 42 | B, a | ← | 42 (clear) | 12 |
| | | | | | 13 | 13 |
| | | | | | 27 | 14 |
| | | | | | 42 | 15 |
| B | ← | 100 (clear) | B, b | ← | 58 (clear) | 16 |
| | | | | | 17 | 17 |
| | | | | | 35 | 18 |
| | | | | | 54 | 19 |
| | | 74 | C, a | ← | 74 (clear) | 20 |
| | | | | | 21 | 21 |
| | | | | | 43 | 22 |
| | | | | | 66 | 23 |
| C | ← | 164 | C, b | ← | 90 | 24 |

While leaves are being scanned sequentially, each accumulator sums families and periodically specifies another point. (With a marginal increase in data handling, the trim can be closed with one accumulator; a pass over the leaves specifies level 2, and then a pass over the nodes of level 2 specifies level 1.)

If the leaves are not in convenient order, a comparable serial pass may require $t - w$ accumulators, one per unspecified node point. (The number can be reduced somewhat if, as mentioned in the previous paragraph, the trim is closed one level at a time.) For example, if the leaf level of Fig. 2.4(a) is given and it is desired to specify the level-1 and level-2 points of Fig. 2.4(b) by a serial pass over the given leaves, ten accumulators are required. Let each accumulator be identified by a point tag. The first leaf, (A, a, 1), is routed to accumulators (a) and (a, 1); the second leaf is routed to accumulators (a) and (a, 2); etc. The last leaf is routed to accumulators (b) and (b, 4).

If the leaves of the array in Fig. 2.4(a) are held in a storage mechanism that permits direct access to any leaf, the serial-pass consideration loses importance. Since it is possible to calculate the position of any desired leaf from its tag (as explained in Sec. 3.6), the leaf order shown in Fig. 2.4(b) can be simulated by skipping about in the array of Fig. 2.4(a). This expedient requires no more accumulators than the most convenient serial pass. In other words, where indexing is applied, an array held in direct-access storage can be processed in the leaf order of any of its transpose arrays. (In some forms of direct-access storage, however, the access delay is a function of physical distance and the serial pass still offers some performance advantage over a nonserial pass.)

Numerical arrays, with leaves identified by indexing, are the typical data structure in the computations of science and engineering. Such arrays are easy to understand and they can be represented, stored, and searched with utmost efficiency. Analysts who work solely with arrays sometimes find it difficult to conceive that data structure can offer much in the way of challenging problems.

The larger truth, nevertheless, is that the genuine challenges of data structure are little glimpsed until one has gone beyond the indexed numerical array to other structures, other ranges, and other methods of naming nodes. In fact, nobody has yet been successful in establishing an adequate terminology for the data structures that fall outside the pale of arrays. At the dawn of the computer era, the notions of scalar, vector, matrix, and general array were waiting to be used. But the people who were dealing with truly complicated data aggregates—principally librarians, statisticians, and accountants—had no common vocabulary. With the scanty data-processing technologies available to them, moreover, it would have been ridiculous for them to spend much time on the potential complexities of their data structures.

It is no accident, therefore, that computers and programming languages were first designed with numerical arrays in mind. Other ranges and structures have had to be forced upon the designers.

## 2.6 Uniform Trims

An array is a uniform trim with base-$r$ structure. Even if base structure is lacking, a uniform trim of height $h$ has $h!$ transposes, as does an array of equal height, but there is one very significant difference: Every transpose of an indexed array is another indexed array, whereas there is no assurance that a transpose of an indexed uniform trim will be properly indexed. For example, consider a two-level indexed uniform trim with two root points of degrees 2 and 4. The transpose of this trim has four root points of degrees 2, 2, 1, and 1. The leaf-tag matrices $\boldsymbol{F}$ and $\boldsymbol{T}$ for trim and transpose are

$$\boldsymbol{F} = \begin{bmatrix} 1 & 1 \\ 1 & 2 \\ \hdashline 2 & 1 \\ 2 & 2 \\ 2 & 2 \\ 2 & 4 \end{bmatrix} \qquad \boldsymbol{T} = \begin{bmatrix} 1 & 1 \\ 1 & 2 \\ \hdashline 2 & 1 \\ 2 & 2 \\ \hdashline 3 & 2 \\ \hdashline 4 & 2 \end{bmatrix},$$

where leaf families are delineated by dotted lines. It is obvious from inspection of $\boldsymbol{T}$ that the third and fourth families of the transpose are not properly indexed.

Inasmuch as the transposes of an indexed uniform trim may turn out to be dubbed, there is often little incentive to use indexing in commercial files, which provide most of the examples of uniform trims. Dubbing becomes the natural mode of naming, and it is assured that the transposes of a dubbed file will also be dubbed. In essence, a uniform trim is an array in which some families are incomplete, and in many of the data processes that involve files this lack of completeness is associated with volatile structure: New members may be inserted and existing members may be deleted from families in the course of the process. All of this testifies more for mnemonic dubbing than for indexing.

A uniform trim consists of an ordered set of leaves and of $h - 1$ levels of additional structure. For the time being, let us simply accept the existence of the leaves and attend to leaf arrangements. Figure 2.5(a) depicts a dubbed uniform trim of height 4 with 12 leaf families; the uppermost family contains one leaf, the next contains two leaves, etc. Leaf tags are omitted, as are the arcs to leaves. In most applications, it is the first $h - 1$ levels that are involved in transposes, effectively reducing the number of interesting tag permutations from $h!$ to $(h - 1)!$. The transpose in Fig. 2.5(b) is based on a (3, 1, 2, 4) permutation: level 3 to level 1, level 1 to level 2, level 2 to level 3, and level 4 unchanged. Leaf families move about in the transpose, but the order within leaf families is not affected.

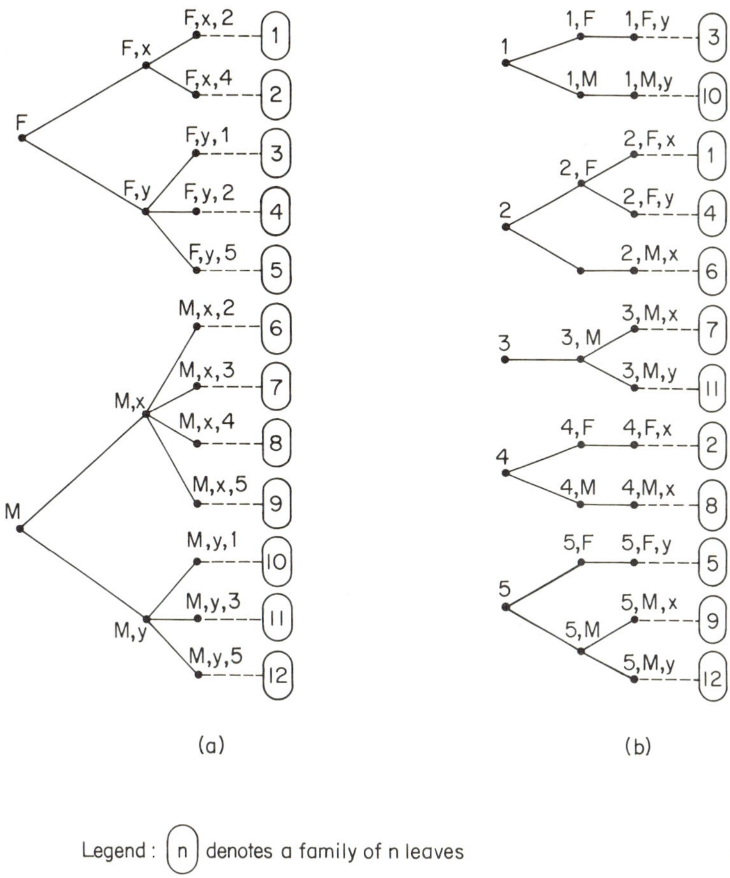


**Fig. 2.5** A dubbed file (a) and one of its transposes (b).

The utility of transposes in the serial accessing of uniform trims was explained in the context of arrays and need not be emphasized again. If

| | | |
|---|---|---|
| (F, M) | encodes | female, male |
| (x, y) | encodes | location $x$, location $y$ |
| (1, 2, 3, 4, 5) | encodes | dept. 1, dept. 2, $\cdots$, dept. 5 |

then the uniform trim of Fig. 2.5(a) is convenient for tabulating leaves by department within location within sex, and the uniform trim of Fig. 2.5(b) is convenient for tabulating leaves by location within sex within department. Figure 2.6 exhibits the weight tree that results when the uniform trim of Fig. 2.5(a) is closed by tallying. The weight tree is easily obtained in a serial pass of file

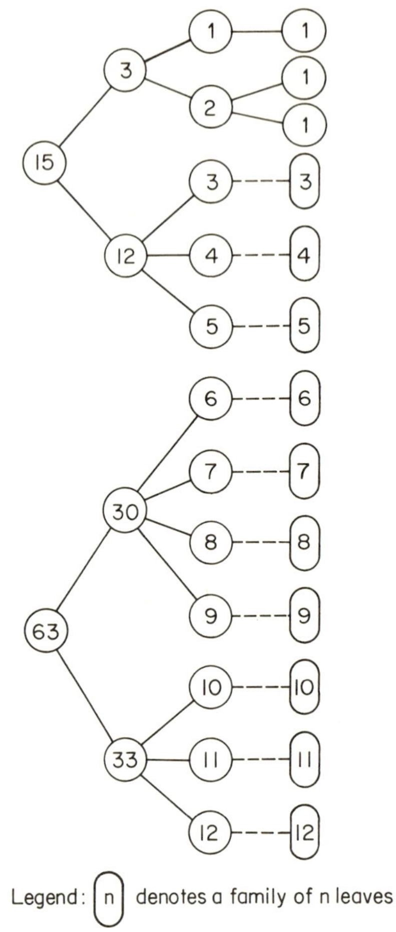


**Fig. 2.6** Weight tree for the file of Fig. 2.5(a).

(a) in the figure; for reasons explained in Sec. 2.5, it is an awkward task to obtain the same tree from file (b).

The term *file* is ordinarily used in a way that does not attempt to show the relationship between the structure of an underlying uniform trim and the order of the leaves. Here, where we are interested primarily in structure, we emphasize that dub tags determine structure and note that the purpose of sorting is merely to arrange leaves in the structural order implied by a set of dub tags. The relationship between these two viewpoints is best clarified by a general discussion of accounting applications.

The typical accounting application defines a population of *items*, an item being an object or a class of events that must be monitored for statutory, obligatory, or control purposes. An item may be an employee, a client, a potential client, an end product, a subassembly, and so on. As the heart of the accounting application, one may envision a large matrix or *master file*. Each row of the master file is a *record*; a record contains the various units of information pertaining to one item. Each column of the master file records one unit of information (some measurement or attribute) for every item. Whereas a file matrix may contain thousands or millions of rows, the number of columns is likely to be in the tens or hundreds. Some of the column vectors may be arbitrary, others numerical, others integral, and still others logical.

The functions involved in maintaining and using a master file usually lead to various complications that do not reveal themselves at first glance. Most of these complications arise out of the following circumstances:

1. The item population is changing,
2. Maintenance and use may involve many different people,
3. Information is used for diverse kinds of analytical needs.

Because record format is carefully planned, the column names are changed infrequently. In view of circumstance 1, however, it is not unusual for new records to be inserted and existing records to be deleted. A user of the master file may possibly be expected to memorize column indices, but he can hardly be expected to mention rows by their indices. There are too many rows, and furthermore the row index of a given record may change as the population changes. It is far more expedient to dub each row by a tag (a name or mnemonic for the item described by a record) and store the tag in the row itself. Because the column that contains these tags (better known as *keys*) constitutes an alphabet, the problem of finding the row index of a record, given the record tag, comes down to a ranking operation in what may be a very large alphabet.

File processing consists of maintenance, routine processing, and analysis. Maintenance includes the updating of record components as well as record insertions and deletion. Updating does not change the number of rows; insertions and deletions may. Routine processing ordinarily consists of the record-by-record preparation of documents such as bills, orders, or check payments. File analysis implies procedures that extract, process, and summarize information from some or all of the records.

In the typical master file many of the columns correspond to categories that can serve to define levels in a dubbed uniform trim. The number of possible trims that can be postulated may be very large. An analysis typically involves the closing of a uniform trim (or subtrim) to form a uniform tree (or subtree). Since the leaves of a postulated trim usually imply another arrangement than that of the master file, a matrix representation of the desired trim is compressed from the master file and transposed into a convenient order for processing. Even if the number of different analyses is modest, a good deal of sorting may be required to effect the transpositions. In the past, various rules of thumb have attributed between one fifth and one third of all the computer processing in accounting applications to sorting.

Sorting is most obligatory where the master file is stored on a medium that requires records to be serially accessed. On the other hand, if the master file can be held in a storage device that permits direct access to any desired record, the sorting can be circumvented (done implicitly, one might say) by accessing records in the order most convenient for analysis of a postulated uniform trim. A similar assertion was made for arrays, but arrays and uniform trims differ in one very salient respect: In an indexed array, the position of a leaf can be calculated from its index tag; in a uniform trim, whether indexed or dubbed, the position of a leaf cannot be calculated from the tag. Hence, to access the leaves of a file in a nonserial order, the file must contain a column (a mapping vector) consisting of *pointers* (row numbers) that lead from record to record in the desired order. That is, the record currently being visited contains (as a component of the mapping column) the row number of the record that should next be visited. The problem is that each postulated uniform trim has a leaf sequence that must be predetermined and recorded in the master file. If the number of required analyses is high, the quantity of additional storage needed for mapping vectors and the task of maintaining mapping vectors can be important considerations. Furthermore, the pointer technique is limited to analyses that are repetitive enough to justify the expense of a mapping column.

Over 80 years ago, Herman Hollerith, a statistician at the U.S. Bureau of the Census, pondered the problem of processing the file matrix that would soon be generated by the Eleventh Census. Here are some excerpts from "An Electric Tabulating System," an article he published in 1889 in *The Quarterly*, a publication of the School of Mines, Columbia University. His observations bear out the assertion that a master file is a spawning ground for analyses. From a structural point of view, of course, each analysis implies a particular uniform trim.

> Few, who have not come directly in contact with a census office, can form any adequate idea of the labor involved in the compilation of a census of 50,000,000 persons, as was the case in the last census, or of over 62,000,000, as will be the case in the census to be taken in June, 1890. . . .
>
> Although our population is constantly increasing, and although at each census more complicated combinations and greater detail are required in the various compilations, still, up to the present time, substantially the original method of compilation has been employed; that of making tally-marks in small squares and then adding and counting such tally-marks. . . .
>
> The work of a census can be divided into two main branches; that of enumeration, and that of compilation or tabulation. In regard to the enumeration, the plan originally adopted at the tenth census, with such splendid results, will substantially be followed in the next census. . . .

The population schedules of the tenth census contained the following inquiries, the replies to which were capable of statistical treatment:

Race or color: whether white, black, mulatto, Chinese or Indian.
Sex.
Age.
Relationship of each person enumerated to the head of the family.
Civil or conjugal condition: whether single, married, widowed, or divorced.
Whether married during the census year.
Occupation.
Number of months unemployed.
Whether sick or otherwise temporarily disabled so as to be unable to attend to ordinary business or duties on the day of the enumeration; what was the sickness or disability?
Whether blind, deaf and dumb, idiotic, insane, maimed, crippled, bedridden, or otherwise disabled. Whether the person attended school during the census year.
Cannot read.
Cannot write.
Place of birth.
Place of birth of father.
Place of birth of mother. . . .

If it is of interest and value to know the number of males and of females in our population, of how much greater interest is it to know the number of native males and of foreign males; or again to know the number of native white males, of foreign white males, of colored males, etc.; or still again, the combination of each one of these facts with each single year of age. All this was done in the tenth census. Many other interesting and valuable combinations were compiled, far surpassing anything of the kind that had ever before been attempted, still, on the other hand, many of the facts enumerated were never compiled at all. Thus, for example, it is to-day impossible to obtain the slightest reliable statistical information regarding the conjugal conditions of our people, though the complete data regarding this is locked up in the returns of the enumeration of the tenth census. . . .

If the data regarding the relationship of each person to the head of the family were properly compiled, in combination with various other data, a vast amount of valuable information would be obtained. So again, if the number of months unemployed were properly enumerated and compiled with reference to age, to occupation, etc., much information might be obtained of great value to the student of the economic problems affecting our wage-earners.

One more illustration will be given. We have in a census, besides the data relating to our living population, records regarding the deaths during the previous year. In both cases we have the information regarding age and occupation. If the living population were tabulated by combinations of age and occupation, and likewise the deaths by ages and occupations, we would then have data from which some reliable inferences might be drawn regarding the effects of various occupations upon length of life. It might even be possible to construct life tables for the various occupations as we now do for the different States and cities. Such information would be of service in relation to life insurance and other problems. Again, it would point out any needed reforms regarding the sanitary conditions and surroundings of any occupation. This is a field of statistical investigation which is as yet almost wholly unexplored.

In this connection it may perhaps be proper to quote from a letter addressed to the writer, in reply to certain inquiries by General Francis A. Walker, the well-known Superintendent of the Tenth Census:

"In the census of a country so populous as the United States the work of tabulation might be carried on almost literally without limit, and yet not cease to obtain new facts and combinations of facts of political, social, and economic significance"....

Heretofore in census and similar compilations essentially one of two methods has been followed. Either the records have been preserved in their proper relations, and the information drawn off by tallying first one grouping of facts and then the next, or the records have been written upon cards or slips, which are first sorted and counted according to one grouping of facts and then according to the next.

To form some idea of the questions involved in the first plan, let us assume that the record relating to each person at the next census be written in a line across a strip of paper, and that such lines are exactly one-half inch apart, it would then take a strip of paper over 500 miles long to contain such records. These must be gone over, again and again, until all the desired combinations have been obtained. This is practically the method followed in compiling the tenth census. On the other hand, if written cards are to be used the prospect is hardly more encouraging. One hundred comparatively thin cards will form a stack over an inch high. In the next census, therefore, if such cards are to be used it will require a stack over ten miles high. Imagine for a moment the trouble and confusion which would be caused by a few such cards becoming misplaced. This method of individual cards was employed in the census of Massachusetts for 1885. The 2,000,000 cards there used weighed about 14 tons. Were the same cards to be used in the next United Sates census it would require about 450 tons of such cards.

In place of these methods it is suggested that the work be done so far as possible by mechanical means. In order to accomplish this the records must be put in such shape that a machine could read them. This is most readily done by punching holes in cards or strips of paper, which perforations can then be used to control circuits through electromagnets operating counters, or sorting mechanism, or both combined....

In a census the enumerator's district forms the statistical unit of area, and a suitable combination is arranged to designate each such district. A card is punched with the corresponding combination for each person in such enumeration districts, and the cards of each district are then numbered consecutively, in a suitable numbering machine, to correspond with numbers assigned to the individual records on the enumerator's returns. This combination of holes, and this number, will serve to identify any card....

As the combination of holes used for designating the enumerator's district are the same for all the cards of that district, a special machine is arranged for punching these holes. This machine is provided with a number of interchangeable punches, which are placed according to the combination it is desired to punch. Five or six cards are then placed in the punch against suitable stops and by means of a lever the corresponding holes are punched through these cards at one operation.

The individual records are now transcribed to the corresponding cards by punching according to a pre-arranged scheme as described above. For this purpose what may be known as a keyboard-punch is arranged, in which the card is held fixed in a frame, while the punch is moved over the card in any direction by means of a projecting lever provided with a suitable knob or handle. Below the knob is a keyboard provided with holes lettered and numbered according to the diagram of the card, and so arranged that when a pin projecting below the knob is over any hole, the punch is over the corresponding space of the card. If the pin is depressed into any hole of the keyboard, the punch is operated and the corresponding space of the card is punched. With such a keyboard-punch it is, of course, apparent that a perfectly blank card may be used, one corner, however, being cut off to properly locate the card in subsequent operations. . . .

In a census the cards as they come from the punching machines would, of course, be arranged according to enumeration districts. . . . such facts as it is desired to know in relation to this unit of area could be counted on the counters, while the cards are at the same time assorted according to some other set of facts, arranging them in convenient form for further tabulations. In this manner, by the arrangement of a judicious "scheme," it will be found that a most elaborate compilation may be effected with but a few handlings of the cards. . . .

## 2.7 Trims

Arrays are characteristic of scientific calculation and files of accounting and census tabulation. But arrays and files are uniform trims. One may well ask, What of trims in general? For the answer regarding nonuniform trims, we must look more closely at the structure of records.

In Sec. 2.6, we assumed that every record in a master file was identical in form. In some applications, however, strict adherence to identical forms is wasteful because too many elements of the master file are null. This is particularly true where the records must contain repeating units of information. For example, consider an employee record that retains, along with other data, the names of employee's dependents. If a large number of columns are set aside for possible names, most of the space provided will go unused. The structure of a fixed-layout record is essentially that of a row vector in a matrix, viz., that of a family of leaves in which each leaf corresponds to one datum. One way to provide greater freedom in record structure is to endow the record with the structure of a trim. The practical effect of this is to permit the leaves that comprise the record to vary in number, in which case the file is said to consist of *variable length* records.

For purposes of illustration, Fig. 2.7 depicts a miniature master file of three records and five fields (units of information) per record. All of the leaf families are identical in dimension and the structure is that of a matrix. The uppermost node of each family is set aside for employee name (which is not entered

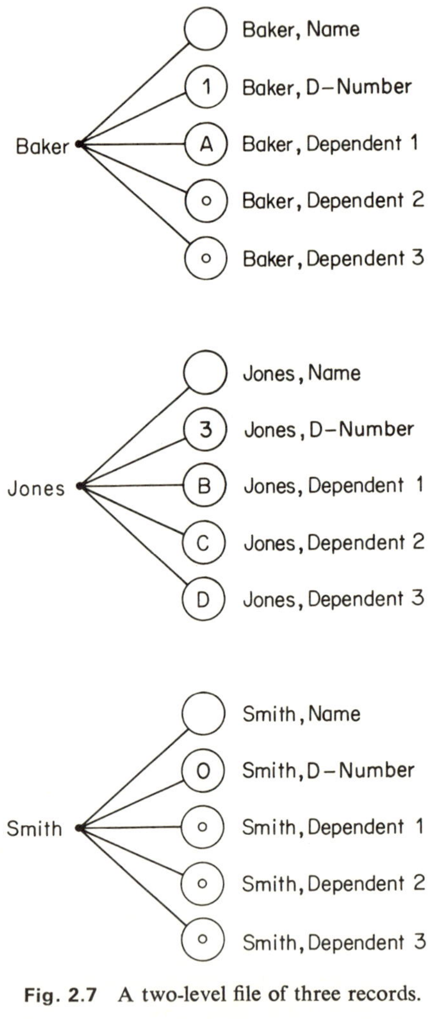


**Fig. 2.7** A two-level file of three records.

for the sake of convenience), the second node for a "D-number" that specifies number of dependents, and the remaining nodes for the names of dependents (for the illustration, the assumed maximum is three and names are shortened

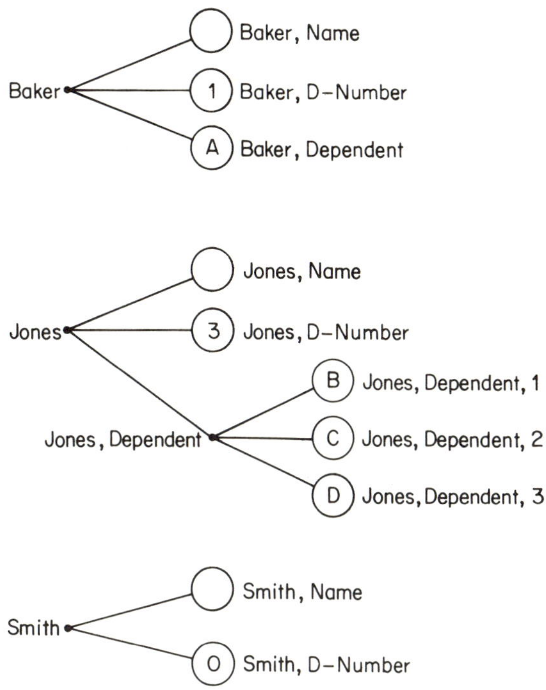


**Fig. 2.8** The file of Fig. 2.7 represented as a trim of three levels.

to one letter to fit the circles). BAKER has one dependent, JONES three, and SMITH none. If records are permitted to have additional structure, the file may take the form of the trim shown in Fig. 2.8. The trim permits fewer leaves than the file at the expense of greater complexity in structure. As a general rule, we shall later see, additional complexity in structure magnifies the problems of storage allocation and search. Nonetheless, records are frequently designed with multiple levels of name structure and stored as variable length vectors to handle the problems occasioned by repeating units of information or by the need to be able to refer to subunits within units (for example, year within a numerical datum that represents a date by month, day, and year). In the literature, records that go beyond the simple structure of a vector are sometimes referred to as *structures*.

The literature also contains references to *list structures*, many of which are trims in the sense that data appear always at the leaves. Since list structures place additional information at the nonleaf nodes, they are discussed as trees in Sec. 2.8.

To jump from records to a context with much larger structures, it is instructive to consider the data aggregates known as libraries. If one is willing to overlook some aberrations, the Library of Congress Classification System and the Dewey Decimal System are instances of dubbing. This being the case, a library may be viewed as a vast trim in which the leaves are documents and the tags are *call numbers*.

## 2.8 Trees

The data processes that generate trees may be usefully divided into two classes.

1. Those that generate trees of predictable structure
2. Those that generate trees of unpredictable structure

Class-1 processes may start with a trim of given structure and form a tree in the course of closing the trim. Class-2 processes start with a scalar and "grow" a tree by appending surtrees. Inasmuch as the trees of classes 1 and 2 pose very different problems in a practical sense, we discuss them separately.

The most elementary class-1 process lends the structure of a given trim to a process-generated tree. For example, base-$r$ trees often arise in the course of a process that closes an array. Each level in a base-$r$ tree of height $h$ can be analyzed as an array. The first level can be treated as a vector, the second level as a matrix, the third level as an array of height 3, etc. Because the base-$r$ tree decomposes so easily and naturally into arrays, it is seldom viewed as a tree at all.

Much the same thing happens in the case of files. Although commercial data processing contains many examples of procedures that obtain trees by closing files, the resulting trees have a uniform structure and their levels can often be treated as independent files with no loss of information. The well-known exceptions are bill-of-materials or parts-explosion applications, wherein the tree structure cannot be overlooked because every node (except perhaps the leaves) contains planning factors needed in the course of computation.

One of the simplest processes for generating a tree starts with a trim, replaces each leaf by a 1, and generates the implied weight tree. Such a process is illustrated for a trim of seven leaves in Fig. 2.9: the original trim appears in (a), the implied summation operators in (b), and the resultant weight tree in (c). Note that the evaluation process must sweep from leaves toward roots; the root level is the last to be fully evaluated. If the trim is of numerical range, the same operators can be applied to the leaves to yield a sum tree, as in (d) of Fig. 2.9. The weight and sum trees in the figure exemplify the kinds of results frequently obtained through tallying and tabulation tasks on very large trims. More often than not, in fact, the trims are uniform and the process is even more systematic than the one illustrated.

Although the process depicted in Fig. 2.9 generalizes with some utility to a few other operators, such as *minimum* or *maximum*, any process based

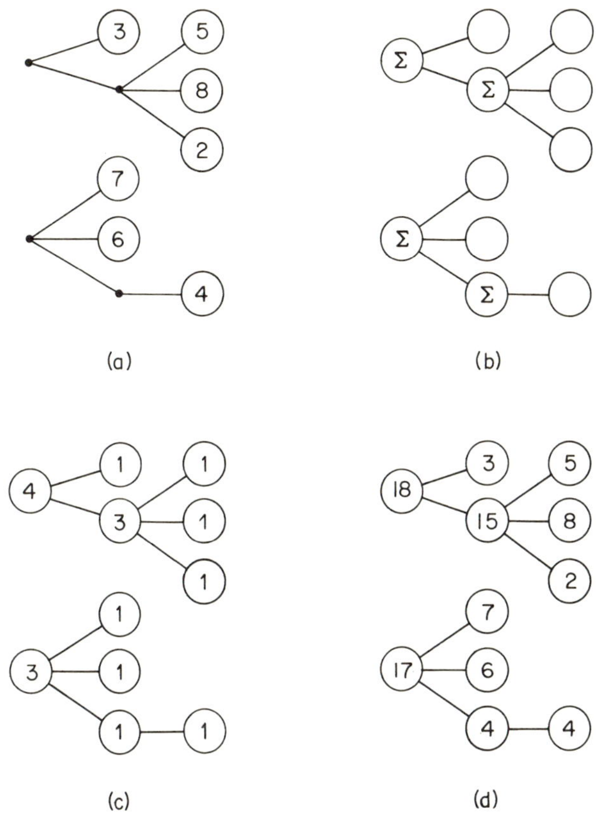


**Fig. 2.9** Two trees obtained by closing trims: (a) numerical trim; (b) summation operators; (c) weight tree; (d) sum tree.

on a single operator is inherently limited. A more complicated process requires the notion of an "algebraic expression" in which leaves are variables and a non-leaf node can consist of any operator from a *vocabulary* that consists of a set of operators. For example, the expression

$$[(e \div f) + h] \times [(a \div b) + (c \times d) + g]$$

is represented as a tree in Fig. 2.10. The variables appear as leaves and the operators as interior nodes. To envision an actual evaluation of the expression, assume that all of the leaf variables have been specified as numbers. Any family of two leaves can be operated by its parent node, whereupon the result of the operation respecifies the parent as a number. This opens the way for further operations, and the process culminates in a number that specifies the root.

Expressions may be permitted when data processes are documented in *high-level* programming languages. The structure of an expression is intrinsic in the process itself. When an expression is executed, the result of interest is the root;

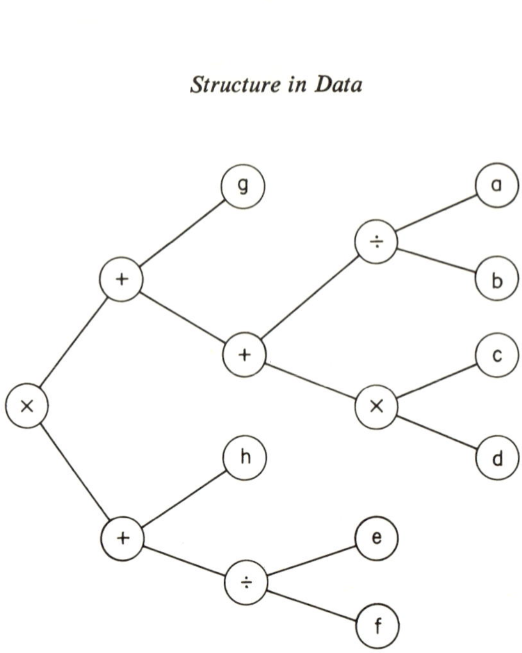


Expression : ((e ÷ f) + h) × ((a ÷ b) + (c × d) + g)

**Fig. 2.10** Example of an expression and its tree.

other interior nodes are merely intermediate results that need not be preserved. A program that documents a complicated data process normally consists of many expressions that are referred to again and again in the course of a sequence that includes conditional branches. Of course, the root of any given expression may appear as a leaf in a subsequently executed expression.

An expression with one operator is a *simple* expression; an expression that contains more than one operator is a *compound* expression. Before a compound expression can be executed by a machine that performs operations serially, the expression must be *translated* into a sequence of simple operations. The fact that every expression can be viewed as a singly rooted tree makes it feasible to systematize this translation process.

The tree of an expression is normally a tree of modest moment. However, a program that consists of $n$ singly rooted expressions can be represented as a tree with $n$ roots. In other words, each expression is a subtree in the program tree. This is to view the program in a static sense. In execution, control must pass from subtree to subtree in an appropriate order. We shall return to this in Chapter 6.

To summarize, trees of given or predictable structure are normally obtained by closing a trim. The structure may be provided by the trim, as is usually the case when uniform trims are closed by elementary processes. Or the structure of the trim may be incidental to the structure of the process, as is the case when complicated processes are documented in expressions. To generalize from both cases, however, we can say that most numerical data processing consists of closing trims.

Class-2 trees, i.e., trees of unpredictable and volatile structure, crop up in algorithms that make structure a function of unpredictable events or incoming data; each time the algorithm is executed, a novel structure may emerge. An algorithm that analyzes possible sequences of moves in a gamelike process may need to store paths lest it explore the same paths again and again; moreover, the algorithm cannot predict which decision an opponent will elect to make. An algorithm that sets out to prove a theorem from previously established theorems has a comparable problem in that it must "learn" to avoid unpromising paths until it finds one that succeeds. Less exotic, but far more common, is the simple example of the vector that changes in dimension, as when a vector represents a dynamic queue.

As a consequence of their structural unpredictability, class-2 trees are exceedingly difficult to process by methods that lend themselves naturally and effectively to arrays and typical files. Because of this, class-2 trees have inspired a body of special techniques known as the field of *list processing*. Since these techniques emerged in the context of unusual applications, the attitudes, performance objectives, and nomenclatures in the field are largely alien to the fields of scientific and commercial processing. Furthermore, the topics herein classified as structure representation (in Chapter 3), tag searching (in Chapter 4), and memory allocation (in Chapter 10) are more thoroughly confounded in list processing than in the case of conventional array and file processing. In view of this, a brief discussion that slights operational practices runs some risk of oversimplification.

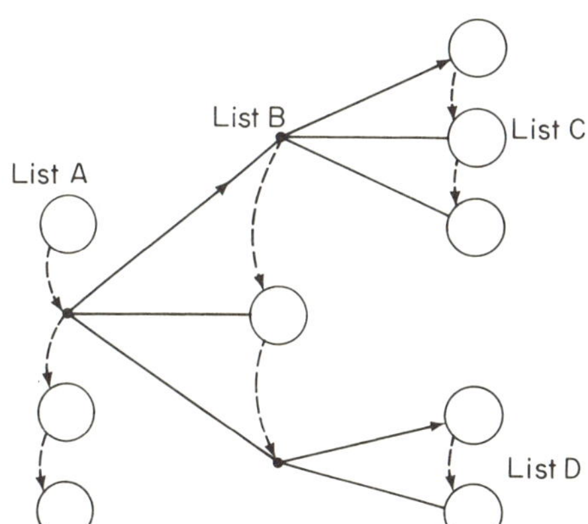


**Fig. 2.11** A list structure depicted as a trim.

A *list* is a family. In a *list structure*, a component of any list may be another list. Letting lists correspond to families, a list structure is seen to be a trim. The schematic trim in Fig. 2.11 represents a list structure of four lists. The trim has three levels because lists *C* and *D* are both components of list *B*, which, in turn, is a component of list *A*.

Three representational practices have often tended to obscure the underlying trims in list structures. First, although the typical list structure places data only at the leaves, search pointers (usually integers designating storage addresses) are placed at other node points for the sake of leaf search (as discussed in Sec. 4.4). The arrows in Fig. 2.11 depict pointers: Dotted arrows represent member-to-member pointers within families, whereas solid arrows represent a pointer from one level to another. In one sense, therefore, every list structure is a tree—or perhaps one should say the combination of a control tree and a data trim. Second, list structures with pairs of pointers have the ostensible appearance of a binary tree; this can obscure the structure of the underlying trim. (Note from Fig. 2.11 that only the uppermost arc to a family plays a role in list representation.) Third, cases sometimes arise in which two path diagrams are permitted to lead to the same leaf. If leaves take more space than pointers, and if two leaves are known to be identical, this is a natural expedient and one that can save space as compared to storing the leaves separately.

A list structure that stores data at every point can represent a data tree. But whether the list structure represents a trim or a tree, the tree diagram is always represented. The advantages of a list structure for storage allocation will become apparent in Chapter 3, but the advantages all stem from the fact that the underlying tree diagram is explicitly represented in the pointers rather than implicitly in an ordering of nodes.

## 2.9 Structurands of Structurands

A completely general structurand, i.e., one whose interior is populated at random by points and circles, is not a thing one expects to be useful. More likely to crop up are systematic generalizations, such as a trim of trees, a tree of trims, a tree of trees. Such generalizations are most conveniently analyzed as hybrid structures.

The most likely combination, the trim of trims, is not a hybrid at all; it is simply another trim of extended height. For example, a vector of compatible vectors is a matrix. A matrix of compatible vectors is an array of height 3, as is a vector of compatible matrices. A matrix of incompatible vectors is a uniform trim of height 3, etc. The trim of trims can provide us with an insight into node representation (which is discussed systematically at the end of Chapter 10). Nodes must be encoded because electronic computers are extremely limited in their functional capabilities: They can process only logical structurands. As a result, unless a structurand is of logical range from the outset, it must be converted into a logical structurand.

Formatting and encoding processes may add to the height of a structurand. For example, if a leaf in a file is chosen to schematically depict a record, the record string must be formatted into fields, the fields encoded in characters, and the characters encoded in zeros and ones—all of which heightens the file by three levels. The effect of encoding a trim is to replace leaves by surtrims and thereby append additional structure. Consider a file with $m$ fields per record, $n$ characters per field as an average, and $p$ logical components per character. If $m = 20$, $n = 6$, and $p = 7$, for example, the logical trim will have $m \times n \times p = 840$ leaves for every record. Except where this additional structure is essential to analysis or exposition, it is best avoided.

## 2.10 Comment

The purpose of this chapter has been to classify and discuss various data structures with the aid of the tree diagram developed in Chapter 1. The discussion proceeded from simple structurands characterized by highly regular structures to those of less systematic structures. It was pointed out that indexed arrays are the characteristic structurands of engineering mathematics and dubbed files are characteristic of accounting analyses. The uniform trim, a category that includes both arrays and files, is the predominant structurand in most data processing.

The term *data processing* alludes to structure in two ways: the data are typically organized as trims, and when documented, the processes reveal the structure of trees. Data processes may vary from utter simplicity to great complexity. A complex process may consist of a sequence of expressions, each of which closes a trim in order to specify a root; the root may then go on to become a leaf in a trim that is subsequently closed by another expression, etc. Methods of documenting such processes are discussed in Chapter 6.

The structural parameters of an indexed array are normally fixed prior to a calculation. The dubbed uniform trim is typically subject to a maintenance procedure that can somewhat modify the number of leaves between successive calculations. Trims or trees that can undergo dramatic changes in structure during calculation give rise to special space-allocation problems that motivated the development of list-processing techniques.

The discussion of vectors and matrices follows K. E. Iverson (1962), who applied the term *structured operand* to arrays and trees. Here, the term is shortened to structurand and given a broader meaning. The word *trim* was coined for the purposes of this book; it is less encumbered than *list structure* or *structure*, the nearest equivalents in the literature. An early discussion of lists and list structures appears in A. Newell and J. C. Shaw (1957). The use of the verb *close* in the sense of generating a tree from a trim is new here. The term *master file* is applied in its conventional sense.

For an approach to trees and list structures that stresses motivation and historical comment, the reader may savor the discussion of information structures by D. E. Knuth (1968). His discussion extends to about 310 pages, of which 75 pages are allocated for answers to exercises.

*Chapter 3*

# STRUCTURE REPRESENTATION

To represent a structurand, it is necessary to represent two different things: a tree diagram and a set of nodes. The present chapter deals solely with the representation of tree diagrams. While it is true that nodes must be given special representations for automatic data processes, they can be discussed simply as numbers or character strings until we reach the topic of encoding in Chapter 10.

The vector and the matrix play an important role in all discussions of representation. For our purposes, the problem of representing structure can be analyzed as the problem of expressing a tree diagram in a vector or matrix.

## 3.1 Introduction

Vectors of dimension $h$ are often useful in summarizing selected aspects of structure. In the *weight vector* $\boldsymbol{w}$ of a given tree diagram, component $\boldsymbol{w}_i$ is specified by the maximum of the point weights at the $i$th level. The weight vector of the diagram in Fig. 3.1 is (8, 6, 4, 2, 1). Component $\boldsymbol{r}_i$ of the *dimension vector* $\boldsymbol{r}$ is specified by the maximum of the family dimensions at the $i$th level; hence, the diagram of Fig. 3.1 has the dimension vector (2, 3, 2, 2, 2). Each component of the *count vector* is a level count; the count vector from Fig. 3.1 is (2, 5, 4, 5, 4). Other information, such as a count of the leaf points at each level, may also be summarized in this way.

Before discussing general methods of representing a tree diagram, it simplifies matters to establish two conventions for ordering points. Points in the diagram of Fig. 3.2 are identified by a *right index*. The right index simply numbers points downward within each level, starting with the first level and moving successively to higher levels until all points are identified. On the other

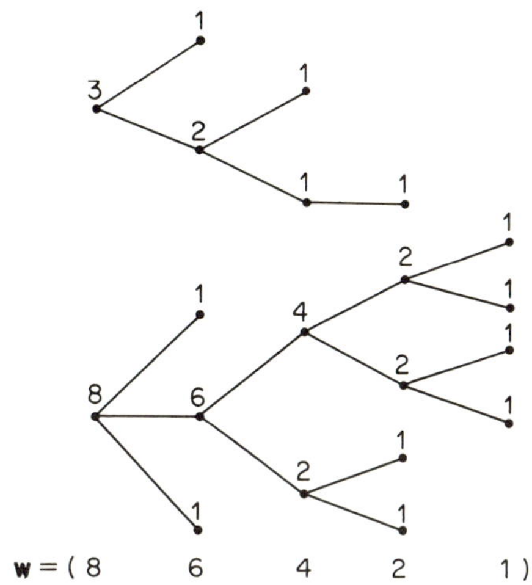


**Fig. 3.1** Tree diagram and weight vector.

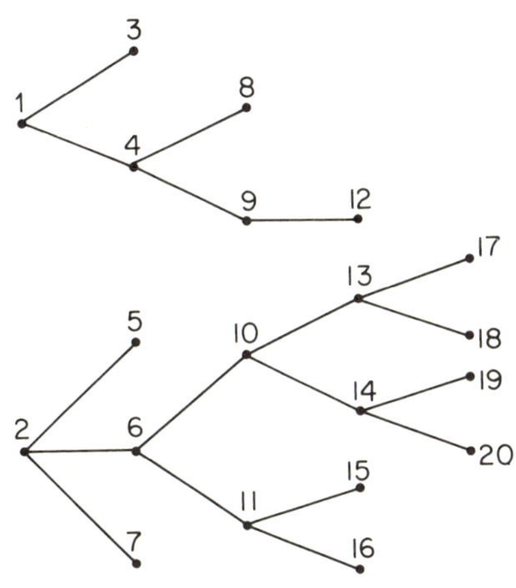

**Fig. 3.2** Tree diagram and right index.

hand, in Fig. 3.3 the points are identified by a *left index*. The left index starts with the uppermost point of the root family; within families, the general direction of indexing is again downward (call this rule I). However, the indexing of point $k + 1$ of a family is postponed until all points reachable from point $k$ of the family have been indexed (rule II). The effect of the left index, therefore, is to sweep out path diagrams, starting with the uppermost path diagram and working downward. Whenever a path diagram is terminated by a leaf point, the sweep resumes with the next point of the partially indexed family selected by rule II. (A rationale for the adjectives *left* and *right* appears in Sec. 3.2.)

As explained in Chapter 1, every point in a tree diagram is the root point

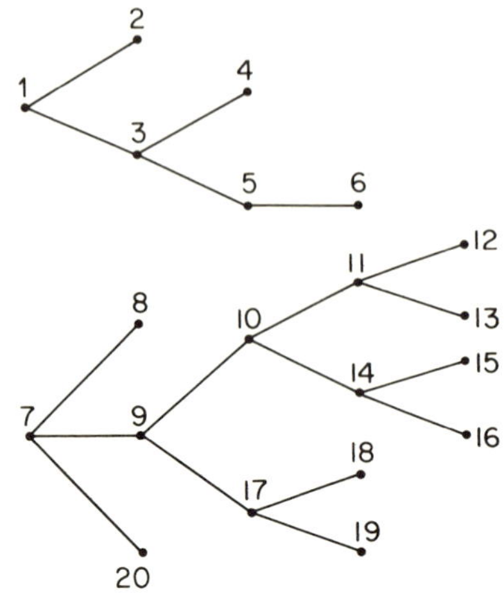


**Fig. 3.3** Tree diagram and left index.

of a subtree diagram. If the nodes of a tree are listed sequentially in left-index order, each node is followed immediately by all of the nodes in its subtree. Left-index order is therefore the most convenient order for subtree analysis.

## 3.2 Tag Matrices

One way to reconstruct a tree diagram from a set of index or dub tags is to maneuver the tags into place, much as though the tags were pieces in a jigsaw puzzle. In the interests of systematic data processing, a better way is to treat the tags as vectors and gather them into a tag matrix of $t$ rows and $h$ columns. Of course, unless the tree diagram is of height 1, its tag vectors are not all compatible. To render them compatible, some may be lengthened—at one end or the other—with components consisting of null characters (or zeros, where one-origin indexing applies). When the tag matrices so obtained are sorted on rows, left-justified tags yield a *left tag matrix* with rows in left-index order, whereas right-justified tags yield a *right tag matrix* with rows in right-index order.

To illustrate this, Fig. 3.4 contains an indexed tree with nodes of the form $p \cdot q$, where $p$ denotes left index and $q$ denotes right index. The corresponding tag matrices, each sorted on rows, are shown below. $\boldsymbol{L}$ denotes the left tag matrix and $\boldsymbol{R}$ denotes the right tag matrix. Corresponding nodes are shown to the left of $\boldsymbol{L}$ and to the right of $\boldsymbol{R}$.

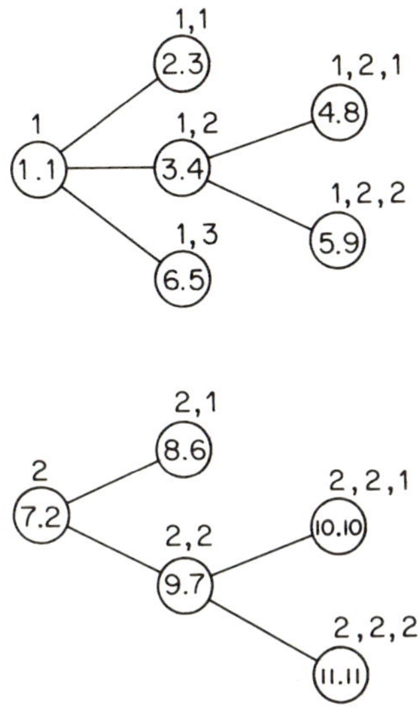


**Fig. 3.4** Illustrative tree.

$$
\begin{array}{c}
p\cdot q \\ 1.1 \\ 2.3 \\ 3.4 \\ 4.8 \\ 5.9 \\ 6.5 \\ 7.2 \\ 8.6 \\ 9.7 \\ 10.10 \\ 11.11
\end{array}
\quad
\begin{array}{c}
\boldsymbol{L} \\
\begin{bmatrix}
1 & \circ & \circ \\
1 & 1 & \circ \\
1 & 2 & \circ \\
1 & 2 & 1 \\
1 & 2 & 2 \\
1 & 3 & \circ \\
2 & \circ & \circ \\
2 & 1 & \circ \\
2 & 2 & \circ \\
2 & 2 & 1 \\
2 & 2 & 2
\end{bmatrix}
\end{array}
\qquad
\begin{array}{c}
\boldsymbol{R} \\
\begin{bmatrix}
\circ & \circ & 1 \\
\circ & \circ & 2 \\
\circ & 1 & 1 \\
\circ & 1 & 2 \\
\circ & 1 & 3 \\
\circ & 2 & 1 \\
\circ & 2 & 2 \\
1 & 2 & 1 \\
1 & 2 & 2 \\
2 & 2 & 1 \\
2 & 2 & 2
\end{bmatrix}
\end{array}
\quad
\begin{array}{c}
p\cdot q \\ 1.1 \\ 7.2 \\ 2.3 \\ 3.4 \\ 6.5 \\ 8.6 \\ 9.7 \\ 4.8 \\ 5.9 \\ 10.10 \\ 11.11
\end{array}
\tag{3.1}
$$

The left index corresponds to row number in a left tag matrix; the right index corresponds to row number in a right tag matrix.

Any tag matrix produced by indexing or dubbing is a complete representation of a tree diagram. Moreover, where advantageous, the rows containing tags of *interior* points (nonleaf points) can be omitted and generated again when needed. The main advantages of the left and right tag matrices stem from their orderly disposition of subtrees and levels. For example, one glance at the first column of matrix $L$ reveals the moments (6 and 5) of the subtrees rooted in level 1. On the other hand, $R$ partitions levels in order (level 1 at the top).

Given a uniform tree diagram, the tags of all the leaf points sink to the bottom in a right tag matrix to form a leaf-level partition that serves as a convenient representation for the structure of a uniform trim. If a sequence of symbols used to distinguish among the members of a point family is called a *tagging alphabet*, we see that column $h$ of a right tag matrix neatly summarizes all the tagging alphabets for a whole tree diagram. From $R_3$, for example, we read the five tagging alphabets used in Fig. 3.4:

$$(1, 2), (1, 2, 3), (1, 2), (1, 2), (1, 2). \tag{3.2}$$

In the case of an indexed tree diagram, the column can be subdivided into families by breaks in ascending sequence. In the case of a dubbed structure, it should be added, sequence breaks do not suffice as a guide; additional information, obtainable from other columns, is needed to delineate families.

The principal advantage of the left tag matrix is that each point is followed immediately by its subtree diagram. If the point occupies level $k$ and its subtree diagram is of moment $m$, then $m$ consecutive rows in the matrix have identical prefixes of length $k$. For example, the node with tag (2, 2) in Fig. 3.4 corresponds to row 9 of $L$. Because the subtree of this node is of moment 3, rows 9 through 11 of $L$ all contain the prefix (2, 2).

Two properties of ordered tag matrices have important implications. First, a tag matrix takes up an appreciable amount of storage space. Second, a structural change, i.e., the insertion or deletion of a point, must be expected to *ripple* about half of the matrix rows into new storage positions. If the matrix contains many rows, maintenance can be time-consuming in an environment that leads to frequent change in structure.

## 3.3 Pointer Matrices

Figure 3.5 presents a tree diagram of moment 14 and height 4, a $14 \times 4$ left tag matrix, and a $14 \times 2$ *pointer matrix* $P$ that contains two classes of elements, viz., row numbers and nulls. Each point in the diagram is represented by one and only one row in $P$; for illustrative purposes, the rows of $P$ are arranged in left-index order. Column 1 of $P$ contains row numbers that serve to chain from point to point within families, and each null in the column signifies the last point in a family (the within-family sequence is downward, as usual). Column 2 of $P$ contains row numbers that chain between levels, the successor of a point on level $k$ always being the first member of its descendant family on level $k + 1$. Each null in column 2 signifies a leaf point, i.e., a point with no descendants.

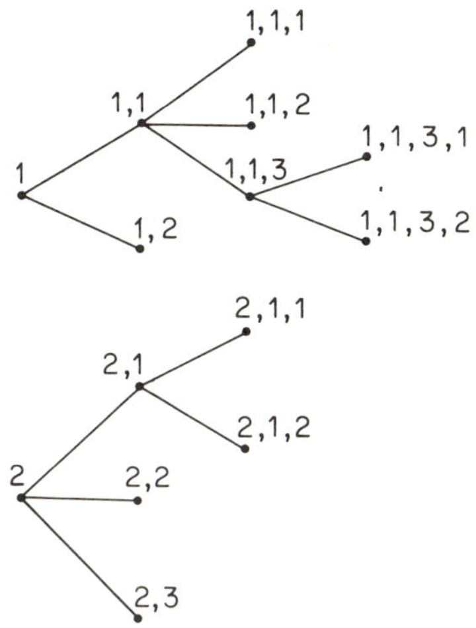


| Row | Left Tag Matrix | | | | Pointer Matrix *P* | |
|---|---|---|---|---|---|---|
| 1 | 1 | 0 | 0 | 0 | 9 | 2 |
| 2 | 1 | 1 | 0 | 0 | 8 | 3 |
| 3 | 1 | 1 | 1 | 0 | 4 | 0 |
| 4 | 1 | 1 | 2 | 0 | 5 | 0 |
| 5 | 1 | 1 | 3 | 0 | 0 | 6 |
| 6 | 1 | 1 | 3 | 1 | 7 | 0 |
| 7 | 1 | 1 | 3 | 2 | 0 | 0 |
| 8 | 1 | 2 | 0 | 0 | 0 | 0 |
| 9 | 2 | 0 | 0 | 0 | 0 | 10 |
| 10 | 2 | 1 | 0 | 0 | 13 | 11 |
| 11 | 2 | 1 | 1 | 0 | 12 | 0 |
| 12 | 2 | 1 | 2 | 0 | 0 | 0 |
| 13 | 2 | 2 | 0 | 0 | 14 | 0 |
| 14 | 2 | 3 | 0 | 0 | 0 | 0 |

**Fig. 3.5** Tree diagram and pointer matrix.

Let $\boldsymbol{d}$ denote the index tag (2, 1, 2) in the tree diagram of Fig. 3.5. The fact that $\boldsymbol{d}_1 = 2$ designates the second member of a family on the first level. Entering $\boldsymbol{P}$ at row 1 (which corresponds to root 1), column 1 points to row 9 (which corresponds to root 2); at this juncture, the conditions implied by $\boldsymbol{d}_1$ are satisfied. Moving on to $\boldsymbol{d}_2$, the pointer in column 2 of row 9 points across levels to row 10; now, the conditions implied by $\boldsymbol{d}_2$ are satisfied. Moving to $\boldsymbol{d}_3$, column 2 of row 10 points across levels to row 11, where column 1 points within the family to row 12. We have arrived at the point sought; all of the implied instructions in $\boldsymbol{d}$ have been carried out.

Although the pointer matrix presents a jumble of information to the eye, it faithfully preserves the structure of a tree diagram.† Its notable property is the complete lack of need for a prescribed order. The contents of any two rows can be interchanged, for example, as long as pointers that refer to the rows are appropriately modified. (Of course, if the content of row 1 is moved to row $n$, every search must start at row $n$.) For example, to swap the contents of rows 7 and 11 in $\boldsymbol{P}$, we must also change 7 to 11 in $\boldsymbol{P}^6$ and 11 to 7 in $\boldsymbol{P}^{10}$. Similarly, were the structure of the tree diagram in Fig. 3.5 changed to admit a new leaf point, the point could be represented as row 15 by appending one row to $\boldsymbol{P}$ and creating or updating pointers. Hence, extensions to the tree diagram have the effect of appending rows to $\boldsymbol{P}$.

To go a step farther, it does no harm for a pointer matrix to have unused rows. If we delete a leaf point from the diagram of Fig. 3.5 and adjust pointers in $\boldsymbol{P}$ accordingly, the row that represented the leaf point merely falls into

† The reader should reconstruct the tree diagram of Fig. 3.5 from $\boldsymbol{P}$, then swap some rows and repeat the exercise.

disuse. Subsequently, the row may be used to represent a point newly entering the structure, or it may even be used to represent a point in an independent structure with a nominal pointer matrix $Q$. In fact, the pointer matrices of two or more tree diagrams may be mingled together in one large *pool* matrix. This can be an advantage if the moment sum of several tree diagrams can be estimated with greater confidence than individual moments. Pointer matrices lend themselves more readily to storage allocation than tag matrices, which must be held intact as individual matrices.

## 3.4 Degree Vectors

The degree of a point, it will be recalled, is the number of arcs that emanate from the point. In a *right degree vector*, point degrees are exhibited in right-index order. The right degree vector of the tree diagram in Fig. 3.2 is

$$(2, 3, 0, 2, 0, 2, 0, 0, 1, 2, 2, 0, 2, 2, 0, 0, 0, 0, 0, 0), \tag{3.3}$$

as the reader may verify by inspection. The dimension of this vector is $t$, the sum of its components is $s$, and it contains $w$ zeros, where $t$, $s$, and $w$ denote tree-diagram moment, degree sum, and weight. Moreover, the right degree vector is a compact representation of the tree diagram as a whole.

To reconstruct a tree diagram from its right degree vector, it is first of all necessary to determine the radix of the tree diagram. But $t$ and $s$ are obtainable, and $r = t - s$ by Eq. (1.1). Hence, for the right degree vector of (3.3), we have $r = 20 - 18 = 2$. After the root points are identified, the count of the second level is found by summing the first $r$ components of the right degree vector. After the second-level points are identified, the count of the third level can be determined, and so on. Each level can be subdivided into families because the degrees of the parents are known.

Although easy to construct, the right degree vector is awkward in an analysis of subtrees. Moreover, in any context that stresses subtrees, point degrees are likely to become available in left-index order. A degree vector in left-index order is called a *left degree vector*. The left degree vector for the tree diagram of Fig. 3.2 (or Fig. 3.3) is

$$(2, 0, 2, 0, 1, 0, 3, 0, 2, 2, 2, 0, 0, 2, 0, 0, 2, 0, 0, 0).$$

In a left degree vector, the component corresponding to point $x$ is followed directly by the components that represent the subtree diagram rooted in $x$. As a result, each of the $t$ subtree diagrams is represented by an infix in the left degree vector. This fact provides the only clue needed for reconstruction of a tree diagram. Because the tree diagram embraces $t$ subtree diagrams, the infix of one subtree diagram must start with each vector component. It remains to determine where each of the $t$ infixes ends.

A subtree diagram is a special case of a tree diagram with the restriction that $r$ must equal 1. Hence, Eq. (1.1) can be written in the form $t - s = 1$. Within a subtree diagram, therefore, the moment must exceed the degree sum by precisely 1, and analysis of a left degree vector will reveal $t$ infixes that satisfy this relationship. Delineation of these infixes will clearly exhibit the structure of the underlying tree diagram. An analysis of the left degree vector for the tree diagram of Fig. 3.2 yields the following pattern:

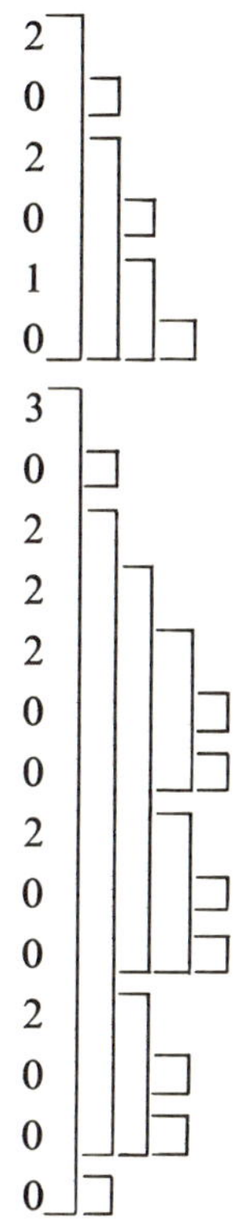


Here there are five levels of brackets, corresponding to the five-level tree diagram. Because the length of each bracket corresponds to the moment of a subtree diagram, the bracket arrangements simulate the structure of the tree. The degree sum within each bracket is less by 1 than the number of bracketed components.

Although the ordered degree vectors are tree-diagram representations commendable for their brevity, they must be considered special-purpose representations for applications that rely on serial scans over a structure. The left degree vector is suitable for a subtree-by-subtree scan and the right degree vector for a level-by-level scan. These vectors are not convenient for unsystematic searches, and they are applicable mainly to static structures.

Although degree vectors provide a compact method of representing tree diagrams, such vectors may lend themselves to futher compaction. For example, the degree vector of an $r$-way tree admits only two values, namely,

$r$ and 0. We can illustrate this for the three-way tree diagram of Fig. 1.6:

Right degree vector: (3, 0, 3, 0, 0, 0, 3, 0, 0, 3, 0, 0, 0, 0, 0)
Left degree vector: (3, 0, 0, 0, 0, 3, 3, 3, 0, 0, 0, 0, 0, 0, 0).

In some contexts, it is more efficient to encode such degree vectors as logical vectors, in this case as

(101000100100000) and (100001110000000).

Also, it may be more efficient to encode $r$ by zero and use positive integers to encode zero infixes in the degree vectors. Then the examples under discussion become

(0, 1, 0, 3, 0, 2, 0, 5) and (0, 4, 0, 0, 0, 7).

In a uniform tree diagram, the points of zero degree (leaf points) all appear on the highest level, and the right degree vector contains a suffix of $w$ zeros. If $w$ is known, therefore, the right degree vector can be truncated to a vector of dimension $t - w$.

## 3.5 Flag Matrices

The methods of representation previously discussed—tag matrices, pointer matrices, and degree vectors—apply to tree diagrams of general structure. We shall now discuss a method that applies only to uniform structures. A uniform tree diagram has the property that its point weights sum to $w$ at each

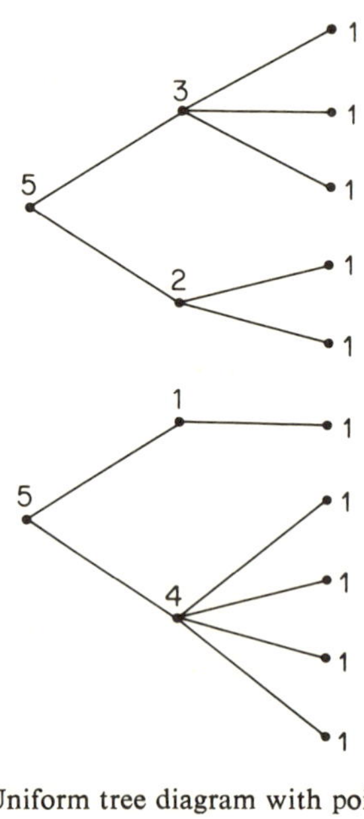


**Fig. 3.6** Uniform tree diagram with point weights.

level. For example, in the tree diagram of Fig. 3.6, the weights at each level sum to 10. The weight of each leaf point is known to be 1, and in the discussion that follows the leaf level is ignored. The weights of each point in the remaining levels can be represented as a logical matrix of $w$ rows and $h - 1$ columns, where each column encodes the weights of a corresponding level. A given weight, say $m$, is encoded as a sequence of $m - 1$ zeros followed by a *flag* that consists of a 1. The flag matrix for the tree diagram of Fig. 3.6 is

$$\begin{bmatrix} 0 & 0 \\ 0 & 0 \\ 0 & 1 \\ 0 & 0 \\ 1 & 1 \\ 0 & 1 \\ 0 & 0 \\ 0 & 0 \\ 0 & 0 \\ 1 & 1 \end{bmatrix}. \tag{3.4}$$

The first column corresponds to the first level of the tree diagram. Although (3.4) does not necessarily provide a more compact representation than a right degree vector, it provides a representation that may be stored conveniently in conjunction with the leaves of a uniform trim.

## 3.6 Dimension Vectors

A base-$\boldsymbol{r}$ tree diagram is completely determined by its dimension vector $\boldsymbol{r}$; each component of $\boldsymbol{r}$ governs the family dimensions of one level. The structure in Fig. 3.7 is a base-(4, 2, 3) tree diagram. Given a base structure, one can calculate the count vector from $\boldsymbol{r}$. The dimension vector (4, 2, 3) leads to a count vector of the form

$$(4, 4 \times 2, 4 \times 2 \times 3) = (4, 8, 24),$$

as is easily verified by inspection of Fig. 3.7. Moreover, point weights are easily calculated. The weight of each root point in Fig. 3.7 is given by $2 \times 3$, the weight of each second-level point by 3, and the weight of each leaf point by 1; the dimension vector (4, 2, 3) therefore yields a weight vector (6, 3, 1).

It is evident that if $\boldsymbol{r}$ denotes a dimension vector of dimension $h$, the compatible weight vector $\boldsymbol{w}$ of a base-$\boldsymbol{r}$ diagram is given by

$$\begin{vmatrix} w_1 \\ w_2 \\ \cdot \\ \cdot \\ \cdot \\ w_{h-1} \\ w_h \end{vmatrix} = \begin{vmatrix} r_2 \times r_3 \times \cdots \times r_h \times 1 \\ r_3 \times \cdots \times r_h \times 1 \\ \cdot \qquad\qquad \cdot \\ \cdot \qquad \cdot \\ \cdot \quad \cdot \\ r_h \times 1 \\ 1 \end{vmatrix}.$$

For example, if $r = (6, 3, 4, 2, 5)$, then

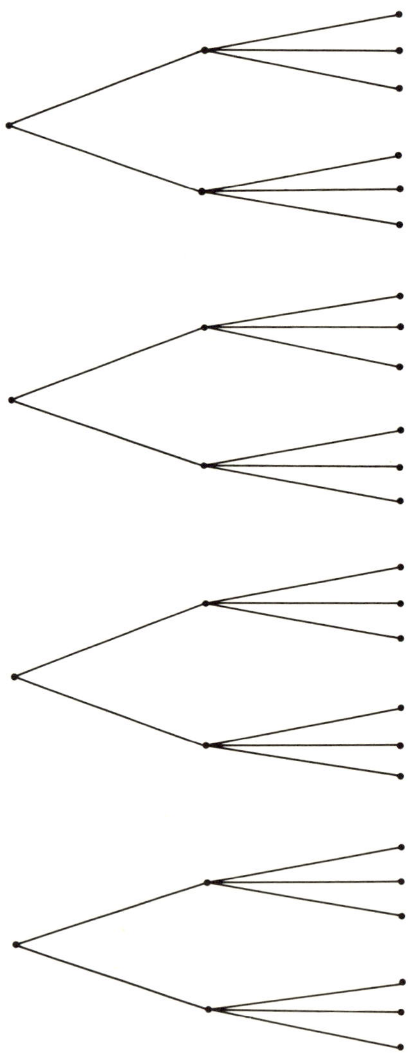

| Leaf-point Tags | Zone Index |
|---|---|
| 0, 0, 0 | 0 |
| 0, 0, 1 | 1 |
| 0, 0, 2 | 2 |
| 0, 1, 0 | 3 |
| 0, 1, 1 | 4 |
| 0, 1, 2 | 5 |
| 1, 0, 0 | 6 |
| 1, 0, 1 | 7 |
| 1, 0, 2 | 8 |
| 1, 1, 0 | 9 |
| 1, 1, 1 | 10 |
| 1, 1, 2 | 11 |
| 2, 0, 0 | 12 |
| 2, 0, 1 | 13 |
| 2, 0, 2 | 14 |
| 2, 1, 0 | 15 |
| 2, 1, 1 | 16 |
| 2, 1, 2 | 17 |
| 3, 0, 0 | 18 |
| 3, 0, 1 | 19 |
| 3, 0, 2 | 20 |
| 3, 1, 0 | 21 |
| 3, 1, 1 | 22 |
| 3, 1, 2 | 23 |

**Fig. 3.7** Base-(4, 2, 3) tree diagram with leaf-point index tags (0-origin indexing).

$$\boldsymbol{w} = \begin{vmatrix} 3 \times 4 \times 2 \times 5 \times 1 \\ 4 \times 2 \times 5 \times 1 \\ 2 \times 5 \times 1 \\ 5 \times 1 \\ 1 \end{vmatrix} = \begin{vmatrix} 120 \\ 40 \\ 10 \\ 5 \\ 1 \end{vmatrix}.$$

To summarize the weight vector calculation, we can write

$$\begin{aligned} \boldsymbol{w}_i &= \prod_{j=1}^{j=h-i} \boldsymbol{r}_{i+j} \qquad i = 1, 2, \ldots, h-1 \\ \boldsymbol{w}_h &= 1. \end{aligned} \tag{3.5}$$

Although (3.5) applies only to base-$\boldsymbol{r}$ diagrams, the resulting weight vector is the same as that obtained by the inspection method explained in Sec. 3.1 for tree diagrams in general.

For dealing with base-$\boldsymbol{r}$ structure, we shall define a *zone index* as an index that starts at the top of a level and numbers downward in the level. With the aid of weight vectors, one can readily calculate the zone index of a leaf point from the index tag of the leaf point. For example, let $\boldsymbol{i}$ denote the index tag vector, and let $k$ denote the associated zone index. Assuming zero-origin indexing, the appropriate value of $k$ can be obtained from $\boldsymbol{i}$ by an expression of the form

$$k = \boldsymbol{w}_1 \boldsymbol{i}_1 + \cdots + \boldsymbol{w}_h \boldsymbol{i}_h. \tag{3.6}$$

If we select tag (2, 0, 1) of Fig. 3.7 as an illustrative $\boldsymbol{i}$, observing first that the relevant weight vector is (6, 3, 1), we have

$$k = (6 \times 2) + (3 \times 0) + (1 \times 1) = 13,$$

as is easily verified by inspection.

The zero-origin zone index $k$ is referred to as the *base-r value* of $\boldsymbol{i}$, and the arithmetic operations of (3.5) and (3.6) are jointly symbolized by $\perp$, the *base value operator*. The base-$\boldsymbol{r}$ value of $\boldsymbol{i}$ will be expressed formally as $\boldsymbol{r} \perp \boldsymbol{i}$. Note that the base value operation employs two vectors and yields a single number. To apply this notation to all of the leaf points of the tree diagram in Fig. 3.7, we have

$$\begin{aligned} (4, 2, 3) &\perp (0, 0, 0) = 0 \\ (4, 2, 3) &\perp (0, 0, 1) = 1 \\ (4, 2, 3) &\perp (0, 0, 2) = 2 \\ &\vdots \\ (4, 2, 3) &\perp (2, 0, 1) = 13 \\ &\vdots \\ (4, 2, 3) &\perp (3, 1, 1) = 22 \\ (4, 2, 3) &\perp (3, 1, 2) = 23. \end{aligned}$$

We have illustrated the base-value operation for the top level of a base-$\boldsymbol{r}$ diagram. It should be obvious that the operation can be applied to any level of such a diagram by merely ignoring the portion of the diagram above the level of interest.

The zero-origin index tags of the leaf points of a base-$\boldsymbol{r}$ tree diagram can be viewed as representations of the integers in a base-$\boldsymbol{r}$ number system. Assuming that the components of $\boldsymbol{r}$ are not all identical, i.e., that the underlying structure is not a base-$r$, height-$h$ structure, the number system is sometimes said to be a *mixed-radix* system.

We have introduced mixed-radix numbers in their most important context, viz., that of converting from index tag to zone index. But mixed-radix problems also occur in conjunction with systems of weights and measures—such as inches, feet, yards, miles—and with systems of currency as well. For example, let (1, 1, 4, 4) represent an integer in a base-(2, 2, 5, 5) number system. Then

$$\begin{aligned}(2, 2, 5, 5) \perp (1, 1, 4, 4) &= (50 \times 1) + (25 \times 1) + (5 \times 4) + (1 \times 4)\\ &= 99.\end{aligned}$$

The vector (1, 1, 4, 4) may express 99 cents in the denominations of half dollar, quarter, nickel, and penny. Thus 99 cents equals 1 half dollar plus 1 quarter plus 4 nickels plus 4 pennies. The weight vector (50, 25, 5, 1) specifies the value of each denomination. Since there are 5 pennies in 1 nickel, 5 nickels in 1 quarter, 2 quarters in 1 half dollar, and 2 half dollars in 1 dollar, an applicable dimension vector is (2, 2, 5, 5). Ten coins are required to yield 99 cents in such a system, and all smaller quantities can be represented with fewer coins.

Inasmuch as the base-value operation employed decimal multiplications and additions, it is possible to encode a decimal integer in a base-$\boldsymbol{r}$ number system by decimal divisions and subtractions. For an example, we shall encode 93 in a (2, 2, 5, 5) system. The applicable weight vector is (50, 25, 5, 1), and the objective at the $i$th step is to subtract out the largest multiple of $\boldsymbol{w}_i$ that provides a nonnegative remainder. Hence,

$$\begin{array}{r|c|l}
50 & 93 & 1 \\
\hline
 & -50 & \\
25 & 43 & 1 \\
\hline
 & -25 & \\
5 & 18 & 3 \\
\hline
 & -15 & \\
1 & 3 & 3 \\
\hline
 & -3 & \\
\hline
\end{array}$$

and the desired number is (1, 1, 3, 3).

Base-2 (binary) systems play an important role in digital computers because they lend themselves well to the logical ON-OFF properties of electronic switching circuits. For example, the logical vector (1, 1, 0, 0, 0, 1, 1) is a seven-digit binary representation of 99. The dimension vector being (2, 2, 2, 2, 2, 2, 2) and the weight vector being (64, 32, 16, 8, 4, 1), it follows that the base-2 value of (1100011) is

$$99 = 64 + 32 + 2 + 1.$$

Commas are typically omitted in displaying logical vectors.

## 3.7 Radix and Height

A base-$r$, height-$h$ tree diagram is dictated by $r$ and $h$. All of the useful properties of base-$r$ structure apply, and the base-value operation is simplified because the weight vector consists of powers of $r$. For example, if $r = 2$ and $h = 7$, the dimension vector is (2, 2, 2, 2, 2, 2, 2) and the weight vector $\boldsymbol{w}$ is given by

$$\begin{aligned} \boldsymbol{w} &= (2^6, 2^5, 2^4, 2^3, 2^2, 2^1, 2^0) \\ &= (64, 32, 16, 8, 4, 2, 1). \end{aligned}$$

Hence, we see that (3.5) reduces to

$$w_i = r^{h-i} \quad \text{for } i = 1, 2, \ldots, h. \tag{3.7}$$

The set of zero-origin index tags for the leaf points of a base-$r$ tree diagram of height $h$ constitutes a base-$r$ polynomial number system in which each integer is encoded in $h$ digits (or possibly less, if leading zeros are suppressed). For example, if $r = 10$ and $\boldsymbol{x} = (2, 0, 1)$, the base-(10, 10, 10) value of $\boldsymbol{x}$ is 201. The base-(3, 3, 3) value of $\boldsymbol{x}$ is $(3, 3, 3) \perp (2, 0, 1)$, which equals $9 \times 2 + 3 \times 0 + 1 \times 3 = 21$.

Of all number systems, the base-10 (decimal) system plays a special role: A scalar number is always assumed to be decimal unless it is explicitly said not to be. For example, the base-value operation was defined to yield a decimal result; a decimal result is what the reader is schooled to expect from an equation.

## 3.8 Comment

The structure of an array is preserved in a dimension vector. The leaf level of an array can be moved about and processed as though it consisted of a vector. As long as the dimension vector is held in readiness, any questions that require leaves to be segregated or identified on a structural basis can be answered with the aid of computations on the dimension vector (as further described in Sec. 4.6). The structural simplicity of the array makes it the "queen" of the structurands.

The structures of other trims and trees cannot be represented as elegantly as those of arrays. The expedient is therefore to represent the given structure in a matrix and exploit the fact that the matrix can easily be represented in its turn. Except in the case of arrays, therefore, vector representation of structure requires two steps: First, contain the structure in a matrix; and, second, represent the matrix as a vector.

To summarize the methods of structure representation discussed in this chapter, we have

| *Array* | *Dimension* | *Structure represented* |
|---|---|---|
| Left tag matrix | $m \times h$ | Any |
| Right tag matrix | $m \times h$ | Any |
| Pointer matrix | $m \times 2$ | Any |
| Left degree vector | $m$ | Any |
| Right degree vector | $m$ | Any |
| Flag matrix | $w \times (h - 1)$ | Uniform |
| Dimension vector | $h$ | Base-$r$ |
| $(r, h)$ | 2 | Base-$r$, height-$h$ |

Most of the nomenclature for these eight arrays is novel, largely because the literature does not address structure as a topic worthy of interest in itself. An exception is the *degree vector* and the distinction between *right* and *left*, which are taken from K.E. Iverson (1962). The *dimension vector* corresponds to his *dispersion vector*. He also introduced the base-value operator symbol and nomenclature, but the definition of *weight vector* given here is more general than the one he gave.

The purpose of this chapter has been to discuss the representation of named tree diagrams without going very far into the reasons for representing tree diagrams in one fashion versus another. The reasons are intimately related to the topic of search, which deserves the separate treatment accorded to it in Chapter 4.

*Chapter 4*

# TABLE SEARCHING

In a *table look-up* operation, one enters a table with an argument, executes a search algorithm that identifies a row in the table, and then extracts desired information from the row. Typically, the table represents a structurand, the argument is a tag, and the desired function is the node that corresponds to the tag. The purpose of this chapter is to characterize the main kinds of tables and search algorithms.

## 4.1 Definitions

A matrix that represents a structurand will be termed a *table* to distinguish it from matrices in general. For example, a table may be formed by appending a column of nodes to a tag matrix. Each of the several methods of representing structure discussed in Chapter 3 leads to a different kind of table; furthermore, variants of these tables may arise to optimize special kinds of searches or to combine various search options. At the minimum, a table consists simply of a node vector, which is usually the appropriate table for representing a base-$\boldsymbol{r}$ trim or tree.

A search algorithm may visit more than one row in the course of locating a desired row. Any visit to a row, including the final visit to the sought-for row, will be called a *probe.* One measure of a search algorithm, useful for rough comparative analyses, is its *probe expectation,* i.e., the average number of rows visited per search. Where each node is sought with equal probability, a *uniform search distribution* is said to prevail. In discussing probe expectations, uniform search distributions will be assumed unless otherwise stated.

After the general principles involved in finding a node become evident, the elaborations required to find a whole family, path, subtree, or subtrim present relatively little difficulty. An emphasis on node search is therefore justifiable in an introduction to search methods.

## 4.2 Sweep Searches

The matrix formed by adjoining a column of $m$ nodes to a tag matrix of $m$ rows will be called a *sweep table*. Since each row in such a table corresponds to a circle in a structurand, we assume that tags and nodes are suitably paired in the rows. With the tree in Fig. 4.1 is one possible example of a left-justified sweep table and the corresponding right-justified sweep table. Any two tags that are consistently justified and null-extended can be matched as continuous character strings.

Given a sweep table and an argument tag, a *row sweep* matches the argument with row-contained tags until either (1) a match is obtained or (2) it is clear that no match will occur. Since table rows can be visited in any sequence, the most efficient sequence many well be determined by the properties of the

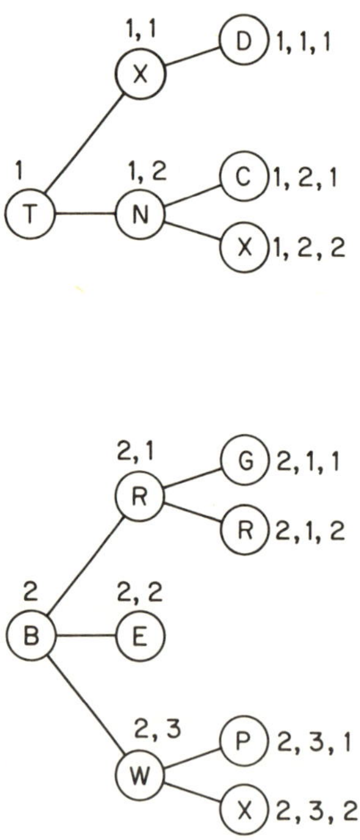


| Row | A left-justified sweep table (node) | | | | A right-justified sweep table: Node vector | Tag matrix | | |
|---|---|---|---|---|---|---|---|---|
| 1 | X | 1 | 1 | ∘ | X | ∘ | 1 | 1 |
| 2 | C | 1 | 2 | 1 | C | 1 | 2 | 1 |
| 3 | R | 2 | 1 | ∘ | R | ∘ | 2 | 1 |
| 4 | R | 2 | 1 | 2 | R | 2 | 1 | 2 |
| 5 | W | 2 | 3 | ∘ | W | ∘ | 2 | 3 |
| 6 | X | 2 | 3 | 2 | X | 2 | 3 | 2 |
| 7 | T | 1 | ∘ | ∘ | T | ∘ | ∘ | 1 |
| 8 | D | 1 | 1 | 1 | D | 1 | 1 | 1 |
| 9 | N | 1 | 2 | ∘ | N | ∘ | 1 | 2 |
| 10 | X | 1 | 2 | 2 | X | 1 | 2 | 2 |
| 11 | B | 2 | ∘ | ∘ | B | ∘ | ∘ | 2 |
| 12 | G | 2 | 1 | 1 | G | 2 | 1 | 1 |
| 13 | E | 2 | 2 | ∘ | E | ∘ | 2 | 2 |
| 14 | P | 2 | 3 | 1 | P | 2 | 3 | 1 |

**Fig. 4.1** An indexed tree and two sweep tables.

device in which the table is stored. A unidirectional sweep is *serial* if a visit to one row is normally followed by a visit to the adjacent row. A serial sweep is *cyclic* if the first row follows the last row in a forward sweep or if the last row follows the first in a backward sweep. In general, a sweep starts at row $j$, where $j$ may either be fixed or be specified anew at each search. It is not unusual for $j$ to be specified by the index of the matching row in the previous search. For a uniform search distribution and a table of $m$ rows, the probe expectation of a row sweep is given simply by

$$E\text{ (row sweep, } m) = \frac{m+1}{2}. \tag{4.1}$$

Although the row sweep has the highest probe expectation of any search to be discussed, it lends itself to serial-access storage media, which tend to offer storage at low cost. Decks of punch cards and reels of magnetic tape are examples of serial-access storage media. Even where direct access to rows is permitted, however, the row sweep has properties that can be useful in some circumstances. The row sweep entails little investment in table preparation; nothing more than consistent formatting of tags is required. Where a structurand is short-lived or contains few nodes, the investment required of a more efficient search may not be justifiable. The serial sweep can be most effective where the search distribution favors a small proportion of nodes with high frequency of use. Assuming a forward sweep from the first row, it is beneficial in such cases to interchange the matching row with its predecessor row. As a result, the often-sought nodes will drift toward the top of the table and reduce the probe expectation for subsequent searches.

Because tables usually contain far more rows than columns, storage-device limitations have traditionally suggested row sweeps. However, the potentialities inherent in a *column sweep* take on increasing interest as hardware technology develops. The nature of a column sweep will be suggested by example. Figure 4.1 provides a tree and a tag-table representation (the table need not be in left-justified format, but this format helps us relate the table to the tree). Figure 4.2 depicts a column sweep on $\boldsymbol{B}$, the tag matrix extracted from the table. Let row 5 of $\boldsymbol{B}$ serve as an assumed argument. The logical selection vector $\boldsymbol{u}$ is initially full (all 1's). In the example, column are examined from left to right. Each examination compares all components of column $\boldsymbol{B}_j$ with the argument vector component $\boldsymbol{a}_j$ corresponding to that column; at every mismatching component in the column, a zero is injected into the selection vector. As columns are swept, the 1's in the selection vector decrease in number. At termination of the column sweep, a 1 in the selection vector $\boldsymbol{u}$ indicates a row that matches the argument. This example culminates in one matching row (row 5).

The tag matrix and the argument can have either left or right-justified format as long as they are consistent, and columns can be examined in any desired order. In sweeping a left-justified tag matrix, however, there is some advantage

Argument $a$: 2 3 ∘

Status of selection vector after n-th column probe

| | Tag matrix $B$ | Start $u$ | 1st $u$ | 2nd $u$ | 3rd $u$ |
|---|---|---|---|---|---|
| 1 | 1 1 ∘ | 1 | 0 | 0 | 0 |
| 2 | 1 2 1 | 1 | 0 | 0 | 0 |
| 3 | 2 1 ∘ | 1 | 1 | 0 | 0 |
| 4 | 2 1 2 | 1 | 1 | 0 | 0 |
| 5 | 2 3 ∘ | 1 | 1 | 1 | 1 |
| 6 | 2 3 2 | 1 | 1 | 1 | 0 |
| 7 | 1 ∘ ∘ | 1 | 0 | 0 | 0 |
| 8 | 1 1 1 | 1 | 0 | 0 | 0 |
| 9 | 1 2 ∘ | 1 | 0 | 0 | 0 |
| 10 | 1 2 2 | 1 | 0 | 0 | 0 |
| 11 | 2 ∘ ∘ | 1 | 1 | 0 | 0 |
| 12 | 2 1 1 | 1 | 1 | 0 | 0 |
| 13 | 2 2 ∘ | 1 | 1 | 0 | 0 |
| 14 | 2 3 1 | 1 | 1 | 1 | 0 |

**Fig. 4.2** Example of column sweep.

in a left-to-right sweep, as may be seen by considering an argument with $k$ nonnull components. After $j$ columns are scanned, where $j \leq k$, the selection vector identifies all nodes in a subtree rooted on level $j$. After scanning $a_1$ and $a_2$ in the example, the selection vector identifies the subtree rooted in node (2, 3). Hence, by simply truncating a search for a single node, a column sweep on a left-justified tag matrix can be made to identify a desired subtree.

To truncate a column sweep is merely to ignore one or more columns during the sweep. A general way of indicating the columns to be ignored can be provided by a *mask vector*, a logical vector compatible with the argument vector. Each column to be swept can be indicated in the mask vector by a 1 and each column to be skipped by a 0. In Fig. 4.2, rows 7 and 11 (level 1 of the tree in question) would be selected, for example, by a column sweep that employed the argument vector (∘, ∘, ∘) and the mask vector (0, 1, 1).

The versatility of the column sweep can be further expanded in a number of ways. One of the useful possibilities would permit selection vectors to be stored and reloaded so that one sweep could start where a previous sweep had ended. Another would permit logical operations between two selection vectors, each of which preserves the result of a search. To date, cost considerations have limited the column sweep to special-purpose roles. Storage devices embodying the column sweep are variously known as *associative memories*, *search memories*, and *parallel-search memories*. The principles of such memories are discussed in Chapter 7.

## 4.3 Skip Searches

Lexical ordering permits one to consult a dictionary by checking an argument term against selected dictionary terms. At each probe, more of the book is excluded from consideration. Dictionary usage suggests the main characteristics of *skip searches*. Skip searches assume a *skip table* consisting of a sorted sweep table, and they require that tags be matched with three-way outcomes. To introduce the skip search by example, let LO, EQ, and HI refer to (1) argument precedes tag, (2) argument equals tag, and (3) argument succeeds tag, respectively.

Consider a hypothetical skip table of 26 rows. Given an argument tag, one form of the skip search starts at row 9:

Probe row 9
- LO: Exclude rows 9 through 26 and probe row 3.
- EQ: Terminate search.
- HI: Exclude rows 1 through 9 and probe row 18.

Probe row 18
- LO: Exclude rows 18 through 26 and probe row 12.
- EQ: Terminate search.
- HI: Exclude rows 1 through 18 and probe row 21.

This stage of the search corresponds to the first level of the probe tree shown in Fig. 4.3. Where applicable, nodes in the tree are identified by a row number, and each node is specified by the number of probes it takes to reach the node. The third node of each family, a dummy node drawn in for analytical purposes, has no counterpart in a row number. (The probe tree is an analytical tool and should not be confused with the original structurand.)

The second stage of the search, if reached, corresponds to the second level of the probe tree. Similarly, the last stage, if reached, corresponds to the third level of the probe tree. The actions required at a second or third stage are identical to those shown for the first stage—except that row numbers have to be changed. For the sake of a smooth illustration, we have chosen a three-way search and a table of convenient length. The first stage deals with $26 = 3^3 - 1$ rows, the second with $8 = 3^2 - 1$ rows, and the third with $2 = 3^1 - 1$ rows. By a simple generalization, each family in the probe tree of a $r$-way search contains $r$ nodes, of which the last is a dummy, and the rule for specifying node values is clear from the example given.

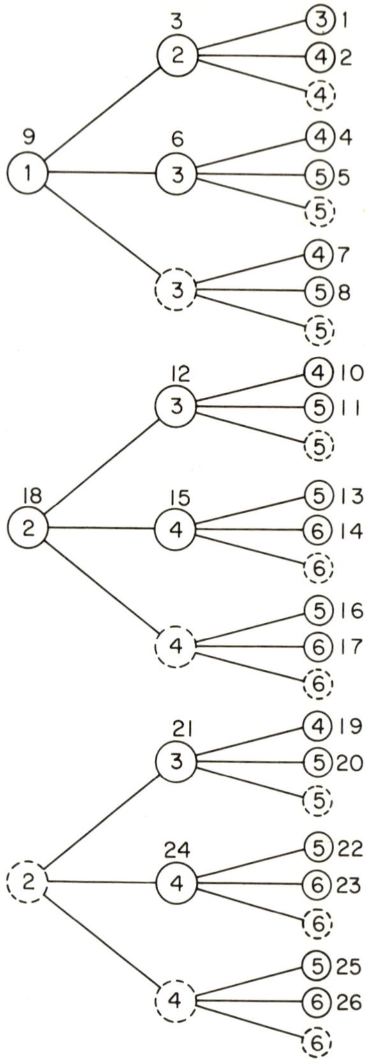


**Fig. 4.3** Probe tree for a 3-way skip table of 26 rows.

A check of the probe tree in Fig. 4.3 shows that 1 family can be reached at the first level, 3 at the second, and 9 at the third. The last search of a family is a serial sweep of 2 nodes, and assuming a uniform search distribution, the probe expectation of the family is $\frac{3}{2}$. Of the three routes to the second level, one involves a single probe; the other routes require two probes. Therefore, on the average, the second level is reached with $(1 + 2 + 2)/3$ or $\frac{5}{3}$ probes. Similarly, the third level is reached with an expectation of $2(\frac{5}{3})$ probes. The number of probes required of all 26 nodes is therefore equal to

$$\begin{aligned} &2(\tfrac{3}{2}) + 6(\tfrac{5}{3} + \tfrac{3}{2}) + 18(\tfrac{5}{3} + \tfrac{5}{3} + \tfrac{3}{2}) \\ &\quad = 26(\tfrac{3}{2}) + 2(3)(\tfrac{5}{3}) + 2(9)(2)(\tfrac{5}{3}) = 109. \end{aligned} \tag{4.2}$$

Note that

$$1 + 2 + 3 + \cdots + (n-2) + (n-1) + (n-1) = \frac{(n-1)(n+2)}{2}.$$

For example, where $n$ is 4 we have

$$1 + 2 + 3 + 3 = \frac{(4-1)(4+2)}{2} = 9.$$

Using this to generalize from (4.2), an $r$-way skip search of $h$ levels is seen to have the probe expectation (for $r > 1$) of

$$E(\text{skip search}, r, h) = \frac{r}{2} + \frac{(r-1)(r+2)}{2}\frac{(r-1)}{r}\left(\frac{\sum_{i=0}^{h-1} ir^i}{r^h - 1}\right). \tag{4.3}$$

It can be shown that

$$\sum_{i=0}^{n} ir^i = \frac{(nr - n - 1)\, r^{n+1} + r}{(r-1)^2}. \tag{4.4}$$

Applying (4.4) to (4.3) and simplifying, we have

$$E(\text{skip search}, r, h) = \frac{(r-1)(r+2)\, hr^{h-1}}{2(r^h - 1)} - 1. \tag{4.5}$$

For the three-way search discussed above,

$$E(\text{skip search}, 3, 3) = \frac{(3-1)(3+2)(3)(3^2)}{2(3^3 - 1)} - 1 = \frac{109}{26},$$

which can be checked by summing nodes in Fig. 4.3.

Equation (4.5) is exact for a table of $r^h - 1$ rows, assuming a uniform search distribution. A rough approximation is given by $rh/2$, which in the above example gives $\frac{117}{26}$. In practice, the number $m$ of rows in a table is seldom conveniently equal to $r^h - 1$, but a useful approximation can still be obtained by taking $h = \log_r (m + 1)$.

By far the most popular version of the $r$-way skip search, the *binary search*, is obtained when $r = 2$. The binary search not only yields a lower probe expectation than other scans, but it is easy to implement. Other skip seaches are of interest mainly where external restraints militate against the binary search. Restraints can arise in various ways, the commonest way being a storage device in which the time required to probe another row is dependent on the location of the row currently being probed.

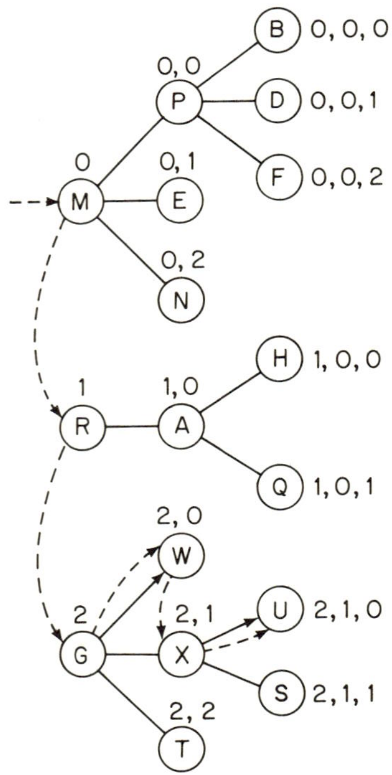


Right tag matrix

| | | | |
|---|---|---|---|
| M | ∘ | ∘ | 0 |
| R | ∘ | ∘ | 1 |
| G | ∘ | ∘ | 2 |
| P | ∘ | 0 | 0 |
| E | ∘ | 0 | 1 |
| N | ∘ | 0 | 2 |
| A | ∘ | 1 | 0 |
| W | ∘ | 2 | 0 |
| X | ∘ | 2 | 1 |
| T | ∘ | 2 | 2 |
| B | 0 | 0 | 0 |
| D | 0 | 0 | 1 |
| F | 0 | 0 | 2 |
| H | 1 | 0 | 0 |
| Q | 1 | 0 | 1 |
| U | 2 | 1 | 0 |
| S | 2 | 1 | 1 |

Sweep table

Mapping vector (level to level); Mapping vector (within families); Vector of tagging alphabets

| | | | | |
|---|---|---|---|---|
| 0 | M | 3 | 1 | 0 |
| 1 | R | 6 | 2 | 1 |
| 2 | G | 7 | ∘ | 2 |
| 3 | P | 10 | 4 | 0 |
| 4 | E | ∘ | 5 | 1 |
| 5 | N | ∘ | ∘ | 2 |
| 6 | A | 13 | ∘ | 0 |
| 7 | W | ∘ | 8 | 0 |
| 8 | X | 15 | 9 | 1 |
| 9 | T | ∘ | ∘ | 2 |
| 10 | B | ∘ | 11 | 0 |
| 11 | D | ∘ | 12 | 1 |
| 12 | F | ∘ | ∘ | 2 |
| 13 | H | ∘ | 14 | 0 |
| 14 | Q | ∘ | ∘ | 1 |
| 15 | U | ∘ | 16 | 0 |
| 16 | S | ∘ | ∘ | 1 |

Rank-path table

| | | | |
|---|---|---|---|
| 0 | M | 3 | 1 |
| 1 | R | 6 | 2 |
| 2 | G | 7 | ∘ |
| 3 | P | 10 | 4 |
| 4 | E | ∘ | 5 |
| 5 | N | ∘ | ∘ |
| 6 | A | 13 | ∘ |
| 7 | W | ∘ | 8 |
| 8 | X | 15 | 9 |
| 9 | T | ∘ | ∘ |
| 10 | B | ∘ | 11 |
| 11 | D | ∘ | 12 |
| 12 | F | ∘ | ∘ |
| 13 | H | ∘ | 14 |
| 14 | Q | ∘ | ∘ |
| 15 | U | ∘ | 16 |
| 16 | S | ∘ | ∘ |

Index-path table

Degree vector

| | | | |
|---|---|---|---|
| 0 | 3 | M | 3 |
| 1 | 1 | R | 6 |
| 2 | 3 | G | 7 |
| 3 | 3 | P | 10 |
| 4 | 0 | E | ∘ |
| 5 | 0 | N | ∘ |
| 6 | 2 | A | 13 |
| 7 | 0 | W | ∘ |
| 8 | 2 | X | 15 |
| 9 | 0 | T | ∘ |
| 10 | 0 | B | ∘ |
| 11 | 0 | D | ∘ |
| 12 | 0 | F | ∘ |
| 13 | 0 | H | ∘ |
| 14 | 0 | Q | ∘ |
| 15 | 0 | U | ∘ |
| 16 | 0 | S | ∘ |

Direct-path table

**Fig. 4.4** A zero-origin indexed tree and three path tables.

For the binary search, (4.5) simplifies to

$$E(\text{skip search}, 2, h) = h\left(\frac{2^h}{2^h - 1}\right) - 1. \tag{4.6}$$

For all but small $h$, say $h < 5$, (4.6) is usefully approximated by $h - 1$. On the average, a table of 1023 rows is searched in about nine probes, a table of 511 rows in about eight probes, etc.

## 4.4 Path Searches

Any search method that uses the components of an argument tag in tracing a path diagram is termed a *path search.* A table that accommodates such a search replaces some or all of the tag matrix by other information, notably mapping or degree vectors.

To facilitate discussion, let the *heir* of a node $x$ of nonzero degree be the first and uppermost descendant of $x$. In the tree of Fig. 4.4, P is the heir of M, B is the heir of P, etc. Moreover, let the *rank path* of a given tag $\boldsymbol{a}$ follow the first level down to root $\boldsymbol{a}_1$, branch to the heir of this root, visit family members until reaching node $(\boldsymbol{a}_1, \boldsymbol{a}_2)$, branch to the heir of this node, etc. The rank path of tag (2, 1, 0) is outlined by dashed lines in Fig. 4.4 (where zero-origin indexing applies, it should be noted). If each node of a tree is a row in a search table, the number of probes required of the rank path to a given node is simply the component sum of the *one-origin* index tag of the node. For example, it takes six probes to reach node (3, 2, 1). The number of probes required of a *direct path* is given by the dimension of the tag vector; that is, the direct path requires one probe per level. A direct path simply follows a path diagram.

The tree of Fig. 4.4 is represented by four search tables. For discussion purposes, all of the tables are in right-index order. The last column of the rank-path table includes the tapping alphabets from the sweep table. The second and third columns constitute a pointer matrix and are therefore familiar from Sec. 3.3.

The character of a *rank-path search* is fairly evident from the rank-path table. An argument tag $\boldsymbol{a}$ of dimension $k$ requires $k$ partial sweeps, one for each family to be visited in tracing a rank path to the desired node. In sweeping the family encountered on level $i$, component $\boldsymbol{a}_i$ of the argument is compared with symbols of the tagging alphabet for the family (as in column 4 of the rank-path table) until equality is reached. Until the argument is exhausted, each sweep culminates in a branch to an heir on the next level, whereupon the search continues in another family. The rank path followed to find U, the node with tag (2, 1, 0), is shown in the tree of Fig. 4.4.

The rows of a family can be chained in any desired order. As in any serial sweep, this freedom can be usefully exploited when some nodes are sought more frequently than others. In fact, the row order of the table can be completely independent of tree order, as was explained for pointer matrices in Sec. 3.3. Although the example in Fig. 4.4 employs an indexed tree, the rank-path search works equally well for dubbed structurands and for structurands that are tagged without any attention to a collating sequence—the reason being that nothing more than two-way (equal or unequal) comparisons are required. The term *rank-path* rightly suggests that each look-up consists of a sequence of ranking operations that effectively yield an index tag from the given argument tag.

An *index-path search* is much the same as a rank-path search but assumes that (1) the argument tag is an index tag and (2) each family is chained in indexing order. Comparisons are therefore unnecessary, and the search proceeds by counting its way through encountered families as directed by the index tag. The required table consists of a pointer matrix and a node vector; as shown by Fig. 4.4, one column can be dropped from the rank-path table to obtain the index-path table. The rank-path and index-path searches are particularly applicable to trees or trims of changing structure.

Where the advantages of chained families are not important, the within-family mapping vector can be dropped, as shown in the direct-path table. Since without this column there is no way of discerning family dimension in a tree diagram of general structure, a degree vector is appended to permit a check for ineligible argument tags. In the direct-path table, each family must occupy consecutive rows and its members must follow one another in tree order. Although the roots are conventionally placed at the top of the table, families as wholes can be located at will. A *direct-path search* is most easily explained with the aid of zero-origin indexing for tags and row numbers. If the argument tag is the vector $\boldsymbol{i}$ (with one-origin indexing for components), the table is entered at row $\boldsymbol{i}_1$, which contains a pointer to an heir on level 2. The pointer is added to $\boldsymbol{i}_2$ to reach the next-visited row, which contains a pointer to an heir on level 3, etc. In general, if we assume a pointer $\boldsymbol{p}_1$ to the first root, a search involves $g$ pointers $\boldsymbol{p}_1, \boldsymbol{p}_2, \ldots, \boldsymbol{p}_g$ for an argument $\boldsymbol{i}$ of dimension $g$. The sought-for row number $k$ is the last term of the sequence

$$(\boldsymbol{p}_1 + \boldsymbol{i}_1), (\boldsymbol{p}_2 + \boldsymbol{i}_2), \ldots, (\boldsymbol{p}_g + \boldsymbol{i}_g). \tag{4.7}$$

The search requires $g$ additions and visits $g$ rows to reach a node on level $g$.

The direct-path search, well suited to static trees, requires a table that is somewhat awkward for trees of rapidly changing structure. In a leaf insertion, the leaf must reside with its family. However, by the expedient of allocating some empty rows to each family, the table can be made to accommodate changes more easily than an ordered tag table.

The index-path and rank-path searches have identical probe expectations. Although it is difficult to generalize about the probe expectation of these searches, a few guidelines can nevertheless be offered. Probe trees for the tree

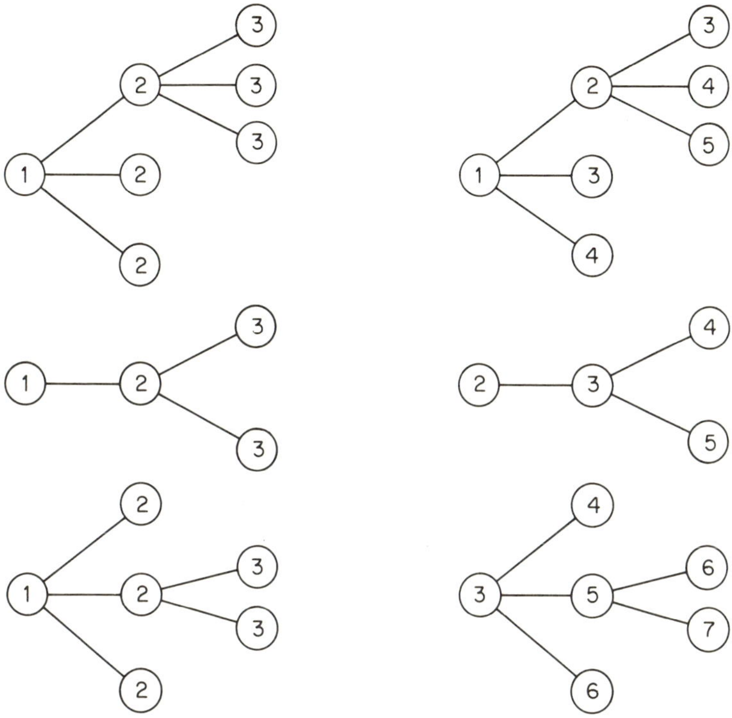


**Fig. 4.5** Probe trees for tree of Fig. 4.4.

of Fig. 4.4 are shown in Fig. 4.5. For a rank path, the probe tree is of sum 67; given a moment of 17, the probe expectation is therefore $\frac{67}{17}$. A similar expectation for the direct path is seen to be $\frac{38}{17}$.

One way to make an informed guess about the probe expectation of a large tree is to simulate the tree by a roughly equivalent base-$r$ tree. Assuming a uniform search distribution, the direct-path expectation for a base-$r$ tree of height $h$ is

$$E(\text{direct path}, r, h) = \frac{hr^h}{r^h - 1} - \frac{1}{r - 1}, \tag{4.8}$$

which yields the mean of a compatible probe tree as a ratio of Eq. (4.4) over (1.9). Since the probe expectation of a direct path is identical to the number of families encountered in a rank path, the expectation for the rank path can be expressed by

$$E(\text{rank path}, r, h) = \frac{r+1}{2}[E(\text{direct path}, r, h)]$$

$$= \frac{r+1}{2}\left(\frac{hr^h}{r^h - 1} - \frac{1}{r-1}\right). \tag{4.9}$$

An inspection of the probe tree of Fig. 4.5 suggests that the $(r, h)$ of a comparable radix tree should fall between (2, 3) and (3, 3). From (4.9), we find that

$$E(\text{rank path}, 2, 3) = \tfrac{51}{14} = 3.6$$

and

$$E(\text{rank path}, 3, 3) = \tfrac{68}{13} = 5.2.$$

The actual expectation of $\frac{67}{17} = 3.9$ is bracketed by these computed values.

In some applications, it is possible to exercise a measure of control over point degrees and therefore to influence the corresponding choices of $r$ and $h$. Although a choice that will minimize (4.9) is difficult to formulate, an approximation can again provide insights. If we confine attention to searches for leaves in a base-$r$ structure, then the probe expectation is given simply by

$$E(\text{leaf rank path}, r, h) = \left(\frac{r+1}{2}\right)h. \tag{4.10}$$

But if $w$ is the number of leaves, then $h = \log_r w$ and

$$E(\text{leaf rank path}, r, h) = \frac{r+1}{2}\log_r w$$

$$= \frac{r+1}{2}\left(\frac{\log_e w}{\log_e r}\right). \tag{4.11}$$

This expression has a minimum for the condition

$$\log_e r - \frac{r+1}{r} = 0. \tag{4.12}$$

The minimum occurs at approximately $r = 3.6$. Therefore, in applying the rank-path searches to arrays, near-optimal probe expectation can be expected of structures with $r$ in the neighborhood of 3 or 4.

From (4.11) we can compute that

$$E(\text{leaf rank path}, 3.6, h) = \frac{3.6+1}{2\log_e 3.6}\log_e w$$

$$= 1.80 \log_e w = 1.25 \log_2 w. \tag{4.13}$$

Since a binary search of $w$ nodes has been shown to take about $\log_2 w - 1$ probes, under typical conditions a rank-path search will require at least 1.25 times as many probes as a binary search. By substituting other values for $r$, E. H. Sussenguth, Jr. (1963) has shown that the expectation is less than $1.5 \log_2 w$

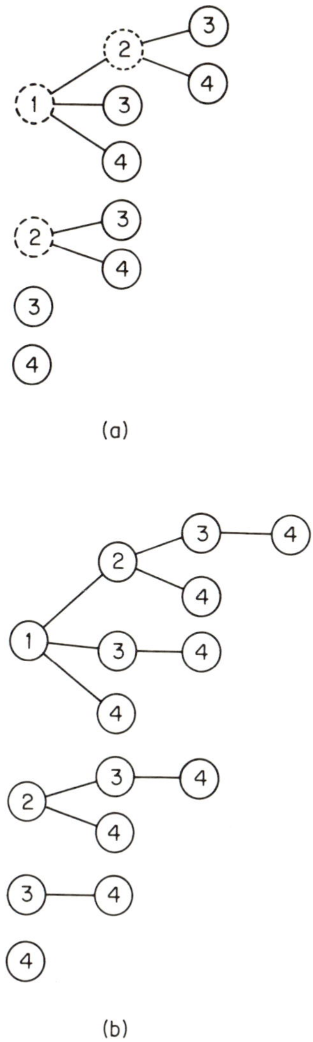


**Fig. 4.6** Two optimal rank-path probe trees: (a) probe tree for 8 leaves; (b) probe tree for 15 nodes.

for $r$ in the range 2 through 8 and less than $2.0 \log_2 w$ for $r$ in the range 2 through 14.

For the conditions we have been assuming, a rank path clearly requires more probes than a binary search. But if the search distribution is nonuniform, so that some nodes are more often sought than others, the rank-path search can exploit this to reduce the probe expectation. Also, a binary-search probe requires a three-way outcome, whereas a ranking probe requires only a two-way outcome. Furthermore, each ranking probe compares two tag components, whereas each binary-search probe matches two tags (they may be vectors). Thus the amount of processing per probe is inherently greater for the binary search than for the rank-path search.

For the unusual applications in which it is possible to exert complete control over the structure of the search tree, Y. N. Patt (1969) has given a method for constructing the optimal probe tree for leaf searches. Figure 4.6(a) illustrates such a tree for eight leaves, of which four have probe length 3 and four have probe length 4. In general, whenever the number of leaves, $w$, equals $2^k$, half of the leaves have probe length $k$ and the remaining half probe length $k + 1$. The probe expectation for this case is $k + \frac{1}{2}$.

To increase $w$ by 1 in the tree of Fig. 4.6(a), a leaf of value 5 is appended to a family. This can be done four times, whereupon $w = (\frac{3}{2})2^3$. Thereupon, to increase $w$ by 1, a family with leaves 4 and 5 is appended to a 3 as a surtree. This can be done four times, at which juncture $w = 2^4$. The generalization to other powers of 2 is obvious. The probe expectation for the general case is given by

$$k + 2 - \frac{3 \times 2^{k-1}}{w} \quad \text{for } 2^k \leq w \leq (\tfrac{3}{2})2^k$$

and

$$k + 3 - \frac{3 \times 2^k}{w} \quad \text{for } (\tfrac{3}{2})2^k \leq w \leq 2^{k+1}.$$

The expectation is not much higher than that of the binary search. A potentially awkward property of the search is that requisite leaf tags vary in dimension from 1 to $k + 1$.

The probe tree in Fig. 4.6(b) is optimal for searching 15 nodes (rather than 8 leaves). The probe expectation of such a tree is identical to that of a binary search. This is interesting in view of the fact that the search employs equal-unequal matches and is applicable to alphameric tags as a result.

## 4.5 Scatter Searches

Any arithmetic or logical formula that transforms tags into integers will be called a *scatter transformation*. For search purposes, the transformation may be chosen to yield integers in some interval vector of dimension $n$, where $n$ is equal to or greater than the number of rows in a given sweep table. A scatter transformation does not possess an inverse transformation for going from integers back to tags and it need not assure a one-to-one mapping from tags to integers. To be useful, however, it should be easy to compute and it must be reasonably successful at scattering tags about in the integer range.

Feasible scatter transformations can be devised for arguments of numerical, integral, or logical range. Since tags are always encoded to a logical range in practice (see Chapter 10), no problem arises except in exposition. Here, to avoid obscuring the important issues by encoding details, the discussion is illustrated with integral tags.

A scatter search comes down to this: A scatter transformation is chosen for a given structurand, whereupon the transformation is used both in constructing a scatter table and in searching the table. It is expected that two or more tags will transform into the same integer in some cases. For a given structurand and transformation, the tags transforming into any given integer

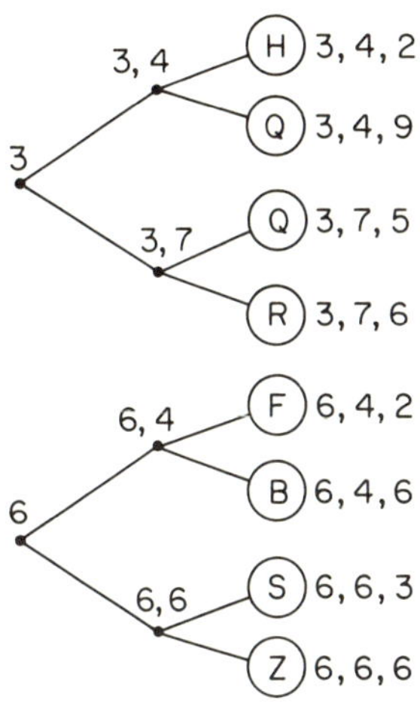


| | | | | |
|---|---|---|---|---|
| 0 | H | 3 | 4 | 2 |
| 1 | Q | 3 | 4 | 9 |
| 2 | Q | 3 | 7 | 5 |
| 3 | R | 3 | 7 | 6 |
| 4 | F | 6 | 4 | 2 |
| 5 | B | 6 | 4 | 6 |
| 6 | S | 6 | 6 | 3 |
| 7 | Z | 6 | 6 | 6 |

**Fig. 4.7** Dubbed file and its sorted sweep table.

are said to form an *equivalence class* for the integer; each tag must belong to exactly one such class. Fortunately, for many feasible transformations the average number of tags per equivalence class is usefully low.

The idea is clear from an example. Figure 4.7 displays a dubbed uniform trim of weight 8 and a sweep table in zone-index order. Consider a scatter transformation that divides the sum of the components in each tag by ten and saves the remainder:

| *Name* | *Sum* | *Remainder* |
|---|---|---|
| (3, 4, 2) | 9 | 9 |
| (3, 4, 9) | 16 | 6 |
| (3, 7, 5) | 15 | 5 |
| (3, 7, 6) | 16 | 6 |
| (6, 4, 2) | 12 | 2 |
| (6, 4, 6) | 16 | 6 |
| (6, 6, 3) | 15 | 5 |
| (6, 6, 6) | 18 | 8 |

Tags (3, 4, 9), (3, 7, 6), and (6, 4, 6) form an equivalence class of three members; tags (3, 7, 5) and (6, 6, 3) form a class of two members. Three other classes are present, each with one tag as a single member. In Table 4.1, each of these five equivalence classes is depicted as a row in a scatter chart. The width of the chart is governed by the number of members in the largest equivalence class. Because chart rows were loaded from left to right while the tag table was being examined from top to bottom, the order within equivalence classes is that retained from the tag table. This within-row order is a convenient one for discussion, but it is not a necessary order.

**Table 4.1**

*Scatter chart*

| | | | |
|---|---|---|---|
| 0 | | | |
| 1 | | | |
| 2 | F(6, 4, 2) | | |
| 3 | | | |
| 4 | | | |
| 5 | Q(3, 7, 5) | S(6, 6, 3) | |
| 6 | Q(3, 4, 9) | R(3, 7, 6) | B(6, 4, 6) |
| 7 | | | |
| 8 | Z(6, 6, 6) | | |
| 9 | H(3, 4, 2) | | |

Now consider a method of finding a leaf in the scatter chart. First the leaf tag is transformed to ascertain a row, and then a serial sweep is undertaken within the row. If the transformation truly scatters, its results take on the approximate character of random numbers from a uniform distribution. Assuming this to be the case, W. P. Heising (1958) showed that class size follows a binomial distribution and can be approximated by the Poisson distribution. Given a set of $m$ arguments and a scatter chart of $m + c$ rows, the probability of a class of $k$ members is therefore given by $P(k; mp)$. Here $m$ corresponds to the number of random drawings and $p = 1/(m + c)$ to the probability at each drawing that the result falls into a given equivalence class. (The notation $P(k; mp)$ is similar to that used in most texts on probability.) We are discussing the Poisson distribution rather than the binomial because it lends itself more conveniently to actual computations.

In an equivalence class of $k$ members, a serial sweep for the first member examines one tag, for the second member two tags, etc. Corresponding to the entire equivalence class there are $k$ serial sweeps requiring $1 + 2 + \cdots + k$ or $k(k + 1)/2$ comparisons. Assume a uniform search distribution and let $x$ denote the average number of comparisons per sweep:

$$x = \frac{\frac{1}{2}\sum_{k=0}^{m} k(k+1)\,P(k;\,mp)}{\sum_{k=0}^{m} kP(k;\,mp)}. \tag{4.14}$$

The comparisons expected of all equivalence classes are summed in the numerator; the members expected of each equivalence class are summed in the denominator.

It is well known from the properties of the Poisson distribution that

$$\sum_{k=0}^{m} kP(k;\,mp) = mp \tag{4.15}$$

and

$$\sum_{k=0}^{m} k^2P(k;\,mp) = (mp)^2 + mp. \tag{4.16}$$

Using these two results, (4.14) reduces to

$$x = \frac{(mp)^2 + 2mp}{2mp} = 1 + \frac{mp}{2}, \tag{4.17}$$

which we can also be written

$$x = 1 + \tfrac{1}{2}\left(\frac{m}{m+c}\right). \tag{4.18}$$

Clearly, $x$ equals 1.5 when $c = 0$ and ranges between 1 and 1.5 when $c > 0$.

**The chained scatter.** One way to convert the scatter chart into a useful search procedure is to form a *chained scatter table* of $m + c$ rows from a tag table of $m$ rows. Construction is in two phases. The first phase differs from the construction of a scatter chart in that only the first-encountered member of each equivalence class is listed in the scatter table, overflows being temporarily shunted aside. In moving the overflows to empty rows of the scatter table, the second phase chains the members of each equivalence class together via a column mapping vector. Thus in Table 4.2, the class with tags (3, 4, 9), (3, 7, 6) and (6, 4, 6) in Table 4.1 occupies rows 6, 0, and 1 of the chained scatter table. In row 6, the mapping vector points to row 0 as the location of another class member; in row 0, the mapping vector points to row 1 as the location of yet another class member. In row 1, the mapping vector contains a null component to indicate the end of a class chain (a convention followed for other chain endings as well).

The second phase in the preparation of a chained scatter table lends itself to various techniques for empty-row selection and mapping vector specification. Note that it is unnecessary, and in fact inefficient, to append a newly encountered overflow to the end of its class chain. It is simpler to insert the overflow ahead of incumbent overflows, which are merely pushed out one place in the chain.

Search in a chained scatter table is identical to search in a scatter chart

**Table 4.2**

*Chained scatter table*

| | *Node vector* | *Tag matrix* | *Mapping vector* |
|---|---|---|---|
| 0 | R | 3 7 6 | 1 |
| 1 | B | 6 4 6 | ∘ |
| 2 | F | 6 4 2 | ∘ |
| 3 | S | 6 6 3 | ∘ |
| 4 | ∘ | ∘ ∘ ∘ | ∘ |
| 5 | Q | 3 7 5 | 3 |
| 6 | Q | 3 4 9 | 0 |
| 7 | ∘ | ∘ ∘ ∘ | ∘ |
| 8 | Z | 6 6 6 | ∘ |
| 9 | H | 3 4 2 | ∘ |

except that the requisite serial sweep is conducted over a chain rather than over a row. In case an argument is not represented in the table, the end-of-chain null in the mapping vector can signal an "unsuccessful" search.

Problems arise when a structurand contained by a chained scatter table is changing in structure; that is, nodes must be deleted or inserted subsequent to initial loading. In deletion, the affected node is found and its status noted. If the node occupies an equivalence class of one member, its row is designated as *empty*. If the node is in a larger class and is not an overflow, it is replaced by the first overflow and the row thus liberated is designated as empty. If the node is an overflow, its row is designated as empty and the class chain is linked around it.

In inserting a node, it is necessary to distinguish between two possible cases: (1) The equivalence class of the new node is already represented in the table, and (2) a new equivalence class must be established. If the class is present, insertion reduces to the problem, already discussed, of pushing an overflow into a chain. If a new class is indicated, the node must be placed at the location indicated by the scatter transformation. If this row is empty, no problem exists. However, if the row is occupied by an overflow in another class, that overflow must be moved. But movement of an overflow is equivalent to a deletion followed by an insertion of type 1—two operations that have already been discussed.

In node insertion it is required to find an empty row. If few rows are vacant and changes have occurred often, this can pose some difficulties. Either a vector of empty-row numbers must be maintained outside the table, or the vacant rows must themselves be chained. As a new equivalence class may break the empty chain, the length of the empty chain can in itself be a serious obstacle to chain repair. This obstacle is easily circumvented for empty rows by a double-chain format that specifies a predecessor as well as a successor. An unused portion of each vacant row can contain the index of the predecessor.

Let the proportion $d$ of occupied rows in a scatter table be the *density* of the table. In a scatter table of $m + c$ rows and $m$ occupied rows, $d$ equals $m/(m + c)$. Under the assumptions used to derive (4.18), the probe expectation of a chained scatter is given by

$$E(\text{chained scatter}, d) = 1 + \frac{m}{2(m + c)} = 1 + \frac{d}{2}. \tag{4.19}$$

As $d$ ranges from 0 to 1, the expectation ranges from 1 to 1.5.

**The open scatter.** The mapping vector of the chained scatter tables is omitted in an *open scatter table.* To insert a node in the table, the scatter transformation indicates the starting point of a cyclic serial sweep for an empty row. To search the table, a similar serial sweep starts from the row nominated by the transformed argument tag. Node deletion is identical to node search except that the row of the node, once found, is cleared or otherwise designated as empty.

The virtue of the open scatter lies in simplicity; insertion, search, and deletion are all straightforward and akin in nature. The open scatter is particularly applicable where the number of insertions and searches are comparable in magnitude.

The open scatter table of Table 4.3 was generated with the same transformation and in the same order as the chained scatter table of Table 4.2. The serial sweeps required in construction were of the lengths shown below:

| *Tag* | *Indicated Row* | *Actual Row* | *Sweep Length* |
|---|---|---|---|
| (3, 4, 2) | 9 | 9 | 1 |
| (3, 4, 9) | 6 | 6 | 1 |
| (3, 7, 5) | 5 | 5 | 1 |
| (3, 7, 6) | 6 | 7 | 2 |
| (6, 4, 2) | 2 | 2 | 1 |
| (6, 4, 6) | 6 | 8 | 3 |
| (6, 6, 3) | 5 | 0 | 6 |
| (6, 6, 6) | 8 | 1 | 4 |
| | | | 19 |

As 19 rows were encountered in inserting 8 nodes, the average insertion in this example swept 19/8 rows. Assuming a uniform search distribution, this example has a probe expectation of 19/8 for searching as well.

Let us turn to the probe expectation of an open scatter search. Under the assumptions used in deriving (4.19), the approximation

**Table 4.3**

*Open scatter table*

| | | | | |
|---|---|---|---|---|
| 0 | S | 6 | 6 | 3 |
| 1 | Z | 6 | 6 | 6 |
| 2 | F | 6 | 4 | 2 |
| 3 | ∘ | ∘ | ∘ | ∘ |
| 4 | ∘ | ∘ | ∘ | ∘ |
| 5 | Q | 3 | 7 | 5 |
| 6 | Q | 3 | 4 | 9 |
| 7 | R | 3 | 7 | 6 |
| 8 | B | 6 | 4 | 6 |
| 9 | H | 3 | 4 | 2 |

$$E(\text{open scatter}, d) = 1 + \tfrac{1}{2}\left(\frac{d}{1-d}\right) \tag{4.20}$$

was derived by G. Schay, Jr., and W. G. Spruth (1962). Equation (4.20) is highly accurate for $d \leq 0.9$. Accuracy falls off as $d$ approaches unity, a matter of little consequence because the expectation rises rapidly and the open scatter is normally avoided for $d \geq 0.95$. For the example of Table 4.3, (4.20) yields 3.

Empirical studies by W. W. Peterson (1957) demonstrated that the probe expectation of the open scatter climbs slowly toward a higher level when the table is repeatedly changed by pairs of node deletions and insertions, a tendency that can be checked, of course, by periodically regenerating an entirely new open scatter table. Strictly speaking, (4.20) applies only where deletions have not affected the scatter table.

One way to combine the search efficiency of the chained scatter with minimal chaining nuisance is to employ a table of $2m$ rows for a trim or tree of $m$ nodes. Since all overflows can be placed in an overflow area of $m$ rows, the problems of inserting new nodes are ameliorated and the desired table can be established in one phase.

The open and chained scatters not only prossess commendably low probe expectations but, as evident from (4.19) and (4.20), their probe performance is a function solely of table density. It follows that they are especially attractive for structurands of large moment or weight. Where nonuniform search distributions prevail, the probe expectations of the scatters can be decreased by ordering members within equivalence classes according to frequence of usage. This is particularly easy to accomplish in the case of the chained scatter.

Scatter searches do not lend themselves to searches for families, subtrees, and the like. In a scatter table, needs for such searchs must be met by other means, e.g., by additional use of mapping vectors.

The scatter searches are, of course, dependent on the availability of transformations that combine a satisfactory degree of scattering with a reasonable amount of processing. No known transformation can guarantee to satisfy both requirements under all conditions. In choosing a general-purpose transformation, one helpful principle to follow is that the transformation should depend on all the information in the argument tag; a transformation that ignores parts of an argument may easily fail to scatter some clusters of tags. Although the least defensible type of general transformation is one that simply selects argument components and adjoins them to yield some representation of a row index, this method can be very effective in special cases. More suitable in general are transformations that employ arithmetic or logical operations, and probably no single operation has been more useful than one that divides a numerical representation of the tag by a prime number and saves the remainder.

The characteristics of most direct-access storage devices dictate a smallest block of storage that can be read in one fetch operation. If the block accommodates several table rows, the scatter transformation, and the pointers in the case of the chained scatter search, are usually addressed at blocks rather than at table rows. (A block is often termed a *bucket* in the literature.) The effect of this modification is to somewhat decrease the probe expectations of the scatter searches, assuming that a probe refers to a block rather than a table row.

## 4.6 Base-Value Calculations

The search table of an indexed array or base-$\boldsymbol{r}$ tree can consist solely of a node vector because node location can be calculated directly from the index tag. As shown in Sec. 3.6, the zero-origin zone indices are equal to the base-$\boldsymbol{r}$ values of the zero-origin index tags. The computation required of a series of searches in a given array can be minimized in a number of ways. First of all, the weight vector $\boldsymbol{w}$ can be computed once and stored. Number-system properties can be exploited if it is desired to systematically visit the nodes of a subarray. The base-(2, 3, 4) array denoted as $F$ in Fig. 4.8 will permit us to give examples. If the leaf level is treated as a node vector $\boldsymbol{n}$ with zero-origin indexing, the nodes themselves specify the vector indices.

The weight vector $\boldsymbol{w}$ of $F$ is (12, 4, 1). The weight of $F$ as a whole is 24. Let $i$ denote the index of $\boldsymbol{n}$, and let $k$ be a component of $\boldsymbol{w}$ to be added to $i$. If we start with $\boldsymbol{n}_0$ and add $k$ to $i$, we visit the nodes

$$\begin{aligned} &\boldsymbol{n}_0, \boldsymbol{n}_{12} && \text{for } k = 12 \\ &\boldsymbol{n}_0, \boldsymbol{n}_4, \boldsymbol{n}_8, \boldsymbol{n}_{12}, \boldsymbol{n}_{16}, \boldsymbol{n}_{20} && \text{for } k = 4 \\ &\boldsymbol{n}_0, \boldsymbol{n}_1, \ldots, \boldsymbol{n}_{23}, && \text{for } k = 1\,. \end{aligned} \tag{4.21}$$

Clearly, by choosing $k$ appropriately, one can visit the first nodes of subarrays.

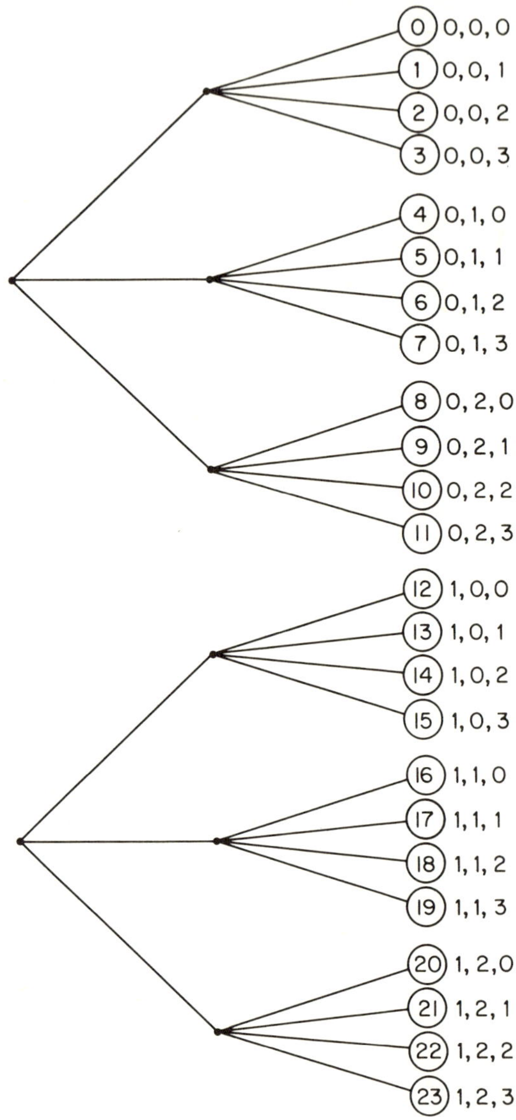


**Fig. 4.8** An array $F$ with dimension vector (2, 3, 4) and leaves specified by the zone index.

Moreover, by starting at an arbitrary point, one can localize the visits to any region of interest. Incrementation by $k$, best known as *indexing* in computer programming, is a search operation of great importance in array processing.

For array $G$ in Fig. 4.9, the (2, 1, 3) transpose of array $F$, we have

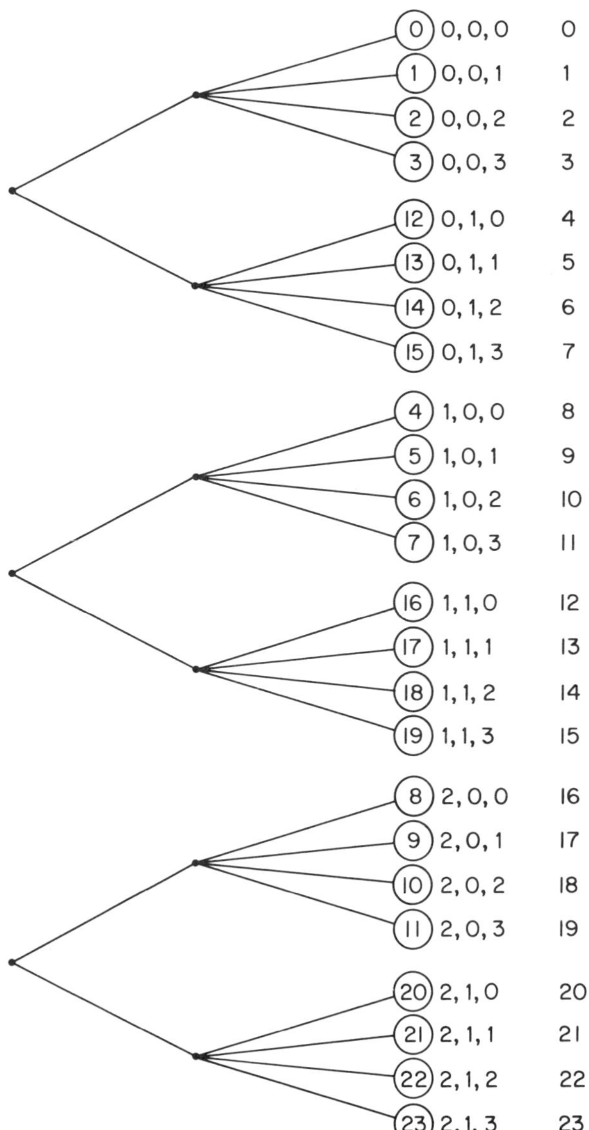


**Fig. 4.9** The (2, 1, 3) transpose array $G$ of array $F$.

$$\boldsymbol{r} = (3, 2, 4) \qquad \text{and} \qquad \boldsymbol{w} = (8, 4, 1).$$

Because the arrangement of leaves in $G$ is different from the arrangement in $F$, the vector $\boldsymbol{n}$ is not the most convenient representation of $G$. However, let vector

$f$ denote a tag in $F$ and let $g$ denote the corresponding tag in $G$. In the mapping-operation sense,

$$g = (2, 1, 3) \int f. \tag{4.22}$$

If we apply the same (2, 1, 3) permutation to the weight vector of $F$, we have

$$(4, 12, 1) = (2, 1, 3) \int (12, 4, 1). \tag{4.23}$$

To refer to $\boldsymbol{n}_i$ given an argument tag $\boldsymbol{g}$, simply use (4, 12, 1) as the applicable weight vector. For example, if $\boldsymbol{g} = (1, 0, 2)$, then

$$i = (4 \times 1) + (12 \times 0) + (1 \times 2) = 6, \tag{4.24}$$

which is the index of the desired node. In general, by suitably permuting the weight vector of $F$, it is possible to calculate position in $\boldsymbol{n}$ from any tag of any transpose of $F$ by methods illustrated in (4.22)–(4.24). With careful analysis, shortcuts of the type illustrated in (4.21) can also be used.

To avoid the multiplications of (4.24), it is possible to use index-tag components as increments for entering precomputed vectors, thereby reducing the arithmetic to additions. The method for doing this has already been discussed in Sec. 4.4 as a direct-path search. However, for base structures, the degree vector of a direct-path table is redundant and should be omitted.

## 4.7 Batch Searches

Where a sequential-access table is to be swept many times during its useful lifetime, and where the nature of the application permits a batch of searches to be conducted at each sweep, the efficacy of the row sweep can be markedly improved. Initially, the table is sorted as a skip table. Subsequently, whenever a set of $q$ transactions becomes available, the set is sorted on argument tags. Assuming a forward sweep, the first argument is matched in a first part of the skip table, the second argument is matched in a second part of the skip table, and so on until all $q$ arguments have been matched. The whole process of searching on $q$ arguments requires at most one complete sweep through the table. In fact, because the process can terminate when the last argument has been matched, a complete pass may not be required over all $m$ rows of the table. If $q = 1$, the probe expectation of a batch search is identical (for a uniform search distribution) to that of the row sweep. But as $q$ increases, the probe expectation rapidly approaches $m/q$. At $q = m$, the probe expectation diminishes to unity.

Notice that the operations required to sort a set of $q$ transactions must be reckoned in the cost of the batch search. As will be seen in Chapter 5, if the transaction set is in haphazard order, sorting will require at least $\log_2 q$ comparisons on each argument tag. Hence, in the limit $q = m$, the batch search is roughly equal in the required number of comparisons to a binary search. In the usual case where $q < m$, the batch search tends to require more comparisons that the binary search. However, the noteworthy advantage of the batch search is that its skip table need not be stored in a random-access device. As a consequence, the batch search is attractive for tables stored on inexpensive storage media (such as decks of cards or reels of magnetic tape) that lend themselves to serial rather than to random access. The batch search has been decisively important in applications requiring periodic maintenance and report-generation passes over accounting files. *Batch processing* is a term often used to allude to this mode of computer usage.

If incoming transactions are not batched and sorted, we have the case $q = 1$, and the probe expectations of the row sweep and the batch search are both given by $(m + 1)/2$. Essentially, this comes about because the batch search is ignoring the properties of the skip table and using it as if it were a sweep table. However, if backward as well as forward access is permitted, the ordering of the skip table can be exploited. A random number of range $m$ admits the integers $0, 1, 2, \ldots, m - 2, m - 1$. For random numbers of range $m$, it can be shown that the absolute value of the difference of two independent observations $j$ and $k$ has the expectation

$$E(|j - k|) = \frac{m - 1}{3m} \simeq \frac{m}{3}.$$

Hence, if rows are equally spaced in storage and if independent searches are conducted by moving in the correct direction from the desired row of one search to the desired row of the next search, approximately one third of table is swept in the average search. Each search starts where the preceding search ended and moves over the fewest possible number of rows.

## 4.8 Subfile Chaining

In the previous sections of this chapter, we have discussed several basic methods of finding a node after the tag of the node has been given as an argument. These methods were discussed in six categories:

1. Sweep searches
2. Skip searches
3. Path searches
4. Scatter searches
5. Base value (for indexed base-$r$ arrays and trees)
6. Batch search (a modification of the sweep).

All of these methods are applicable where their tables are housed in direct-access storage, but only the sweep and the batch searches are applicable where tables are housed in serial-access storage. The base-value method is specialized for base-$r$ structures and the path searches are most suitable for structurands of several levels. Skip searches and scatter searches, the other two categories, are particularly applicable to master files housed in direct-access storage. The rest of this chapter is concerned with important embellishments for master files that are organized as skip or scatter tables.

Most master files require a large quantity of storage capacity. A reel of magnetic tape is an example of a serial-access storage medium, and a read/write device that permits reels to be mounted and dismounted can provide capacity for the largest master file. A device that consists of a battery of revolving disks and one or more movable read/write heads that can be positioned to numbered locations provides a good example of a large-capacity direct-access storage mechanism. (The nature of these devices is explained more fully in Chapter 7.) Practically speaking, one of the important properties of most large-capacity disk devices is that the time required for access to location $n$, given that the head is already positioned at location $m$, depends to some extent on the physical separation between locations $m$ and $n$. As a result, the total time required for a sequence of probes depends in part on the actual locations that have to be visited. Although this can have important implications for application planning, here we can do little more than draw attention to the existence of a practical problem.

Where we are solely concerned with presenting the principles of node search, we can start with a dubbed vector and represent it by a skip table of two columns: One column contains dub tags and the other contains nodes. It is often convenient to think of the master file introduced in Sec. 2.6 as a dubbed vector; a node in the vector consists of a long character string that embraces all of the record except the dub tag, and the structure in the string can be ignored as long as one is solely interested in searching or sorting nodes on the given set of dub tags. A scatter table can be similarly simplified, although one extra column must be appended to the table to accommodate the chained scatter. If we are to remark further about search, however, we must delve into the fields of the record itself.

In some applications, after a record $R$ is located by a skip or scatter search, a set $S$ of additional records needs to be processed in conjunction with $R$. For example, if $R$ is the record of a manager, all of the employees that report to the manager may constitute the set $S$. One way to relate $S$ to $R$ is to append a mapping vector to the table and chain the members of $S$ to $R$. Typically, the last record in the chain points back to $R$, thereby closing a loop for all employees in the manager's department. Essentially, the loop provides for efficient search of a subfile. The cost of the technique lies in (1) the marginal storage required for the pointer column and (2) the additional probes required each time the table is revised to insert or delete records.

Unless the structure of the file changes very slowly, the significance of 2 outweighs the significance of 1. If several columns of pointers are appended to facilitate subfile searches, the maintenance involved in moving a record becomes high, and it becomes important to emphasize techniques that either avoid or delay the need to ripple records in the table at every instance of insertion or deletion. In any case, each insertion or deletion requires patching in the chains that are directly involved with the record. The number of probes required in patching can be minimized by doubling the number of pointer columns, thereby permitting each chain to point backward as well as forward.

Subfile chains are particularly useful in applications that deal with the planning and control of manufactured parts and subassemblies.

## 4.9 Multiple Keys

A master file housed in direct-access storage is typically maintained as a skip or scatter table and one particular field in the record, the *primary key*, serves the role of the dub tag. The file is likely to be used in two distinctly different ways:

1. Consult an individual record quickly.
2. Go through the file for periodic reporting purposes.

In use 1, the problem is to find a record promptly, either to consult the information therein or to update the information; for example, an inventory amount may be consulted or revised. In use 2, the problem is to access the records of the file in some desired order, at the same time achieving a high rate of information flow (the creation of paychecks is an example in the context of personnel files).

Having studied the properties of scatter tables, we know that they can be efficacious for use 1. If they are to serve for use 2, a pointer column must be appended to permit chaining through the records in the desired order. By batching information concerning structural changes, it may be feasible to perform all necessary maintenance on the chain in the course of the periodic-reporting pass itself. Pointer columns can also be used, if necessary, for skip tables, but note that order on the primary key is an inherent property of the skip table. Where the practical characteristics of direct-access devices make seek times a function of distance, a pass of a skip table in primary-key order is likely to achieve the highest possible data rate.

We have been considering record look-up and periodic reporting in the context of a primary key. But suppose that a master file is employed by two or more applications, each of which focuses attention on a different key. The key that governs the generation of the skip or scatter table is called the primary key, whereas the other keys are usually known as *secondary keys*. A mapping vector will permit periodic-reporting processes to chain through a file in secondary-key order, but additional measures must be taken before records can be consulted quickly on the basis of their secondary keys. In the absence of special measures, the only recourse is the sweep search, a pathetically inefficient method for truly large master files.

A method of amending the scatter table to provide for searches on secondary keys is described by L. R. Johnson (1961). The method employs two mapping vectors, rather than one, in conjunction with the chained scatter. The expectation of the chained scatter is lengthened by one probe. The maintenance involved in structural changes is nontrivial (by now it should be clear that pointer columns have this inherent disability), but as with all chained scatters, this maintenance can be greatly reduced by allocating a separate and additional storage area for overflow records. Another way of ameliorating the maintenance problem is to forego the search performance of the primary key and treat all keys as secondary keys.

A competitive method of supplementing the skip table to provide for searches on secondary keys is to create a *tag file* for each secondary key. Each tag file consists of two columns, a tag column and a pointer column, and has the same number of rows as the master file. A tag file is ordered on its tag column; hence, it can be entered with the aid of a skip search. Each tag in the file is accompanied by a pointer that specifies the location of the associated record in the master file. The tag files require additional storage and they require maintenance whenever structural changes alter the master file. They can be useful at the time of periodic reporting as well as at times of individual record look-up.

## 4.10 Inverted Files

Queries that involve information in an unpredictable subset of the records in a file are not easily managed by any of the search methods that we have been discussing for direct-access storage devices. An example of such a query might take the form, "Who are the Ph.D.'s with occupation code $C$ at geographical location $Z$?" The possible variety among such questions is large enough to frustrate efforts that attempt to improve search performances using pointer columns and arrangements based on ordered tags. In other words, it is not feasible to strive for optimal searches because the fields involved in a query are diverse and unpredictable. A more promising approach is to look at practical methods of simulating the column sweep.

We have been assuming a storage device that permits direct access to table rows (i.e., records) and delivers a whole row at each access. To examine a field, under this assumption, it is necessary to fetch the record that contains the field. Since the record may contain dozens of fields, this can be a cumbersome and inefficient way of examining individual fields. In light of this, unforeseen queries are more readily answerable given a master file matrix that is stored column by column rather than row by row. The transpose that results is reasonably well suited to questions involving a few fields. If records contain 100 fields and a question involves 3 fields, only 3 percent of the columns must be swept to pinpoint the records needed in answering the question. If the query involves a substantial proportion of the fields, the transpose loses its inherent advantage over the original skip table. One of the problems with the transpose is that it is awkward to maintain.

A more convenient scheme is provided by the *inverted file*. This can take a number of different forms that differ in detail, but the general idea is illustrated by the schematic in Fig. 4.10, where an inverted file is shown supplementing the master file. The inverted file consists of a set of vectors. The first component of each vector consists of an attribute value for some field of the master-file records, and the remaining components of the vector consist of pointers that identify the locations of records that contain the given attribute value. There may be several or many vectors for any given field; in Fig. 4.10, field $j$ is shown with three vectors and field $k$ with four vectors.

Within each vector, we assume, the pointers are ordered in ascending sequence. As a result, it is easy to sweep several relevant vectors simultaneously and determine the intersection or union set of all relevant pointers. In this way, the locations of all relevant records are determined before the master file is consulted. For example, if there is a vector for Ph.D., another for occupation code $C$, and still another for geographical location $Z$, the intersection of the pointers in the three vectors will identify all of the records that need to be consulted to determine the names of the Ph.D.'s with code $C$ at location $Z$.

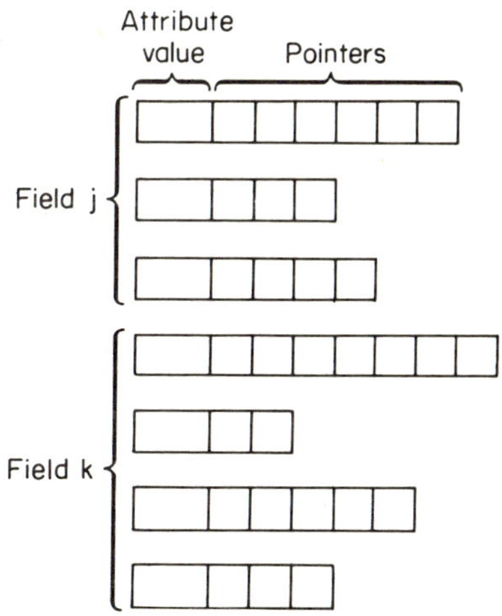


**Fig. 4.10** Schematic of an inverted master file.

By systematically inverting every field in the master file, it is possible to entirely dispense with the master file. This possibility is of interest mainly in very specialized applications, the reason being that the inverted file is an awkward tool for routine processing involving record updating or periodic reporting. In most cases, the inverted file can be limited to a subset of all fields and used as a helpful adjunct to a conventional file. As such, it adds to storage requirements and maintenance costs; in return, it enhances search capabilities and permits the information in the file to be exploited for a wider variety of purposes.

## 4.11 Comment

Nomenclature for search table and search method is particularly chaotic. The terms *sweep search*, *skip search*, and *path search* are not established in the literature. Neither is the trick of referring to a table by the name of the corresponding search technique. The term *scatter search* is emerging but has more often been called a *key-transformation* search or, less formally, *hash addressing*. The binary search is the only search in Chapter 4 that has a fully accepted name.

Although *table* has a number of drawbacks as a technical term, it is not easy to find a convincing substitute. As defined here, the term is not inconsonant with the ways in which programmers typically use it. *Key*, *primary* versus *secondary key* and *inverted file* are accepted terms.

A version of the rank-path search is described by R. de la Briandais (1959) in the context of character-by-character searches on variable-length character strings (English words). The rank-path search is inefficient for structures with large families, the worst case being a long vector. In the context of ordered numerical vectors with frequent insertions and deletions, the use of doubly chained binary search trees has received considerable attention, for example, P. F. Windley (1960), T. N. Hibbard (1962), H. A. Clampett, Jr. (1964), and S. R. Arora and W. T. Dent (1969). Since these chained versions of the binary search involve high-low-equal comparisons, we would classify them as skip searches that pay a penalty in additional storage to expedite insertions and deletions.

C. W. Bachman and S. B. Williams (1964) discuss a system for subfile chaining with reference to master files. In the list structure context, A. J. Perlis and C. Thornton (1960) define a *threaded list* that is applicable to multilevel trims; each within-family chain terminates with a pointer to the family's parent point (rather than with a null). Their approach is a variation on the list conventions of A. Newell and J. C. Shaw (1957) and Shaw et al. (1958).

Skip searches are used in such a wide variety of circumstances that it is difficult for an introduction to convey their importance. In the method of Sec.

4.3, the row number for a probe on the succeeding level can be calculated because families are equal in dimension, but if pointers are supplied, families can vary in dimension. Moreover, if tags are accompanied by pointers to record nodes, rather than by the records themselves, search speed can be improved by placing some or all of the tag levels in a storage device with faster access than provided for the records.

*Chapter 5*

# TABLE SORTING

Sorting is an adjunct to searching. When files, numerical arrays, or input transaction tables are sorted, the motivation is always to heighten the efficacy of subsequent search operations. Because of the decisive role that sorting plays in batch processing, the subject of sorting has been disciplined by a good deal of analysis and practical experience. This chapter is not a complete survey of sorting methods but rather a discussion of methods that have gained the most recognition on the basis of merit.

Most of the sorting methods to be discussed accrue information by matching tags. In exposition, it simplifies matters to illustrate with the simplest possible tags, notably positive integers.

## 5.1 Linear Sorts

A vector of dimension $n$ has $n - 1$ pairs of adjacent components. In the first stage of a *bubble sort*, components are swept in reverse order and a comparison is made between the components of each pair. After each comparison, the components of the pair in question are interchanged, if necessary, to endow the smaller component with the lower vector rank. By the end of the first stage, the smallest integer has bubbled to the top of the vector and can be excluded from further consideration. Stage 2 is identical except that $n - 2$ rather than $n - 1$ pairs are compared; stage 3 is identical except that $n - 3$ pairs are compared; etc. At most, $n - 1$ stages can be required, but early termination is permitted after a stage with no transpositions. The bubble sort is illustrated in Table 5. 1 for a vector of dimension six.

The *selection sort* involves at most one interchange per stage. In stage 1, the position of the smallest component is ascertained by $n - 1$ comparisons; at each comparison, one comparand is the smallest component yet processed.

**Table 5.1**

*Examples of three linear sorts*

| | | *Stage* | | | | |
|---|---|---|---|---|---|---|
| *Sort type* | *Given vector* | 1 | 2 | 3 | 4 | 5 |
| Bubble | 5 | ② | 2 | 2 | 2 | |
| | 4 | 5 | ③ | 3 | 3 | |
| | 8 | 4 | 5 | ④ | 4 | |
| | 2 | 8 | 4 | 5 | 5 | |
| | 6 | 3 | 8 | 6 | 6 | |
| | 3 | 6 | 6 | 8 | 8 | |
| | | | Sorted area | | | |
| Selection | 5 | 2 | 2 | 2 | 2 | 2 |
| | 4 | 4 | 3 | 3 | 3 | 3 |
| | 8 | 8 | 8 | 4 | 4 | 4 |
| | 2 | 5 | 5 | 5 | 5 | 5 |
| | 6 | 6 | 6 | 6 | 6 | 6 |
| | 3 | 3 | 4 | 8 | 8 | 8 |
| Insertion | 5 | 5 | 5 | 5 | 5 | 2 |
| | 4 | 4 | 4 | 4 | 2 | 3 |
| | 8 | 8 | 8 | 2 | 3 | 4 |
| | 2 | 2 | 2 | 3 | 4 | 5 |
| | 6 | 3 | 3 | 6 | 6 | 6 |
| | 3 | 6 | 6 | 8 | 8 | 8 |
| | | | Sorted area | | | |

The minimium component, once located, is interchanged with the first component in the vector and henceforth ignored. Stage 2 repeats the process for a vector suffix of dimension $n - 1$, stage 3 for a vector suffix of dimension $n - 2$, etc. Exactly $n - 1$ stages are required to select $n - 1$ components (the $n$th component is positioned by exclusion). Table 5.1 provides an example.

An infix of a numerical vector $x$ is called a *train* if $x_i \leq x_{i+1}$ for each pair in the infix. Each stage in an *insertion sort* lengthens an existing train by one. Given a number to be inserted in the train, the point of insertion is determined by comparisons made in sweeping the string; a forward sweep will be assumed.

Each component smaller than the given number is moved up one position during the course of the sweep, thus creating any empty position for the number at the proper insertion point. The insertion sort requires $n - 1$ stages because a train of length 1 is given at the outset. An example is given in Table 5.1.

To sort a vector of dimension $n$, the selection sort requires $n(n - 1)/2$ comparisons. If the vector is in backward order, the worst case, the bubble and insertion sorts require an identical number. For random order, it can be shown that the bubble sort requires fewer comparisons because less than $n - 1$ stages are expected. Since the stages saved are the stages with the fewest comparisons, the practical effect is rather insignificant. For random order, however, the number of comparisons expected of the insertion sort approximately equals half the number required of the selection sort. For random and haphazard numbers, the insertion sort is the most useful of the sweep sorts. The bubble sort has special utility, on the other hand, for vectors that are nearly ordered at the outset.

The number of comparisons required of the insertion sort can be reduced by using the binary search to locate the point of insertion at each stage. Since a portion of the vector will have to be displaced one position to make room for the insertion, the binary search is interesting if components can be moved faster than they can be compared. (Also, see Sec. 5.5.)

The *odd-even transposition sort* proceeds by half-stages. During the first half of a stage, each component with an odd index is compared to its successor, if one exists, and if necessary the pair is interchanged to bring the lower component forward. During the second half-stage, each even-numbered component is compared to its successor and, if necessary, an interchange occurs as in the previous half-stage. The sort of a vector of dimension $n$ must end in $n$ half-stages. Subsequent to the initial half-stage, however, the process can end at the first half-stage that involves no interchange. An example is given in Table 5.2.

**Table 5.2**

*Transposition sort example*

| | | *Stage* | | | | |
|---|---|---|---|---|---|---|
| *Vector index* | *Given vector* | 1 | 1.5 | 2 | 2.5 | 3 |
| 1 | 5 | 4 | 4 | 2 | 2 | 2 |
| 2 | 4 | 5 | 2 | 4 | 3 | 3 |
| 3 | 8 | 2 | 5 | 3 | 4 | 4 |
| 4 | 2 | 8 | 3 | 5 | 5 | 5 |
| 5 | 6 | 3 | 8 | 6 | 6 | 6 |
| 6 | 3 | 6 | 6 | 8 | 8 | 8 |

Each stage of this sort takes $n - 1$ comparisons, as can easily be verified. Each half-stage averages $(n - 1)/2$ comparisons. Since a maximum of $n$ half-stages is required in the worst case (a backward-ordered vector), the maximum number of comparisons is again $n(n - 1)/2$. For random data, the expected number of half-stages decreases, but for our purposes, worst-case conditions are sufficiently indicative of performance. The transposition sort, such as the bubble sort, is particularly suited to the sorting of partially ordered data.

It is a potential advantage of the odd-even transposition sort that all comparisons at each half-stage can be executed in parallel. The sort is at a disadvantage, on the other hand, if executed by serial data passes; in this case, each half-stage requires a full pass of the data, and the amount of data to be handled is roughly twice the amount required of a bubble sort in sorting a backward-ordered vector.

The sort methods discussed in this section are *linear* in the sense that the number of comparisons per item is some linear function of $n$. It needs to be stressed that the number of comparisons is only one of the parameters to be considered in evaluating a sorting method. Other measures need to be applied, in practice, to assess the utility of a given sorting method. For example, where storage is at a premium, a linear method may be preferable to a method that requires fewer comparisons but takes more space.

## 5.2 Column Sorts

Let $\boldsymbol{M}$ be an $m \times n$ matrix of range $\boldsymbol{\iota}^0(r)$. Let $j$ denote the column index of $\boldsymbol{M}$, and let $d$ denote an integer in the range of $\boldsymbol{M}$. Consider $\boldsymbol{M}_j$, the $j$th column of $\boldsymbol{M}$, and a compatible logical vector $\boldsymbol{u}$ that contains a 1 for each component in $\boldsymbol{M}_j$ equal to $d$ and a 0 for each component unequal to $d$. Then the matrix obtained in compressing the columns of $\boldsymbol{M}$ by $\boldsymbol{u}$ is called the *class-$(j, d)$ matrix* of $\boldsymbol{M}$. A maximum of $nr$ class matrices are possible. Of the following matrices,

$$\underset{\boldsymbol{K}}{\begin{bmatrix} 2 & 3 & 2 \\ 2 & 6 & 3 \\ 1 & 4 & 8 \\ 3 & 5 & 6 \\ 2 & 2 & 0 \\ 0 & 4 & 3 \end{bmatrix}} \quad \underset{\boldsymbol{D}}{\begin{bmatrix} 2 & 3 & 2 \\ 2 & 6 & 3 \\ 2 & 2 & 0 \end{bmatrix}} \quad \underset{\boldsymbol{E}}{\begin{bmatrix} 3 & 5 & 6 \end{bmatrix}} \quad \underset{\boldsymbol{F}}{\begin{bmatrix} 2 & 6 & 3 \\ 0 & 4 & 3 \end{bmatrix}}$$

$\boldsymbol{D}$ is the class-(1, 2) matrix, $\boldsymbol{E}$ the class-(2, 5) matrix, and $\boldsymbol{F}$ the class-(2, 3) matrix of $\boldsymbol{K}$.

In a *column sort*, the matrix $\boldsymbol{M}$ has a counterpart in the characters that represent a tag matrix. The tag matrix is sorted to desired order by repeatedly forming class matrices and concatenating them by column. The idea should be clear from an example.

The given matrix of Table 5.3 is of range $\iota^0(4)$. For a matrix of $n$ columns,

**Table 5.3**

*Column sort example*

| | *Stage* | | | |
|---|---|---|---|---|
| | 0 | 1 | 2 | 3 |
| Matrix | 3 0 2 | 3 1 0 | 3 0 2 | 0 2 0 |
| at | 1 3 1 | 0 2 0 | 2 0 2 | 0 3 2 |
| end | 2 1 3 | 1 3 1 | 3 1 0 | 1 3 1 |
| of | 0 3 2 | 2 2 1 | 2 1 3 | 2 0 2 |
| stage | 3 1 0 | 3 0 2 | 0 2 0 | 2 1 3 |
| | 0 2 0 | 0 3 2 | 2 2 1 | 2 2 1 |
| | 2 2 1 | 2 0 2 | 1 3 1 | 3 0 2 |
| | 2 0 2 | 2 1 3 | 0 3 2 | 3 1 0 |
| Derived | 2 | 2 | 2 | |
| dimension | 2 | 2 | 1 | |
| vector | 3 | 2 | 3 | |
| | 1 | 2 | 2 | |

the column sort requires $n + 1$ stages. Stage 0, a preparatory stage, inspects the rightmost column of the matrix to determine the number of rows required of each class matrix in stage 1. For the range of the matrix in Table 5.3, this stage ascertains dimensions 2, 2, 3, 1 for digits 0, 1, 2, 3, respectively. It follows that the class matrices to be formed in stage 1 should start in rows 1, 3, 5, and 8 of an empty matrix. The allocation vector needed in stage $i + 1$ is always formed in stage $i$.

Stage 1 inspects the rightmost column of the original matrix in forward order, moving each row of the old matrix to the next vacant row in the appropriate class-(3, $d$) matrix. At the end of the stage, all class matrices are complete and in order on the rightmost column. The matrix resulting from stage 1 becomes the input to stage 2, which goes on to form the class-(2, $d$) matrices. Similarly, stage 3 forms the class-(1, $d$) matrices from the matrix given by stage 2. The column sort shown in the example terminates at stage 3.

The number of stages in a column sort is solely a function of the number of columns to be classified. Storage is required for two matrices, those of stage $k$ and of stage $k + 1$. Stage 0 of the sort, and the dimension vector as well, can be eliminated if enough extra storage is provided for the class matrices of each stage. In punched-card-sorting machines, where the column sort finds important use, this extra storage is physically realized in the form of bins that fill under the watchful eye of an operator.

The column sort is a rather convenient way to manually arrange cards. The term *sorting* apparently came into vogue in the context of column sorting. In its generalized versions, the column sort is sometimes called a *radix sort*. The range of the sort can be implemented to take in a whole collating sequence. Moreover, the sort range permits optional values of $r$. Where $r$ is a parameter that can be controlled, fewer passes can be realized by treating a larger radix at each pass. For example, $r = 100$ would take fewer stages than $r = 10$.

## 5.3 Logarithmic Sorts

A numerical vector $\boldsymbol{x}$ is an ascending train if $\boldsymbol{x}_i \leq \boldsymbol{x}_{i+1}$ for every pair of adjacent components. A descending train is analogously defined, although here the discussion will assume ascending trains.

Computers are designed to compare two operands at a time. Therefore, a two-way merge is a merge that repeatedly compares leading components from two input trains and appends a chosen component of the pair to an output train. Three merging methods will be introduced in their two-way realizations. Later, it will be shown that these schemes can be generalized to reduce the number of passes over the data.

Of the methods to be discussed, the most intuitive is the *balanced merge*. At its simplest, the method takes the form of the *train doubler*, which is demonstrated in Table 5.4 for a vector of dimension 8. Each merging stage of the doubler yields a matrix of which each row is a train. The process starts with a matrix of one column and ends with a matrix of one row. Row dimension is doubled, and column dimension halved, at each stage.

Let $n$ denote the dimension of the initial column vector. If $n$ is a power of 2, as in the example of Table 5.4, then the number of required merge stages is given by $\log_2 n$. Because each stage moves $n$ components, the number of components moved is $n \log_2 n$. If the input to stage $i$ is preserved until stage $i$ terminates, storage for $2n$ components is required. One comparison is required to produce a train of length 2, at most three comparisons are required to produce a train of length 4, and, in general, at most $(g - 1)$ comparisons are required to produce a train of length $g$. This is equivalent to saying that at least $n/2$ comparison are saved at the first stage, $n/4$ at the second, $n/8$ at the third, etc. Hence there are fewer comparisons than moves, the number of comparisons for $\log_2 n$ stages being at most

$$n\left[\log_2 n - \left(\frac{1}{2} + \frac{1}{4} + \cdots + \frac{1}{n}\right)\right],$$

which is approximately equal to $n \log_2(n/2)$.

**Table 5.4**

*Doubler merge example*

| | *Merge Stage* | | |
|---|---|---|---|
| *Given vector* | 1 | 2 | 3 |
| 5 | | | |
| 0 | | | |
| 3 | | | |
| 8 | | | |
| 6 | 05 | | |
| 7 | 38 | | |
| 9 | 67 | 0358 | |
| 1 | 19 | 1679 | 01356789 |

Table 5.4 depicts the doubler in a form that emphasizes its simplicity, not in a manner appropriate for serial-access storage devices. Consider four devices 1, 2, 3, and 4 that can only be read or written (recorded) in a forward direction; in view of these restrictions, all return to initial positions at the close of each stage. Let the given vector be contained on device 1, as in Table 5.5. In stage 0, the vector on device 1 is swept: half of the components (trains of length 1) are recorded on device 2 and half on device 4. In stage 1, devices 2 and 4 are swept and pairs of trains are successively merged; the trains produced are alternately stored on devices 1 and 3. In stage 2, the trains produced in merging from devices 1 and 3 are alternately recorded on devices 2 and 4. The pattern thus established in stages 1 and 2 continues until one train eventuates on device 1 or 2.

Let a *maximal* train be a train contained in no train of greater length. Thus the vector (6, 3, 4, 4, 8, 5, 7, 2) contains four maximal trains: (6), (3, 4, 4, 8), (5, 7), and (2). At the cost of one extra comparison for each component written, stage 0 can write maximal trains rather than strings of length 1. This can be helpful in reducing the required number of stages, particularly if the data are partially ordered at the outset.

Stage 0 corresponds to what is called an *internal pass* in conventional computer sorting programs. The internal pass may create trains of some fixed length, say $f$, where $f$ is a function of the amount of high-speed memory available to the computer. Or the internal pass may guarantee trains of at least length $f$, but continue building on each train until memory contains $f$ components that

**Table 5.5**

*Example of doubler merge with serial-access devices*

| Phase | Relevant content | | | | Train length |
|---|---|---|---|---|---|
| | Device 1 | Device 2 | Device 3 | Device 4 | |
| Initially | 5, 0, 3, 8, 6, 7, 9, 1 | | | | |
| Stage 0 | | 5, 3, 6, 9 | | 0,8,7,1 | 1 |
| Stage 1 | [0, 5] [6, 7] | | [3, 8] [1, 9] | | 2 |
| Stage 2 | | [0, 3, 5, 8] | | [1, 6, 7, 9] | 4 |
| Stage 3 | [0, 1, 3, 5, 6, 7, 8, 9] | | | | 8 |

are comparatively lower than the last component written for the train. For randomly ordered data, B. J. Gassner (1967) has shown that this method yields trains of expected length $2f$; for partially ordered data, the increase in train lengths can be much more dramatic.

**Table 5.6**

*Example of two-way oscillating merge*†

| Phase | Relevant content | | | | Length of new trains |
|---|---|---|---|---|---|
| | Device 1 | Device 2 | Device 3 | Device 4 | |
| Initially | 5, 0, 3, 8, 6, 7, 9, 1 | | | | |
| Stage 0.0 | 5, 0, 3, 8, 6, 7, 9, 1 | | (5) | (0) | 1 |
| Stage 1.0 | 5, 0, 3, 8, 6, 7, 9, 1 | (0, 5) | | | 2 |
| Stage 0.1 | 5, 0, 3, 8, 6, 7, 9, 1 | 0, 5 (3) | | (8) | 1 |
| Stage 1.1 | 5, 0, 3, 8, 6, 7, 9, 1 | 0, 5 | (3, 8) | | 2 |
| Stage 2.0 | 5, 0, 3, 8, 6, 7, 9, 1 | | | (0, 3, 5, 8) | 4 |
| Stage 0.2 | 5, 0, 3, 8, 6, 7, 9, 1 | (7) | | 0, 3, 5, 8 (6) | 1 |
| Stage 1.2 | 5, 0, 3, 8, 6, 7, 9, 1 | | (6, 7) | 0, 3, 5, 8 | 2 |
| Stage 0.3 | 5, 0, 3, 8, 6, 7, 9, 1 | (9) | 6, 7 (1) | 0, 3, 5, 8 | 1 |
| Stage 1.3 | 5, 0, 3, 8, 6, 7, 9, 1 | | 6, 7 | 0, 3, 5, 8 (1, 9) | 2 |
| Stage 2.1 | 5, 0, 3, 8, 6, 7, 9, 1 | (1, 6, 7, 9) | | 0, 3, 5, 8 | 4 |
| Stage 3.0 | 5, 0, 3, 8, 6, 7, 9, 1 | | (0, 1, 3, 5, 6, 7, 8, 9) | | 8 |

†The trains formed at each phase are parenthesized.

Another access strategy is employed in the *oscillating merge*. An example of a two-way oscillating merge for eight input items is shown in Table 5.6. As is evident from the example, stage 0 is accomplished in four and stage 1 in two partial passes of the data. (The four phases of stage 0 are named 0.0, 0.1, 0.2, and 0.3; other stages are similarly named.) The final stage, stage 3 in this example, is similar to the last stage of the doubler merge.

The number of components recorded is identical to that required of the doubler, but it is an advantage of the oscillating merge that input data are not obliterated. With devices that can read backward as well as forward, both methods can avoid much of the repositioning implicit in the examples of Tables 5.5 and 5.6. Of the two methods, however, the oscillating merge is the one most critically dependent on the positioning capabilities of the available devices. For example, most magnetic-tape devices are designed to permit one or the other of two classes of operations:

1 Class I: a. Write a block, forward
b. Read a block, forward
c. Rewind the reel

2 Class II: a, b, c, and d. Read a block, backward

The oscillating merge is feasible with class-II but not with class-I devices.

The two-way merge examples are summarized in Table 5.7. In the examples, stage 0 yielded trains of length 1; in general, we may visualize initial

**Table 5.7**

*Two-way balanced and oscillating merges compared*†

| | *Relevant content* | | | |
|---|---|---|---|---|
| *Phase* | *Device 1* | *Device 2* | *Device 3* | *Device 4* |
| | | *Two-way balanced merge* | | |
| Stage 0 | | Four trains‡ | | Four trains‡ |
| Stage 1 | [2] [2] | | [2] [2] | |
| Stage 2 | | [4] | | [4] |
| Stage 3 | [8] | | | |
| | | *Two-way oscillating merge* | | |
| Stage 0.0 | Eight trains‡ | | [1] | [1] |
| Stage 1.0 | Eight trains‡ | [2] | | |
| Stage 0.1 | Eight trains‡ | [2] [1] | | [1] |
| Stage 1.1 | Eight trains‡ | [2] | [2] | |
| Stage 2.0 | Eight trains‡ | | | [4] |
| Stage 0.2 | Eight trains‡ | [1] | | [4] [1] |
| Stage 1.2 | Eight trains‡ | | [2] | [4] |
| Stage 0.3 | Eight trains‡ | [1] | [2] [1] | [4] |
| Stage 1.3 | Eight trains‡ | | [2] | [4] [2] |
| Stage 2.1 | Eight trains‡ | [4] | | [4] |
| Stage 3.0 | Eight trains‡ | | [8] | |

†Brackets designate a train and the number inside the brackets indicates the number of initial trains in the designated train.

‡Each of these initial trains could be represented by [1].

trains of any length, with the two-way balanced and oscillating merges still halving the number of trains at each merge stage.

Table 5.8 illustrates a so-called *polyphase merge* for sorting eight trains by two-way merges with only three serial-access devices. In step 0, the eight given trains are dispersed in a prescribed way. Subsequent steps reduce the number of trains to one; of these, however, only the final step moves all the data. Reading upward from the last step, the maximum number of trains per step on any device is 1, 1, 2, 3, 5, 8. This pattern is from the Fibonacci sequence

$$0, 1, 1, 2, 3, 5, 8, 13, 21, \ldots, \tag{5.1}$$

a sequence in which by definition the leading elements are 0 and 1 and each succeeding element is equal to the sum of its two predecessors. In a polyphase merge, each step liberates one serial-access device. For two-way merging, the number of trains dispersed in step 0 must be a term in the Fibonacci sequence. One of the known ways to disperse the right number of trains is to include, if necessary, *dummy* trains that are suppressed in the last merging step.

Assuming eight initial trains, each of length 1, it can be verified from Tables 5.5 and 5.8 that the two-way balanced and polyphase methods write 32 and 33 components, respectively. Studies indicate that the polyphase merge attains its storage advantage at a relatively small penalty in the required amount of data movement. The increase in data movement is related to the fact that the trains being merged are of varying lengths.

**Table 5.8**

*Two-way polyphase merge example for eight initial trains*†

| | *Relevant Content* | | |
|---|---|---|---|
| *Phase* | *Device 1* | *Device 2* | *Device 3* |
| Initially | [1] [1] [1] [1] [1] [1] [1] [1] | | |
| Step 0 | | [1] [1] [1] | [1] [1] [1] [1] [1] |
| Step 1 | [2] [2] [2] | | [1] [1] |
| Step 2 | [2] | [3] [3] | |
| Step 3 | | [3] | [5] |
| Step 4 | [8] | | |

†Bracketed numbers indicate train length in units of initial trains.

## 5.4 Performance Criteria

In a discussion of sorting fundamentals, the need for clarity justifies the use of simple examples. In practice, the things being sorted are usually table rows, the comparisons involve the matching of character strings, and two or more basic methods may be combined in an attempt to obtain near-optimal performance from available equipment.

One testimonial to the importance of sorting is found in the carefully wrought sorting programs made available by most computer manufacturers. Because these are for general-purpose use, they are designed to yield commendable performance over a wide spectrum of application parameters and equipment configurations. The classical approach has been to form initial trains within the memory of the computer and to disperse these trains to serial-access storage areas (such as magnetic-tape devices). This is done at stage 0 (the *internal sort*) with the aid of insertion or two-way merging algorithms. The remaining stages (the *external sort*) read trains from storage areas, merge the trains, and disperse longer trains to other areas: the applicable reading and writing patterns following from an $r$-way generalization of the two-way balanced, oscillating, or polyphase methods that have been discussed. For the $r$-way merge, an analogy to the numerical comparison in a two-way merge is an operation that selects the minimum of $r$ numbers.

If $2r$ serial-access devices are available, and stage 0 disperses trains to half of them (say to the even-numbered devices), then stage 1 can execute an $r$-way balanced merge, reading from the $r$ even-numbered devices and dispersing longer trains to the $r$ odd-numbered devices. Stage 2 merges from odd-numbered to even-numbered devices, and so on, until one train is obtained. If $d$ trains are dispersed in stage 0, the number of stages subsequently required is given by $\log_r d$ (rounded up).

To perform the $r$-way merge, at least one component from each nonexhausted input train must be available in the main memory of the computer. The *active* component of an input train is the first-read component not yet chosen for the current output train. As long as no input trains have been exhausted, there are $r$ active components. Assuming that the output train is to be in ascending order, it is required to find a minimum, say $x$, among the active components, append $x$ to the output train, and replace $x$ (i.e., obtain another active component) from the input train that provided $x$. The result is an $r$-way merge.

An $r$-way merge is no more efficient, in the sense of comparisons, than a two-way merge. The only advantage in $r > 2$ is that it reduces the number of times that data must be passed to and from auxiliary storage. This can be important in the case of direct-access storage devices, where increasing use is being made of larger values of $r$.

An $r$-way oscillating merge requires $r + 2$ serial-access devices. The reader may determine the merging pattern by generalizing from the example given for $r = 2$.

An $r$-way polyphase merge requires $r + 1$ serial-access devices. To generalize from the two-way polyphase merge, it is customary to introduce the $r$-generalized Fibonacci numbers $f_{j,r}$, which yield a different sequence of integers

**Table 5.9**

*Values of $f_{j,r}$, the r-generalized Fibonacci numbers (from $f_{0,1}$ through $f_{14,5}$)*

| $j$ \ $r$ | 1 | 2 | 3 | 4 | 5 |
|---|---|---|---|---|---|
| 0 | 1 | 0 | 0 | 0 | 0 |
| 1 | 1 | 1 | 0 | 0 | 0 |
| 2 | 1 | 1 | 1 | 0 | 0 |
| 3 | 1 | 2 | 1 | 1 | 0 |
| 4 | 1 | 3 | 2 | 1 | 1 |
| 5 | 1 | 5 | 4 | 2 | 1 |
| 6 | 1 | 8 | 7 | 4 | 2 |
| 7 | 1 | 13 | 13 | 8 | 4 |
| 8 | 1 | 21 | 24 | 15 | 8 |
| 9 | 1 | 34 | 44 | 29 | 16 |
| 10 | 1 | 55 | 81 | 56 | 31 |
| 11 | 1 | 89 | 149 | 108 | 61 |
| 12 | 1 | 144 | 274 | 208 | 120 |
| 13 | 1 | 233 | 504 | 401 | 236 |
| 14 | 1 | 377 | 927 | 773 | 464 |

**Table 5.10**

*Constructive definition of $C_{b,j,r}$ for $r = 4$*

| $j$ \ $b$ | 1 | 2 | 3 | 4 |
|---|---|---|---|---|
| 0 | 0 | 0 | 0 | 0 |
| 1 | 0 | 0 | 0 | $f_{0,4}$ |
| 2 | 0 | 0 | $f_{0,4} + f_{1,4}$ | $f_{1,4}$ |
| 3 | 1 | $f_{0,4} + f_{1,4} + f_{2,4}$ | $f_{1,4} + f_{2,4}$ | $f_{2,4}$ |
| 4 | $f_{0,4} + f_{1,4} + f_{2,4} + f_{3,4}$ | $f_{1,4} + f_{2,4} + f_{3,4}$ | $f_{2,4} + f_{3,4}$ | $f_{3,4}$ |
| 5 | $f_{1,4} + f_{2,4} + f_{3,4} + f_{4,4}$ | $f_{2,4} + f_{3,4} + f_{4,4}$ | $f_{3,4} + f_{4,4}$ | $f_{4,4}$ |
| 6 | $f_{2,4} + f_{3,4} + f_{4,4} + f_{5,4}$ | $f_{3,4} + f_{4,4} + f_{5,4}$ | $f_{4,4} + f_{5,4}$ | $f_{5,4}$ |
| ⋮ | ⋮ | ⋮ | ⋮ | ⋮ |

for each positive value of $r$. The general nature of such a series can be seen from the region covered in Table 5.9. The $r$th series starts with $r - 1$ zeros followed by a 1; each subsequent term is formed by summing the previous $r$ terms.

A merging pattern for an $r$-way polyphase merge can be obtained from a matrix of the form shown in Table 5.10 for $r = 4$. The column index $b$

identifies serial-access devices. Column 1 consists of the Fibonacci series for $r = 4$, and columns 2, 3, and 4 are obtained from $f_{j,4}$ as shown. Each table row is a possible initial-train distribution pattern for an $r$-way polyphase merge. The numerical values for $r = 4$ are shown in Table 5.11, which should be compared with the four-way polyphase merge example of Table 5.12. This example starts with five tape reels containing 15, 14, 12, 8, and 0 trains, respectively, and

**Table 5.11**

*Distribution table for $r = 4$*

| $j$ \ $b$ | 1 | 2 | 3 | 4 |
|---|---|---|---|---|
| 0 | 0 | 0 | 0 | 0 |
| 1 | 0 | 0 | 0 | 0 |
| 2 | 0 | 0 | 0 | 0 |
| 3 | 1 | 0 | 0 | 0 |
| 4 | 1 | 1 | 1 | 1 |
| 5 | 2 | 2 | 2 | 1 |
| 6 | 4 | 4 | 3 | 2 |
| 7 | 8 | 7 | 6 | 4 |
| 8 | 15 | 14 | 12 | 8 |
| 9 | 29 | 27 | 23 | 15 |
| ⋮ | ⋮ | ⋮ | ⋮ | ⋮ |

**Table 5.12**

*Example of four-way polyphase merge of 49 trains with 5 tape units*

| Merge step | Tape unit | | | | | | | | | | Write unit | Units rewound | Number of trains written |
|---|---|---|---|---|---|---|---|---|---|---|---|---|---|
| | $T_1$ | $T_2$ | $T_3$ | $T_4$ | $T_5$ | $T_1$ | $T_2$ | $T_3$ | $T_4$ | $T_5$ | | | |
| | 1 | 0 | 0 | 0 | 0 | | | | | | | *All* | |
| 5 | | | | | | | | | | | $T_1$ | | 1 |
| | | 1 | 1 | 1 | 1 | 0 | | | | | | $T_2$, $T_1$ | |
| 4 | | | | | | | | | | | $T_2$ | | 1 |
| | | | 2 | 2 | 2 | 1 | 0 | | | | | $T_3$, $T_2$ | |
| 3 | | | | | | | | | | | $T_3$ | | 2 |
| | | | | 4 | 4 | 3 | 2 | 0 | | | | $T_4$, $T_3$ | |
| 2 | | | | | | | | | | | $T_4$ | | 4 |
| | | | | | 8 | 7 | 6 | 4 | 0 | | | $T_5$, $T_4$ | |
| 1 | | | | | | | | | | | $T_5$ | | 8 |
| | | | | | | 15 | 14 | 12 | 8 | 0 | | *All* | |

reduces the number of trains to one in five merging steps. The example assumes that the tape devices do not possess read-backward capabilities. If the devices have such capabilities, the number of rewinds can be reduced.

Although the balanced, oscillating, and polyphase merges provide effective ways of applying serial-access devices in sorting, they do not necessarily minimize the amount of data moved in a given sorting task. All are reasonably efficient on this score, and in practice, operational considerations weigh more heavily than theoretical optimums. Nevertheless, circumstances do arise in which $n$ trains of various lengths are held in auxiliary storage, one train per storage area, and the question arises how best to form one long train, given a capability to support $r$-way merges ($r < n$). Under the circumstances, $r$-way merging requires $r + 1$ access devices, $r$ for inputs and one for the output. The movement of data in such a merging sequence can be depicted and analyzed with the aid of an $r$-way tree diagram.

If $w^*$ trains are to be merged with an $r$-way merge capability, the process can be represented by an almost $r$-way tree in which each leaf is specified by the amount (or proportion) of data in a train and parent nodes are specified by family sums. A three-way example for ten trains of lengths 10, 6, 5, 5, 3, 3, 2, 2, 2, 2 is depicted in Fig. 5.1.

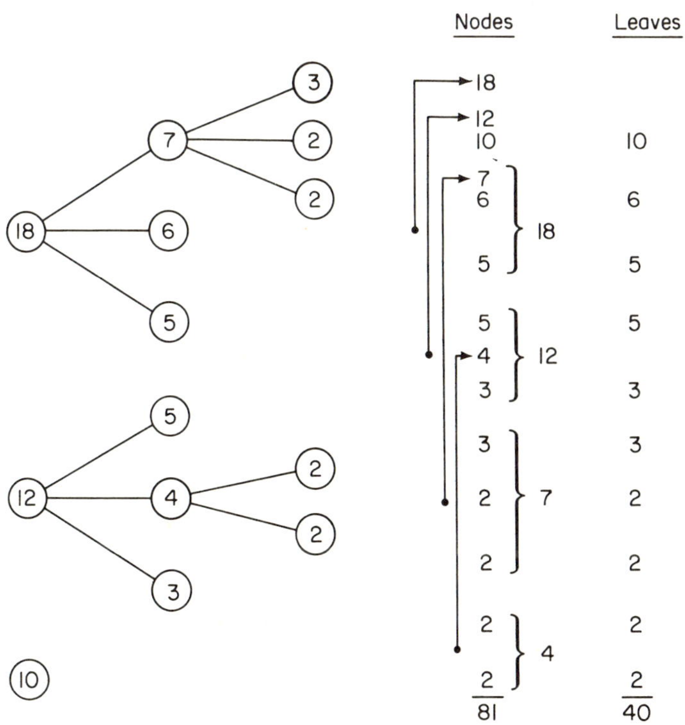


Fig. 5.1 A merge tree of minimum sum.

To find the tree of minimal sum, the leaves are ranked from high to low, as shown. By (1.6), the smallest family must contain two leaves. From the given leaves, the rest of the tree is generated in four steps. At each step, a node is generated and inserted into the provisional vector in a position that preserves numerical order. The right degree vector can be generated at the same time, a simple matter and one not shown in the example of Fig. 5.1. The sum (in this case 81) of a tree formed in this way was shown to be minimal by D. A. Huffman (1952). The minimal property of the tree is intuitive in that the minimum node of level $i$ is never smaller than the maximum node of level $i + 1$, and a family of least dimension is at the top level.

A minimal tree can be useful, for example, in planning a merge operation for a large set of tape reels, assuming one train per reel. More generally, it is a tool for analyzing data-handling operations and has applicability to searching and encoding as well as merging.

## 5.5 Comment

For early treatments of the polyphase sort and oscillating sort, see R. L. Gilstad (1960) and S. Sobel (1962). The column sort and the balanced merge have origins that predate the electronic digital computer. Most discussions of sorting use the terms *string* or *sequence* rather than *train*. Unfortunately, the former terms are finding wide usage in more general contexts.

In *tag sorting*, the tags—accompanied by row numbers—are sorted independently of the nodes. After the tags are ordered, the row numbers form a permutation vector that indicates the desired order of the nodes.

In emphasizing the basic properties of linear sorts and contrasting them with logarithmic merge sorts, we have attempted to provide the reader with useful benchmarks for comparison. However, this is to oversimplify. One possible method of approaching merge performance without the merge penalty in work space is advanced by D. L. Shell (1959) and R. B. Lazarus and R. M. Frank (1960); the basic idea is to improve on exchanging by moving items much farther in the early stages of the sort. Methods of improving insertion performance by generating a chained binary tree are discussed in P. F. Windley (1960) and T. N. Hibbard (1962). H. Nagler (1959) and A. Bayes (1968) treat a generalization of the column sort that employs partial passes over serial-access devices in a manner that is rather suggestive of the oscillating merge. P. Hildebrandt and H. Isbitz (1959) discuss a binary column sort that takes advantage of the binary radix to simplify storage allocation.

The number of comparisons in a balanced merge can be minimized by taking advantage of the trains that exist at the outset. For random data, the number of comparisons expected of such a strategy is discussed by L. J. Woodrum (1969).

# Chapter 6

# STRUCTURE IN PROGRAMS

A data process starts with given tables, performs a sequence of operations—thereby producing additional tables from the given tables—and terminates with one or more result tables. A procedure for carrying out a data process is a *program.* The prerequisites for a program are (1) a set of operations and (2) a set of rules for prescribing a data process as a sequence of operations. A set of operations and a set of rules, taken together, is a *programming language.*

After the notion of an operation has been discussed, illustrative operations and rules are introduced. Program structure is then illustrated using examples of programs. The salient structural characteristics of a few programming languages are related to the illustrative language.

## 6.1 Arguments and Functions

Here are two excerpts from a handbook of mathematical tables.

| $n$ | $1/n$ |
|---|---|
| 1 | 1.00000 |
| 2 | 0.500000 |
| 3 | 0.333333 |
| 4 | 0.250000 |
| 5 | 0.200000 |
| 6 | 0.166667 |
| . | . |
| . | . |
| . | . |

| $d$ | $\pi d^2/4$ |
|---|---|
| 1 | 0.785398 |
| 2 | 3.14159 |
| 3 | 7.06858 |
| 4 | 12.5664 |
| 5 | 19.6350 |
| . | . |
| . | . |
| . | . |

(6.1)

In each table, the first column contains values of an argument and the second column yields values of a function of the argument, in this case, the reciprocal of $n$ or the area of a circle of diameter $d$.

In typical handbook usage, one scans the first column with an argument value, finds the row of that value, and then moves right to read a function value from the second column. This enter-search-read procedure is an example of table look-up by a skip search.

The reciprocals and areas in (6.1) are represented with a precision of six significant decimal digits. Because most fractions lead to an infinite series in decimal notation, most reciprocals cannot be represented exactly. For example, the reciprocal of 3 is the infinite series

$$\frac{1}{3} = \frac{3}{10} + \frac{3}{100} + \frac{3}{1000} + \frac{3}{10{,}000} + \frac{3}{100{,}000} + \frac{3}{1{,}000{,}000} + \cdots,$$

which can also be expressed as

$$\frac{1}{3} = 3 \times 10^{-1} + 3 \times 10^{-2} + 3 \times 10^{-3} + 3 \times 10^{-4} + 3 \times 10^{-5} + 3 \times 10^{-6} + \cdots.$$

In (6.1), this series is terminated at the sixth decimal place. Every fraction, if carried out far enough, leads to a cycle of repeating digits in decimal notation. The reciprocals of 2, 4, and 5 "come out even," i.e., with the very special one-digit cycle of zero. In the case of 7, the reciprocal leads to a six-digit cycle:

$$\frac{1}{7} = 0.142857\ 142857\ 142857 \cdots.$$

In a decimal system, the reciprocal of $n$ always comes out even if $n$ can be factored into powers of 2 and 5.

The user of a handbook can extend the utility of most tables by scaling an argument and appropriately rescaling the corresponding value. For example, to find the square of 0.6, the user scales 0.6 into the form $6 \times 10^{-1}$, enters a table of squares with the argument 6, and multiplies the value 36 by the square of $10^{-1}$ (which equals $10^{-2}$ because exponents add in multiplication). All of this is similar to the task of *pointing off* results obtained with a slide rule or desk calculator.

Now consider the second table in (6.1), which yields the area of a circle. Because $\pi$ cannot be written exactly, even as a fraction, the values in the area table are all rounded values. Inasmuch as engineers seldom measure the radius of a circle with six-digit precision, a table of six digits suffices for most purposes. ($\pi$ has been determined with great precision—to 100,000 decimal places, at latest report.) However, the decimal point and the six digits cannot both be aligned. A neater table ensues with a form of scientific notation that represents all values as fractions and preserves the decimal-point position by an exponent of ten. Hence, 12.5664 can be written as $0.125664 \times 10^2$. Still more conveniently, a *floating-point* notation abbreviates to 0.125664E2, or a similar format, in which case the table becomes

| *Argument* | *Value* | |
|---|---|---|
| 1 | 0.785398E0 | |
| 2 | 0.314159E1 | |
| 3 | 0.706858E1 | (6.2) |
| 4 | 0.125664E2 | |
| . | . | |
| . | . | |
| . | . | |

The zero column and the decimal points in (6.2) can be omitted if the position of the decimal point is elsewhere stated. E is just a delineator.

A handbook table may involve two arguments, in which case each value of the function intersects a row and a column. Let the arguments $m$ and $n$ be octal digits and the function their octal product. Then we have the base-8 multiplication table of (6.3):

| $m$ \ $n$ | 0 | 1 | 2 | 3 | 4 | 5 | 6 | 7 | |
|---|---|---|---|---|---|---|---|---|---|
| 0 | 0 | 0 | 0 | 0 | 0 | 0 | 0 | 0 | |
| 1 | 0 | 1 | 2 | 3 | 4 | 5 | 6 | 7 | |
| 2 | 0 | 2 | 4 | 6 | 10 | 12 | 14 | 16 | |
| 3 | 0 | 3 | 6 | 11 | 14 | 17 | 22 | 25 | (6.3) |
| 4 | 0 | 4 | 10 | 14 | 20 | 24 | 30 | 34 | |
| 5 | 0 | 5 | 12 | 17 | 24 | 31 | 36 | 43 | |
| 6 | 0 | 6 | 14 | 22 | 30 | 36 | 44 | 52 | |
| 7 | 0 | 7 | 16 | 25 | 34 | 43 | 52 | 61 | |

In the language of previous chapters, $(m, n)$ is a zero-origin index tag and the table is a matrix. The decimal equivalent of an octal entry can be obtained by a base value operation. For example, applying the principles of Sec. 3.6 to the largest entry in the table, we see that $(8, 8) \perp (6, 1) = 49$.

Algebra familiarizes us with two ways of defining a function; one way defines by equation, the other by table. Many functions that are awkward to represent by equation can easily be defined by setting forth a table. (Note that in communicating by equation, one normally assumes a knowledge of addition and multiplication, two operations that are defined with the aid of tables.) Functions defined by tables are not unusual in commerce; transportation charges and actuarial tables provide well-known examples. Examples also occur in the substitution process of cryptography. Cryptanalysts sometimes speak of enciphering and deciphering as *encoding* and *decoding*, terms that lend themselves rather well to the substitution processes that occur in everday data processing.

An argument need not be a number; it may be, for example, a letter or a string. A well-known code with some phonetic utility is as follows:

| *Argument* | *Value* |
|---|---|
| *a* | ABLE |
| *b* | BAKER |
| *c* | CHARLEY |
| *d* | DOG |
| ⋮ | ⋮ |
| *z* | ZEBRA |

Here the decoding process is unusually easy: The argument is the first letter of the value. As discussed in Chapter 10, some methods of representing characters involve more than one stage of encoding, in which case the first stage may encode each alphameric character by two decimal digits. The general idea is suggested with a hypothetical collating sequence:

| *Argument* | *Value* |
|---|---|
| blank | 00 |
| A | 01 |
| B | 02 |
| ⋮ | ⋮ |
| Z | 26 |
| ? | 27 |
| & | 28 |
| ⋮ | ⋮ |
| 0 | 50 |
| 1 | 51 |
| ⋮ | ⋮ |
| 9 | 59 |

In mathematics, the term *function of n* is often given a general denotation, say $F(n)$. For a table of squares, one can write $F(n) = n^2$. In defining the mathematical function that underlies a table, an equation leaves unspecified the practical considerations that concern precision, scaling, rounding, and formatting. Also, many defining equations invoke exponential or trigonometric functions; i.e., they do not reduce the definition to $+$, $-$, $\times$, and $\div$. In the case $F(n) = n^2$, the expression $n^2$ is computationally direct; the easiest way to find the square of $p$, ordinarily, is to carry out the multiplication $p \times p$. It is worth noting, however, that addition is the only operation needed in forming a table of squares. The sum of the first $n$ odd integers is equal to $n^2$, that is,

$$1 + 3 + 5 + \cdots + (2n - 1) = n^2, \tag{6.4}$$

and each addition in the sequence of (6.4) leads to a square.

With a handbook of tables for elementary functions, an engineering student may reasonably hope to finish in 1 hour an assignment that could take 10 hours to calculate entirely by hand. Because he understands the nature of the functions, usage of the tables is natural for him. At a later date, let us suppose, the student, now an aircraft designer, is faced with a sequence of computations that involve 10 million times the effort required of a homework exercise. Moreover, quite unrealistically, let us assume that the engineer is assigned 10,000 obedient and willing clerks to help him with the computation. The clerks know how to add, subtract, multiply, and divide, but they do not understand mathematics, and they must be explicitly directed at each step that involves an arithmetic operation or table look-up.

The engineer is at first astonished, and later appalled, at the magnitude of the communication problem that confronts him. The clerks and he share few words and little notation sufficiently unambiguous for the documentation of step-by-step procedures. With the aid of training exercises, he may hope to expand the common vocabulary, but he is far from sure which words or symbols to teach. Even were a vocabulary settled, the engineer intuitively suspects that he cannot prepare dozens or hundreds of interrelated procedures without admitting blunders and glaring inefficiencies. Someone suggests that he teach the clerks engineering mathematics. At first, this strikes him as a perceptive suggestion, even though it does not appear to be feasible. Later, he decides it is off the mark: Much of the work of preparing systematic procedures would persist even if the clerks could become engineers overnight.

By hypothesis, we have confronted a hapless engineer with some of the problems inherent in using a digital system. In terms of today's technology, the 10,000 clerks take the form of an electronic digital computer and the procedures that instruct the computer are called computer programs. Today, moreover, human beings do not have to express the numerical methods required of a design computation in the language of computer programs. (Such programs are tedious to write and awkward to read, largely because they do not subordinate detail.) A design computation can be programmed in a more convenient language, a so-called "high-level" language, and the high-level program can be translated into a computer program by the computer (under the direction of a computer program called a translator).

A high-level language is far more suitable for man-to-man communication than a computer language. An introduction to the structure of programs is therefore well advised to use a subset of a high-level language for illustrative purposes. The subset to be presented in Sec. 6.2 is oriented more toward operations of general interest than toward the operations needed in mathematical computation. It is based on the work of K. E. Iverson (1962) to suggest a common language for hardware, software, and computer applications.

## 6.2 Illustrative Operations

A left-pointing arrow will denote specification. Hence, the statement $z \longleftarrow 1$ specifies the scalar variable $z$ by 1. Similary, the statement $z \longleftarrow x$ specifies $z$ by the value of $x$, and the statement $z \longleftarrow x + y$ specifies $z$ by the sum of $x$ and $y$. Within a statement, the portion to the right of the arrow is an *expression*. An expression may be a constant (sometimes called a *literal*), an argument variable, a function of one or more constants, a function of one or variables, or a function of both constants and variables.

For a statement of the form

$$z \longleftarrow x + y,$$

$x$ and $y$ are often called the *operands* and $z$ the *result*. Because it requires two operands, addition is a *dyadic* operation. An operation that requires only one operand is a *monadic* operation. An example of a monadic operation is absolute value. The absolute value $|x|$ of a number $x$ is the maximum of $x$ and $-x$.

Recall that the set of values that may be assumed by a variable is the *range* of the variable. As explained in Chapter 2, a logical variable can take either 0 or 1 as its value, an integral variable can take any integer as its value, and a numerical variable can take any rational number as its value. In the context of a known character set, an arbitrary variable can consist of any string. Logical variables form a subclass of the integral variables, which in turn form a subclass of the numerical variables, which in their turn are a subclass of the arbitrary variables. Consequently, an operation defined for arbitrary variables holds for all variables, an operation defined for numerical variables holds for integral and logical variables, and an operation defined for integral variables holds also for logical variables.

The four arithmetic operations are of limited utility in explaining or documenting most data processes. A more useful set of operations is listed in Table 6.1. Although chosen with pedagogic needs in mind, and therefore tightly limited in the total number of operations, the set opens the way for concise documentation of a variety of data processes. Most people who work with data have encountered these operations in one context or another, although they may not be accustomed to seeing the operations expressed in a formal notation.

Table 6.1 shows the general form in which each operation is to be symbolized, provides a word or term that can refer to the operation in exposition, indicates the range of the argument or arguments, and indicates the range of the result. Some of the operations in Table 6.1 are self-explanatory and many of the others have been explained in previous chapters. The discussion here can therefore be brief.

The minimum and maximum operations are perhaps more intuitive for positive numbers than for negative. For example,

## Table 6.1

*A set of operations*

| | Operation | Descriptor | Argument Ranges | Result Range |
|---|---|---|---|---|
| 1 | $\bar{u}$ | Complement | Logical | Logical |
| 2 | $x \lfloor y$ | Minimum | Numerical | Numerical |
| 3 | $x \lceil y$ | Maximum | Numerical | Numerical |
| 4 | $-y$ | Negation | Numerical | Numerical |
| 5 | $x + y$ | Addition | Numerical | Numerical |
| 6 | $x - y$ | Subtraction | Numerical | Numerical |
| 7 | $x \times y$ | Multiplication | Numerical | Numerical |
| 8 | $x \div y$ | Division | Numerical | Numerical |
| 9 | $\lvert y \rvert$ | Absolute value | Numerical | Numerical |
| 10 | $\lfloor y \rfloor$ | Floor | Numerical | Integral |
| 11 | $\lceil y \rceil$ | Ceiling | Numerical | Integral |
| 12 | $x^y$ | Exponent | Numerical | Numerical |
| 13 | $\log_x y$ | Logarithm | Numerical | Numerical |
| 14 | $m \mid n$ | Residue of $n$ modulo $m$ | Integral | Integral |
| 15 | $a = b$ | Equal | Arbitrary | Logical |
| 16 | $a \neq b$ | Not equal | Arbitrary | Logical |
| 17 | $x < y$ | Less than | Numerical | Logical |
| 18 | $x \leq y$ | Less than or equal | Numerical | Logical |
| 19 | $x > y$ | Greater than | Numerical | Logical |
| 20 | $x \geq y$ | Greater than or equal | Numerical | Logical |
| 21 | $\mathbf{r} \perp \mathbf{m}$ | Base value | Integral | Integral |
| 22 | $\mathbf{r} \top n$ | Base representation | Integral | Integral |
| 23 | $\mathbf{m} \int \mathbf{b}$ | Mapping | Integral; arbitrary | Arbitrary |
| 24 | $\mathbf{a} \,\iota\, \mathbf{b}$ | Ranking | Arbitrary | Integral |
| 25 | $\boldsymbol{\iota}^k(n)$ | Interval vector | Integral | Integral |
| 26 | $\boldsymbol{\alpha}^k(n)$ | Prefix vector | Integral | Logical |
| 27 | $\boldsymbol{\omega}^k(n)$ | Suffix vector | Integral | Logical |
| 28 | $\mathbf{a}, \mathbf{b}$ | Catenation | Arbitrary | Arbitrary |
| 29 | $\mathbf{u}/\mathbf{b}$ | Compression | Logical; arbitrary | Arbitrary |
| 30 | $k \uparrow \mathbf{b}$ | Rotate left | Integral; arbitrary | Arbitrary |
| 31 | $k \downarrow \mathbf{b}$ | Rotate right | Integral; arbitrary | Arbitrary |
| 32 | $k \overset{\uparrow}{\circ} \mathbf{b}$ | Shift left | Integral; arbitrary | Arbitrary |
| 33 | $k \underset{\downarrow}{\circ} \mathbf{b}$ | Shift right | Integral; arbitrary | Arbitrary |
| 34 | $\rho\mathbf{b}$ | Vector dimension | Arbitrary | Integral |
| 35 | $\mu\mathbf{B}$ | Number of rows | Arbitrary | Integral |
| 36 | $\nu\mathbf{B}$ | Number of columns | Arbitrary | Integral |
| 37 | $a_i$ | Select component $i$ | Arbitrary; integral | Arbitrary |
| 38 | $\mathbf{B}^i$ | Select row $i$ | Arbitrary; integral | Arbitrary |
| 39 | $\mathbf{B}_j$ | Select column $j$ | Arbitrary; integral | Arbitrary |
| 40 | $\mathbf{B}^i_j$ | Select element $i, j$ | Arbitrary; integral | Arbitrary |

$$2\lfloor 4 = 2; \quad -2\lfloor -4 = -4; \quad 2\lfloor -2 = -2; \quad 2\lfloor 2 = 2.$$

$$2\lceil 4 = 4; \quad -2\lceil -4 = -2; \quad 2\lceil -2 = 2; \quad 2\lceil 2 = 2.$$

Negation places a minus sign before a variable and thereby accomplishes a sign reversal. If a number is negative, negation makes it positive, and vice versa. An example of negation occurs in $x\lceil(-x)$, which serves to define the absolute value of $x$. The floor of $x$, designated by $\lfloor x \rfloor$, is the maximum integer not exceeding $x$. The ceiling of $x$, designated by $\lceil x \rceil$, is the minimum integer not exceeded by $x$. If $x$ is an integer, both operations yield $x$ as the result. For example,

$$\lfloor 3.4 \rfloor = 3; \quad \lfloor 2.0 \rfloor = 2; \quad \lfloor -3.4 \rfloor = -4;$$

$$\lceil 3.4 \rceil = 4; \quad \lceil 2.0 \rceil = 2; \quad \lceil -3.4 \rceil = -3.$$

In the course of integer arithmetic, division may lead to a nonintegral quotient. The floor and ceiling operations can be useful in choosing an integer result.

Let $m$ and $n$ be integers, and let $m \geq 1$. The residue of $n$ modulo $m$, written $m \mid n$, is given by

$$n - (m \times \lfloor n \div m \rfloor).$$

This function is most intuitive for nonnegative $n$, in which case the residue is equivalent to the remainder in $n \div m$, e.g.,

$$\begin{array}{ll} 10 \mid 0 \quad = 0 & 3 \mid 3 = 0 \\ 10 \mid 1 \quad = 1 & 3 \mid 4 = 1 \\ 10 \mid 8 \quad = 8 & 3 \mid 5 = 2 \\ 10 \mid 344 = 4 & 3 \mid 6 = 0 \\ 10 \mid 146 = 6 & 3 \mid 7 = 1. \end{array}$$

However, unless a negative $n$ is an exact multiple of $m$, the nonnegative result yielded by $m \mid n$ is not equal to the remainder $r$ (which is negative), but to $m - r$. Thus,

$$\begin{array}{ll} 10 \mid -3 \quad = 7 & 3 \mid 2 = 2 \\ 10 \mid -1 \quad = 9 & 3 \mid 1 = 1 \\ 10 \mid -8 \quad = 2 & 3 \mid 0 = 0 \\ 10 \mid -344 = 6 & 3 \mid -1 = 2 \\ 10 \mid -146 = 4 & 3 \mid -2 = 1. \end{array}$$

Because the residue of $n$ modulo $m$ is not affected by adding multiples of $m$ to $n$, one way to find the residue of a negative $n$ is to treat a positive number obtained by adding a multiple of $m$ to $n$. The residue operation is useful in specifying the positive readings of a counter that returns to zero after $m$ "+1" or "−1" operations. For example, after $n$ miles of travel, the typical automobile logs a reading of $100{,}000 \mid n$ miles.

The complement $\bar{u}$ of a logical variable $u$ is defined as follows:

$$\bar{u} = 1 \quad \text{if } u = 0$$

and

$$\bar{u} = 0 \quad \text{if } u = 1.$$

To obtain the complement of a logical structurand, we simply replace the 0's by 1's and the 1's by 0's.

In the literature on data processing, it should be emphasized, the equal sign is used in at least three ways: (1) in its algebraic sense, (2) as an operator in expressions, and (3) in some programming languages for denoting specification. We avoid the third, and the reader can distinguish between the first and second from the context (as in the next paragraph) of equation versus expression.

The operations involving $=$, $\neq$, $<$, $\leq$, $>$, and $\geq$ are called *relational operations* because they assert a relation between two operands. If the asserted relation is true, the result is 1; if false, the result is 0. Here are some examples:

| *Statement* | *Value of u if x = 3, y = 2, z = 1* |
|---|---|
| $u \longleftarrow x = y$ | 0 |
| $u \longleftarrow y > z$ | 1 |
| $u \longleftarrow x = (y + z)$ | 1 |
| $u \longleftarrow x < (y + z)$ | 0 |
| $u \longleftarrow (x = y) \neq (y > z)$ | 1 |

The relational operations can be useful in expressing the conditions under which a switch is to turn on or off.

The base-value operation was explained in Sec. 3.6, and the base-representation operation $\boldsymbol{r} \top n$ was illustrated but not symbolized. A base-$\boldsymbol{r}$ value operation yields an integer; a base-representation operation takes an integer and expresses it in base $\boldsymbol{r}$. Thus

$$(2, 2, 2) \perp (1, 0, 1) = 5,$$

whereas

$$(2, 2, 2) \top 5 = (1, 0, 1).$$

The mapping and ranking operations were introduced in Sec. 2.3, as was interval vector and compression. The prefix vector operation $\boldsymbol{\alpha}^k(n)$ yields a logical vector of $k$ ones followed by $n - k$ zeros. Hence $\boldsymbol{\alpha}^3(5) = (1, 1, 1, 0, 0)$. The operation $\boldsymbol{\alpha}^0(n)$ produces a *zero vector* of dimension $n$ and the operation $\boldsymbol{\alpha}^n(n)$ a *full vector* of dimension $n$. The suffix vector operation $\boldsymbol{\omega}^k(n)$ yields a logical vector of $n - k$ zeros followed by $k$ ones, Thus $\boldsymbol{\omega}^2(6) = (0, 0, 0, 0, 1, 1)$.

The operation $k \uparrow \boldsymbol{a}$ rotates the vector $\boldsymbol{a}$ to the left (or up) by $k$ positions; the operation $k \downarrow \boldsymbol{a}$ rotates it to the right (or down) by $k$ positions. In rotation, components displaced at one end move to the other end. The shift operations are similar but $k$ zeros enter at one end to replace the components dislodged at the other end, as shown by the following examples:

$$2 \uparrow (4, 5, 6, 7, 8) = (6, 7, 8, 4, 5); \qquad 2 \overset{\uparrow}{\circ} (4, 5, 6, 7, 8) = (6, 7, 8, 0, 0).$$

$$2 \downarrow (4, 5, 6, 7, 8) = (7, 8, 4, 5, 6); \qquad 2 \underset{\downarrow}{\circ} (4, 5, 6, 7, 8) = (0, 0, 4, 5, 6).$$

A convention that assumes $k = 1$ whenever $k$ is omitted is useful in the interval-vector, prefix-vector, suffix-vector, rotation, and shift operations.

The dimension operation $\rho \boldsymbol{a}$ yields the dimension of vector $\boldsymbol{a}$. The catenation operation $\boldsymbol{a}, \boldsymbol{b}$ combines the operand vectors $\boldsymbol{a}$ and $\boldsymbol{b}$ to form a new vector of dimension $(\rho \boldsymbol{a}) + (\rho \boldsymbol{b})$. For example,

$$(2, 5, 4), (8, 3) = (2, 5, 4, 8, 3).$$

The dimension operations $\mu A$ and $\nu A$ for matrices are mnemonic in the sense that the $\mu$ and $\nu$ transliterate into $m$ and $n$.

A set of operations will be called a *vocabulary*. The 40 operations in Table 6.1 constitute a rather useful vocabulary and one that is easily learned, largely because many of the operations are already familiar. By far the most difficult operations of the 40 are addition, subtraction, multiplication, and division—most of us have a tendency to forget how many years we spent learning these four.

Consider the first $n$ positive integers $1, 2, 3, \ldots, n$. A step-by-step procedure for obtaining the product of these integers is documented in program 1 of Fig. 6.1. The program deals with two variables, $i$ and $p$, and an argument $n$ that must be given as an integer before the procedure can be used. The program contains five statements, each of which is identified by a statement number at the left of the program box.

Statements 1, 2, 3, and 5 of program 1 are specification statements. In program 1, the argument $n$ is assumed to be given as an integer; in statements 1 and 2, therefore, the variables $p$ and $i$ are specified by this integer.

In statement 3, the expression prescribes subtraction of a constant from a variable; in statement 5, the expression prescribes multiplication of a variable by another variable. To indicate that statement 4 is a *branch* statement, a colon replaces the arrow. A comparison statement cannot change the value of a variable; its sole function is to admit flexibility in the execution sequence of a program. A comparison statement of the general form $a : b$ is assumed to be able to ascertain the truth or falsity of any of the relations, that is, $=$, $\neq$, $<$, $\leq$, $>$, or $\geq$.

An entry point in a program is represented by an arrow incident to the program box. In program 1, the entry occurs at statement 1, which sets $p$ to the value of $n$. In the absence of other guidance, the execution sequence of a program passes downward, in this example to statement 2, which sets the variable $i$ to $n$. The main section of the program starts with statement 3, which decreases $i$ by 1. This statement highlights a significant difference between

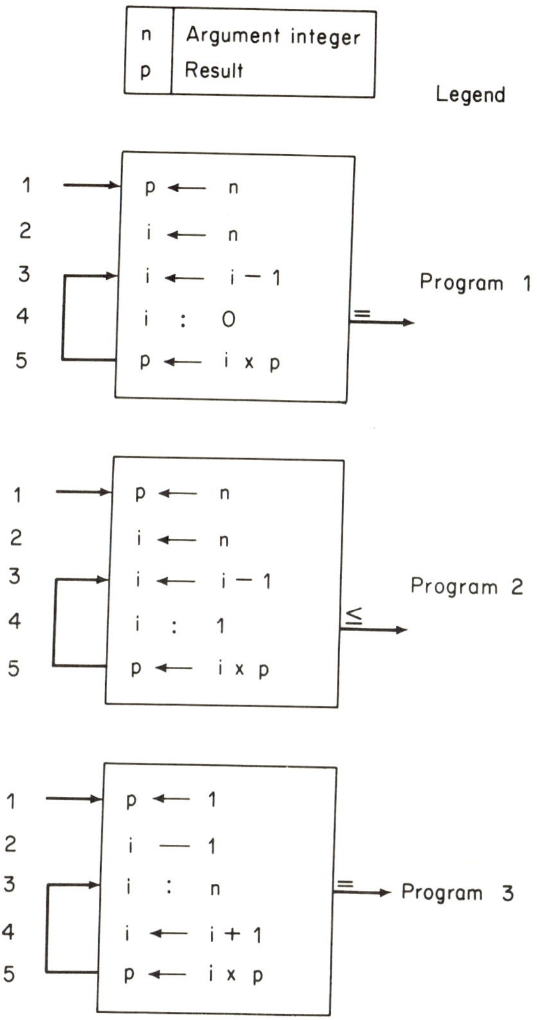


**Fig. 6.1** Three programs for obtaining the product of the first $n$ positive integers.

statements and equations: As an equation, the statement would be inconsistent; as a statement, it merely says to reduce the value of $i$ by 1 and then denote the new value by $i$. For a physical analogy, one may view the variable $i$ as if it were an accumulator in a desk calculator.

Statement 4 compares the value of $i$ to zero. Thereupon, the execution sequence becomes contingent on the result of the comparison. If $i$ is equal to zero, the sequence follows the emergent arrow marked $=$; if not, the sequence passes downward. An emergent arrow may return to another statement, or as in the present example, it may point outward and thereby indicate an end to the execution seqence. In execution, therefore, program 1 terminates when $i$ reaches zero.

If reached, statement 5 multiplies $p$ by $i$ and the result then respecifies $p$. An arrow emerging from a specification statement must be followed unconditionally: Statement 3 always follows statement 5 in an execution of program 1. Statements 3, 4, and 5 form a *loop;* if program 1 is executed, this loop will be traversed again and again until statement 4 finds $i$ equal to zero.

Until one becomes extremely adept at reading programs, the surest way of grasping a program lies in trial executions. For example, choose $n = 4$ and follow the values of $p$ and $i$ in program 1. After execution of statement 1, $p =$ 4 and $i$ is still indeterminate; after statement 2, $i = p = 4$. Here is a complete execution of the program:

| *Statement No.* | $p$ | $i$ |
|---|---|---|
| 1 | 4 | |
| 2 | 4 | 4 |
| 3 | 4 | 3 |
| 4 | 4 | 3 |
| 5 | 12 | 3 |
| 3 | 12 | 2 |
| 4 | 12 | 2 |
| 5 | 24 | 2 |
| 3 | 24 | 1 |
| 4 | 24 | 1 |
| 5 | 24 | 1 |
| 3 | 24 | 0 |
| 4 | 24 | 0 |

(6.5)

At termination, $p = 4 \times 3 \times 2 \times 1 = 24$, as is appropriate to the avowed purpose of the program. As a practical matter, however, the final multiplication by $i = 1$ is superfluous; if the logic of the program can be modified to omit this multiplication and still function properly for the case $n = 1$, fewer statements will be executed.

Program 2 contains a modification that saves one multiplication over program 1. Statement 3 of program 2 terminates execution as soon as the condition $i \leq 1$ is satisfied. Program 2 will surely terminate, therefore, at any time that $i = 0$ or $i = 1$. It is worth noting that the only case in which $i$ can become zero is when $n = 1$. Because of this, were statement 3 written to terminate on $i = 1$, the case $n = 1$ would admit a logical error and the program would loop on the faulty sequence $i = 0, -1, -2, \ldots$. (Logical errors are "bugs" in programmer jargon, and faulty loops a garden variety.) In tests on the validity of a program, correct results from typical and "reasonable" cases may not suffice; atypical extremes, such as 0 and 1, may still give rise to difficulties.

Programs 1 and 2 are designed to yield the product of the first $n$ positive integers. Neither is intended to cope with blunders, such as negative $n$, although, of course, the programs could be amended to provide a separate exit for these cases. As it stands, program 1 responds to $n < 1$ by going into an endless loop, whereas program 2 exits at once, leaving $p = n$ as a possibly misleading result.

Because addition and multiplication are so defined that

$$a + b = b + a \tag{6.6}$$

$$a + (b + c) = (a + b) + c \tag{6.7}$$

$$a(b + c) = ab + ac, \tag{6.8}$$

we know that addition is *commutative* (6.6), addition is *associative* (6.7), and multiplication is *distributive over* addition (6.8). Similarly, multiplication is commutative and associative; subtraction is neither commutative nor associative; addition is not distributive over multiplication, that is

$$a + bc \neq (a + b)(a + c);$$

and so on. We are speaking here in an algebraic context that holds, of course, for integers. In a context of numerical ranges, Eqs. (6.6)–(6.8) may not hold because of rounding. This is conspicuously the case for (6.8).

Because multiplication is an associative and commutative operation, one can form the product $1 \times 2 \times 3 \times \cdots \times n$ in any order desired. Program 3 is similar to program 1 but deals with positive integers in low-to-high rather than high-to-low order. The variables $p$ and $i$ are initially set to 1 (statements 1 and 2), the end-of-program occurs when $i = n$ (statement 3), and $i$ is increased by 1 (statement 4) at each passage of the loop. Only statement 5 is unchanged from program 1.

In algebra, *n factorial* is written ! and defined as follows:

$$\begin{aligned} n! &= 1 \times 2 \times 3 \times \cdots \times n \quad && \text{if } n > 0 \\ n! &= 1 && \text{if } n = 0. \end{aligned} \tag{6.9}$$

The proviso $0! = 1$ in (6.9) helps to simplify and generalize many algebraic definitions. A procedure for obtaining $n!$ is given in program 4 of Fig. 6.2, which contains one comparison (statement 2) that is absent from program 3.

A program is expected to embody a sequential ordering of statements that leads to a correct execution. As to the means or timing of statement execution, it says nothing; in this regard, it is as abstract as a mathematical equation. A program does not claim to provide the only possible sequential ordering of statements; in program 1, for example, statements 1 and 2 can be interchanged without affecting the outcome in any way. Moreover, a program does not con-

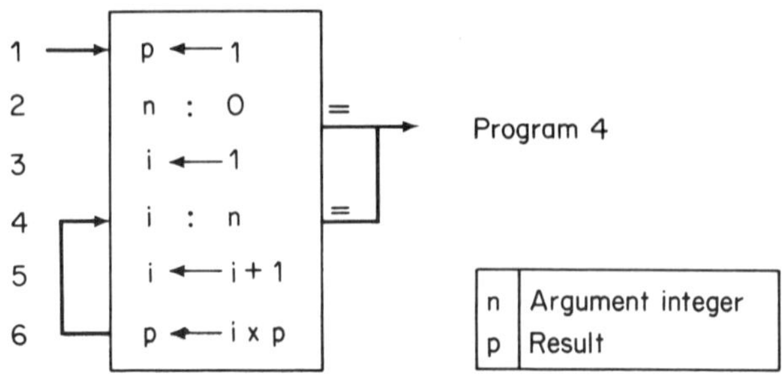


**Fig. 6.2** Program for factorial *n*.

cern itself with the degree to which statements can be executed in parallel: Statements 1 and 2 can obviously be executed in parallel. There are so many ways to write most programs that it is unprofitable to attempt general criteria for a "best" program. A program is a means of communication; a suitable program, like a suitable essay, communicates its intended message to a chosen audience in a language that is appropriate to both message and audience. At this point, we merely assume that neatness, clarity, and simplicity are attributes that enhance the merit of a correct program.

The function of a legend is to heighten the intelligibility of a program. The legend should describe the arguments and the result, at the very least, and it may be helpful to describe temporal operands that appear and disappear within execution. Some methods of programming intersperse the legend declarations within the program proper, it should be added.

In some cases, it is difficult or impossible to write a program without crossing one branch line by another. The need to cross lines can be minimized, to a large extent, by judiciously using both sides of the program box for branch lines. For programs that are sufficiently complex to require crossed lines, it

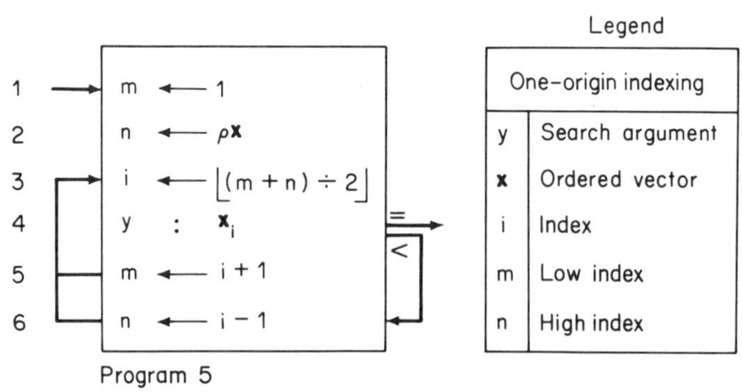


**Fig. 6.3** Program for binary search of numerical vector.

may be preferable to resort to a branching convention that dispenses with lines altogether and indicates the branches by a more formal type of branch statement. This becomes necessary, rather than optional, if the program is intended for man-to-computer communication. For the time being, we are more concerned here with man-to-man communication.

For a more convincing example of a program for man-to-man communication, consider the binary search documented in program 5 (see Fig. 6.3). The search is to be conducted on a numerically ordered vector $\boldsymbol{x}$ for a tag $y$. In statements 1 and 2, two boundary indices $m$ and $n$ are set to the low and high values, respectively, of the index $i$. Statement 3 selects $\boldsymbol{x}_i$ at or near the waist of the vector by obtaining the floor of the average of $m$ and $n$. Statement 4 compares component $\boldsymbol{x}_i$ with the argument tag. If the tag proves to be lower than the selected component, the high boundary index is lowered (statement 6); if the tag proves to be higher, the low boundary index is raised (statement 5); in either case, the search resumes at statement 3. If tag and component are equal, the search ends on statement 4 and $i$ indicates the desired component.

This program can be executed correctly by anybody who knows the meaning of specification and branch statements and the definition of the addition, subtraction, division, floor, vector-dimension, and vector-selection operations. Insofar as execution is concerned, it is unnecessary to know anything about a binary search. Most of the searching and sorting methods of Chapters 4 and 5 can be comparably expressed with programs of a dozen statements or less, although the merge sorts may take more unless the "housekeeping" operations are oversimplified.

The realm of mathematical computation also provides a large number of functions that can be readily expressed. These can arise, for example, in the context of complex-number arithmetic, trigonometric functions, algebra-of-sets operations, algebra-of-matrices operations, and pseudo-random number generation. Most engineering fields have a variety of special functions that can be expressed in short programs. However, as mentioned previously, the operations of Table 6.1 were selected more for general interest than for applicability to mathematical functions.

## 6.3 Compound Expressions

By algebraic convention, the tacit multiplications in the equation

$$z = mx + ny$$

are assumed to be performed before the addition. Parentheses can alter the order and the meaning, as in the equations

$$r = m(x + ny) \qquad \text{and} \qquad s = m(x + n)y.$$

The algebraic rule is that multiplication and division take precedence over addition and subtraction unless another order is indicated by the use of parentheses. Moreover, exponentiation takes precedence over multiplication and division.

In programming, where operators tend to be greater in number and some operators are less familiar as a consequence, the precedence rules of algebra have less to recommend them. In our programs here, expressions will be evaluated with a right-to-left rule that performs operations sequentially from the right unless another order is indicated by parentheses. Hence, the two statements

$$p \longleftarrow m + n \times q$$
$$p \longleftarrow m + (n \times q)$$

are equivalent, as are the two statements

$$p \longleftarrow (m + n) \times q$$
$$p \longleftarrow q \times m + n.$$

We hasten to observe that operands are not commuted by the right-to-left rule. The statement $i \leftarrow i - 1$ means that 1 is to be subtracted from the value of $i$; it does not mean that $i$ is subtracted from 1. Variables retain their given order even though operations are performed from right to left. Consequently, an expression containing noncommutative operations, such as subtraction and division, can be interpreted without ambiguity. The statements

$$k \longleftarrow m - n - p - q$$
$$k \longleftarrow m - (n - (p - q))$$

are equivalent by the rule.

The rule accommodates itself to monadic as well as dyadic operations. In the case of absolute value, floor, ceiling, and complementation, the operators themselves can serve the function of parentheses, as in the expressions

$$|x - y|, \quad \lceil m \div n \rceil, \quad \lfloor q \div 2 \rfloor, \quad \bar{u}, \quad \text{and} \quad \overline{u \lfloor v}.$$

In such cases, the enclosed or barred expression is evaluated and finally subjected to the monadic operation itself. Negation is distinguished from subtraction by the absence of a left-hand operand or by a pair of adjacent operators, as in the following examples:

$$x \longleftarrow y$$
$$k \longleftarrow p \times -q$$
$$m \longleftarrow p + -q$$
$$n \longleftarrow p - -q.$$

An expression that calls for more than one operation is a *compound expression.* An expression of one operation is a *simple expression.* By employing compound expressions, it is usually possible to document a data process with fewer statements than required by simple expressions. Moreover, in some cases a human being can more readily recognize the essential nature of a process from a compound expression than from a series of simple expressions.

The right-to-left rule has some novel properties; we now show one of them. An equation of the familiar form

$$y = c_n x^n + c_{n-1} x^{n-1} + \cdots + c_2 x^2 + c_1 x + c_0 \tag{6.10}$$

is a polynomial in $x$. The $c$'s are termed the coefficients, and if $c_n$ is nonzero, the polynomial is of degree $n$. Note that the decimal number system expresses integers as a polynomial in which $x = 10$. If $y$ is the integer 3465, (6.10) takes the form

$$3465 = 3 \times 10^3 + 4 \times 10^2 + 6 \times 10^1 + 5.$$

Numerical analysts make considerable use of polynomials in calculating functions of one variable. A set of constant coefficients is given, and $y$ is approximated from (6.10) for any value of $x$ within some useful range. In this context, (6.10) is often written in the order

$$y = c_0 + c_1 x + c_2 x^2 + \cdots + c_n x^n. \tag{6.11}$$

To evaluate this equation term by term requires $n$ additions and $2n - 1$ multiplications (of which $n - 1$ are required to form the successive powers of $x$).

The number of multiplications can be nearly halved by Horner's rule for arranging the computation. For example, if $n = 3$, then (6.11) is

$$y = c_0 + c_1 x + c_2 x^2 + c_3 x^3.$$

By factoring out $x$, this can be written in the form

$$y = c_0 + x(c_1 + x(c_2 + x(c_3))), \tag{6.12}$$

which requires three additions and three multiplications. If we express (6.12) by the statement

$$y \longleftarrow c_0 + x \times c_1 + x \times c_2 + x \times c_3, \tag{6.13}$$

the right-to-left rule automatically instructs us to perform all operations in the correct order. The nature of the computation becomes vividly clear. In fact, the contrast between (6.10) and (6.13) highlights the gulf that exists between algebra and data processing. Equation (6.10) is meant to reveal the essential abstract properties of a polynomial ; for a reader familiar with the right-to-left rule, the statement (6.13) can serve to reveal the nature of a polynomial computation.

## 6.4 Vocabulary Expansion

The operations of Table 6.1 are chosen from a larger and more highly generalized set suggested by K. E. Iverson. One way to extend a vocabulary is to enlarge the set of operations; another way is to make each operation more powerful by systematic generalization. Nobody appears to have gone as far as Iverson in suggesting such generalizations. His most effective approach to generalization permits operands to be structured.

Let $\oplus$ denote a dyadic operation. An operation of the form $\oplus/\boldsymbol{x}$ represents a sequence

$$x_1 \oplus x_2 \oplus \cdots \oplus x_{\rho x} \tag{6.14}$$

in which the operations are executed from right to left. The first-executed operation yields an intermediate result that becomes one of the operands in the second execution, etc. For example, $+/\boldsymbol{x}$, $\times/\boldsymbol{x}$, $\lfloor/\boldsymbol{x}$, and $\lceil/\boldsymbol{x}$ yield the sum, product, minimum, and maximum of a numerical vector $\boldsymbol{x}$. Such operations are called *reduction* operations because the operand is a vector and the result a scalar. *Pair* operations of the form $\boldsymbol{x} \oplus \boldsymbol{y}$ are also permitted. This case assumes vector compatibility and $\rho x$ executions of the form

$$\begin{gathered} x_1 \oplus y_1 \\ x_2 \oplus y_2 \\ \vdots \\ x_{\rho x} \oplus y_{\rho x}. \end{gathered} \tag{6.15}$$

The result is a vector compatible with $\boldsymbol{x}$ and $\boldsymbol{y}$. Iverson also generalizes pair operations for any two compatible arrays or trees.

Reduction operations can be further generalized if care is taken to indicate the vector to be reduced. For example, a reduction across the rows of a numerical matrix $X$ yields a result vector of dimension $\mu X$; a reduction down the columns yields a result vector of dimension $\nu X$. As a useful example of reduction, we may note that the *parity* of a logical vector is said to be *even* if the vector contains an even number of 1's and *odd* otherwise. The expression $\neq/\boldsymbol{u}$ equals 1 if $\boldsymbol{u}$ is of odd parity and zero if $\boldsymbol{u}$ is of even parity, as the reader may verify.

Pair operations on vectors can be further generalized for incompatible vectors if the shorter vector is repeatedly catenated to form a vector of sufficient length. If the longer vector is of dimension $n$, a scalar operand is therefore repeated $n$ times to achieve compatibility. If $\boldsymbol{x} = (1, 2, 3, 4, 5)$,

$$6 + \boldsymbol{x} = (6, 6, 6, 6, 6) + \boldsymbol{x} = (7, 8, 9, 10, 11),$$

and, in a more general case,

$$(6, 0) + \boldsymbol{x} = (6, 0, 6, 0, 6) + \boldsymbol{x} = (7, 2, 9, 4, 11).$$

Selection operations can be generalized by permitting indices to be vectors. If $\boldsymbol{a}$ = (A, B, C, D, E) and $\boldsymbol{i}$ = (1, 3, 5), then

$$\boldsymbol{a}_{\boldsymbol{i}} = (\text{A, C, E}).$$

Rotation and shift can be generalized for matrix rows or columns and, if so desired, $k$ could be replaced by a vector whose components pertain individually to corresponding rows or columns.

The purpose of systematic generalization is to greatly enhance the power of a vocabulary at a modest increase in the number of rules to be learned. One of the objectives of generalization is subverted if every user is forced to learn the marginal rules. As long as he is content with a basic set of operations, e.g., the set in Table 6.1, it should not matter to a user that the set generalizes. A basic vocabulary does not lend itself to generalization by chance, of course; a suitable framework for generalization must have guided the designer of the basic vocabulary.

Unfortunately, no matter how well his basic vocabulary generalizes, the person engaged in data processing must expand his vocabulary. The reason, which has probably occurred to the reader by now, is that every program written in a basic vocabulary defines a new operation. In the data-processing sense, program 4 defines a "FACTORIAL $n$" operation and program 5 defines a "$y$ BINARY SEARCH $\boldsymbol{x}$" operation. Before these programs can be used in longer programs, it is necessary to know exactly what functions they embody. To avoid expanding a basic vocabulary is essentially to avoid using programs in more than one context. This will not suffice in practice; analysts and programmers in every specialized discipline want to refer again and again to programs of particular interest to their field. This is to say that they want to expand upon their basic vocabulary, to regard the programs they and their colleagues write as investments that repay over a long period of time, and to bring ever more data-processing potential within their grasp. After it is granted that the programs written in a given vocabulary define a new vocabulary, no practical limit can be placed on the number of useful operations in a vocabulary.

Although matrix multiplication is an important operation in numerical analysis and in many engineering computations, we include it here simply as an example of a fairly complicated operation that applies in many computations and is therefore an operation in the vocabulary of many people. If $X$ and $Y$ are numerical matrices and $\nu X = \mu Y$, their matrix product is a new matrix, say $\boldsymbol{Z}$, such that $\mu \boldsymbol{Z} = \mu X$, $\nu \boldsymbol{Z} = \nu Y$, and

$$Z^i_j \longleftarrow +/(X^i \times Y_j) \tag{6.16}$$

for each $i$, $j$ pair. Note that (6.16) contains two vector operations: a pair multiplication [see Eq. (6.15)] followed by a reduction addition [see Eq. (6.14)]. In other words, row $X^i$ is multiplied by column $Y_j$, component by component, and the products are summed. For example, if

$$X = \begin{bmatrix} 2 & 2 & 0 & 1 \\ 2 & 1 & 1 & 3 \end{bmatrix} \quad \text{and} \quad Y = \begin{bmatrix} 2 & 0 & 1 \\ 1 & 2 & 3 \\ 3 & 1 & 2 \\ 2 & 3 & 4 \end{bmatrix},$$

then

$$Z = \begin{bmatrix} 8 & 7 & 12 \\ 14 & 12 & 19 \end{bmatrix},$$

as is easily verified by carrying out the vector multiplications and reductions. To verify that $Z^1_1 = 8$, take the first row of $X$ and the first column of $Y$ and write out all implied operations:

$$(2 \times 2) + (2 \times 1) + (0 \times 3) + (1 \times 2) = 8.$$

One method for evaluating the product of two matrices $X$ and $Y$, as expressed with the aid of vector operations, is shown in program 6 (see Fig. 6.4).

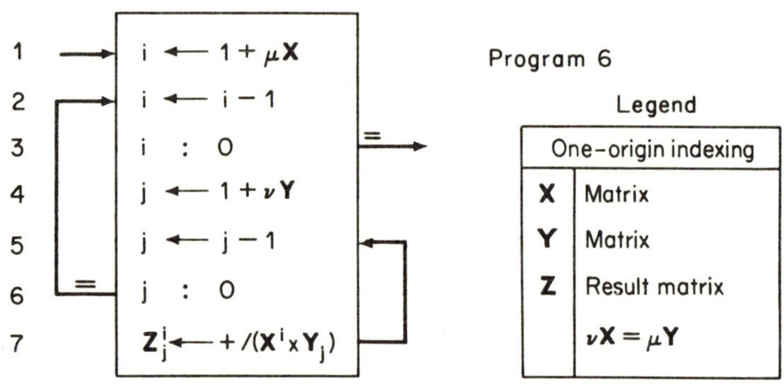


**Fig. 6.4** Matrix multiplication (vector operations permitted).

The reader of this program need know nothing of the mathematical properties of matrix multiplication; the program simply tells *how* to process the matrices. Statements 1 and 4 initialize, statements 2 and 5 decrease, and statements 3 and 6 test index variables. Statement 7 calls for a pair operation (multiply two vectors) followed by a reduction operation (vector summation). Clearly, program execution calls for $\mu X \times \nu Y$ executions of statement 7.

Program 7 of Fig. 6.5 goes into Table 6.1 detail by expressing the matrix multiplication entirely in operations on scalars. An additional indexing variable in needed. Inspection of index ranges will quickly reveal that statement 11 is executed $\mu X \times \nu Y \times \nu X$ times. (In light of this, the reader who elects to manually check the program should choose small dimensions for the test

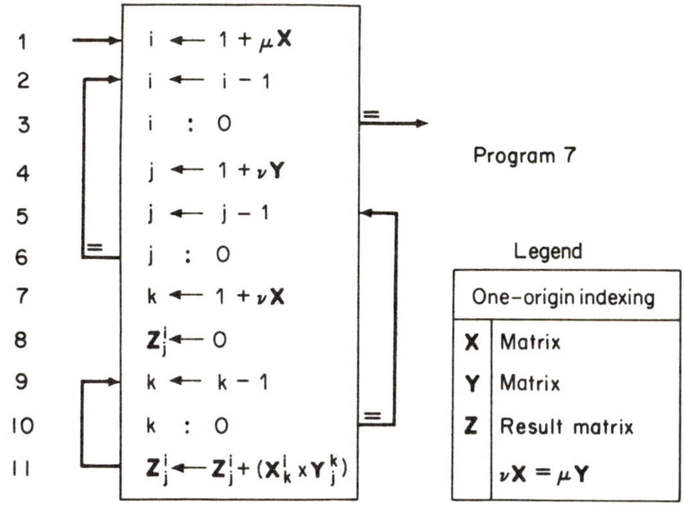


**Fig. 6.5** Matrix multiplication with scalar operations.

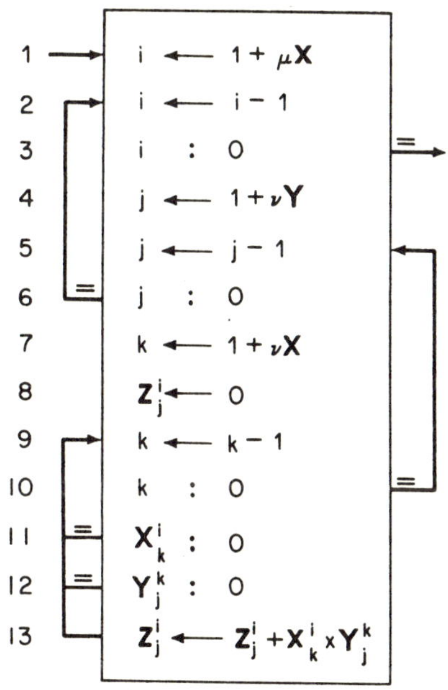


Program 8

**Fig. 6.6** Matrix multiplication with tests for zero operands (same legend as Program 7).

matrices!) In a program written at a suitable level of detail, special requirements can be documented without difficulty. For example, program 8 (see Fig. 6.6) is identical in result to program 7, but it omits a multiplication if either the multiplier or multiplicand is equal to zero.

## 6.5 Primitive Vocabularies

Since new operations can be defined ad infinitum by writing programs, we cannot go far in discussing large vocabularies. It is more instructive to turn to primitive vocabularies where operations are few in number and extraordinary in their simplicity. For discussion purposes, let us examine some of the principles of Boolean algebra.

Let $u$, $v$, and $w$ denote logical variables and consider an algebra of three operations. In terms of the complement, minimum, and maximum operations from Table 6.1, the postulates of Boolean algebra can take the following form.

I. Two complementations leave a variable unchanged:

$$\overline{(\bar{u})} = u. \tag{6.17}$$

II. Minimum (maximum) is commutative.

$$u \lfloor v = v \lfloor u; \qquad u \lceil v = v \lceil u. \tag{6.18}$$

III. Minimum (maximum) is associative:

$$u \lfloor (v \lfloor w) = (u \lfloor v) \lfloor w; \qquad u \lceil (v \lceil w) = (u \lceil v) \lceil w. \tag{6.19}$$

IV. Minimum is distributive over maximum, and vice versa:

$$\begin{aligned} u \lfloor (v \lceil w) &= (u \lfloor v) \lceil (u \lfloor w); \\ u \lceil (v \lfloor w) &= (u \lceil v) \lfloor (u \lceil w). \end{aligned} \tag{6.20}$$

V. Self-minimization (maximization) leaves a variable unchanged:

$$u \lfloor u = u; \qquad u \lceil u = u. \tag{6.21}$$

VI. One and 0 are identity elements for $\lfloor$ and $\lceil$:

$$u \lfloor 1 = u; \qquad u \lceil 0 = u. \tag{6.22}$$

VII. Zero and 1 are dominant elements for $\lfloor$ and $\lceil$:

$$u \lfloor 0 = 0; \qquad u \lceil 1 = 1. \tag{6.23}$$

VIII. A complement simulates a dominant element:

$$u \lfloor \bar{u} = 0; \qquad u \lceil \bar{u} = 1. \tag{6.24}$$

IX. De Morgan's laws:

$$\overline{u \lfloor v} = \bar{u} \lceil \bar{v}; \qquad \overline{u \lceil v} = \bar{u} \lfloor \bar{v}. \tag{6.25}$$

Where variables have logical ranges, minimum and maximum are sometimes likened to multiplication and addition. This is misleading because Boolean algebra exhibits a consistent duality that fails when ordinary algebra is applied to 0's and 1's (the likeness breaks down in the right-hand equations of IV, V, VII, and IX). However, the imperfect analogy is motivated by a certain amount of utility. If + denotes maximum, if the minimum symbol is elided (as the multiplication symbol often is), and if minimum is given precedence over maximum, equations can be written more compactly. For example, (6.20) becomes

$$u(v + w) = (u + v)(u + w); \qquad u + vw = uv + uw.$$

In Boolean algebra, an asserted equivalence between two expressions in the same variables can be checked by comparing columns of a *truth table*. The truth table is constructed to yield the 0 and 1 outcomes of both expressions under all possible value combinations for the variables. (This method of proof is seldom feasible in ordinary algebra.) As an example of a truth table, we show that the two expressions $(u \lceil v) \lfloor (\bar{u} \lceil \bar{v})$ and $(u \lfloor \bar{v}) \lceil (\bar{u} \lfloor v)$ are equivalent:

| 1 | 2 | 3 | 4 | 5 | 6 | 7 | 8 | 9 | 10 |
|---|---|---|---|---|---|---|---|---|---|
| $u$ | $v$ | $\bar{u}$ | $\bar{v}$ | $u \lceil v$ | $\bar{u} \lceil \bar{v}$ | $u \lfloor \bar{v}$ | $\bar{u} \lfloor v$ | $(u \lceil v) \lfloor (\bar{u} \lceil \bar{v})$ | $(u \lfloor \bar{v}) \lceil (\bar{u} \lfloor v)$ |
| 0 | 0 | 1 | 1 | 0 | 1 | 0 | 0 | 0 | 0 |
| 0 | 1 | 1 | 0 | 1 | 1 | 0 | 1 | 1 | 1 |
| 1 | 0 | 0 | 1 | 1 | 1 | 1 | 0 | 1 | 1 |
| 1 | 1 | 0 | 0 | 1 | 0 | 0 | 0 | 0 | 0 |

(6.26)

At the start, only the two leftmost columns contain 0's and 1's. Note that these columns manage to exhaust all possible $u$, $v$ values. Remaining columns are filled in as exercises in complement, minimum, and maximum operations. Because columns 9 and 10 are identical, the two expressions in question have been proved equivalent. Incidentally, using relational operations, this *exclusive or* function of columns 9 and 10 can be written $u \neq v$.

There are 4 functions of one logical variable, 16 functions of two logical variables, and $2^{(2^n)}$ functions of $n$ logical variables. Any logical function can be expressed in the operations complement, minimum, and maximum. Many different but logically equivalent expressions can be written for a typical function. As a result, equation simplification is an important topic in Boolean algebra. Moreover, if a function is defined by a truth table, methods are known for writing an equation from the truth table.

In Boolean algebra, which deals only with logical operands, minimum is customarily known as *and* and maximum as *or*. Since minimum, maximum, and complement are functions that can be reliably realized in electronic circuits, many digital computers have been designed with AND, OR, and NOT circuits. From the designer's standpoint, rotation and shift operations, residue operations (obtained by binary counters), and encoding operations are the first level of vocabulary expansion. If timing questions are subordinated, the behavior of a computer can be documented as a program written in these operations. Brevity will be served, however, by employing the vector generalizations of (6.14) and (6.15) and various other operations in Table 6.1, for example, the relational operations $=$ and $\neq$.

To specify $w$ for any of the four basic functions of one logical variable $u$, the statements $w \leftarrow 0$, $w \leftarrow u$, $w \leftarrow \bar{u}$, and $w \leftarrow 1$ suffice. The first of these may be called the *zero function*, the second the *identity function*, and the fourth the *full function*. To define these functions we need a matrix of 2 rows and 4 columns:

| $u$ | 0 | 1 | 2 | 3 |
|---|---|---|---|---|
| 0 | 0 | 0 | 1 | 1 |
| 1 | 0 | 1 | 0 | 1 |

To define all 16 basic functions of two logical variables (say $u$ and $v$), we need a matrix of 4 rows and 16 columns. The 4 rows exhaust all possible values of $u$, $v$ and the 16 columns give the desired results in each case:

| $u$ | $v$ | 0 | 1 | 2 | 3 | 4 | 5 | 6 | 7 | 8 | 9 | 10 | 11 | 12 | 13 | 14 | 15 |
|---|---|---|---|---|---|---|---|---|---|---|---|---|---|---|---|---|---|
| 0 | 0 | 0 | 0 | 0 | 0 | 0 | 0 | 0 | 0 | 1 | 1 | 1 | 1 | 1 | 1 | 1 | 1 |
| 0 | 1 | 0 | 0 | 0 | 0 | 1 | 1 | 1 | 1 | 0 | 0 | 0 | 0 | 1 | 1 | 1 | 1 |
| 1 | 0 | 0 | 0 | 1 | 1 | 0 | 0 | 1 | 1 | 0 | 0 | 1 | 1 | 0 | 0 | 1 | 1 |
| 1 | 1 | 0 | 1 | 0 | 1 | 0 | 1 | 0 | 1 | 0 | 1 | 0 | 1 | 0 | 1 | 0 | 1 |

(6.27)

The functions defined by these 16 columns are represented in the following statements:

| *Column* | *Statement* | *Column* | *Statement* |
|---|---|---|---|
| 0 | $w \leftarrow 0$ | 15 | $w \leftarrow 1$ |
| 1 | $w \leftarrow u \lfloor v$ | 14 | $w \leftarrow \overline{u \lfloor v}$ |
| 2 | $w \leftarrow u \lfloor \bar{v}$ | 13 | $w \leftarrow \bar{u} \lceil v$ |
| 3 | $w \leftarrow u$ | 12 | $w \leftarrow \bar{u}$ |
| 4 | $w \leftarrow \bar{u} \lfloor v$ | 11 | $w \leftarrow u \lceil \bar{v}$ |
| 5 | $w \leftarrow v$ | 10 | $w \leftarrow \bar{v}$ |
| 6 | $w \leftarrow (u \neq v)$ | 9 | $w \leftarrow (u = v)$ |
| 7 | $w \leftarrow u \lceil v$ | 8 | $w \leftarrow \overline{u \lceil v}$ |

The functions defined by columns 1 and 7 are *and* and *or*; the functions defined by columns 14 and 8 are known as *nand* (not and) and *nor* (not or). As is well known, all 16 functions can also be generated by expressions in nand operations (the same can be said for nor operations). Practically speaking, this means that a computer can be designed from either NAND or NOR circuits (that is, the designer need not use *and*, *or*, and *complement*). Having reached down to two very primitive vocabularies, each consisting of one operation, it is interesting to note that both are unintelligible to all but a very practiced eye. *And*, *or*, and *complement* carry over far more intuitive meaning from linguistic contexts than do *nand* and *nor*.

Program 9 is meant to show how switching circuits can be used to add two unsigned binary numbers. In a binary number, the only digits are 0 and 1 (*bi*nary digi*ts* are called *bits*). The basic addition table states that

$$0 + 0 = 0$$

$$0 + 1 = 1$$

$$1 + 0 = 1$$

$$1 + 1 = 0 \quad \text{with a carry of 1.}$$

In this binary representation, an integer can be treated as a logical vector. Let $\boldsymbol{u}$ and $\boldsymbol{v}$ be two such logical vectors, and let them be compatible. A right-to-left serial addition process may involve carries, and the truth table that applies in the $i$th position to yield a sum digit $s_i$ is shown in Table 6.2.

**Table 6.2**

*Truth table for binary addition*

| *Carry in to position i* | $u_i$ | $v_i$ | $s_i$ | *Carry out from position i* |
|---|---|---|---|---|
| 0 | 0 | 0 | 0 | 0 |
| 0 | 0 | 1 | 1 | 0 |
| 0 | 1 | 0 | 1 | 0 |
| 0 | 1 | 1 | 0 | 1 |
| 1 | 0 | 0 | 1 | 0 |
| 1 | 0 | 1 | 0 | 1 |
| 1 | 1 | 0 | 0 | 1 |
| 1 | 1 | 1 | 1 | 1 |

Program 9 of Fig. 6.7 shows a method for carrying out the addition bit by bit. Statement 1 clears a carry bit $c$ to zero. Statements 2–4 count backward through the vector components and terminate the addition process. Statement 5 forms a sum bit using two exclusive-or operations. Statement 6 forms a carry bit using maximum and minimum operations. The reader can easily check the validity of statements 5 and 6 with Table 6.2. If so desired, the exclusive-or operations in statement 5 can be written in maximum, minimum, and complementation operations by (6.26).

It may be suggested that the addition in statement 2 and the subtraction

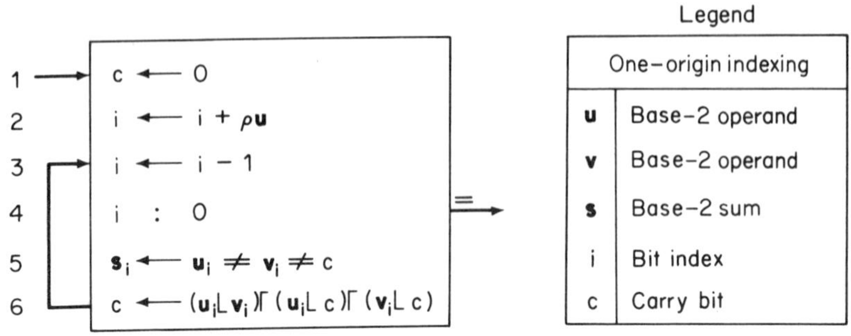


Program 9

**Fig. 6.7** Binary bit-by-bit addition of nonnegative numbers.

in statement 3 are operations of equal complexity to binary addition itself; hence, the program assumes operations similar to the one it purports to describe. In describing processes, however, it is often good tutorial license to describe or illustrate a point with the least distracting means at hand. The easiest way to define a short word may be to choose a few longer words. Statements 2, 3, and 4 simply provide one way of representing a binary counter. The program can be made more realistic by rotating the vector one place at each iteration, in which event statements 5 and 6 can always refer to the first component of each vector.

## 6.6 Programming Languages

Let $S$ denote the set of all possible programs that could be written in vocabulary $V$, and consider the problem of expressing members of $S$ with a character set $C$. We have deliberately avoided this problem by introducing the notion of a program in the context of man-to-man communication. More often than not, however, programs are intended for man-to-computer communication, and the problem is entirely a practical one.

If the programs of $S$ are to be systematized for a typical character set $C$, the use of conventional mathematical notion will be severely limited, special type faces will be precluded, and keybord/printer characteristics may be expected to rule out the use of subscripts and superscripts. As a consequence, all of the structural elements of a program have to be represented by strings. In fact, the program will take the form of one long character string, and elements within this long string must be delineated by convention. Conventions are also needed for representing names, legend declarations, structure in compound expressions, branches, and vocabulary extensions. These conventions, in conjuction with the vocabulary $V$, are what is usually meant by a programming language.

The names are needed to denote or identify argument variables, result variables, operations, programs, and statements referred to in other statements (the name of a statement is usually known as a *label*). It must be possible to distinguish between argument variables and argument literals. To provide a conveniently large set of possible names, most programming languages permit a name to be a string of several characters or more. Such a string is sometimes termed a *symbol*. Name ranges may be variously limited as one means of distinguishing among object classes.

The class of recognizable structurands, the manner in which structure is to be represented, and tagging disciplines (e.g., the indexing origin) may be fixed for the language. If there are options, the user must be given a way of expressing his choice. In any case, the language must systematize the legend so that dimensions and ranges can be "declared" for each argument structurand.

The rules for forming compound expressions must be made explicit, as must conventions for expressing branches. One way of expressing branches is in a statement that yields the number of the next statement to be executed. For example, let $\rightarrow k$ denote an unconditional branch to the statement of label $k$. A conditional branch can be represented by generalizing $k$ as a relational statement. Using program 5 as an example, statement 4 might take the form

$$\rightarrow (7 \times y = \boldsymbol{x}_i) + 6 \times y < \boldsymbol{x}_i, \tag{6.28}$$

assuming right-to-left evaluation. If $y$ is smaller than $\boldsymbol{x}_i$, then (6.28) yields 6 and a branch is taken to statement 6; if $y$ is equal to $\boldsymbol{x}_i$, then (6.28) branches to "statement 7," which is outside the program and can therefore represent program termination (the 7 could be any integer above 6). If $y$ is greater than $\boldsymbol{x}_i$, then (6.28) yields a zero and this can denote continuation at the next statement (statement 5 in the example given).

A basic vocabulary can be extended by defining new operations as supplementary programs and then *calling* these programs as needed. Calling is a generalization of branching that involves two branches, one to the called program and another that brings control back to the calling program.

After a programming language has been systematized, *source* programs in the language can be translated into *target* or *object* programs in a simpler language. The target language will usually be a language based on the instruction set of a digital computer. The nature of a computer language will become more evident in Chapter 7. Here we merely remark that a computer language is limited to simple expressions and to a vocabulary consisting primarily of scalar addition, subtraction, multiplication, and division operations. Usually, the arithmetic operations are represented by a variety of instructions that permit a number of different number formats.

Various practical considerations have to be given due consideration in the design and use of a language. These involve the collating sequence, which if not defined in the source language will be determined by the target language; the control of input and output devices; the conveniences provided in debugging and modifying a source program; the messages used to inform of rule violations in the source language; etc. The importance of such considerations will become clearer in subsequent chapters.

## 6.7 Language Contrasts

FORTRAN (FORmula TRANslator) and COBOL (COmmon Business Oriented Language) are two programming languages widely used for man-to-computer communication. The details of a high-level programming language may vary somewhat with the year of design and the target computer system. Here we merely remark upon structural characteristics of the languages, highlight the differences, and mention a few other languages that depart from FORTRAN and COBOL in interesting ways.

FORTRAN, which is oriented toward the computational needs of science and engineering, was designed primarily for operations on numerical arrays. The symbols +, −, *, /, and ** denote scalar addition, subtraction, multiplication, division, and exponentiation, respectively. Numbers are represented either as fixed-format integers or fixed-format floating-point fractions, and the language requires the programmer to distinguish between integer and floating-point variables. Constants with a decimal point are assumed to be numerical; constants without a decimal point are assumed to be integral. Each variable is named by a character string consisting of one letter followed by as many as five other letters or digits (if the first letter is I, J, K, L, M, or N, the variable is assumed to be integral).

As in algebra, parentheses combine with operation precedences to indicate the order in which an expression is evaluated. Where parentheses are lacking, multiplication and division take precedence over addition and subtraction, and exponentiation takes precedence over multiplication and division. An element in an array of height $h$ is denoted by the name of the array followed by parentheses that enclose $h$ integral indices separated by commas. An index can be a constant, a variable, a variable plus or minus a constant, a constant times a variable, or a constant times a variable plus or minus another constant. Hence,

BSIX (2, J, K*L − 3)

is a legitimate way of referring to an element in a numerical array BSIX of height 3.

Specification is denoted by the equal sign. A branch to statement $n$ is symbolized by GO TO $n$. (Lowercase letters are ours; FORTRAN uses only uppercase.) In an unconditional branch, $n$ is a given label (labels are integral). An ASSIGN statement, executed prior to the GO TO statement, can alter the value of $n$, thereby permitting one kind of conditional branching. Another kind is of the form

$$\text{GO TO } (\boldsymbol{n}_1, \boldsymbol{n}_2, \ldots, \boldsymbol{n}_m), i \tag{6.29}$$

where $i$ is an integral variable of range $1, 2 \ldots, m$ and $\boldsymbol{n}$ is a vector of statement labels. If executed, the statement of (6.29) branches to the statement with label $\boldsymbol{n}_i$. Still another kind of conditional branching employs a statement of the form

$$\text{IF } (x)\ \boldsymbol{n}_1, \boldsymbol{n}_2, \boldsymbol{n}_3$$

where $x$ denotes an expression that yields an integer and $\boldsymbol{n}_1$, $\boldsymbol{n}_2$, and $\boldsymbol{n}_3$ denote statement labels. The branch taken is to $\boldsymbol{n}_1$ if $x < 0$, to $\boldsymbol{n}_2$ if $x = 0$, and to $\boldsymbol{n}_3$ if $x > 0$.

A DO statement assists in component-by-component operations on arrays. In the statement

$$\text{DO } n\, i = \boldsymbol{m}_1, \boldsymbol{m}_2, \boldsymbol{m}_3$$

$n$ is a label, $i$ is an indexing variable, and $\boldsymbol{m}_1$, $\boldsymbol{m}_2$, and $\boldsymbol{m}_3$ are integer constants or variables. DO $n$ requests execution of all statements down to and including a statement of label $n$. The request is honored repeatedly, the first time with $i = \boldsymbol{m}_1$, the second time with $i = \boldsymbol{m}_1 + \boldsymbol{m}_3$, the third time with $i = \boldsymbol{m}_1 + 2\boldsymbol{m}_3$, and so on as long as $i \leq \boldsymbol{m}_2$. After $i$ exceeds $\boldsymbol{m}_2$, control passes to the first statement following the DO loop. If $\boldsymbol{m}_3$ is omitted, $\boldsymbol{m}_3 = 1$ is assumed. Although GO TO, IF, and DO statements are "executed" in the sense that they provide for branching during execution, they do not affect the values of variables.

In FORTRAN, a *function* is a subprogram that yields a scalar and a *subroutine* a subprogram that yields more than one value. The FORTRAN vocabulary can be expanded by named functions or subroutines. A function name can be used in expressions much as though it were an arithmetic operator. On the other hand, a subroutine must be invoked by a CALL statement that names the subroutine and tenders a vector of arguments. After the subroutine is executed, control returns to the statement following the invoking statement.

The DIMENSION, EQUIVALENCE, and COMMON statements are not executable statements, but rather a means of declaring information. Via a DIMENSION statement, the dimensions of one or more arrays can be listed. As a result of the statement, storage is allocated for each of the listed arrays. An EQUIVALENCE statement is a means of requesting that two or more variables in a main program be allocated the same space; a person who understands the flow of the program can thereby conserve on storage requirements. The COMMON statement is analogous but applies to subroutines as well as to the main program.

FORTRAN has grown; its four principal "dialects" are known as FORTRAN I, II, III, and IV; in general, each new dialect has brought additional capabilities to the language. For example, FORTRAN I did not have the EQUIVALENCE and COMMON statements or subroutine-calling capabilities. FORTRAN IV introduced logical relations comparable to operations 15 through 20 in Table 6.1; also, it permits logical variables to be named, stored, and treated as operands for *and* and *or* operations.

The standard FORTRAN vocabulary includes sine, cosine, arctangent, square root, exponentiation to the natural base, natural logarithm, and common logarithm. It also includes absolute value, maximum, minimum, ceiling, residue, transfer of the sign of one argument to the absolute value of another, and an operation that subtracts the minimum of two arguments from the first-mentioned argument. Such operations are denoted by mnemonic character strings. Some operations take different names for the integral and numerical modes; moreover, a FLOAT operation is defined to convert from integral to numerical and an IFIX operation from numerical to integral.

As the acronym implies, COBOL is primarily a language for file-maintenance, voucher-preparation, and summary-tabulation applications. The assumed structurands are dubbed files and indexed arrays; files and arrays may be of arbitrary or integral range. In the case of an indexed array, all elements must be declared of identical range; in the case of a file matrix, the ranges of columns may be declared individually. In any case, a declared range consists of the number of alphameric characters or decimal digits needed (with an upper limit of 18 characters). All arithmetic is integer arithmetic with an option for rounding, and decimal points may be edited into results before printing.

Compound expressions follow the same general rules as in the case of FORTRAN. The FORTRAN notation for arithmetic operations can be used, as can the equal sign for specification. Array elements are referred to much as in FORTRAN. Whereas the design of FORTRAN shows a keen concern for efficient floating-point computations, the design of COBOL reflects a comparable concern for efficient use of storage areas and input/output devices.

The COBOL *word*—which contains from 1 to 30 letters, digits, or hyphens—is used for several naming purposes. Variables are denoted by COBOL words. For example, SPECIAL-OVERTIME-PAY-ADJUSTED can denote a field in a record. This can be useful, and those who want a shorter name can have it. English equivalents for the symbols +, −, *, /, ** are also provided, permitting statements that can be read as English (although the writing process itself is rather tightly constrained). This serves to enhance the readability, if not the intelligibility, of many statements. Somewhat less convincingly, the designers classify names and literals as *nouns*, operations as *verbs*, expression groupings as *sentences*, and sentence groupings as *paragraphs*. A degree of redundancy can thereby creep into COBOL manuals: The writers speak of operations as well as verbs, of operands and results as well as nouns, and of expressions as well as sentences and compound sentences. The fact that COBOL has a good deal of structural kinship with FORTRAN (and many other languages) tends to be obscured.

In FORTRAN and COBOL, subscripts cannot be subscripted and subroutines cannot call on themselves. In these languages, moreover, storage areas are allocated to a program at translation time, which precedes execution time. In ALGOL, a more general and elegant array-processing language than FORTRAN, subscripts can be subscripted, subroutines can call on themselves, and storage can be allocated "dynamically" at execution time. ALGOL assumes lowercase as well as uppercase letters and, as in the case of COBOL, the designers gave some thought to the needs of man-to-man communication. For several years, ALGOL has been an accepted language for algorithms in the *Communications of the Association for Computing Machinery*.

The literature in the computing field has given a good deal of attention to *list-processing* languages that emphasize trees and trims, pointer matrices, and dynamic storage allocation. In PL/I, a newcomer on the language scene, one can perceive heritages from FORTRAN, COBOL, ALGOL, and the list-processing languages. Provision is made for arrays, for files, and to some extent for trees and trims. Dynamic storage allocation is provided. Pair-by-pair operations [Eq. (6.15)] are provided for compatible structurands. In view of its many capabilities, PL/I poses something of a tutorial problem; different classes of potential users may be concerned with different capabilities of the language. This is being met by emphasizing different features of the language for FORTRAN users and COBOL users. The designers also contemplated the need for subsets of the language, thereby permitting new users to gain experience with a nucleus of the language before attempting to absorb the entire language.

In the case of FORTRAN, COBOL, ALGOL, and PL/I, the designers anticipated that source programs would be translated into a target language prior to execution on a computer. The designers were less concerned with the length of a source program than with the storage requirements and running times of the target program. In some system environments, particularly those in which a computer user communicates directly with the computer from a keyboard and his statements are translated into the target language and executed immediately, optimal efficiency is a function of source-program brevity as well as of target-program efficiency. K. E. Iverson and his colleagues have modified his original language (which we sampled in Table 6.1) to produce a very succinct man-to-computer language called APL. The basic structurand is the array, which can be of arbitrary, numerical, or logical range. The user is not required to distinguish between the integral and numerical range. Wherever possible, operators are given both a monadic and a dyadic meaning. Expressions are evaluated from right to left except where otherwise indicated by parentheses. New operations can be named and defined, whereupon they can be used in the same way as existing operations. Branch statements are similar to the form shown shown in (6.28), the difference being that null denotes "continuation" and zero denotes "exit." Operations are generalized along the lines indicated by (6.14) and (6.15). The user is not concerned with the details of storage allocation. For debugging purposes, the user may obtain execution traces of the form shown in (6.5). Most of the operations of Table 6.1, together with others not shown therein, constitute a basic vocabulary. The character set includes a modest set of special symbols and Greek letters to permit some continuity with the usages shown in Table 6.1. The language is easy to learn because it avoids ad hoc rules. Careful thought has been given to the special cases—such as zero dimensions—that inevitably arise in generalized usages for operations. (A scalar is "dimensionless" in APL, a technical classification that we did not attempt to explore in Chapter 2.)

## 6.8 Comment

Much has been written about FORTRAN, COBOL, and ALGOL; basic reports are J. W. Backus et al. (1957), J. E. Sammet (1962), and P. Naur (1960). For a description of the goals and design directions in PL/I, see G. Radin and H. P. Rogoway (1965). List processing from the PL/I viewpoint is discussed by H. W. Lawson (1967). Much of APL is introduced in Iverson (1966).

Instructional books, manuals, and primers on the above-mentioned languages abound. For example, manuals on FORTRAN, COBOL, PL/I, and APL are available through branch offices of the IBM Corporation. Herein, we have introduced program structure at a very elementary level. For an introduction to many of the formal constructs of programming languages, the reader may consult P. Wegner (1968). A thorough introduction to Boolean operations is provided, among others, by F. E. Hohn (1966).

For illustrative material we have returned to Iverson's work of the early 1960's, essentially as reported to the Fall Joint Computer Conference of 1962 in a paper entitled "A common language for hardware, software, and applications." In this choice, we are guided by four motives: (i) the idea of a common language for the whole data system is congenial to the purposes of this book; (ii) the right-to-left evaluation rule and the special character font bring out stimulating contrasts that would otherwise be missed; (iii) the operations can be presented without amplifying on the discussion of structurands in Chapter 2; and (iv) a graphic portrayal of programs complements the graphic approach to structure in Chapter 1. We hope to have captured the spirit of the approach, which we believe has unrealized potentialities for man-to-man communication. A full adherence to detail seems unnecessary here because Iverson has subsequently made changes and gone on to design APL, a language for man-computer communication that also has merit for man-to-man communication.

A tree diagram is a special case of a construct known as a "directed graph." In a directed graph, more than one arc may lead into a given vertex—a circumstance that is not permitted in a tree diagram. Since the flow of execution in a branching program is an example of a directed graph, it deserves emphasis that the static program, considered as a structurand, is a tree. The salient property of the tree in question is, of course, that subtrees correspond to statements and the leaves in branch statements are merely pointers to other statements. Many other examples of directed graphs can be handled as trees by analogous means.

For practice with the operations of Sec. 6.2, we suggest the following. Let $A$ be an arbitrary matrix, $X$ a numerical matrix, and $b$ an arbitrary vector. Write programs that will (1) yield the transpose of $A$; (2) fill $A$, row by row and element by element, with component $b_1$, rotating $b$ to the left after each copy operation; (3) obtain the maximum of the row minima in $X$; (4) obtain a vector of the indices of the distinct elements in $b$; (5) obtain a $u$ such that $u/b$ yields an alphabet of maximum dimension.

*Chapter 7*

# TASK MECHANIZATION

To write a program is to define an operation; to execute a program is to accomplish a task. A complicated operation can be documented by a program in less complicated operations; analogously, a complicated task can be synthesized out of less complicated tasks.

In any given technology, some primitively simple tasks can be performed more rapidly, reliably, and inexpensively than others. The purpose of this chapter is threefold: first, to introduce primitive tasks that lend themselves well to known technologies; second, to discuss ways in which primitive tasks can be coordinated to perform complicated special-purpose tasks; and third, to identify the properties of the general-purpose digital computer that justify the adjective *general purpose*.

## 7.1 Storage and Decision Elements

**Storage element.** Any two-state device that can be held to a given or specified state and interrogated regarding its status is a *storage element*. Since one state can represent 0 and the other state 1, a storage element is said to have the capacity for one bit (binary digit) of information. Let the state of a storage element be denoted by a logical variable, say $q$. Assuming that $q$ is defined at the periodic points in time $\ldots, t-1, t, t+1, \ldots$, the successive states may be denoted by $\ldots, q(t-1), q(t), q(t+1), \ldots$. Storage elements may be classified by the number of inputs provided: A representative element may have 0, 1, or 2 inputs.

A storage element with no input is best known as a *read-only element*. This element will be symbolized by $N$ to suggest its no-input nature.

A one-input storage element has its place as a *delay element* that holds each incoming bit for one time period. Let $D$ symbolize such an element, and let $d$ denote its single input. The functional behavior of a $D$ element can be summarized in a table that shows state $q$ at time $t + 1$ as a function of input $d$ at time $t$:

| $d(t)$ | $q(t + 1)$ |
|---|---|
| 0 | 0 |
| 1 | 1 |

The state of a delay element is solely dependent on the input at the preceding time period. We take the convention that if the input were "up," the element stores a 1, and if "down," the element stores a 0.

The roster of storage elements can be completed by an *RS element* with two inputs, an $R$ input that *resets* the element to its 0 state and an $S$ input that *sets* the element to its 1 state. The $RS$ element is defined in the following table, wherein $r$ denotes a logical signal at the $R$ input and $s$ a logical signal at the $S$ input:

| $r(t)$ | $s(t)$ | $q(t + 1)$ |
|---|---|---|
| 0 | 0 | $q(t)$ |
| 0 | 1 | 1 |
| 1 | 0 | 0 |
| 1 | 1 | Undefined |

If the reset and set signals are both down at time $t$, the state of the $RS$ element holds unchanged at time $t + 1$. For the two cases in which one input is up at time $t$ (the second and third rows of the table), the outcomes are clear from the table. An "undefined" state at time $t + 1$ ensues if both inputs are up at time $t$. In practice, engineers may find it advantageous to define this state, for example, by specifying it as $\overline{q(t)}$, the complement of $q(t)$. We are assuming, of course, that any storage element is designed to permit an informative output.

**Decision element.** A device with one binary-valued output and one or more binary-valued inputs is a *decision element* if the output is a known function of the inputs. In the ideal sense, a decision element takes no time to make a decision and therefore provides no storage. The sole purpose of a decision element is to receive one or more input bits and to yield one output bit.

One possible decision element is a NOT element that has one input and complements this input in the output. To express additional elements, we employ the reduction convention of Eq. (6.14) in conjunction with the symbols $\wedge$ and $\vee$ for the Boolean functions *and* and *or* (which for logical variables are identical to the minimum and maximum of Chapter 6). Let the logical vector $\boldsymbol{u}$ denote the inputs to, and the logical scalar $w$ denote the output from, a decision element. Four important decision elements are as follows:

| | *Decision Statement* | *Element Name* | *Result* |
|---|---|---|---|
| 1. | $w \leftarrow \wedge/\boldsymbol{u}$ | AND | *w is* 0 *unless* ***u*** *is* a full vector |
| 2. | $w \leftarrow \vee/\boldsymbol{u}$ | OR | *w* is 1 unless ***u*** is a zero vector |
| 3. | $w \leftarrow \overline{\wedge/\boldsymbol{u}}$ | NAND | Complement *w* in 1 |
| 4. | $w \leftarrow \overline{\vee/\boldsymbol{u}}$ | NOR | Complement *w* in 2 |

Logicians have shown that all functions of logical variables can be expressed with AND, OR, and NOT elements. Logical designers and circuit designers also make use of the fact that any logical function can be realized by NAND (or NOR) elements. We confine ourselves to AND, OR, and NOT elements here because they are more intuitive than NAND and NOR elements.

In practice, a parameter of interest is the allowable number of inputs, that is, the maximum dimension of ***u***. Engineers refer to this as element *fan in*. Since the output of a decision element serves as an input to other decision elements, another consideration of interest is *fan out*, the number of inputs that can be fed by the output of a given element.

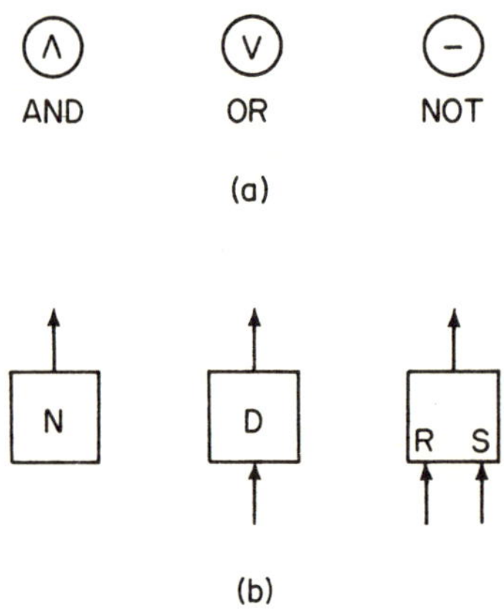


**Fig. 7.1** Conventions for depicting decision elements and storage elements: (a) decision elements; (b) storage elements.

Later, we resort to elementary schematic diagrams to suggest ways in which primitive storage elements and decision elements can be organized to perform larger tasks. In these diagrams, a decision element will be depicted by a circle, inputs by incident arrows, and the output by an emergent arrow. The element class will be designated by the symbols $\wedge$ for AND, $\vee$ for OR, and $-$ for NOT, as shown in Fig. 7.1(a). Storage elements will be depicted by squares, as shown in Fig. 7.1(b). The letter or letters in a square designate the element class and, in the case of an *RS* element, distinguish between the two inputs as well.

## 7.2 Remarks on Element Devices

Devices that implement storage and decision elements are typically designed to exploit nonlinear phenomena. To illustrate principles, we review a few phenomena and devices.

In the electrical circuit of Fig. 7.2(a), the electromotive force of a battery provides a voltage rise of $E$ volts. In series with the battery is a resistor of $R$ ohms. By convention the flow of current in the circuit is from the higher battery voltage around to the lower battery voltage, and by Ohm's law the amperes through the circuit are given by $E/R$. When $I$ amperes flow through a resistance of $R$ ohms, the voltage drop across the resistance is $IR$ volts. In the example, $IR$ is identical with $E$ because there is only one resistance.

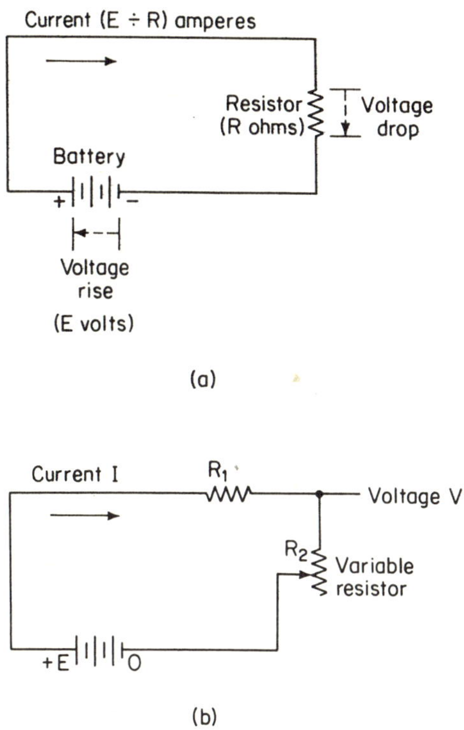


Fig. 7.2 Electrical circuits: (a) battery and resistor; (b) battery, resistor, and variable resistor in series.

In the circuit of Fig. 7.2(b), two resistors are connected in series. The first has a fixed resistance of $R_1$ ohms. The resistance $R_2$ of the second can be varied by an external agency. For a given setting of $R_2$, a current $I$ equal to $E/(R_1 + R_2)$ amperes will flow in the circuit. The voltage drop, say $V_2$, across the second resistance is given by

$$V_2 = IR_2 = \frac{E}{R_1 + R_2}(R_2) = \left(\frac{R_2}{R_1 + R_2}\right)E = rE.$$

When $R_2$ approaches zero, $r$ and $V_2$ approach zero; when $R_2$ approaches infinity, $r$ approaches unity and $V_2$ approaches $E$. Moreover, the current $I$ approaches zero as $R_2$ approaches infinity and reaches its maximum when $R_2$ drops to zero.

In a suitable mode of operation, the variable resistance can constitute a two-position switch; the switch is *open* when $R_2$ is very high and *closed* when $R_2$ is very low with respect to $R_1$. By a simple convention, say that a maximum represents 1 and a minimum represents 0, either the voltage drop $V_2$ or the current $I$ can be employed as a binary-valued signal. To achieve a high switching rate, obviously $R_2$ must be amenable to rapid change.

**Mechanical switches.** The essential features of a single-pole switch are shown in Fig. 7.3(a). In the double-throw context, a conductive pole with an insulated handle throws to either of two conductive contacts, completing an upper circuit in the up position and a lower circuit in the down position. In the exhibit, a lamp provides a visible indication whenever the pole is down. In

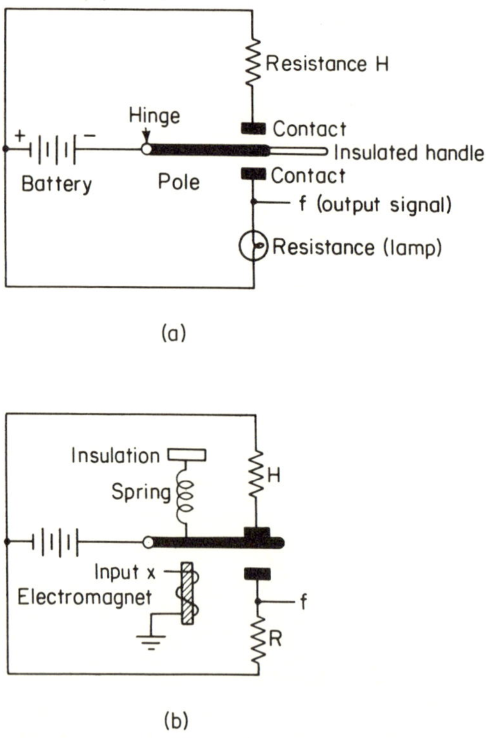


**Fig. 7.3** Schematic switch and relay: (a) manual switch; (b) relay.

single-throw usage, up is associated with OFF and down with ON. This requires resistance $H$ to be very high, a condition easily satisfied in practice by an air gap between the pole and the lower contact. When the switch is OFF, no current flows through the lamp and the voltage $f$ is at maximum battery potential. When the switch is ON, the voltage $f$ is at minimum battery potential, there is a voltage drop across the lamp, and current flows through the lamp.

Manually operated switches are useful in computing systems, as elsewhere, to turn on power. They may also be employed in incidental ways for communication of digital information, as when an operator at a central panel represents 0 or 1 by moving a switch to the up or down position.

**Relays.** The pole of a relay is held at one throw until pulled to the opposite throw by a flow of current in an electromagnet. In Fig. 7.3(b), the holding force is spring tension; when the voltage at $x$ is high, current flowing in the electromagnet pulls the pole down and the voltage at $f$ falls to its minimum. The circuit in the figure is an *inverter*; if voltages $x$ and $f$ are considered logical variables, their logical relation is summarized in the statement $f \leftarrow \bar{x}$.

The *nor* function can be obtained from a relay by providing the electromagnet with independent windings for the inputs $x_1, x_2, \ldots, x_n$. Because $f$ is down if any input is up, the relevant statement is $f \leftarrow \overline{\vee/\mathbf{x}}$.

Where engineering tolerances permit, a *nand* function can be obtained with similar windings. In this case the spring must provide just enough tension to resist $n - 1$ positive inputs but not to resist $n$ positive inputs. The appropriate statement is

$$f \leftarrow \overline{\wedge/\mathbf{x}}.$$

As the tension of a spring is affected by age, usage, temperature, gravitational pull, and other factors, such a circuit actually has little to recommend it.

Using well-known methods, the *and* and the *or* functions can be obtained with one relay per input variable. Two or more relays in series constitute an *and* circuit; to complete the circuit, all relays must be energized. If the relays are connected in parallel, the circuit can be completed by energizing any one or more of the relays, and an *or* function is obtained.

Although relays have found wide application in telephony and in electrical accounting machines, they are relatively slow and large in size. The switching time of a fast relay is in the neighborhood of a millisecond (one-thousandth of a second). In modern computers, the use of relays is narrowly confined to units with very modest requirements for speed, as is the case in some input/output devices.

**Diodes.** Any two-terminal device with high forward conductivity and low reverse conductivity can be classed as a *diode*. The most useful diodes for switching purposes are produced from semiconductor materials. Where diodes are symbolized, as in Fig. 7.4, the arrow points in the direction of high con-

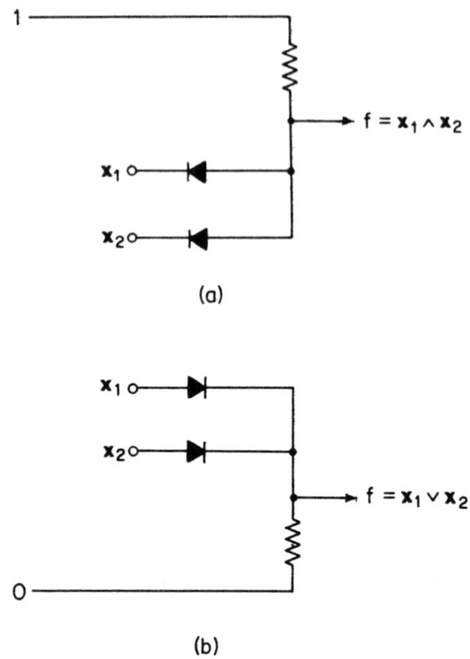


**Fig. 7.4** Ideal diode circuits: (a) diode AND; (b) diode OR.

ductivity. An ideal diode is assumed to have zero forward resistance and infinite backward resistance. Although actual diodes can only approximate ideal diodes, the ideal is useful for expository and analytical purposes.

Assume a system with two voltage levels, denoted by 1 and 0, for signal potentials. In the circuit of Fig. 7.4(a), $f$ is at potential 0 unless both inputs are at potential 1, in which case no current flows and $f$ is at potential 1. The circuit therefore yields the *and* function. In the circuit of Fig. 7.4(b), $f$ is at potential 0 only if both inputs are at potential 1; this circuit yields the *or* function. Although the number of inputs normally exceeds two, in practice the number is limited by the nonideal characteristics of available diodes.

**Vacuum tubes and transistors.** A two-terminal vacuum tube is a diode; it conducts when the cathode is negative with respect to the plate and it does not conduct when the applied voltages are reversed. The operating behavior of the tube can be greatly modified by placing additional terminals called *grids* between the cathode and the plate. In a *triode*, tube conductivity is influenced in a nonlinear way and over a useful operating range by changes in the voltage applied to a single grid. A small rise (drop) in grid voltage can effect a large rise (drop) in tube conduction. As a result, the tube acts as a variable resistance that is governed by a voltage signal applied to the grid. If the plate is connected through a resistor to a fixed potential, the plate voltage will drop (rise) as conduction rises (falls). The plate voltage amplifies and complements the signal applied to the grid. To obtain other logical functions, it is necessary to employ either more grids or more triodes.

Although the transistor offers more circuit flexibility than the vacuum tube, the logical capabilities of the two are closely analogous. Also, both are useful for signal amplification. Nonetheless, the transistor has several compelling advantages over the vacuum tube. The semiconductor transistor is smaller, dissipates far less power, is less fragile, and has a longer life than the vacuum tube. Its smaller size permits shorter leads and contributes to faster switching rates. Moreover, semiconductors lend themselves to batch-fabrication manufacturing and packaging processes, a property extremely significant to economy of production. The switching times of diodes and transistors are measured in nanoseconds (a nanosecond is $10^{-9}$ second).

**Magnetic devices.** A flow of current in a conductor creates a magnetic field whose polarity depends on the direction of current flow. If a field of sufficient intensity is brought to bear on unmagnetized ferromagnetic material of suitable thickness and composition, the material takes on the character of a magnet. If the field is brought to bear on a magnet of coinciding polarity, little happens; but should the applied field oppose the magnet, two outcomes are possible. If the field is sufficiently strong, the magnet will undergo a complete reversal in polarity. If the current is insufficient, the disturbed magnet will fall back to its initial state as the current subsides. This nonlinear behavior is useful for *RS* storage elements.

When a conductor cuts through the field of a magnet, as by physical motion of the conductor relative to the magnet, a transient current is induced in the conductor. The direction of the current is determined jointly by the field and the direction of relative motion. A related effect is observed when the conductor is stationary with respect to the magnet but the state of the magnet is changing, for example, when the magnet is reversing its polarity or, to a lesser degree, when its state is disturbed but not reversed.

The typical *magnetic core* consists of a ferrite substance in the shape of a toroid with an outside dimension of a fraction of an inch. In the cores depicted in Fig. 7.5, a clockwise magnetization is assumed to represent 1 and the opposite magnetization a 0. The core is set to state 1 by a directional current and reset to state 0 by a current of opposite direction. As shown, the windings employ a full turn, although a similar effect may be achieved by a half-turn, i.e., by merely passing the winding through the core.

One magnetic-core configuration, not exhibited, employs three windings: one to carry the current needed to set the core, another to carry the current needed to reset the core, and one to sense a change of state from 1 to 0. The core is first set or reset, as desired. Then, to interrogate the core, a reset pulse

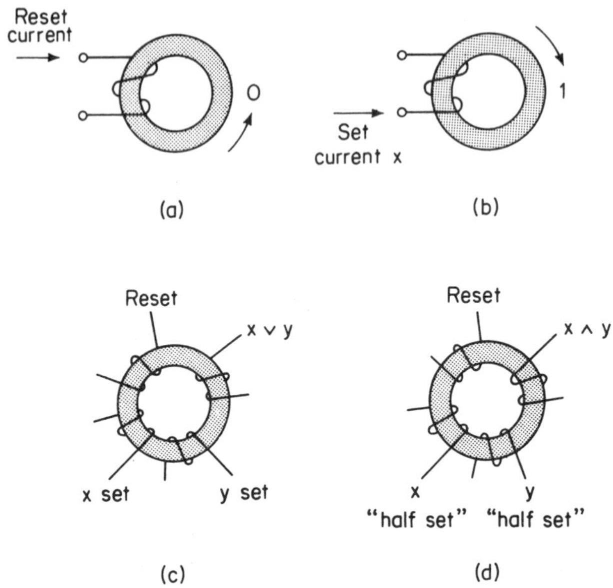


**Fig. 7.5** Magnetic core principles: (a) reset current produces counterclockwise magnetization; (b) set current produces clockwise magnetization; (c) set/reset cycle yields output pulse if core is set by $x$ or $y$ in set portion of cycle; (d) set/reset cycle yields output pulse if $x$ and $y$ are jointly pulsed in set portion of cycle.

is applied. If the core is in state 0, the sense line is quiescent; on the other hand, if the core is in state 1, the resultant change of state induces an informative pulse on the sense line. Because the interrogation is destructive for a set core, a 1 output must be followed by a set pulse to restore the core. The configuration can be simplified by using a common winding for reset and set functions, in which case the functions are distinguished by the two possible directions for current flow.

The core can be adapted to switching purposes by using a two-phase set and reset cycle in conjunction with multiple set windings: Fig. 7.5(c) provides an example of an *or* circuit. In the set phase, either the $x$ set winding, the $y$ set winding, or both are energized to set the core. In the reset phase, the core is reset and the winding labeled $x \vee y$ is sensed. Various other functions can be generated by altering the windings.

A more important application of cores is illustrated by the *and* circuit of Fig. 7.5(d). Again a set/reset cycle is employed, but in this case each of the two set windings carries half the current needed to set the core. Thus two *half-set* pulses must coincide to set the core. Reset provides an informative output pulse, as before. Again the reset winding can be eliminated if *half-reset* pulses are created by reversing the direction of current in the $x$ and $y$ windings. Relative to transistors and diodes, cores switch slowly and are difficult to cascade into complex circuits. These limitations have restricted their use to special-purpose contexts. However, since roughly 1954, the magnetic core has reigned as an economical and reliable means of implementing large arrays of storage elements. The time required to load or interrogate a storage element in the array context is in the neighborhood of a microsecond (one-millionth of a second).

To magnetize a small region on the surface of a suitable ferromagnetic substance is essentially to record a miniature bar magnet. Denoting polarities by 0 and 1, each bar serves to store one bit of information. In writing the bars, the surface and the electromagnetic write head must undergo motion relative to each other. In reading, i.e., in sensing the bars, motion is again provided and informative currents are induced in an electromagnetic read head. In practice, one device often serves jointly as a read/write head. Surfaces for ferromagnetic material may be provided by reels of plastic tape, by cylinders (drums), by disks, by cards, etc. In normal usage, drums and disks are rotated continuously, whereas motion is imparted to magnetic tapes and cards whenever necessary for the execution of read or write operations.

Magnetic surfaces serve as a relatively inexpensive means of storing large volumes of information. Along the line or "track" that passes under a read/write head, densities in the neighborhood of $10^3$ to $10^4$ bits per inch are typical. Given a track versus head motion of $10^2$ inches per second, a fairly representative speed, the data rate per head is $10^5$ to $10^6$ bits per second. An $n$-fold increase in the data rate can be obtained by sweeping $n$ tracks in parallel, but cost-performance considerations have usually limited $n$ to about ten.

A magnetic core is a circuit component with permanent windings; it can be set and reset whenever necessary. Because a magnetic bar is generated by a write head and subsequently never changed, it cannot perform switching functions. The bar can be read as many times as necessary and finally, at the end of its useful life, erased along with all other bars in some defined region of a magnetic surface. Erasure or obliteration, usually accomplished jointly with a writing process, frees the surface for the recording of new information.

**Electronic time scales.** In discussing elemental devices, we deal with an unfamiliar time scale. Useful units of time and their definitions are summarized below:

| *Unit* | *Definition* |
|---|---|
| Millisecond | $10^{-3}$ second |
| Microsecond | $10^{-6}$ second |
| Nanosecond | $10^{-9}$ second |

The nanosecond and the microsecond are much too brief to have intuitive meanings. It lends them a measure of operational significance to invoke the speed of light (186,000 miles per second). Roughly speaking, a nanosecond is the time required for light to travel 1 foot. The speed of electrical signals in an isolated copper wire is of the same order of magnitude as the speed of light (rules of thumb put signal propagation at about two thirds the speed of light). In a circuit where near-nanosecond switching is sought, therefore, short connectors are essential. Hence, as switching devices become faster, natural laws demand that they become smaller as well.

The fastest semiconductor devices now used in digital computers switch in the near-nanosecond range. This is impressive when compared with the near-millisecond switching times of the relay calculators of the 1940's. Technology offers few parallels to this millionfold increase in speed.

## 7.3 Registers, Decoders, and Counters

**Registers.** Whereas a storage element holds one bit, a register of $n$ elements provides storage capacity for a logical vector of dimension $n$. The capabilities of a register depend on the constituent elements and the way in which they are connected together. For example, a serial register may provide for an input at one point, an output from one point, and internal connections from element to element. The most representative case, the circulating register, is suggested by the four delay elements of Fig. 7.6(a). The control signal is assumed to be normally up, in which case the stored vector circulates. The register can be cleared to zeros by holding the control signal down for a period of four or more bit times. To load the register, signals are routed to the input while the control line is down.

Delay registers have been implemented in various ways, for example, by acoustic delay lines, electrical delay lines, and tracks on the rotating surface of a magnetic drum or disk. Rotating tracks have an advantage over delay lines in that information bits need not be sensed and reshaped at each cycle. Moreover, because a read/write head is essential to a track only during reading or writing cycles, a movable head can service more than one track.

The main disadvantage of the circulating register accrues from its access limitations. If the register stores a logical vector of dimension $n$ and a short infix of the vector is needed at an arbitrary time, nearly $n/2$ bits of irrelevant information, on the average, precede the infix to the output point. If the pattern of register accesses is predictable to a useful degree, the contents can sometimes be arranged to reduce the average delay. Another way to reduce the average wait is to tap the circulating loop at more than one point and select among the output points in reading from the register. In general, however, the employment of $k$ outputs per circulating register seems to lack much advantage over $k$ single-output registers of dimension $n/k$.

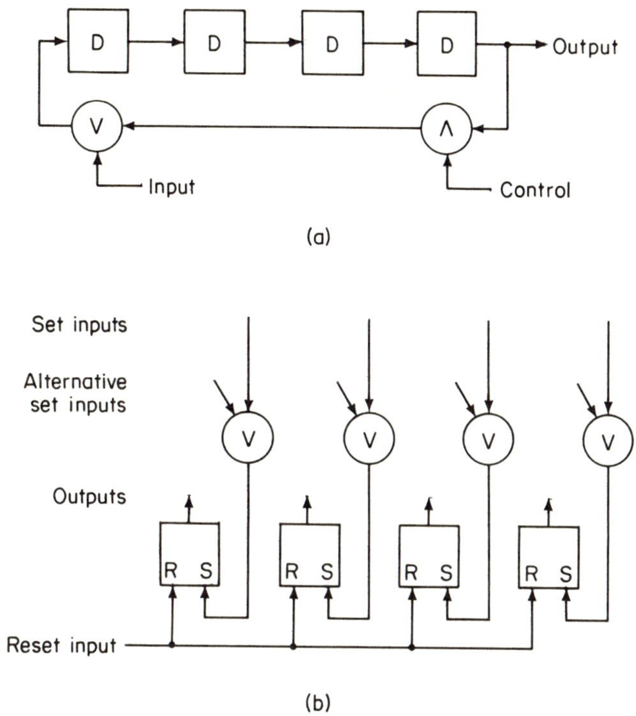


**Fig. 7.6** Registers with (a) serial and (b) parallel access.

A register with parallel inputs and outputs is shown in Fig. 7.6(b). It can be cleared by bringing up the reset line and it can be set by signals from either of two sources. In practice, it may be feasible to have more than two sources. Note that before setting the register, it is required that all elements of the register be reset. The loading of a parallel register therefore involves a twin reset/set cycle.

In Fig. 7.7, each RS element is attended by a delay element. If the RS elements constitute the *main* register, the *D* elements may be said to constitute a *companion* register. In the absence of signals, the main register holds information unchanged. A reset signal will clear the main register. As before, a reset signal followed by a group of set signals will load the register. On the other hand, a reset pulse followed at one unit in time by a restore pulse simply routes the companion delay register back into the main register; the net effect, in this case, is nonproductive. However, by modifying connections from AND to OR elements, the register can perform a rotation of the form $k \uparrow \boldsymbol{u}$ (or $k \downarrow \boldsymbol{u}$) in Table 6.1. In this case, the restore line is a *rotate line* and a rotation of $k$ places in a fixed direction (left or right) is executed at each reset/rotate cycle. To shift rather than rotate, end connections may be omitted.

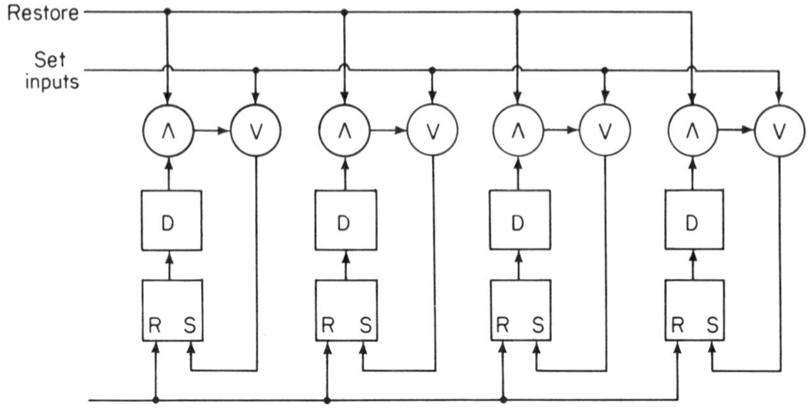


**Fig. 7.7** Register with companion delay register.

The simplest circuit for rotation moves the register contents, say ***u***, one place in one direction. All possible rotations can be obtained by a sequence of such operations (but some rotations will be very slow). The simplest shift register capable of any desired shift must respond to two commands, i.e., shift right one and shift left one. This implies two command lines and two AND elements at the output of each delay element. A similar approach can improve the speed of rotation operations. Since the simplest shift registers are not very fast, additional lines may be included to gain speed. For example, the number of cycles for a $k$-place shift in a long register becomes a logarithmic function of $k$ if command lines are provided for shift 1, shift 2, shift 4, shift 8, etc. It is possible to envision a shift line and connection set for each possible $k$, but circuit complexity and cost considerations usually militate against this solution.

In a computer, the processing of a word normally occurs while the word is enroute from one register to another. In Fig. 7.8, means are shown for moving the content of register B to register A (assuming as usual that register A has been cleared). It is a matter of interposing more decision elements in the data path to modify the content of B, say by ORing (or with more decision elements by adding) the output of a third register C (not shown) to B while B is enroute to register A. In fact, the use of delay elements might permit register A to replace register C; A would provide one operand, B the other operand, and the result would return to A.

Before leaving the subject of registers, we comment that registers can be designed with both serial and parallel properties. For example, a shift register can be designed to accept bits serially and yield a parallel output. A serial-to-parallel register can be useful in assembling information from a relatively slow device and, whenever the register becomes loaded, in passing its contents to a

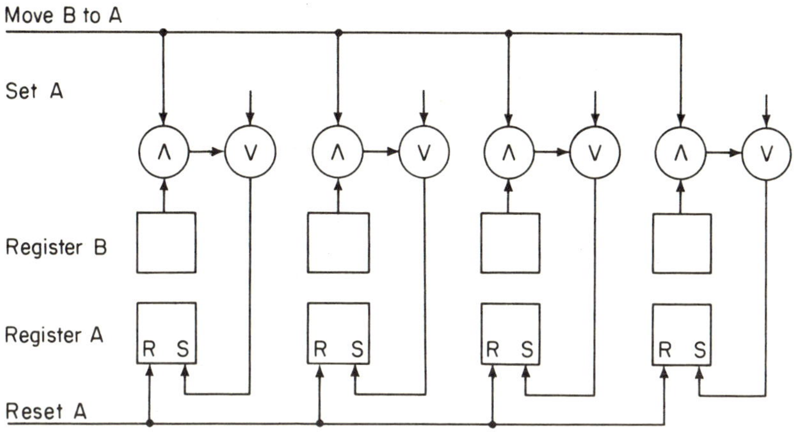


**Fig. 7.8** Registers A and B with path from B to A.

faster device. Conversely, parallel-to-serial registers are useful for passing information to relatively slow devices.

**Decoders.** During passive storage, and in the course of register-to-register transfers, efficiency usually demands that control information be compactly encoded. (Later, examples will be provided in the command fields and address fields of computer instructions.) But when the time comes to instruct circuits, a less efficient encoding is needed. A decoder circuit responds to an encoded field by bringing up one of its $n$ output lines. Let a *unit-k vector of dimension m* be a vector that contains zeros except for a 1 in the $k$th position. Assuming zero-origin indexing, Fig. 7.9 illustrates a decoder for passing from the first 16 binary numbers to their corresponding unit vectors. A logical vector $\boldsymbol{u}$ of dimension 4 encodes an input $k$ to the decoder, whereupon the output is a unit-$k$ vector of dimension 16. Two lines are provided for each input bit, one for a given digit and another for its complement. The circuit is termed a *level decoder* because every AND element is connected to each input bit position. There are 16 different functions for a four-input AND element, and the 16 are arranged so that the vector $\boldsymbol{u}$ is a binary representation of the integers 0, 1, 2, . . . , 15.

The level decoder has the virtue of simplicity, but its use may be limited by fan-in considerations. In Fig. 7.9, each AND element has only four inputs but the number must increase if the decoder is to be enlarged. Fan-in restrictions can be circumvented by employing a *tree decoder* with more than one level. A tree decoder with three levels and 16 outputs is depicted in Fig. 7.10. This decoder employs more AND elements than the previous decoder, and the fan-in is two instead of four. Where $m$ is large, an alternative to the tree decoder is a *twin decoder* in which two tree decoders feed the rows and columns

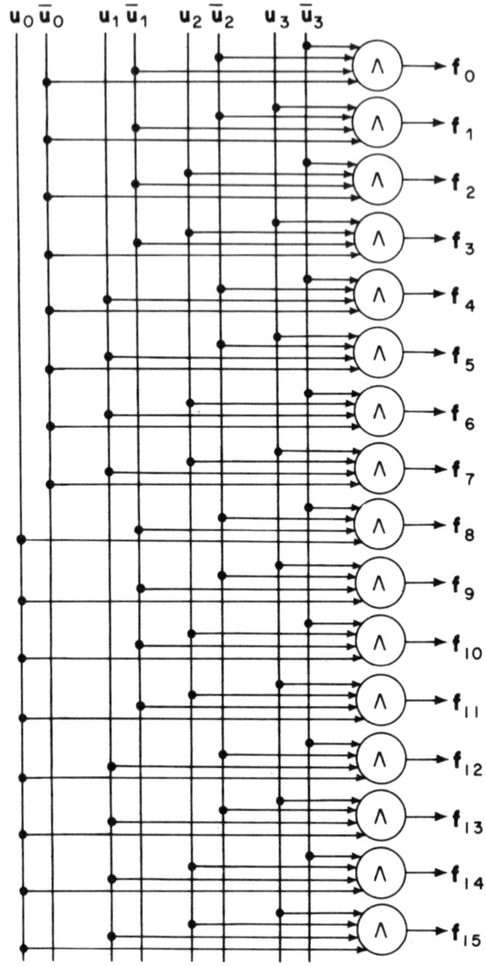


Fig. 7.9 Level decoder for determining a unit vector of dimension 16 from the vector $\boldsymbol{u}$ which encodes $j$ as a binary number.

of a rectangle of AND elements. In the twin decoder of Fig. 7.11, the tree decoders are each of one level, but this need not be the case in general.

In general, the numbers of elements required of the three kinds of decoders are given by the following expressions, wherein $n$ denotes the number of input pairs, $2^n$ is the number of outputs, $p + q$ must equal $n$, and each of the integers $n$, $p$, and $q$ is greater than unity:

| *Decoder* | *Elements Needed* | *Inputs per Element* |
|---|---|---|
| Level | $2^n$ | $n$ |
| Tree | $2^{n+1} - 4$ | 2 |
| Twin | $2^n + (2^{p+1} - 4) + (2^{q+1} - 4)$ | 2 |

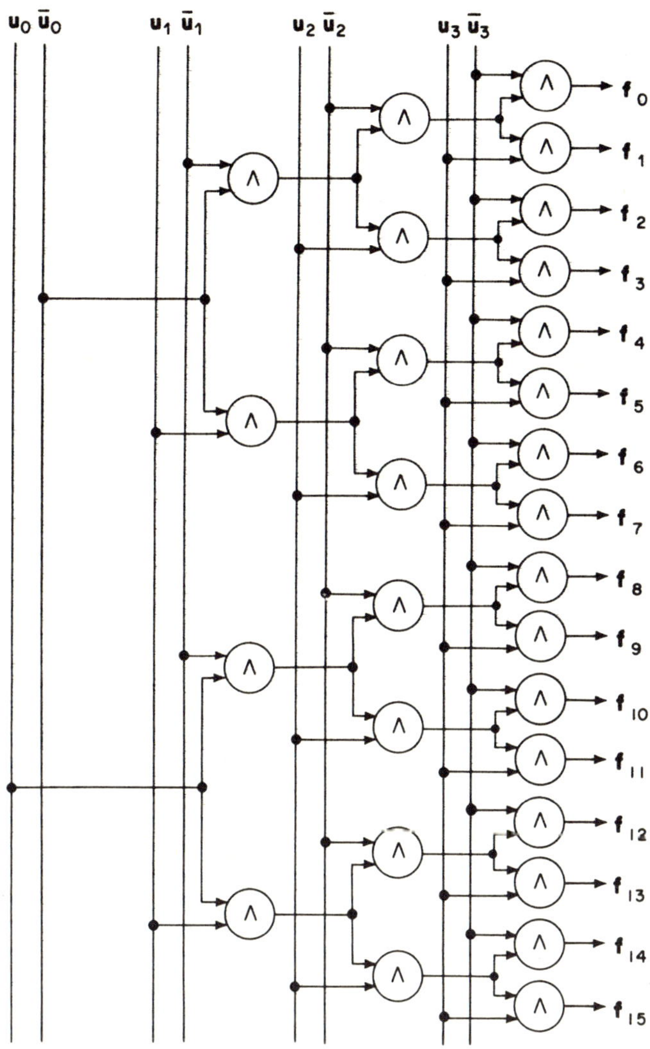


**Fig. 7.10** Tree decoder of three levels.

The elements in the twin decoder are at a minimum when input pairs are divided as equally as possible between $p$ and $q$; this can be assured by taking $p = \lfloor n \div 2 \rfloor$ and $q = \lceil n \div 2 \rceil$. Accordingly, the level decoder (Fig. 7.9) should have 16 elements, the tree decoder (Fig. 7.10) should have 28 elements, and the twin decoder (Fig. 7.11) should have $16 + (8 - 4) + (8 - 4) = 24$ elements. These results may be verified by inspection.

As $n$ grows large, the number of elements required of a twin decoder approaches that of a level decoder, whereas the tree decoder requires about twice

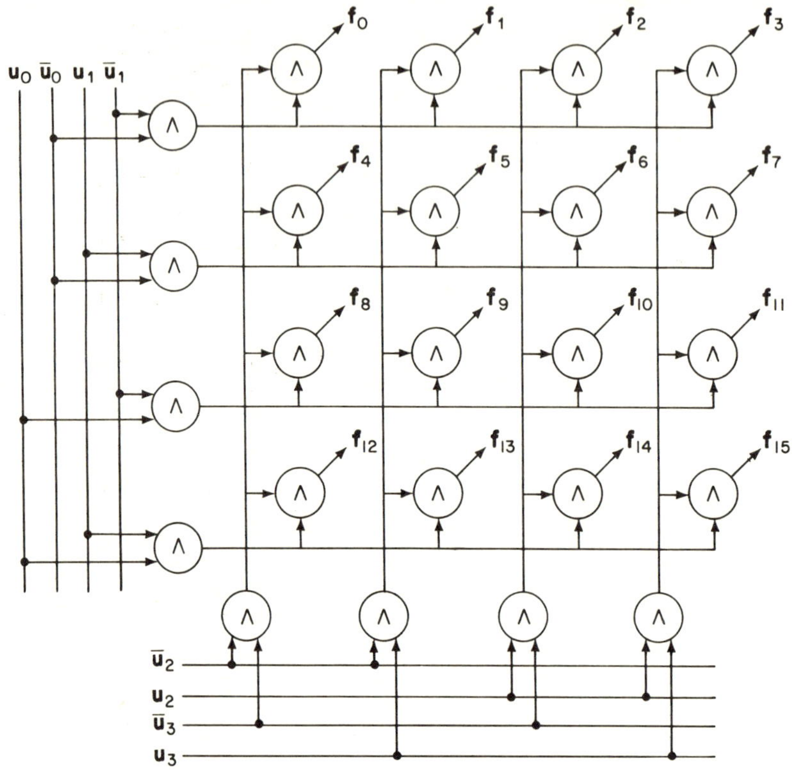


**Fig. 7.11** Twin decoder.

the number. The level decoder gains its advantage in the assumption of $n$-way fan-in for its decision elements. The twin decoder, on the other hand, gains an advantage through the assumption of large ($2^p$-way and $2^q$-way) fan-outs for elements at the leaves of its marginal tree decoders. These assumptions naturally have an important bearing on the engineering design of a decoder. For elements of the tree decoder, a fan-in and a fan-out of two suffices. Semiconductor diodes, transistors, and magnetic cores have been used as decision elements in decoders.

**Counters.** An $n$-state counter is a unit that can step through an interval vector of dimension $n$. A counter is either designed to count up or to count down: A unit designed for the first option counts up to $n - 1$ and then starts over at zero; a unit designed for the second option counts down to zero and then starts over at $n - 1$. Counting modulo $n$ is equivalent, clearly, to stepping through an interval vector that is bent into a loop. Inasmuch as each component of the interval vector is associated with a position in the loop, the count at a given time can be designated by a 1 in a unit vector. Thus in a *ring* *counter* of $n$ stages, a unit vector of dimension $n$ is stored in a rotation register. Each one-place rotation is equivalent to stepping the counter by 1. The ring counter is particularly applicable where $n$ is small and an output signal is desired at known counts. For example, if a processing cycle requires $n$ time periods and various events must be triggered at each period, a ring counter of $n$ stages can be used to trigger desired control signals.

Where outputs are desired for few counter values, the *binary counter* is less cumbersome than a ring counter. In the binary counter, as its name suggests, counts are encoded as binary integers. A three-stage binary counter of RS storage elements and decision elements is shown in Fig. 7.12. This counter adds 1 each time the input is pulsed. When the count reaches 111, an incoming 1 propagates through the stages and emerges as an overflow, having cleared the counter back to zero. An overflow signal is thus generated at every eighth input pulse. Decision elements can be attached to the stage outputs to detect an arbitrary count, say $m$, where $m < 8$.

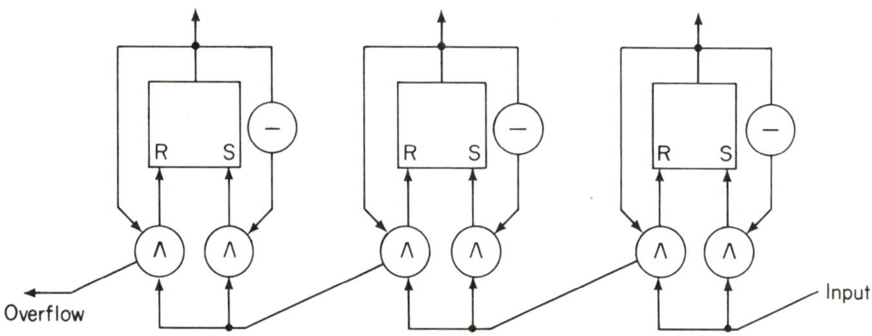


**Fig. 7.12** Three-stage binary counter.

Were AND elements ideal, all stages in this counter would respond together to an incoming "add 1" signal. Because decision elements are not ideal in practice, the carry propagation line simulates a delay line to some extent. Hence, an overflow signal follows in time the input signal that occasioned it. This delay need not interfere with counting accuracy, but it may diminish the value of the counter as a source of control signals. Many methods of reducing such delays have been developed.

## 7.4 Arithmetic Units

Each stage in a binary counter concerns itself with two values: a resident value (augend bit) and an incoming signal. One of the inputs to the least significant stage is normally an external signal, whereas the comparable input at each of the other stages is a carry from the stage below. The typical stage of a binary adder, on the other hand, treats of three inputs: an augend bit, an addend bit, and a *carry-in* bit. From these, the stage generates two outputs, a sum bit and a *carry-out* bit, as required by the truth table of Fig. 7.13. An illustrative network for realizing the truth table is also shown. This two-level circuit is but one of many capable of effecting binary addition. By employing more levels, the number of decision elements can be reduced (at some penalty in elapsed time).

| a | b | c | r | s | Legend |
|---|---|---|---|---|---|
| 0 | 0 | 0 | 0 | 0 | a : augend bit |
| 0 | 0 | 1 | 0 | 1 | b : addend bit |
| 0 | 1 | 0 | 0 | 1 | c : carry in |
| 0 | 1 | 1 | 1 | 0 | r : carry out |
| 1 | 0 | 0 | 0 | 1 | s : sum bit |
| 1 | 0 | 1 | 1 | 0 | |
| 1 | 1 | 0 | 1 | 0 | |
| 1 | 1 | 1 | 1 | 1 | |

(a)

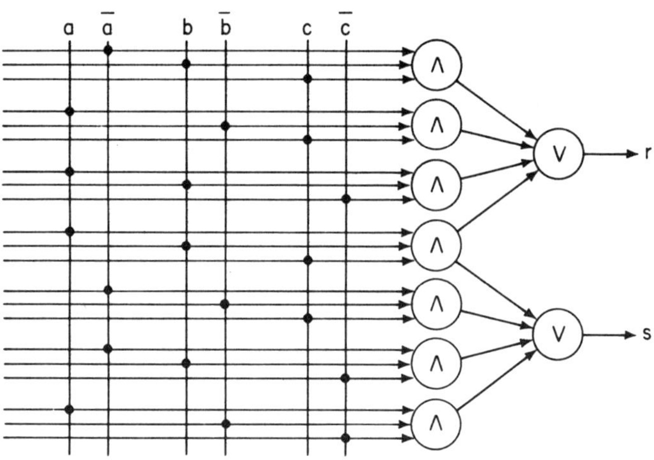


(b)

**Fig. 7.13** Binary addition; (a) truth table and (b) possible circuit.

Assuming that augend, addend, and sum is each assigned a register, the serial-access scheme, suggested in Fig. 7.14(a), rotates the augend and addend digits to a one-stage adder. The carry input to the adder is provided by a storage element. Since the addition proceeds on bits of increasing significance, the

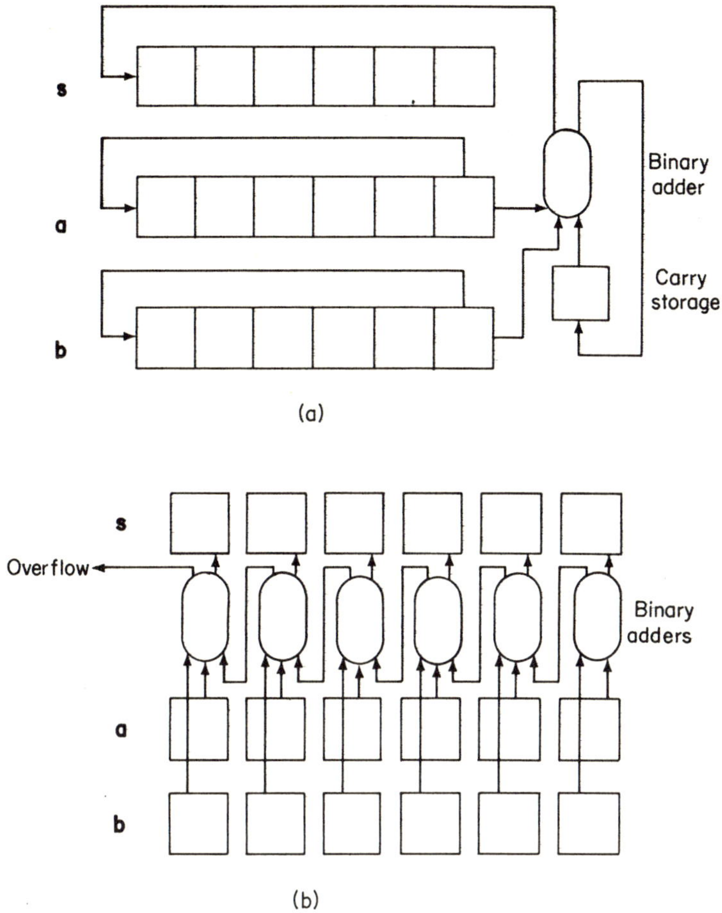


Fig. 7.14 (a) Serial and (b) parallel add units for six-bit numbers.

carry bit goes to carry storage and the sum bit to a rotating register. A serial unit of this kind is especially congenial to delay-line registers.

In any case, the speed of a serial adder is apt to be limited by the rotation time. This limitation can be relaxed by employing parallel-access registers and one adder per bit position, as in Fig. 7.14(b). The limiting factor in addition time becomes the carry process rather than the rotation operation. But since the carry process itself need not involve storage elements, the bottleneck has been isolated in a network of decision elements. The more nearly ideal are the available decision elements, the faster is the carry process. Moreover, when the carry process is closely examined, it becomes evident that the empirical delays of nonideal elements can be considerably reduced by judicious use of additional decision elements. Several methods of reducing carry times are described in the literature on computers. The circuits of Fig. 7.14 are often modified to return the sum from register ***s*** to register ***a*** (in some cases ***s*** is simulated by empirical delays). In this operating mode, register ***a*** is called an accumulator.

For a binary operand, a one-placed left shift corresponds to multiplication by 2 and a one-place right shift to division by 2. If the product of a multiplicand and a multiplier is to be obtained by summing appropriate multiples of the multiplicand, the multiples may be obtained by shifting and additions can be controlled by testing multiplier bits. One well-known method employs a double-length shift register as an accumulator ***a***. The operands are assumed to be of equal lengths. Initially, the most significant half of ***a*** is cleared and the least significant half holds the multiplier. The multiplicand, held in register ***b***, is aligned with the parallel adders and with the most significant half of ***a***. At each summation cycle, the accumulator is shifted right one place, moving the least significant bit out into a storage element *d*. If *d* receives a 1, the multiplicand is added into the accumulator; if it receives a 0, the addition is skipped. Following the last cycle, a terminal shift brings the double-precision product into its proper position in the accumulator.

For an example, we multiply 9 by 11. The operands are encoded as four-bit unsigned binary numbers. The product is formed in an eight-bit accumulator ***a*** and the accumulator spills into element *d* at each shift. The multiplicand is held in register *b*.

| | *a* | *d* | *b* |
|---|---|---|---|
| Initially | 0 0 0 0 1 0 1 1 | 0 | 1 0 0 1 |
| Cycle 1 | 0 0 0 0 0 1 0 1 | 1 | 1 0 0 1 |
| | 1 0 0 1 | | |
| | 1 0 0 1 0 1 0 1 | | |
| Cycle 2 | 0 1 0 0 1 0 1 0 | 1 | 1 0 0 1 |
| | 1 0 0 1 | | |
| | 1 1 0 1 1 0 1 0 | | |
| Cycle 3 | 0 1 1 0 1 1 0 1 | 0 | |
| Cycle 4 | 0 0 1 1 0 1 1 0 | 1 | 1 0 0 1 |
| | 1 0 0 1 | | |
| | 1 1 0 0 0 1 1 0 | | |
| Terminal shift | 0 1 1 0 0 0 1 1 | | |

The base-2 value of 0 1 1 0 0 0 1 1 equals $64 + 32 + 2 + 1$, i.e., 99, as it should. Although we have been neglecting signs, the product sign can be determined directly from the operand signs.

In all addition and subtraction operations on signed magnitudes, the result magnitude is either the sum or the difference of the two operand magnitudes. If *b* and *c* are two magnitudes (unsigned numbers) and $b > c$, then the difference $b - c$ can be obtained by adding a suitable "complement" of *c* to *b*. Using four-digit decimal numbers as examples, the difference 6543 − 4321 is equivalent to

$$\begin{aligned}6543 + (10^4 - 4321) - 10^4 &= 6543 + (5679) - 10^4 \\ &= 12{,}222 - 10^4 \\ &= 2222 + 10^4 - 10^4 \\ &= 2222.\end{aligned} \tag{7.1}$$

The expressions in parentheses are called the *ten's complement* of 4321. After the ten's complement of 4321 is available, the desired difference can be obtained by merely adding 6543 to 5679 and then ignoring the overflow.

Although complementation has been widely used to systematize algebraic addition and subtraction, the principle has many practical facets and a very long discussion is required to treat the subject at the level of competitive techniques. In the first place, it is usually impractical to require that magnitude relations be known; it simplifies matters to always complement one operand—the right-hand operand, say—and then correct the result if no overflow occurs (this has the additional advantage that only one register needs to possess complementing capabilities). For example, to find the difference 4321 − 6543,

$$\begin{aligned}4321 + (10^4 - 6543) - 10^4 &= 4321 + 3457 - 10^4 \\ &= 7778 - 10^4 \\ &= -(10^4 - 7778) = -2222.\end{aligned} \tag{7.2}$$

Here, the lack of overflow testifies that 7778 needs to be recomplemented and that the result is opposite in sign to that of (7.1).

In dealing with radix-10 numbers, the *nine's complement* can be obtained without borrowing. Using this convention, the difference 6543 − 4321 is equivalent to

$$6543 + (9999 - 4321) - (9999),$$

which can also be written

$$\begin{aligned}6543 + (5678) - (10^4 - 1) &= 12{,}221 - 10^4 + 1 \\ &= 2221 + 1 + 10^4 - 10^4 \\ &= 2222.\end{aligned} \tag{7.3}$$

Because the overflow out of the high-order position (which has the value $10^4$) can be interpreted as a command to add 1 into the least significant position, the overflow is often called an *end-around carry*. If the result has to be recomplemented, then 1's cancel and no end-around carry is required. By analogy with (7.2), the difference 4321 − 6543 is obtained as

$$\begin{aligned}4321 + (9999 - 6543) - 9999 &= 4321 + 3456 - 9999 \\ &= 7777 - 9999 \\ &= -(9999 - 7777) = -2222.\end{aligned} \tag{7.4}$$

The complementation principles generalize readily for radix-$r$ numbers, in which case we speak of $r$'s complements and $(r - 1)$'s complements. In the radix-2 case, the 1's complement can be obtained by merely complementing a logical vector. In any radix, the convenient way of forming the $r$'s complement is usually to form the $(r - 1)$'s complement and add 1.

From Chapter 1, we know that a string of $n$ binary 1's has the value

$$2^{n-1} + 2^{n-2} + \cdots + 2^1 + 2^0 = 2^n - 1.$$

This equivalence can be used, in conjunction with subtracting by adding complements, to reduce the number of additions in binary multiplication. Multiplication by such a string can be accomplished with one subtraction, one $n$-place shift and one addition.

The idea is easily explained—and has often been implemented—in the context of two-bit multiplier groups (radix-4 digits) and uniform shifts of two: The applicable rules are given in Table 7.1. After an addition cycle, the partial product is always correct; after a subtraction cycle, it is too small by four times the multiplicand until shifted two places to the right, whereupon it is too small

**Table 7.1**

*Rules for summing the multiplicand x in radix-4 multiplication, assuming uniform two-place right shifts in the partial product*†

| Multiplier digit (radix 4) | Binary code | Appropriate operations | |
|---|---|---|---|
| | | Initially or following add cycle | Following subtract cycle |
| 0 | 00 | Add 0 | Add $x$ |
| 1 | 01 | Add $x$ | Add $2x$ |
| 2 | 10 | Add $2x$ | Subtract $x$ |
| 3 | 11 | Subtract $x$ | Subtract 0 |

*Example* ($b$ denotes multiplicand):

| | $q, a$ | $d$ | $t$ | $b$ |
|---|---|---|---|---|
| Initially | 000001011 | 00 | 0 | 01001 |
| Cycle 1 | 000000010 | 11 | | 01001 |
| | 10111 | | | |
| | 101110010 | | 1 | |
| Cycle 2 | 111011100 | 10 | | 01001 |
| | 10111 | | | |
| | 101001100 | | 1 | |
| Terminal cycle | 111010011 | | | |
| | 01001 | | | |
| | 01100011 | | 0 | |

†If the last cycle employs subtraction, the terminal shift is followed by addition of $x$.

by one times the multiplicand. The rules in the last column of the table take this into account. If the last cycle leads to a subtraction, the terminal shift must be accompanied by a terminal addition.

Where two multiplier digits are to be employed, one needs a binary adder for a prefix stage in the accumulator. To multiply 9 by 11, as before, assume that the multiplicand 9 is encoded in five bits; this permits doubling by a left shift. For control purposes, a storage element $t$ is set at subtract cycles and reset at add cycles. When $t$ is set, right shifts must bring in 1's on the left. (The 2's complement of $\boldsymbol{b}$ is 1 0 1 1 1.) Table 7.1 completes the example.

This method nearly halves the time of multiplication for long operands. It is readily generalized to the octal radix by employing a triple of the multiplicand $x$, which may be formed at the start by adding $2x$ to $x$. Additional data paths and controls are, of course, required. Generalization to higher radices is possible, but at the price of mounting complexity in registers, paths, and controls. Other shortcuts in multiplication have been proposed and used. However, the method cited is not only very practical, but it introduces the principles needed to understand other methods, including those that employ nonuniform shifts.

If multiplication is to be performed by successive additions, rapid addition is clearly important to multiplication. One scheme for hastening a known sequence of additions employs the *carry save* (CS) principle and encodes the partial sum jointly as a CS sum vector and a carry vector. Each stage in a carry/save adder is independent of the other stages. Each has three inputs: a CS-sum digit, a carry digit, and an addend digit. Each has two outputs, a CS-sum digit and a carry digit. After each CS addition, the carry vector is shifted left by one stage.

The idea is illustrated in Table 7.2 for the following decimal summation:

$$\begin{array}{r} 0\,9\,9\,9\,9 \\ 0\,9\,9\,9\,9 \\ 0\,4\,5\,0\,1 \\ 0\,4\,5\,0\,3 \\ \hline 2\,9\,0\,0\,2. \end{array}$$

The numbers are summed from the top down. At the first CS cycle, 0 9 9 9 9 is added to 0 9 9 9 9, but the carries are not propagated. The carry vector is shifted left for the second CS cycle, which sums 0 4 5 0 1. After three CS addition cycles, the carry vector is assimilated with the CS sum by a conventional addition. In this way, $n$ numbers can be summed in $n$ cycles followed by a single carry process.

Note that the carry vector must be a logical vector: Two decimal digits plus a carry digit obviously cannot exceed 19. The method, which generalizes without difficulty to other radices, has found some application in high-performance multiply units.

**Table 7.2**

*Addition of four decimal integers with three carry/ save* (CS) *adds and one conventional add*

| | CS *add 1* | CS *add 2* | CS *add 3* |
|---|---|---|---|
| Addend | 09999 | 04501 | 04503 |
| Saved carries in | 00000 | 11110 | 11000 |
| CS sum in | 09999 | 08888 | 13499 |
| Saved carries out | 01111 | 01100 | 00001 |
| CS sum out | 08888 | 13499 | 28992 |

| | *Add 4* |
|---|---|
| Addend | 00010 |
| Augend | 28992 |
| Final sum | 29002 |

Because division is the most complicated arithmetic operation executed in a digital computer, we shall be content to illustrate principles with decimal examples and positive fractions. Longhand division generates one quotient digit at a time by subtracting a suitable multiple from a partial dividend. A "suitable" multiple is the largest multiple that does not drive the partial dividend negative. Initially, the partial dividend is the whole dividend; at the close, the partial dividend is the remainder. If the result must be a fraction, the magnitude of the dividend is required to be smaller than the magnitude of the divisor (thereby avoiding overflow).

For example, $0.590738 \div 0.663 = 0.891$ with a remainder of 0.000005.

```
            0.891
0.663)0.590 738
        530 4
        -----
         60 33
         59 67
        -----
           668
           663
        -----
           005
```

The accomplish this division without employing multiples, we can resort to subtracting, counting, and shifting. Thus, if 663 is subtracted from 5907 eight times, from 6033 nine times, and from 668 one time, the quotient and remainder are obtained as before. The problem, of course, is to determine when to halt a series of subtractions. In *restoring division*, the series is halted at (1) nine subtractions or at (2) a negative partial dividend—whichever occurs first. In the latter event the partial dividend is restored to a positive status by addition of the divisor. This addition, like the subtraction that occasioned it, is useless work insofar as the numerical process is concerned; it serves a control function only.

In *nonrestoring division*, the control function is served more efficiently. The partial dividend is permitted negative as well as positive encodings. As before, the divisor is subtracted from positive partial dividends until stopped by event 1 or 2. After event 2, restoration is omitted, but subsequent to a shift, the negative partial dividend is further diminished by a series of divisor adds. For the negative partial dividend, addition plays a role analogous to subtraction from a positive partial dividend.

Nonrestoring division easily generalizes to radix $r$. Because the gain over restoring division rises as $r$ becomes smaller, nonrestoring division is the basic method for binary division. For radix 2, the method yields one quotient bit for each subtraction or addition. Techniques have been described by which the method can be extended to produce more than one quotient bit per add cycle, but these go beyond the scope of our discussion.

An arithmetic unit capable of addition, subtraction, multiplication, and division needs various facilities for decoding, rotating, shifting, complementing, adding, counting up, and counting down. To sequence these facilities, it must be able to execute sequential processes that are governed by clock signals, overflow signals, ring counters, sign bits, and the like. The engineering design of an arithmetic unit becomes even more complicated if the operands and results are represented in floating-point notation, as they usually are in high-speed computers.

## 7.5 Memory Units

**Planes.** As we have seen, the primary function of a register is to store a logical vector. By extension, a set of registers capable of storing a logical matrix will be called a *plane*. Although registers are often designed to perform secondary functions such as shifting, this is seldom the case for planes. Typically, the sole functions of a plane are to store information and to communicate with one or more registers. No topic is more important to the digital computer industry than storage, and the industry has responded with a considerable variety of storage devices. As a consequence, the field is rife with practical classifications that are useful in given contexts but that are essentially impediments to a functional analysis. Here we do no more than emphasize a few basic and suggestive models.

A simple $2 \times 2$ plane is shown in Fig. 7.15. The plane consists of four RS elements, three AND elements per RS element, one OR element, and a trio of control lines per row and column. Simultaneous up conditions on the row-$i$ reset (set) line and the column-$j$ reset (set) line will write a 0 (1) in storage ele-

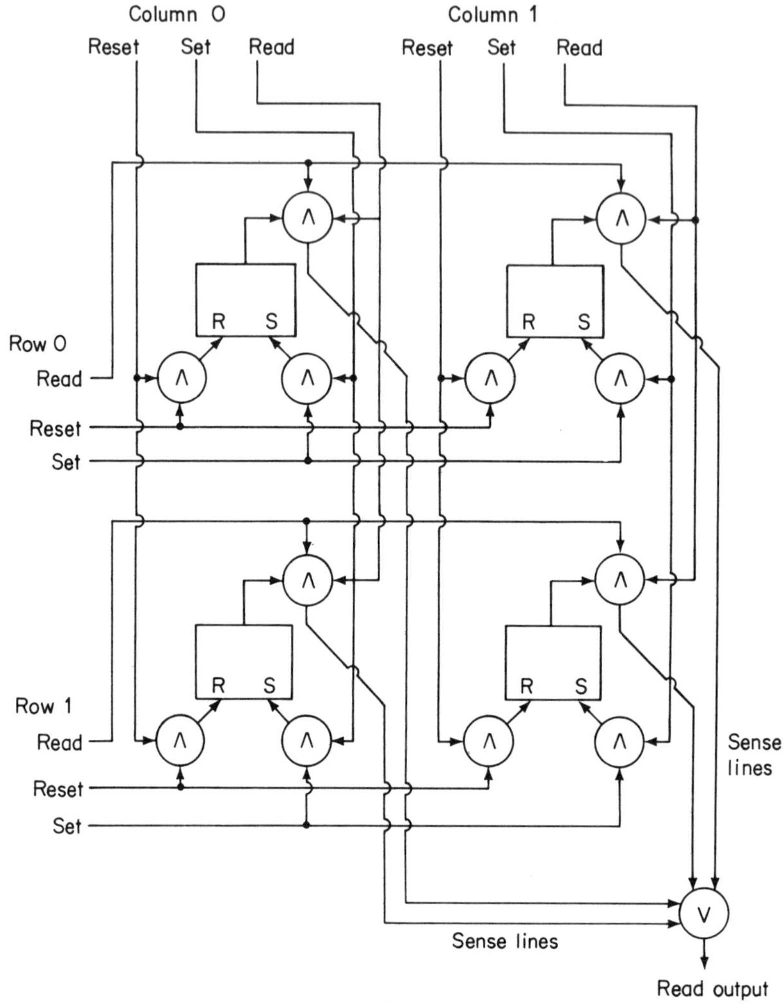


**Fig. 7.15** $2 \times 2$ element-organized plane with the NDR (non-destructive read) property.

ment $i, j$. This is easily verified by inspection. In much the same way, simultaneous signals on the row-$i$ and column-$j$ read lines will send the status of element $i, j$ to the OR element and yield an appropriate output. Because read and write are closely analogous operations, convenience is served by jointly designating them as *accesses*.

The model is said to possess a *nondestructive read* (NDR) property because the status of a storage element is not affected by a read operation. Moreover, the plane is said to be *element-organized* because read access is limited to one element at a time. It may be noted, however, that an entire row (or column) can be written simultaneously and that the read limitation is imposed by the treatment of sense lines. This limitation is relaxed in the 3 × 2 plane of Fig. 7.16, which is said to be *row-organized* because access is always to a row. The plane possesses a *destructive read* (DR) property in that the functions of a read line are subordinate to those of a reset line.

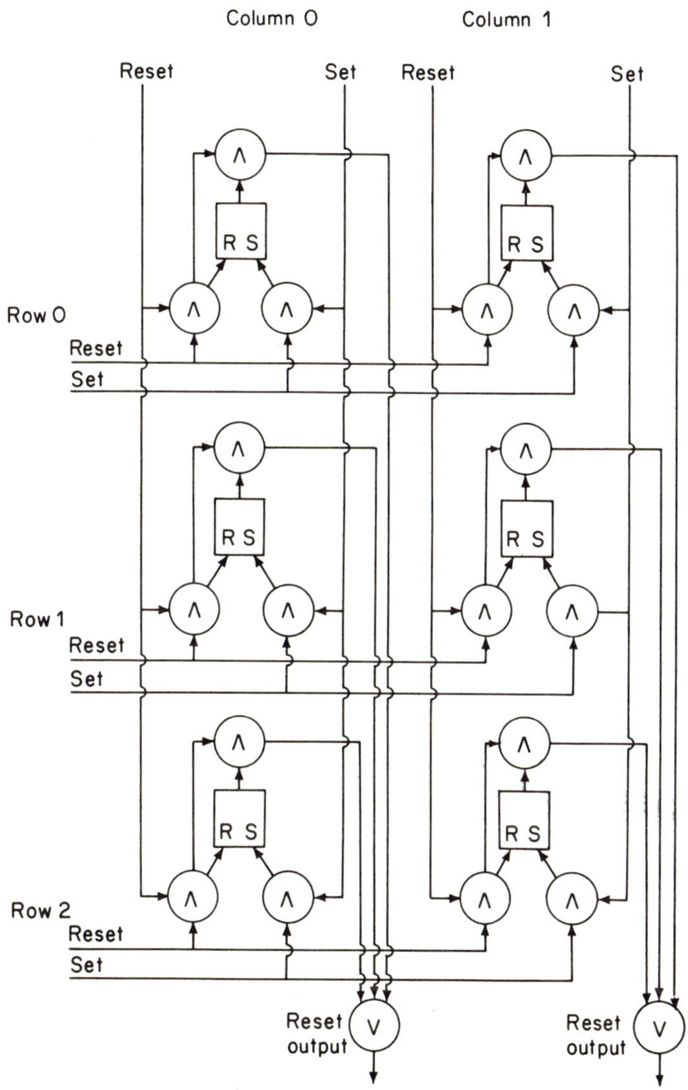


**Fig. 7.16** 3 × 2 row-organized plane with the DR (destructive read) property.

To read row *i* in this plane, all column reset lines and the row-*i* reset line are brought up. Thus the RS elements in row *i* are reset at the same time as the row is being read at the output. The output is saved in a register and from there written back into row *i* by placing signals simultaneously on the row-*i* set line and the set lines of all columns that produced a 1 output. It is to be noted that the act of reading a row requires the row to be cleared and that writing can be accomplished as a slight variation of reading. Another possible way of writing is to place simultaneous signals on the row-*i* reset line, the row-*i* set line, the column reset lines corresponding to 0's, and the column set lines corresponding to 1's. Because a column-organized plane employs the same principles as a row-organized plane, one need not be shown. Moreover, by suitably compounding the design principles, a plane can be jointly row- and column-organized. The plane in Fig. 7.17 differs from the two previously discussed in that it possesses the read-only (RO) property. Here the control lines are reduced to the minimum of one per row.

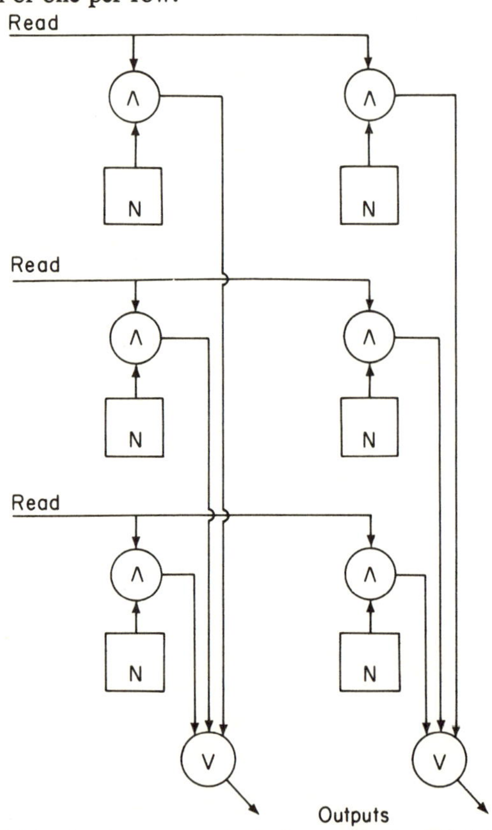


**Fig. 7.17** 3 × 2 row-organized plane with the RO (read-only) property.

Of the three models described, the NDR array in a row-organized mode lends itself well to transistor flip-flops, the DR plane to magnetic cores, and the RO plane to semiconductor diodes as well as a number of other devices. To suggest the simplicity that can be attained with cores, Fig. 7.18 shows two small DR planes for magnetic cores threaded by wires. Assuming that a core switches under six units of current but not under three units, a core in Fig. 7.18(a) is read by pulsing three units of current through its column wire and three units through its row wire (in the reset direction): This is the well-known *coincident-current* principle. If set to 1, the core flips to the opposite state and sends an informative pulse down the sense wire; if set to 0, the informative pulse does not materialize. Writing is accomplished by simultaneous current pulses, each with a magnitude of three units in the set direction, on the selected column and row wires. Previous comments on clearing and writing apply.

In the row-organized plane of Fig. 7.18(b), row $i$ is read simply by pulsing

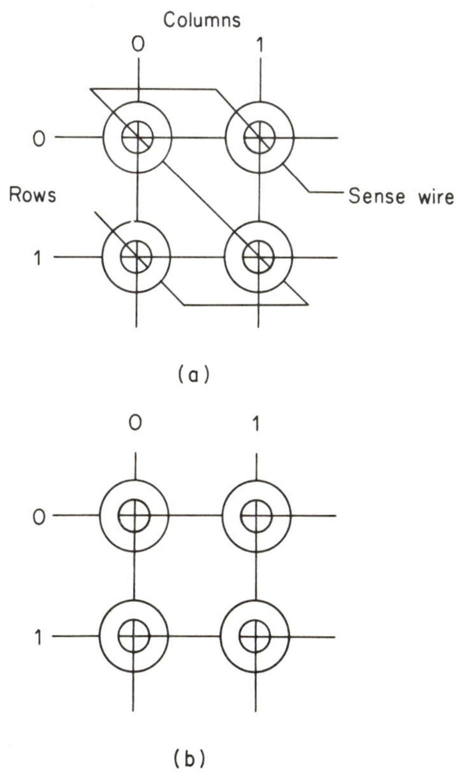


**Fig. 7.18** Illustrative windings for a $2 \times 2$ core plane: (a) element-organized core plane; (b) row-organized core plane (column wires function as sense wires in reading).

it in the reset direction with six or more units of current. The tolerances here are less critical and, in practice, speed may be gained by using more than six units of current. In reading, the column wires function as sense wires. In writing, the coincident-current principle is employed by pulsing row $i$ and all of the columns wherein a 1 is to be stored. The designer has some latitude in choosing pulse strengths, moreover. For example, row $i$ may be pulsed by four units (set direction), the 0 columns by two units (reset direction), and the 1 columns by two units (set direction). In this choice, the cores outside row $i$ are disturbed by only two units of current, whereas they would be disturbed by three units in the case of an element-organized plane.

In read-only planes, a storage element may consist of no more than an electrical coupling between a row and a column wire. Various ways of using inductive and capacitive coupling have been tried. Semiconductor diodes can also be used; for example, the word-organized diode plane shown in Fig. 7.19 stores a $3 \times 2$ matrix. A pulse on row $i$ yields an output pulse from each column that is coupled to the row by a diode. The high back-resistance of the diodes prevents pulses from sneaking into other rows and thereby causing false outputs. It will be noted that the illustrated plane functions as a table look-up decoder; a unit-vector input is encoded at the output in a manner determined by the stored matrix. In fact, one high-speed RO plane can provide a versatile

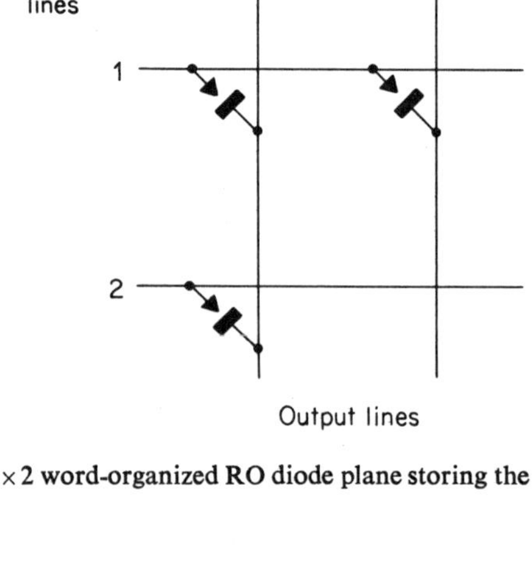


**Fig. 7.19** $3 \times 2$ word-organized RO diode plane storing the matrix $\begin{pmatrix} 01 \\ 11 \\ 10 \end{pmatrix}$.

way of systematizing a whole set of decoding needs. The RO plane therefore finds considerable use in providing patterns of control signals for computers.

**Memories.** Conceptually, a *memory unit* is a set of identical registers. The straightforward way to implement a memory is to start with a row-organized plane, in which case each row serves as a memory register. The *n* registers in a memory are normally identified by the integers 0, 1, 2, . . . , $n - 1$. In practice, the content of a register is called a word. In a typical memory, one register can be read or loaded per operating cycle. Memory registers, seen as logical vectors, are usually designed to be compatible with registers in the arithmetic unit of the computer.

A memory implemented by a row-organized plane requires at least one extra register for the word about to be loaded or read, one signal source per column, and one signal source per row. Because the plane usually contains far more rows than columns, signal strength is a problem mainly in the case of columns. Where it suffices to access the rows in sequence, the row signals can be triggered by a ring counter, as in the schematic of Fig. 7.20 for a $16 \times 6$

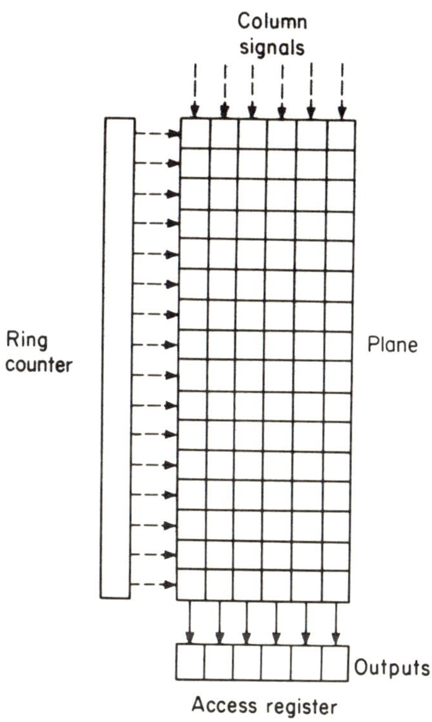


**Fig. 7.20** Schematic of a $16 \times 6$ row-organized memory with sequential access.

row-organized memory. The requisite control lines, not shown in detail, are suggested by the dashed lines. At each access the ring counter steps to its next state, stepping down or up as determined by its design. A memory of this type provides for sequential row access.

Although sequential access someitmes plays a role in optimizing performance versus cost, many contexts require a memory that affords direct access to any row. To achieve this, the memory must be supplemented by an *address register* and an *address decoder*, as shown in the schematic of Fig. 7.21. A row-organized memory of this kind, often said to possess a *random access* property, permits the user to access any row during any memory cycle.

Parallel access to the bits of a word, with its advantage for speed, can also be attained with element-organized planes. With element-organized planes, parallel access to words of $b$ bits each can be obtained by accessing $b$ planes in parallel. A memory based on this approach is shown in the schematic of Fig. 7.22. The capacity of the memory is 16 words of six bits each. The first bit of each stored word resides in plane 0, the second in plane 1, etc. The six planes are traversed by common sets of row lines and column lines. A one-bit output

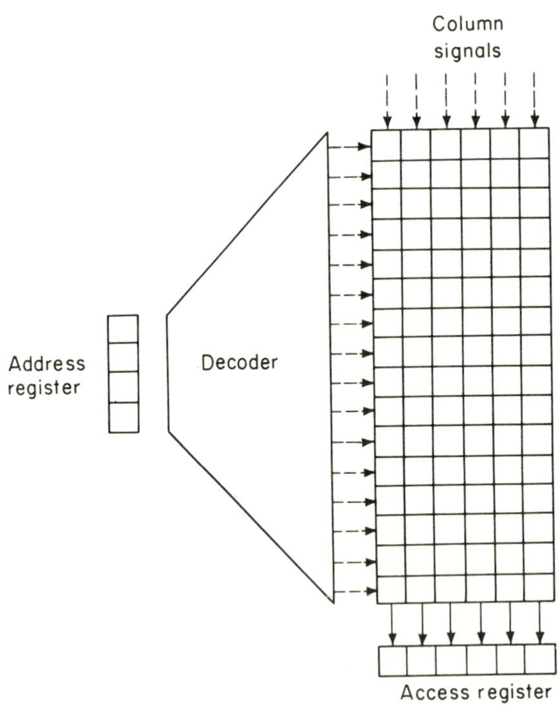


**Fig. 7.21** Schematic of 16 × 6 row-organized memory with random access.

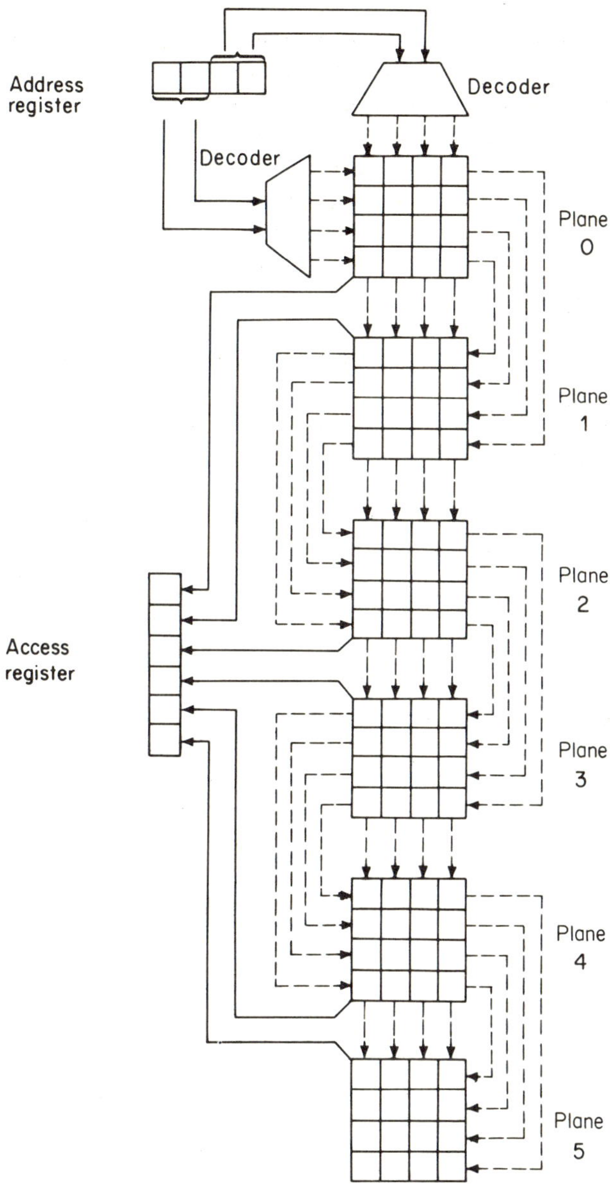


**Fig. 7.22** Schematic of a random-access memory with six element-organized 4 × 4 planes.

is sensed from each plane. The binary address is split into prefix and suffix and fed to two decoders, the prefix to one decoder and the suffix to the other decoder. Although two decoders are required, the total number of decoder outputs is smaller than in the comparable memory of Fig. 7.21.

Note that the bottom row lines of even-numbered planes go to the top row of odd-numbered planes. As a result, the planes can be stacked by an accordion fold that shortens wires and eases threading of the magnetic cores. It is with this topology in mind that core memories of this type are called *three-dimensional* memories. In a three-dimensional memory, part of the address decoding function is performed within the core planes themselves. However, a two-dimensional configuration usually has speed advantages over the three-dimensional pattern. In any case, decoding is only one of several factors to be considered in an engineering analysis of cost and performance.

In the memories thus far described, access to a word requires that the word be designated by its address. On the other hand, in a *search* memory (also known as *associative* memory, *parallel search* memory, or *content-addressable* memory) word selection is contingent on a match between the word and a given logical vector called the *argument*. The argument may pertain to the desired word in whole or in part.

One possible search memory is suggested by the schematic of Fig. 7.23. To start with, this memory has the column controls, decoder, sense outputs, and access register of a word-organized plane; moreover, reading and writing in an addressable mode is permitted. Beyond this, the plane is assumed to be designed in such a way that columns can be read into a column register. Assuming that it suffices to inspect columns sequentially, column addressing is accomplished by a ring counter that scans from left to right.

As explained in Sec. 4.2, the search proceeds by treating one column at each step. During a step, all bits of a selected column are matched with the corresponding bit in the argument (unless the column is accompanied by a zero in the mask register, in which case the step is to be skipped). After each search step, the detector register preserves the search status by storing at 1 for each row that continues to match the masked argument. At the outset of a search, the detector register stores a full vector. The initial read brings out the first column, mask bit, and argument bit. If the mask bit is 1, each element of the column is compared (by decision elements not shown) with the argument bit; for each mismatching row, the corresponding element of the detector register is reset to zero. Steps repeat for successive columns until the entire plane has been scanned, at which point the detector register contains a 1 for each matching row.

If the user wishes to fetch the matching rows in memory-address order, the next action is to obtain the address of the uppermost matching row. This is far from a trivial problem, at least where high speed is important, and is too specialized to treat here. Required is a unit that can specify the number of leading zeros in the detector register, i.e., a unit that may be termed a *zero prefix count encoder*. The encoder finds the address of the uppermost matching row, resets the corresponding bit in the detector register, and sends the address to

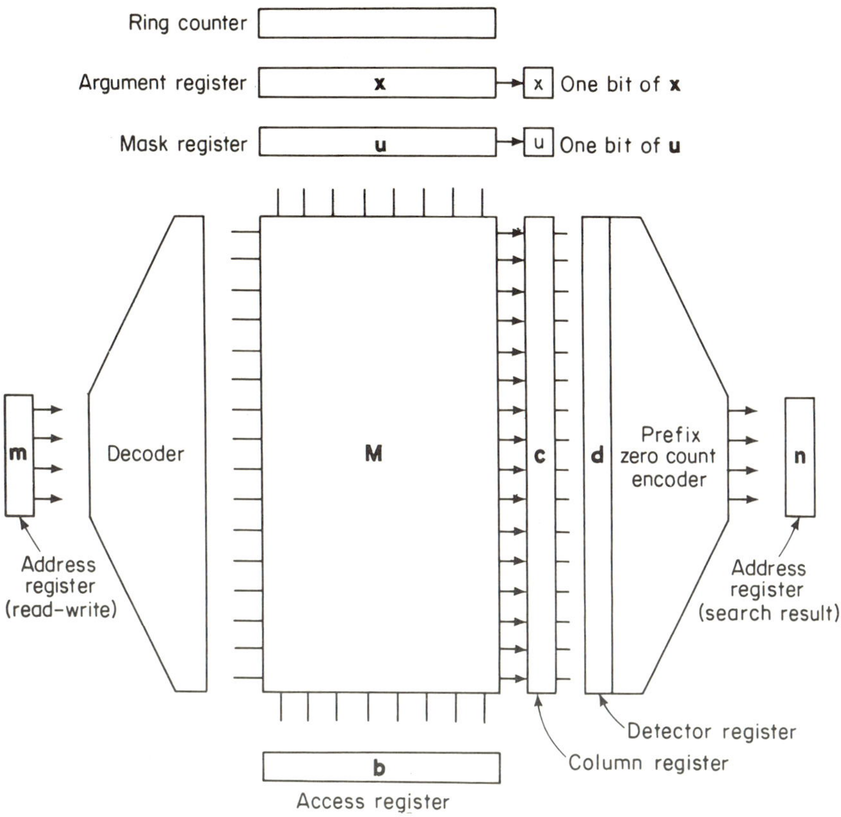


**Fig. 7.23** Schematic of a search memory based on a word-organized, column-organized plane.

the address register. The word is fetched to the access register, whereupon the encoder can go on to find the address of the next matching row.

Consider a set, say $S$, of one or more search-memory rows that has been identified by searching on a masked argument. Typically, the objective is to read out the rows of $S$, one at a time. At the time a row is read, its address being known, the row content can be changed by following the fetch with a write. In some cases, to be sure, the only information of interest is the number of rows in $S$. And only the addresses of the rows in $S$ are of interest where the search memory serves as an address look-up device for records stored in a coordinate memory.

Unemployed search-memory rows are presumably flagged in a column set aside for distinguishing between "used" and "not used." To find a row that can be newly allocated, it suffices to mask out all other columns and search for

0 or 1, as appropriate, in the flag column. The address of the uppermost (lowest address) responding row becomes available, whereupon the row is loaded and flagged as used.

Although a search memory is a complicated device in any technology, known restrictions that characterize the intended applications may permit design engineers to simplify the functional schematic shown in Fig. 7.23. The design of a search memory is usually considered to be at its simplest where the intended applications assure that no more than one row will respond to a search. This is a severe assumption: It means, for example, that unused rows must be identified by auxiliary means (for example, by a list or chain of addresses). However, it is in restricted designs that the greatest simplicity has been attained and search times have been most successfully minimized through parallelism.

On the other hand, several algorithms that can complicate the schematic by providing additional search-memory functions have been described. A. D. Falkoff (1962) has analyzed methods of finding extrema (minimum or maximum) in a given set $S$. In addition to the mask and argument registers, a *plurality counter* is necessary to inform whether there are 0, 1, or more than 1 responses in a search. If a search for equality is termed a *simple search*, a search for *nearest below* or *nearest above* a given argument may require several simple searches. In some of these algorithms, it is necessary to preserve the contents of the detector column in a spare register. This opens up possibilities that could well be useful in other contexts by permitting the state of the detector register after search A to become the initial state for search B. For example, if search A isolates one set and search B another, the combined search of A followed by B can isolate the intersection of the two sets.

Search memories have not been widely used to date, largely for two reasons. First, the magnetic-core technology has been highly developed for coordinate memories; core memories with a capacity of tens or hundreds of thousands of words and a random access time in the neighborhood of 1 microsecond set the rigorous standard against which search memories must be measured. Second, surprisingly few applications invoke the marginal facilities of a search memory more than sporadically—yet, to justify the additional cost, such facilities must be used heavily. One well-known application of search memories is cited in Chapter 10.

## 7.6 Auxiliary Storage Units

A random-access core memory that holds hundreds of thousands of words is entirely too small to hold the library of programs and data of a typical digital system. Moreover, since much of the information in the library is inactive for relatively long interims between periods of use, cost considerations militate for less expensive means of storage during the interims. This need is met by auxiliary storage units (also known as backup stores or auxiliary stores).

Although a deck of punch cards can be convenient for storing a small volume of information, e.g., a program that is being debugged, the magnetic recording of suitable surfaces has become a more important technology for storing large quantities of information. As explained earlier, magnetic recording (writing) and reading is dependent on relative motion between a read/write head and the recorded surface. Three surface configurations have been particularly successful, namely, magnetic tapes, drums, and disks.

In the magnetic-tape unit, a reel of narrow coated tape is unwound past a stationary read/write head, the mechanics being similar to that of an audio tape recorder. Typically, these units have been designed for seven, eight, or nine tracks along the tape, with a cross section of one bit from each track representing an alphameric character. As a consequence, the reading/recording rate is usually described in terms of $x$ characters per second. Information is recorded in long character strings called *blocks* and adjacent blocks are separated by an unrecorded gap. The simplest command to a tape unit is a request to read one block in the forward direction; the tape unit reads the block and stops on the gap. Typical designs provide a *backspace* command that facilitates block rereading. Some tape units are designed to permit reading in the reverse direction as well as the forward direction. In nearly all cases, tape units are designed to write in the forward direction only; that is, the write command assumes that the newly written block will become the last valid block on the tape. (Economical engineering tolerances make it difficult to assure that a block can be repeatedly read, modified, and rewritten between two valid blocks.) Hence, a typical file-updating process reads the master file from one tape unit and writes a new version of the master file on another tape unit. Batch-processing modes of operation (see Sec. 4.7), which dominated in the 1950's and reigned important in the 1960's are based on tape-contained files. With interchangeable reels of magnetic tape, the storage capacity of a computer is effectively unlimited.

Today's technology supports tape reels with about 10 tracks, $10^3$ or more bits per inch in the recorded track, a read/write motion of over $10^2$ inches per second, and start/stop times of a few milliseconds between blocks. These parameters mean that bursts of information can be read or written at rates of hundreds of thousands of characters per second.

Its serial-access property severely limits the utility of magnetic tape as auxiliary storage for the files of many applications. Rotating magnetic drums with stationary read/write heads have commendable access properties but the cost per unit of recording area tends to be rather high. A stack of magnetic disks, with disks mounted at intervals along a rotating column, can provide more recording surface than a drum—but at some penalty in the form of longer access times. Envision a vertical column (with disks stacked one above another) and an arm with two read/write heads that can straddle a disk to service either the top or bottom surface. In the slowest disk devices, the time required to access a record may have three mechanical components:

1. An up-or-down movement of the arm to the appropriate disk
2. A lateral movement of the arm inward to the appropriate track of the disk
3. A *rotational delay* during which the desired sector of the track appears at the head

The average access time of early disk devices was in the neighborhood of one-half second, with component 1 accounting for the bulk of the time. Later developments have served to eliminate the first component, for example, by providing a comb of arms, one arm per pair of surfaces. With such a configuration, the appropriate arm and head can be selected electronically. If there are *n* surfaces in a stack, the comb arrangement has the additional advantage that the *n* tracks (identically located on *n* different surfaces) can be serially accessed without any head movement, thereby maintaining a high bit rate for a significant length of time.

Although auxiliary storage of one form or another is absolutely essential for file-processing applications, it is also often needed in program compilations and array computations. Direct-access devices (disks or drums) are particularly important for inventory applications and program libraries. Since few of the programs are needed at any given time, they are most economically held in auxiliary storage. However, since it is often impossible to predict which program or program segment will next be needed, direct-access storage is more efficacious than serial-access storage for program storage.

## 7.7 Input/Output Units

Loosely speaking, an input process is any process that yields *machine-readable* information. The classic examples of input mechanisms are keyboards. These have been operated in conjunction with card punches, paper-tape perforators, and magnetic-tape recorders, and they have even been connected directly into arithmetic and logical units. A dial switch (as in the telephone) can be an input device. In record-keeping applications, dependence on the keyboard has been somewhat diminished by developments in mark sensing, in character recognition devices for standardized fonts (first in conjunction with magnetic inks), and, more recently, in character recognition devices for hand-lettered characters. In process-control applications, heavy reliance is placed on suitable instrumentation and direct inputs from analog-to-digital converters.

The most recent addition to input technologies comes in conjunction with video displays. The graphic device is designed so that the tip position of an incident *wand* or *light pen* can be communicated to the computer memory as input. As a consequence, a human being can select among a set of alphamerically presented alternatives (such a set is best known as a *menu*) simply by pointing to the desired alternative. More dramatically, if the human being draws a pattern with the wand, the pattern can be interpreted as a sequence of discrete point positions in a fine grid. That is, human beings can enter numerical representations of diagrams or patterns directly to the digital system. Although it would be incautious to guess at the rate of acceptance of this input method until more cost-oriented experience is available, the method permits a man-machine relationship that could be congenial to creative designers in many fields.

To this day, the principal output device is the impact printer, which is familiar, in one form or another, to everyone. Impact printers do not require special paper, they produce high-quality output, and they yield extra carbon copies at competitive costs. It is useful to make a distinction between the character printer, exemplified by the typewriter and teletypewriter, and the line printer, which prints a number of characters in parallel. Impact line printers have been held to about 2000 lines per minute by mechanical limitations. By employing chemical or electrical principles (that involve burning, deposition, or the like), nonimpact printers can be designed to print over 10,000 lines per minute—but in general at a penalty in quality, convenience, or cost.

Much attention has been given to other forms of output for specialized applications. Mechanical plotters, driven by digital-to-analog converters, are in routine use, e.g., to draw isobars on weather maps. Video displays, roughly comparable to television displays in quality, are gaining acceptance as a means of displaying alphameric information, e.g., in response to a query concerning a record of a file. The display is quiet, prompt, and in many contexts more convenient than a printed output. Moreover, the display can present diagrams, patterns, statistical charts, and the like in a form that encourages rapid comprehension. Still another method of answering standardized classes of queries is via telephone: Audio recordings of English words are stored under program control and the numerical or alphameric answer is couched in English by a computer program. This method assures privacy, an important advantage in some application environments.

## 7.8 Clocks and Transmission Lines

Digital computer circuits are usually arranged with a semblance of tree-diagram form, so that decision elements on a given level act more or less in unison as they feed signals to an adjacent level. By analogy to the tree diagram, a complicated circuit is often said to have *h levels of logic*, where *h* is a parameter that depends on circuit design. If $b$ denotes the practical delay of a decision element, that is, the maximum number of nanoseconds required for a decision element to act and propagate a decision to an adjacent level, then at most $bh$ nanoseconds are required for a circuit of $h$ levels to act. It is in the interest of systematic design and reliability to choose decision elements with comparable delays. In any case, the observed delay of an element may vary somewhat under differing circumstances. Since a digital system may contain tens or hundreds of thousands of decision elements, and each of these elements may make many billions of decisions per day, designers must plan conservatively for delays.

The typical system design includes an oscillator that serves as an electronic clock. The oscillator output is shaped and used to delineate time periods known as *clock times* or *machine cycles*. The machine cycle may dip into the range 10 to 100 nanoseconds for a high-speed computer and the range 100 to 1000 nanoseconds for other computers. Let $c$ denote the period of a machine cycle. For control purposes, the designers may start with the machine cycle and define a series of periods, say $c, d, e, \ldots$, where $d$ is a multiple of the machine cycle, $e$ is a multiple of $d$, etc. In general, the more cycles in the series and the more systematically that tasks are made to coincide with cycles, the more the system is said to be *synchronous*.

Ideally, an *asynchronous* design would fix none of the time parameters, each task would finish its work with a completion signal, and tasks would start whenever prerequisite completion signals permitted. In practice, computer systems are synchronous in varying degrees, and high-performance systems tend to be less synchronous than systems of modest performance. The designers usually choose a product $bh$ that fits within a machine cycle $c$. A multiple of $c$ (say something near $10c$) is selected as a memory cycle, and computer-instruction executions are reckoned in units of memory cycles. Because auxiliary-storage and input/output tasks require much longer time periods, these tasks are handled on an asynchronous basis.

The transmission lines that move information from register to register, and the accompanying control lines, are among the most highly engineered units of a digital computer. The number of units is carefully minimized and each unit is synchronously allocated on a *time-slot* basis, where the time slot is typically a machine cycle. Line lengths are a critical factor in high-performance machines.

Within a digital computer, information is not only moved on a time-slot basis but control bits can be routed in parallel with data bits. This contrasts with the remote-transmission case, wherein control and data information are typically intermixed over the same communication channel and activities are essentially asynchronous. The contrast leads to a rather different set of technological problems.

## 7.9 The Digital Computer

Herman Hollerith's innovative punched-card machines for sorting and tallying (see Chapter 2) presaged a long and productive period of development in electrically driven devices for keying, reproducing, classifying, sorting, adding, multiplying, punching, and printing. Until 1948, when the first electronic calculating punch was announced, such machines were constructed solely from mechanical or electromechanical components.

In these electrical accounting machines, as they came to be called, each type of machine is designed to perform one class of functional tasks (in some cases, more than one function is embodied in a machine). The details of a function are indicated via the wires or patchcords of a plugboard. A file is stored as a deck of punched cards, each record being represented by one or more cards. A data-processing job involves input, intermediate, and output decks; the job is accomplished by passing decks through one functional machine after another, as required by the nature of the job. Decks are moved manually from machine to machine.

This functional approach to processing is less applicable to scientific and engineering computations than to accounting jobs. It lends itself to the construction of mathematical tables that can be obtained by progressive operations, one example being a table of squares—in summing odd integers, another square is obtained with each addition. But in computations involving trigonometric and exponential functions, complex numbers, result-dependent branches, searches for minimums or maximums, subarray searches, and thousands of intermediate numbers per final result, the digital accounting machines can be awkward and slow. For many years, scientists found more intuitive appeal in the possibilities of analog devices. For example, in 1925, Vannevar Bush, an electrical engineer at the Massachusetts Institute of Technology, spearheaded the construction of a large analog calculator from electric motors and mechanical parts. Variables were represented by angular rotations of gears. In an improved model, started in 1935 and completed during World War II, variables could be represented by voltages. Because the machine was useful for ballistics computations, its completion was a secret until the end of the war.

In 1937, George Stibitz, a mathematician in the Bell Telephone Laboratories, and Howard Aiken, a graduate student in physics at Harvard University, independently started thinking of ways of achieving a higher degree of automaticity in digital calculation. Stibitz's ideas led to a series of electromechanical calculators that were controlled by relays and instructed by paper tape; the first of these, designed for a class of complex-number computations, was completed in 1940. In 1939, the International Business Machines Corporation undertook to build a more ambitious machine proposed by Aiken. The Automatic Sequence

Controlled Calculator, Mark I, went into service in 1943 and was presented to Harvard in 1944. Data entered Mark I in the form of punched cards and results were punched into cards. The operations of the machine were controlled by information recorded on paper tapes. In the relay calculator, program loops could be simulated by paper-tape loops that moved under the control of a main tape. The dependence on tape loops placed a rather severe restriction on the class of algorithms that could be sequenced automatically.

In 1942, John Mauchly, a physicist at the Moore School of Electrical Engineering of the University of Pennsylvania, drafted an informal report on the possibilities of building an electronic computer. In April 1943, Mauchly and J. Presper Eckert gave a presentation to the director of the Ballistic Research Laboratory, Aberdeen Proving Ground, Army Ordnance Corps. In June, the Moore School entered into a contract to build an electronic calculator. ENIAC (Electronic Numerical Integrator and Computer) was completed in 1946. It contained over 18,000 vacuum tubes and successfully demonstrated the feasibility of electronic computers.

Although ENIAC performed arithmetic operations at rates that far surpassed any prior machine, the setup operations required before undertaking a new job were very time-consuming. The machine was costly to build, operate, and maintain, and its storage capacity was inadequate for many computational processes. By 1944, the designers were already at work part time on plans for an improved machine. A contract for an additional study was worked out with the Ballistic Research Laboratory, and in September 1945 Eckert and Mauchly submitted a formal report on plans for a second computer to be called EDVAC (Electronic Discrete VAriable Computer). For historical insights, we quote from the introduction to the report:

> 1.0 Historical Comments
>
> The Ballistic Research Laboratory of the Aberdeen Proving Ground is forced, by the nature of its work, to carry out numerical computations which are notable both for their volume and for the variety and complexity of the procedures employed. Of necessity, the Laboratory has become an important computing center. To expedite its work, it has sought improved techniques for the use of existing equipment and has fostered the development of new devices for "mechanizing" and speeding up the processes of numerical computation.
>
> In August, 1942, J. W. Mauchly summarized briefly, in memorandum form, the advantages to be expected from an electronic high-speed computer such as could reasonably be developed at the time. Capt. Herman H. Goldstine, of the Ballistic Research Laboratory, and Col. Paul N. Gillon, of the Office of the Chief of Ordnance, became interested in the possibilities of such a device for the Laboratory. Mauchly and J. P. Eckert, Jr. then wrote out a tentative technical outline of a machine which would be capable of numerically integrating trajectories for firing tables and which would handle other computing

jobs of similar complexity. J.G. Brainerd then incorporated this material into a report which was submitted to the Ballistic Research Laboratory. The United States Government then entered into a contract with the University of Pennsylvania, to have the Moore School of Electrical Engineering carry out research and development on electronic calculating devices for the Ballistic Research Laboratory. The project was set up under the administrative supervision of Dr. Brainerd with Mr. Eckert as chief engineer and Dr. Mauchly as principal consultant; Captain Goldstine was appointed to take technical cognizance of the project for the Laboratory.

Under this contract, a staff at the Moore School has, since July 1, 1943, worked continuously on the design and construction of electronic computing devices. A first machine, the Electronic Numerical Integrator and Computer (ENIAC) has been designed and constructed, and will soon be put into operation. It was necessary, in order to complete a task of this magnitude in little more than two years, to fix the design at an early date and to concentrate thereafter on production and testing.

During this latter period of work on the ENIAC, it became more and more evident that close scrutiny should be given to the way in which the high speed of electronic devices could be utilized in computing machines. It became apparent that serial operation was in general advantageous, and that when serial methods were used wherever possible the equipment was used most efficiently. Hence, in January, 1944, a "magnetic calculating machine" was disclosed, wherein the successive digits of a number were transmitted in timed sequence to a central electronic computing circuit and similarly returned to magnetic storage. An important feature of this device was that operating instructions and function tables would be stored in exactly the same sort of memory device as that used for numbers. The electronic switching means for such a machine were already disclosed—the ENIAC function tables use one form of such a switch.

The invention of the acoustic delay line memory device by Eckert and Mauchly early in 1944 provided a way of obtaining large high-speed storage capacity with comparatively little equipment. An automatic electronic calculating machine was then planned, using the delay line device for the "internal" memory, and using the somewhat lower speed magnetic devices only for input and output mechanisms.

It was clear that this new machine would, with much less equipment, easily handle problems beyond the intended scope of the ENIAC. Therefore, by July, 1944 it was agreed that when work on the ENIAC permitted, the development and construction of such a machine should be undertaken. This machine has come to be known as the EDVAC (Electronic Discrete VAriable Computer).

Although pressure of work on the ENIAC has made it impossible to conduct much experimental work on the EDVAC, all of the essential components to be used in the EDVAC are known to work. In designing a specific machine, however, a great number of decisions must be made—decisions as to quantity and proportion of various parts, and decisions as to which of several possible methods shall be employed. During the past year, many questions of this sort have been considered in a series of discussions held just for this purpose.

During the latter part of 1944, and continuing to the present time, Dr. John von Neumann, consultant to the Ballistic Research Laboratory, has fortunately been available for consultation. He has contributed to many discussions on the logical controls of the EDVAC, has prepared certain instruction codes, and has tested these proposed systems by writing out the coded instructions for specific problems. Dr. von Neumann has also written a preliminary report* in which most of the results of earlier discussions are summarized. In his report, the physical structures and devices proposed by Eckert and Mauchly are replaced by idealized elements to avoid raising engineering problems which might distract attention from the logical considerations under discussion.

It must be emphasized that final decisions on many questions cannot yet be made. In many cases, closer study of alternative circuit designs of further experimental data will be necessary before intelligent choices can be made. The discussions that have been held have served an essential purpose by formulating the important questions and indicating what experimental data is pertinent to their answers.

### 1.1 Contrast of the EDVAC with the ENIAC

The EDVAC and the ENIAC have very little in common. Although they are both electronic digital computing machines, the resemblance ends there. A few salient contrasts will emphasize this. In many respects the ENIAC is an electrical analogue of mechanical computing machines: it has decade counters instead of decade gear wheels, and all the decimal digits of a given number are added simultaneously as in any mechanical adding machine. Multiple channels and multiple equipment are necessary to do this. In the EDVAC, the various digits specifying a number will be transmitted serially through a single channel. Switching equipment is consequently simplified and reduced. Moreover, the storage or memory elements to be used in the EDVAC are entirely different from those used in the ENIAC. A typical unit, involving about 10 vacuum tubes, can be made to hold many digit sequences in definite time relationships.

In fact, the EDVAC will have an internal high-speed memory capacity for about 2,000 ten-digit decimal numbers, while the ENIAC accommodates only 20. Nevertheless, the EDVAC is expected to require only one-tenth as much equipment as the ENIAC. As a consequence, the solution of wide classes of non-linear partial differential equations will be easily managed in the EDVAC, whereas such problems can be carried out on the ENIAC only with the aid of a much slower external memory capacity in the form of punched cards.

Another important contrast between the ENIAC and the EDVAC is this: To change over from one type of problem to another, the ENIAC must be prepared by setting numerous switches and plugging in many interconnecting cables, while the EDVAC will be set up automatically and electronically for each new problem. Indeed, the EDVAC will store its operating instructions in exactly the same manner as it stores numbers. The total storage capacity will

*First draft of a report on the EDVAC: June 30, 1945.

> be at the disposal of the operator to allocate as he wishes—part to operating instructions, part to tables of functions, and part to the numbers which enter into and come out of the various calculations.
>
> The input and output devices for the two machines are also different. The ENIAC reads from IBM cards, and results are punched into IBM cards. It is expected that the EDVAC will read from a steel wire or tape on which the required information has been recorded by magnetic means, and that the output data will be magnetically recorded on steel wire. Typewriters for preparing such wire and for printing from wire records will be provided. Records on steel wire are less bulky and more easily and automatically handled than stacks of separate cards. Also, higher reading and recording speeds are attainable with steel wire than with cards or with paper tape. Sorting problems, for which cards have always been considered desirable, are also done expeditiously using wire.
>
> The EDVAC will be, then, a mathematical tool of much greater power and scope than the ENIAC. At the same time it will be physically smaller and easier to service.
>
> Finally, much attention has been given to the question of "coding the problem" so as to simplify the work of the mathematician who must "instruct" the machine as to what he wants done in symbols which the machine "understands." On this topic and many others the project staff at the Moore School has benefited greatly from conferences with and work done by Dr. John von Neumann, acting as consultant to the Ballistic Research Laboratory....

It is explicit in the report that computer instructions were to be units of information akin to problem data in format; therefore, instructions could mingle with data in storage and, if so desired, serve as data. The computer was not only to be automatically sequenced, it was to be controlled by a stored program. Although the Chief of Ordnance imposed a Confidential classification on the September report until 1947, many of the new ideas were discussed at a special summer session held by the Moore School in the summer of 1946. By this time, at the Institute for Advanced Study at Princeton, New Jersey, von Neumann was planning a faster computer. The stored-program concept received its classic formulation in a well-known IAS report of June 1946, by A. W. Burks, H. H. Goldstine, and J. von Neumann.

The development engineering required to implement the new ideas posed critical problems for several years. Also open to investigation was the potential range of applications for computers. The work at the Bell Laboratories, Harvard, the Moore School, and Princeton soon inspired computer-design projects at several university and industrial laboratories; the rationale for most of these projects was clearly scientific computation. Among those who foresaw a wider role for computers were Eckert and Mauchly. In 1946, they formed a partnership and went on to design UNIVAC (UNIVersal Automatic Computer, later known as UNIVAC I). This computer was at least as applicable to accounting applications as to mathematical computation. The general-purpose electronic computer entered the market place in March 1951, when the first-completed UNIVAC was formally accepted by the U.S. Bureau of the Census.

Some of the interesting design features of UNIVAC and two other rather early computers are summarized in Chapter 8. But to conclude this chapter of computer building blocks, we can hardly do better than discuss the organization of the EDVAC itself. In exploiting new and very shaky technologies, the designers carefully chose to implement the basic ideas of a computer in exceptionally straightforward ways. In so doing, they achieved a machine that was distinguished more by its conceptual clarity and simplicity than by its efficiency. The clarity suits our immediate objective, which is to view a whole computer, and the simplicity suits a secondary objective, which is to establish a standard of comparison for organizational innovations in subsequent computers.

The EDVAC described here is documented in a final contract report of 1949. Although a decimal machine was alluded to in 1945, EDVAC took shape as a serial binary computer. Moreover, the machine went into operation in 1950 with various changes to the design in the final contract report, and it was later modified several times before being removed from service on December 19, 1962. In any case, it was the plan for EDVAC that exerted influence at the time and is of interest in retrospect.

EDVAC memory consisted of 128 acoustic delay lines, each holding a sequence of 384 bits. Each delay line required a tank of mercury, and each bit in the line was represented by the absence or presence of a pulse of acoustic energy. As a bit emerged from the end of a tank, its electrical image was formed, returned to the head of the tank, and reentered in the acoustic image. Because electrical pulses travel much faster than sonic pulses, the return trip took relatively little time, and a given sequence of 384 bits, once loaded, could be circulated indefinitely. The storage elements were synchronized by an electronic clock that generated 1 million pulses per second, and each sequence of bits traversed its delay line once every 384 microseconds.

The 384 elements in a delay line were grouped into eight sections of 48 elements each. Four of the 48 elements were not available to the user; the other 44 stored a *word* of information. The word would represent an instruction or a number. Each of these 1024 (i.e., $8 \times 128$) memory words was given a location number, that is, an address, from the integers 0 through 1023. The choice of 1024 locations (as opposed to an even 1000, say) was based on the relation $1024 = 2^{10}$; which is to say that 1024 addresses could be represented by binary integers of ten bits.

Let the bits in a word be indexed 1 through 44. The formats of instructions and operands are shown in Fig. 7.24. Each instruction contains four ten-bit addresses—denote them $\boldsymbol{a}_1$, $\boldsymbol{a}_2$, $\boldsymbol{a}_3$, and $\boldsymbol{a}_4$—and a four-bit command. The command specifies an operation; the addresses provide the locations of two operands, the location at which to store the result, and the location of the next instruction to be executed. An operand consists of a 43-bit binary fraction (bits 1 through 43) and a sign (represented by bit 44).

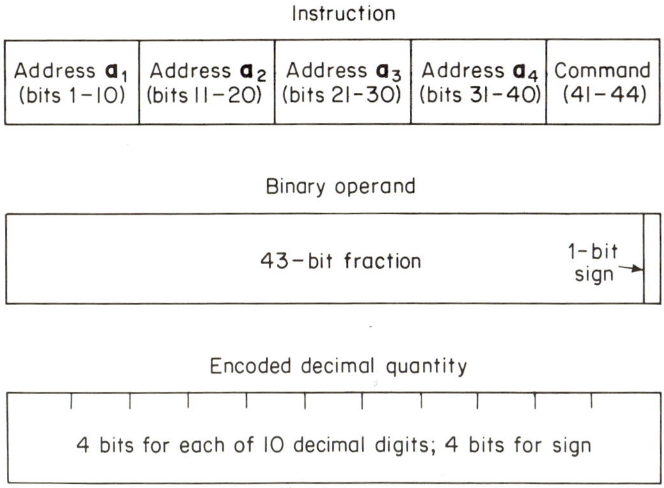


**Fig. 7.24** EDVAC word formats.

The 11 EDVAC instructions are summarized in Table 7.3. ADD and SUBTRACT are self-explanatory. MULTIPLY yields a 43-bit rounded product, while MULTIPLY EXACT yields an 86-bit exact product. Just as two $n$-digit decimal fractions, when multiplied, yield an exact product of at most $2n$ significant decimal digits, so two 43-bit binary fractions yield a product of at most 86 significant bits. The most significant half of the product is stored in location $\boldsymbol{a}_3$ and the least significant half in location $\boldsymbol{a}_3 + 1$. DIVIDE yields a rounded 43-bit quotient, and the remainder is lost. In DIVIDE EXACT, however, the unrounded quotient is stored in location $\boldsymbol{a}_3$ and the remainder in location $\boldsymbol{a}_3 + 1$.

COMPARE is similar to SUBTRACT except that the fraction of the difference is not saved and the choice of a next instruction is contingent on the sign of the difference. If the sign is positive, the next instruction is obtained from location $\boldsymbol{a}_4$ in the usual manner. If the sign is negative, a branch is taken and the next instruction is obtained from location $\boldsymbol{a}_3$.

HALT diverts the computer from automatic status to manual status. After execution of a HALT, the computer idles until the operator manually depresses a *start key* on the console, whereupon automatic sequencing resumes with the instruction at the location specified by $\boldsymbol{a}_4$ of the HALT instruction. VISUAL positions a spot of light on the face of one of three possible cathode-ray oscilloscopes. If designed with suitable image persistence, such a device permits curves to be plotted for visual or photographic purposes.

EXTRACT provides options for shifting the word from location $\boldsymbol{a}_1$, masking this shifted word with a word from location $\boldsymbol{a}_3$, and returning the result to location $\boldsymbol{a}_3$. The word at $\boldsymbol{a}_1$ remains unaltered. Among other uses, this instruction facilitates conversions between binary numbers and numbers consisting of binary-coded decimal digits.

## Table 7.3

*EDVAC instructions*

| Command | Nature of words specified by addresses in instruction | | | |
|---|---|---|---|---|
| | $a_1$ | $a_2$ | $a_3$ | $a_4$ |
| ADD | Augend | Addend | Sum | Next instruction |
| SUBTRACT | Minuend | Subtrahend | Sum | Next instruction |
| MULTIPLY | Multiplicand | Multiplier | Rounded product | Next instruction |
| MULTIPLY EXACT | Multiplicand | Multiplier | Product—upper half (lower half in $a_3 + 1$) | Next instruction |
| COMPARE | Minuend | Subtrahend | Next instruction (if sum negative) | Next instruction (if sum positive) |
| DIVIDE | Dividend | Divisor | Rounded quotient | Next instruction |
| DIVIDE EXACT | Dividend | Divisor | Quotient (remainder in $a_3 + 1$) | Next instruction |
| HALT | Irrelevant | Irrelevant | Irrelevant | Next instruction |
| VISUAL | *X*-axis position | *Y*-axis position | Select one of three scopes | Next instruction |
| EXTRACT | Operand to be shifted | Shift and mesh control | Operand and masked result | Next instruction |
| WIRE | First applicable location† | Wire control (with options) | Last applicable location | Next instruction |

†One read option permits an address to accompany each word on wire; in this option, $a_1$ is ignored and reading proceeds until an address from wire agrees with $a_3$.

WIRE selects one of three possible magnetic devices; indicates whether to write, read, or skip words; and indicates whether to wind the spool forward or backward. The number of words involved in a WIRE operation can be determined by $a_1$ and $a_3$, the addresses of the first and last memory locations involved in the execution. However, if each word on wire is preceded by a ten-bit binary address, an option permits the recorded address to indicate the memory register associated with the word. If this option is used, the operation continues until an address from wire agrees with $a_3$ of the WIRE instruction. (In the outcome, magnetic tapes replaced the planned magnetic wires.)

With these 11 instructions in mind, we can appreciate the EDVAC schematic in Fig. 7.25. The computer communicates with input and output devices, holds instructions and intermediate results in storage devices, and executes arithmetic instructions. Three one-word *storage registers*, implemented by short delay lines, support each adder; registers and adder are duplicated for the sake of er-

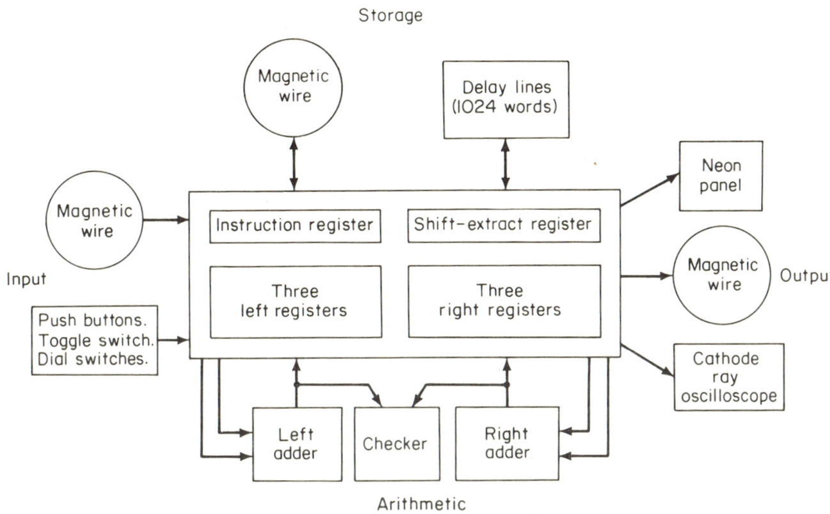


**Fig. 7.25** Schematic of functional EDVAC units.

ror detection. Moreover, a one-word *instruction register* holds an instruction during the period of its execution, and a one-word *shift/extract register* facilitates shifting and masking.

The magnetic wire served three functions. From a spool of magnetic wire, information could be read into the system, and, in fact, the only other means of input was provided by pushbuttons and switches at the operator's console. Switches at the console permitted the instruction register to be loaded manually (this was essential in starting a computation), permitted a word to be loaded into any desired delay-line location, permitted computation to be manually initiated or halted, and permitted the operator to specify one of four options for the computer in the event of sum overflow or of quotient overflow.

In multiplication of two fractions, the product must be a fraction. In addition and subtraction on signed fractions, however, the result may not be a fraction. Similarly, in division with fractions, the quotient may not be a fraction. Because EDVAC words accommodated fractions only, overflow had to be guarded against, or at least planned for, by the user. For sum overflow, the four options were (1) ignore the overflow, (2) halt, (3) branch to an instruction stored by console switches, or (4) branch to the instruction at an address indicated by the console switches. The options available for quotient overflow were similar.

EDVAC had three means of communicating to its environment. First, the magnetic wire could be used for output, in which case the rewound spool was removed to an auxiliary device for printing. Second, curves could be exhibited on the cathode-ray oscilloscopes. Finally, a panel of neon bulbs provided visual information useful in maintenance, program testing, and monitoring manual operations.

As indicated in Fig. 7.25, EDVAC provided two media for storage of instructions and operands. Each of the 1024 word locations in delay-line memory could be addressed by instructions. The memory was augmented by an auxiliary storage of magnetic wire under EDVAC control.

The eight EDVAC internal one-word registers were not addressable by the user's program and functioned solely during instruction execution. The miscellaneous counters and storage elements needed to store information for control circuits are not shown in Fig. 7.25.

Although EDVAC was a binary computer, it does not follow that input and output had to consist of binary numbers. A stored program could effect the necessary conversion between binary and decimal numbers, assuming that each digit of the decimal number was suitably encoded.

EDVAC was a serial computer. First, the execution of a given instruction ended before another instruction was fetched from the 1024-word memory. Second, in moving a word, one bit was moved at a time, starting with the sign bit. Additions and subtractions were performed serially on pairs of bits from two words. Third, multiplication was achieved by 43 repeated additions, and division was achieved by 44 repeated subtractions.

In a delay-line memory, the time required to fetch a word from the memory to an arithmetic register, or to return a register word to memory, is dependent on the temporal alignment of the word with respect to some physical access point. If the delay lines are 8 words in length, up to 8 words can pass the end of a given line before a desired word has been obtained. On the average, 4.5 words will pass, and at the minimum, 1 word will pass. Because the EDVAC delay lines were synchronized with the electronic clock, 1 bit emerged from a delay line each microsecond and 1 word emerged each *word time* of 48 microseconds. To estimate effective operating times for arithmetic operations, the word times required of four memory accesses (instruction, two operands, and result) pertained. These four accesses took 4, 18, or 32 word times—equivalent to 192, 864, and 1536 microseconds, respectively—for the minimum, average, and maximum cases. An addition or subtraction could be performed during the word time in which the second operand moved from memory to internal register. Thus the average ADD or SUBTRACT took 18 word times. Because 42 extra word times were needed to effect 43 additions, the average MULTIPLY took 60 word times.

DIVIDE took one more word time than MULTIPLY. Because it did not return a difference to memory, COMPARE took fewer word times than SUBTRACT. Table 7.4 gives the minimum, average, and maximum times (in microseconds) required to fetch and execute all EDVAC instructions. Clearly, memory access time was a very significant factor in EDVAC performance, and particularly so for instructions requiring little adder time, e.g., ADD, SUBTRACT, COMPARE, or EXTRACT.

One way for an EDVAC user to improve on the average of 4.5 word times per memory reference was to carefully plan the memory locations of his operands and instructions with timing in mind. By getting down in the neighbor-

**Table 7.4**

*EDVAC operating times*

| *Command* | *Microseconds required* | | |
|---|---|---|---|
| | *Minimum* | *Average* | *Maximum* |
| COMPARE, EXTRACT, VISUAL | 192 | 696 | 1200 |
| ADD, SUBTRACT | 192 | 864 | 1536 |
| MULTIPLY | 2208 | 2880 | 3552 |
| DIVIDE, DIVIDE EXACT, MULTIPLY EXACT | 2256 | 2928 | 3600 |
| HALT | | | |
| WIRE | About 35,000 per word transversed | | |

hood of 1.5 word times per reference, a user could triple EDVAC's speed. Although it could substantially reduce the running time of a problem, this placed a burden on the user and lengthened program-preparation time. The designers made the time saving possible when they chose to have each instruction specify the address of its successor. Given a memory technology for homogeneous memory-access times, the designers undoubtedly would have omitted field $a_4$ and required the instructions of a program to reside one after another in consecutive locations. Lest the shortcomings of the delay-line memory be overemphasized, it should be noted that EDVAC's greatest technological advance lay in its mercury delay line. With less than one-fifth of the vacuum tubes of an ENIAC, EDVAC far surpassed ENIAC in flexibility and roughly equaled it in arithmetic speed.

Tens of thousands of electronic digital computers have been built since 1949, all with a remarkable kinship to EDVAC. Although 20 years of hindsight make it easy for us to spot regions for improvement, it is only fair to add that the EDVAC designers were aware of some of the bottlenecks themselves. The delay-line memory is too slow, the adders are too seldom busy, the machine is too serial. The duplicated arithmetic unit pays rather dearly for error detection. The instruction set is too limited; the memory is too small; the input/output scheme was rather inadequate. Moreover, the system would prove to be tedious to program. Chapters 8, 9, and 10 are largely concerned with methods subsequently developed to improve the versatility and performance of digital computers.

## 7.10 Comment

We select a few additional references from the huge literature applicable to this chapter. The rapid development of magnetic-core memories can be seen from J. W. Forrester (1951), W. N. Papian (1953), E. D. Foss and R. S. Partridge (1957), and E. L. Younker (1957). For an early report on disk storage, see T. Noyes and W. E. Dickinson (1957). For trends in solid-state circuits, see R. A. Henle (1956), G. J. Pom and R. L. Crosby (1956), H. S. Yourke and E. J. Slobodzinski (1957), D. P. Masher (1960), and E. M. Davis et al. (1964).

A few books with relevance to this chapter are R. K. Richards (1955, 1957), M. Phister, Jr. (1958), W. Buchholz (1962), Y. Chu (1962), G. A. Maley and J. Earle (1963), and H. H. Hellerman (1967). H. J. Gray (1963) has given a short but very informative discussion of ENIAC. I am indebted to a personal communication from M. H. Weik, Jr., for information that "the power was removed forever from the EDVAC at the Ballistic Research Laboratories at the Aberdeen Proving Ground, Md., on December 19, 1962".

*Chapter 8*

# TASK SEQUENCING

The design of a digital computer enables complicated data-processing tasks to be fashioned from large numbers of simple tasks. If $Z$ is a complicated task and $A$ is a primitive task, numerous tasks of decreasing complexities intervene between $Z$ and $A$ in the typical data-processing system. Since a large number of $A$'s are typically required by $Z$, the time required to accomplish $Z$ is ultimately a function of (1) the time required by an $A$, (2) the efficacy of the algorithms that relate $Z$ to $A$, and (3) the parallelism or overlap attained with tasks. In this chapter, we are largely concerned with 3, the purpose being to further delineate the kinds of tasks that characterize most systems and summarize the main lines of development that have led to increasing degrees of task overlap.

## 8.1 Historical Introduction

The EDVAC progress report of September 1945 mentioned a pending decision between two serial bit-processing schemes. In the first, a word would represent a binary operand; in the second, a word would represent an operand of binary-encoded decimal digits. Although the decision went to the former, an alphameric generalization of the latter scheme reappeared in UNIVAC, which handled each character internally as seven serial bits. Akin to EDVAC in its delay-line memory, UNIVAC relied on magnetic tapes for both auxiliary storage and input/output. Up to ten magnetic-tape units could be attached to the system. Input instructions and data were separately recorded on tape at keyboard-to-tape and card-to-tape devices; results were mustered out from tape at tape-to-printer and tape-to-card devices. An electric typewriter at the computer console permitted programs to print messages to the operator, who could key in appropriate answers from a set of planned responses.

Although the first few UNIVAC's were delivered to the government, one soon went to the Metropolitan Life Insurance Company. For activities with huge tabulating and accounting applications, the significance of the general-purpose magnetic-tape UNIVAC was comparable, one might say, to the significance for scientists of Mark I, ENIAC, and EDVAC together—here was a promise of breakthrough after 60 years of functionally specialized punched-card processing. Thus in 1948, the Society of Actuaries established a Committee on New Recording Means and Computing Devices. In 1952, the committee tendered a report that contains five guideposts. These guideposts, which may be considered a manifesto for business data processing with computers, are still informative.

## Guideposts

So by actually trying to apply an electronic computer to the practices of one company, we evolved some guiding principles. These were:

1. An electronic computer should be applied to the whole job, not to some separately departmentalized piece of it. With such machines to work with it becomes a matter of sound economics to get as many things as possible done from one handling of the policy information regardless of whether or not such work is now being performed in one department or in several departments. We must remember that one of the reasons we have separate departments is that we cannot reasonably expect clerical groups to become thoroughly familiar with all the details in many different procedures. Therefore, we have to parcel out assignments, someone to calculate the dividends, someone else to figure loans. Now these machines have marvelous memories. They remember everything you tell them to do, down to the minutest detail, and what is often even better, they remember only what you tell them. Accordingly, the idea of breaking down a whole job in pieces in order to assign it to separate departments in manageable sizes requires much re-examination.

2. Small jobs should be combined with others. Electronic computers can be given the procedures for handling many different jobs and can switch over from one job to another with no elaborate change-over operation. This makes possible the mechanization of many areas in which the volume is now too small to warrant mechanical methods. Also, it appears to make possible the use of powerful machinery of this kind in smaller companies where the desired volume of work can be created by bringing together many different kinds of activities.

3. Source records should be consolidated. One of the most expensive phases of a computer operation is the "make ready" costs. There is a relatively large amount of work involved to get the proper information into the machines. Often it must be extracted from different card records, converted into the

punched hole form or magnetic tape form which the machine requires, batched up into controllable consignments, shipped to another department, proof-checked for completeness in the receiving department, and scheduled for machine processing. A great deal of this cost can be avoided by reducing the number of different places from which the information must be collected and, of course, if that information is kept in machinable form in the first place an expensive conversion operation is avoided.

4. Make all calculations at one time. It adds little if anything to the cost of an electronic computer operation to double or triple the amount of arithmetic which the computer is required to do with the information it has received. Once the information is in the machine, practically every useful figure should be developed, even though it may not now be customary to develop any such figures.
5. Use a self-checking machine. These computers apply a long series of operations automatically, move from policy to policy automatically, change the procedures automatically. In a short space of time they run through thousands of calculations. Certainly, we do not want to wait until after a large amount of work was done to find out that at an unknown point the machine had failed to recognize a signal or had inadvertently lost some of the information. On the other hand, we do not want to build in so many external clerical type checks, controls, and comparisons that we defeat the whole idea of automatic operation. Accordingly, machinery which controls and checks its own operation is highly desirable. If anything goes wrong it would not require an analysis of a very complicated machine, hours later, in order to set it right again.

To generalize this excerpt for many other applications, it suffices to substitute the word *record* for the word *policy*.

Despite the fact that the magnetic wires planned for EDVAC did not materialize, the decision to use magnetic recording for auxiliary storage was prophetically right. Although UNIVAC did not satisfy engineers and scientists as long as its designers may have hoped, its magnetic-tape auxiliary storage opened up an accounting-application market that proved mightier than the market for scientific computation. Within a few years after the Bureau of the Census accepted its UNIVAC, a majority of existing computers were being justified primarily for accounting applications. Batch processing (see. Sec. 4.7) has been based largely on tape-contained files. With interchangeable reels of magnetic tape, the auxiliary storage capacity of a computer is effectively unlimited. The guideposts clearly reveal that the digital computer encouraged users to generalize their concept of *tasks*. The computer would open up new vistas because (1) data processes could be sharply consolidated and (2) task switching could be effected rapidly.

Whenever an operable program is loaded into the memory of an electronic digital computer, the computer becomes a special-purpose machine for the class of tasks defined by the program. Conceptually, a computer is said to be general-purpose because a given memory-resident program can be replaced by simply reading another program from either an auxiliary storage or input device. Practically speaking, however, the interval of time elapsing between the last-executed instruction of one program and the first-executed of the next program is dependent on many factors, some of which have had an important bearing on the design of digital systems. Among these factors are the search capabilities and reading rates of auxiliary storage devices. Auxiliary storage units that can be removed from a device and replaced—magnetic-tape reels, for example—open the way for off-line keyboard, card reading, or printing operations. This permits faster data rates at program execution time but interposes manual operations that are likely to be slow.

Later sections discuss some of the schemes that have been used to achieve a reasonable minimum in the cost of idle facilities due to slow setup/setdown activities. Also to be discussed are methods of overlapping tasks. In Chapter 6, we pointed out that programs are algorithmic documents that do not treat of timing considerations per se. It is in the task, i.e., the execution of the program, that timing comes directly into play. This is not to say that the form of a program cannot affect execution times; it is simply to say that the author of a program must understand the machine environment in which the program is to be executed before he can judge between one form and another. In making such a judgment, the author is essentially stepping beyond the realm of the program to design a task.

Many of the considerations involved in efficient task handling were brought into the open by the designers of early computers. Since the basic timing concepts tend to be illustrated one by one in various of yesterday's computers, we shall return for a moment to the EDVAC and then discuss selected features of the UNIVAC, IBM 702, and IBM 704.

The EDVAC was an example of a highly synchronous computer with a serial-access memory. The machine cycle was 1 microsecond. Instructions and operands were fetched (or stored) one bit at a time. Given an ADD instruction and its operands, one pair of operand bits was processed at each machine cycle (bit time) and the addition was typically completed in a word time. The arithmetic circuits were frequently idle, however, because of the many word times elapsing in memory accesses and the absence of central registers for holding operands from one operation to another. Moreover, no arithmetic could be executed during exchanges between memory and storage.

The UNIVAC was designed around a serial-access memory (the best technology available) similar to that of EDVAC. The memory consisted of 100 delay lines, each storing 10 words. A word could hold 12 alphameric characters, or 11 decimal digits with appended sign, or 2 instructions. Since a character was represented by a code of 7 bits (6 for data, 1 for parity checking), each delay line contained more bits than in the EDVAC case. To compensate, the clock rate was increased to 2.25 million pulses per second, yielding a machine cycle of about 444 nanoseconds. When control pulses are accounted for, each word was equivalent to 13 characters (91 bits) and the word time was 40.4 microseconds, which is roughly comparable to the EDVAC word time.

In arithmetic operations, the 12 characters of an operand word were interpreted as 11 decimal digits and a sign. Each instruction (there could be two per word) contained an operation code and the memory address of an operand word. The second operand was obtained from a central register, and the result remained in a central register. Instruction words were addressed successively by an instruction counter that counted until reset by a successful branch.

The UNIVAC design went beyond that of EDVAC to have four central registers that could be used in various ways to preserve operands from one instruction execution to the next. To permit the programmer to manage these registers, more instructions were defined than in the case of EDVAC. UNIVAC was endowed with a 10-word register to facilitate the movement of tables or records from one memory area to another. It also had two 60-word buffer memories—one for tape input, one for tape output; once launched, a magnetic-tape read or write operation could proceed independently of internal processing. Internal processing had to be suspended during memory-buffer transfers, but since these transfers took relatively little time, the elapsed time for an application with a smooth balance among reading, writing, and processing activities approached the time required for processing alone. If reading or writing outweighed internal processing, an application was said to be computer-limited.

UNIVAC proved to be computer-limited on many scientific applications. It was more attuned to accounting applications, even though the fixed-length word and fixed-length tape block (60 words) were a programming nuisance and a performance handicap.

In the field of accounting applications, the first major competitor to UNIVAC was the IBM 702 Data Processing Machine. The 702 was introduced with a 10,000-character memory constructed of cathode-ray tubes. An important contribution of the 702 was the introduction of the variable-field-length (VFL) mode of operation. A 702 instruction consisted of five characters, but an operand field could be of any practical length. This simplified programming and encouraged efficient use of memory.

The 702 design also permitted the user to tie several kinds of input/output units into one unified system. Card readers, card punches, and line printers—as well as magnetic-tape devices—could be modularly attached to the processing unit and operated *on-line* under program control. By eliminating some of the manual steps that were previously required, the on-line mode of operation helped to reduce the elapsed time from arrival of job data to delivery of job results. Each card reader, punch, or printer in a 702 system was accompanied by a buffer that could communicate with the main memory. The buffers imaged a card or print line and permitted the slow mechanical actions of readers, punches, or printers to overlap other system activities. The buffering provision did not apply to magnetic tapes; the 702 designers made block length a parameter to be specified by the programmer.

The 702 designers employed a 7-bit character code similar to that in UNIVAC, a 1-microsecond machine cycle, a 23-microsecond character cycle, and a 5-character instruction. The 7 bits of a character were held in 7 different cathode-ray tubes that were accessed in parallel during a character cycle. To supplement the main memory, 2 accumulator storage units, each with a capacity of 512 characters, were provided. The accumulators were constructed of the same tubes as memory and were synchronized with memory. The character cycle was subdivided into fetch, arithmetic, and store phases of 6, 9, and 8 microseconds, respectively.

A statement of the form $x \leftarrow x + y$ was executed serially by character. In one character cycle, a digit of $x$ and a digit of $y$ were fetched, added, and the sum digit returned to $x$. The ADD instruction assumed that $x$ was held in a designated accumulator and $y$ was held in memory; the ADD MEM instruction assumed the opposite. Operands were signed; there were analogous instructions for subtraction; differences were obtained by complementing the operand $x$ and, if necessary to obtain a true result, recomplementing the result $x$.

With exceptions for a few special characters, the 7-bit IBM 702 code allocated a 4-bit subset for the representation of decimal digits. The 2 additional bits, i.e., the *zone*, needed for alphameric representation could be ignored in arithmetic operations. The seventh bit, the parity bit, was checked in data transmission. The sign of a numerical field in memory was not represented by a separate character, as in the UNIVAC case, but by a code in the zone of the low-order decimal digit. For arithmetic instructions, the zone codes served to delineate operands in memory. In an accumulator, on the other hand, a field was demarcated by a special character at the high-order end of the field, and the accumulator sign was separately stored.

Where EDVAC was serial by bit, the 702 was serial by character—with the difference that the 702 accommodated directly to fields of application-determined length, a noteworthy advantage for accounting applications. The time required to fetch and execute a 702 instruction was a function of the number of required character cycles. Where recomplementation was unnecessary, an addition leading to a result of $n$ digits required $n + 6$ character cycles: 5 cycles to fetch and interpret the instruction, $n$ cycles to perform the addition, and 1 cycle for control operations (such as sensing the accumulator mark). An additional $n + 1$ character cycles were required if the result had to be recomplemented.

Since the character-cycle organization of the 702 teamed harmoniously with VFL decimal arithmetic, the 702 design was to have a pervasive influence on subsequent computers intended for accounting applications. The machine was not intended for scientific computation. To glimpse the kind of word-cycle organization that is appropriate to applications with heavy computational loads, we consider a very different type of computer.

In science and engineering, it is easy to postulate computations that require many billions of additions and multiplications. The rates at which a computer can add, multiply, and fetch from memory are therefore matters of utmost concern. In their report of 1946, Burks, Goldstine, and von Neumann analyzed the possibilities of a computer in which the bits of a word would move in parallel between a memory and a parallel binary arithmetic unit. Subtraction would be performed by complementation and addition. An Institute for Advanced Study (IAS) computer, later developed as an embodiment of ideas in the report, used a cathode-ray-tube memory and stored negative numbers in the two's-complement form. Binary multiplication was executed by repeatedly shifting a partial product and adding the multiplicand; whenever a zero was encountered in the multiplier, time was saved by skipping the addition.

As an example of an IAS-influenced computer, consider the IBM 704. Announced in 1954, the 704 was a redesign of an earlier computer, the IBM 701. The 704 employed a magnetic-core memory, the 701 a cathode-ray-tube memory; the 704 provided instructions for binary floating-point arithmetic as well as fixed-point arithmetic, whereas the 701 did not.

The principal functional units and data paths in the 704 processing unit are depicted in Fig. 8.1. As the memory word contained 36 bits, the typical register held 36 data bits and the typical data path routed 36 bits. A fixed-point operand consisted of a sign and a 35-bit fraction. There were four main registers. All communication with magnetic core memory was through the *storage register*. Sums were placed in the *accumulator register*. The next instruction to be executed was held in the *instruction register*. Also, there were three *index registers*, each of 15 bits. An instruction of 36 bits typically contained three fields: (1) an encoded operation symbol, (2) a memory address (a binary integer of 15 bits), and (3) a 3-bit *tag* that could identify an index register. The instruction execution sequence was governed by the program counter, which counted until respecified by a successful branch instruction.

Assuming that $x$ was held in the accumulator and $y$ in the memory, two memory cycles were required for fixed-point execution of a statement of the general form $x \leftarrow x + y$. The first cycle (*instruction cycle*) obtained an instruction from memory; the second cycle (*execution cycle*) brought $y$ to the storage register, routed the contents of the accumulator and the storage registers to the parallel binary arithmetic unit, and returned the sum to the accumulator.

During an instruction cycle, the address of $y$ did not go directly to the address register from the storage register; instead, it went through the arithmetic unit. At the same time, if an index register had been identified in the tag field of the instruction, the register contents went to the arithmetic unit to be added to the address. Thus, if $y$ were a vector and the instruction ad-

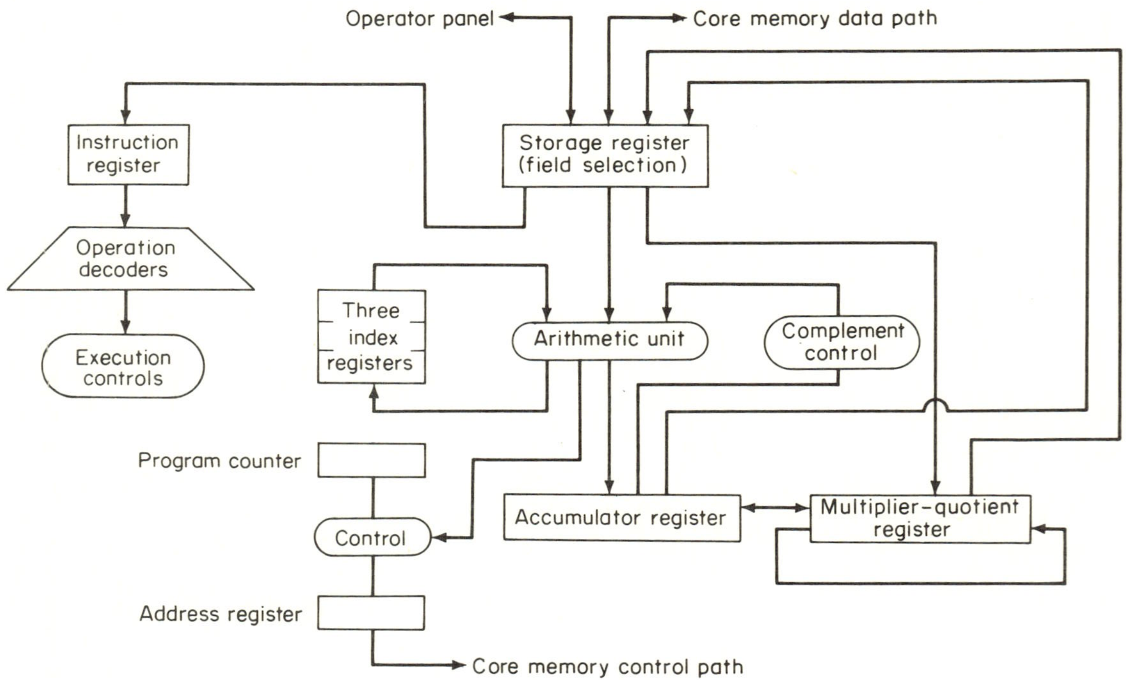


**Fig. 8.1** Principal functional units in a central processing unit (IBM 704 simplified).

dressed the first component of $y$, and if $i$ were held in index register, the statement $x \longleftarrow x + y_i$ was executed. In this case, the instruction was said to be *indexed*. If the add instruction were followed by instructions for index modification and conditional comparison, a short and very simple program loop could sum the vector.

The accumulator, jointly with the *multiplier/quotient* (MQ) *register*, possessed shift capabilities. (The latter register also possessed capability for left rotation.) In division, these two registers initially held a double-length dividend, whereas the storage register held the divisor. The accumulator held the partial dividend, which at conclusion constituted the remainder; quotient bits were left-shifted into the MQ register. In multiplication, the multiplicand was held in the storage register, the multiplier bits were right-shifted from the MQ register, and the partial product was developed in the accumulator. Right shifting brought the least significant half of the double-length product into the MQ register. Fixed-point multiply, fixed-point divide, and all floating-point operations required more than one memory-cycle time for execution. A memory cycle in the read-and-restore core memory completed its fetch about half way through the cycle. The other half of the cycle sufficed for adding operands in fixed-point addition and subtraction. In multiply or divide, two additions could be performed during each elapsing memory cycle of the operation.

The magnetic core memory of the 704 could be accessed every 12 microseconds. A fixed-point addition (or any similar instruction that required two memory cycles) was executed in 24 microseconds. The arithmetic unit became available every 6 microseconds. In fixed-point multiplication, 20 memory cycles (240 microseconds) were set aside for the required operations (which included an instruction fetch, an index addition, an operand fetch, and 35 full-length additions). As a result, the 704 was about 10 times faster than the planned EDVAC at fixed-point multiplication and, under average conditions, about 30 times faster at fixed-point addition.

The effectiveness of the 704 was further increased by the index registers, a memory with up to 32 times the capacity of the EDVAC memory, and instructions for floating-point arithmetic. (Floating-point arithmetic was one of the later improvements to the EDVAC design, incidentally.) All in all, the 704 circuits decoded about 8 times as many different instructions as in the case of the planned EDVAC.

For input/output operations, the 704 design assigned the MQ register the role of a buffer register and delegated the responsibility for memory-MQ transfers to the stored program. During such operations, therefore, much of the power of the central processing unit (CPU) went unused. Although some degree of overlap in processing and input/output was achievable, the MQ restrictions tended to idle the CPU during magnetic-tape operations.

The potential of a digital computer is limited by the rate at which information can flow between the memory and the CPU. There are many techniques for exploiting the potential, as we see later, but the rate itself is a fundamental parameter. The UNIVAC moved information bit by bit, the 702 moved 7 bits in parallel, and the 704 moved 36 bits in parallel. It was evident enough that the 702 approach had merit for accounting applications and the 704 approach for scientific computation. But two basic problems remained. First, few large digital computer installations can escape a job mix that includes both character processing and floating-point arithmetic. For example, program compilation, which consists heavily of character processing, is significant in nearly all installations. Second, the economical direction for performance improvement in a 702-like machine frequently led to a buffered balance between word-by-word memory accesses and character-by-character arithmetic. By the decade of the 1960's, technology offered enough modularity in memory capacities and speeds and enough economy in decision elements to support feasible solutions to both problems. In IBM's System/360, for instance, one instruction set is implemented over a wide spectrum of different performance levels. Most of the properties of parallel binary arithmetic are retained in the form of base-16 arithmetic, serial decimal arithmetic is easily provided in the base-16 framework, and alphameric characters are encoded in 8 bits.

## 8.2 Overlapped Operations

The typical computer has one program counter. When the computer is "running," its control circuitry deals with an incoming stream of instructions and launches executions one at a time. Functionally speaking, an arithmetic operation may involve four activities: (1) fetch the instruction from memory, (2) fetch two operands from memory, (3) perform arithmetic, and (4) store the result to memory. In the EDVAC, these activities occur serially and explicitly in the course of each arithmetic instruction. However, the introduction of a central accumulator—together with *load-accumulator* and *store-accumulator* instructions—simplifies the typical activities to (a) fetch the instruction, (b) fetch one operand, and (c) perform arithmetic. The UNIVAC employed the simplification, which is more efficacious for most computational loops. (Moreover, UNIVAC fetched two instructions at a time, a technique that has often been used in modified or generalized forms.)

**Look-ahead.** If an instruction stream is to consist largely of arithmetic instructions, a reasonable goal is a system design that will keep the arithmetic unit busy a high proportion of the time. Toward this end, one way to accelerate the stream is to overlap activities a, b, and c by performing a and b for instruction $n + 1$ while c is being executed for instruction $n$. This so-called *look-ahead* technique was not attempted in the IBM 704, which employed the arithmetic unit for indexing purposes, but it has since been used in high-performance computers by providing a separate unit for indexing arithmetic and extra buffer registers for instructions and operands. If the arithmetic unit is made sufficiently fast, it may be useful to generalize the idea of look-ahead, e.g., to overlap a for instruction $n + 2$, b for instruction $n + 1$, and c for instruction $n$.

Several factors prevent look-ahead from being a smoothly synchronous affair. First of all, arithmetic instructions may vary in required execution time. Moreover, the stream can contain instructions that

I. Load, modify, or test index registers
II. Branch conditionally upon index content
III. Branch conditionally upon accumulator state
IV. Store accumulator or index content
V. Control input/output

Since V, and I and II, need not affect the arithmetic unit, they can be picked out of the stream and handled on an overlapped basis. But III leads to the fundamental problem that limits the potential of look-ahead: The branch path to take is determined in an unpredictable way by the computational process itself. Essentially, the look-ahead designer has three choices: (i) curtail the look-ahead stream when a branch on data is encountered, (ii) follow one path and correct matters if it turns out to be the wrong path, or (iii) follow both paths until the correct path is known. Solution iii is very expensive, whereas ii may improve on i at reasonable cost.

The other look-ahead problem concerns IV, the store-to-memory instructions. Some guarantee must be provided by which an anticipatory fetch from memory location $m$ obtains current information (to guard against the possibility that the arithmetic unit is developing a result destined for $m$). The problem is conceptually simple, but solutions can be significant in terms of either extra equipment or of performance loss.

Fixed-point multiplication and division, and all four floating-point arithmetic operations, take longer in execution than fixed-point addition or subtraction. A great deal of developmental effort has been invested in algorithms and circuits that accelerate arithmetic operations, and the improvements have been impressive. In the IBM 704, for example, the carry in binary addition was treated as a process that took 36 units of time, 1 unit per adder stage; this treatment made the carry time a linear function of the number of stages. Designers soon noted that by using more circuitry, they could reduce the carry time to a logarithmic function of the number of stages. Such an approach might, for example, subdivide a 36-bit binary adder up as follows:

1. Twelve sections of three stages each
2. Three groups of four sections each
3. One word of three groups

Operand bits corresponding to each section may be thought of as a base-$2^3$ digit, to each group as a base-$2^{12}$ digit, and to each word as a base-$2^{36}$ digit.

The carries generated by all digits of a given base are determined in parallel: (1) base-2-generated carries are determined, (2) base-8-generated carries are determined, (3) base-$2^{12}$-generated carries are determined, and (4) the carry out of the whole arithmetic unit is determined. The information assembled in this treelike process is then filtered back to the leaves: (5) the carry into each base-$2^{12}$ digit is determined, (6) the carry into each base-8 digit is determined, and (7) the carry into each base-2 digit is determined. This general scheme is known in the literature as *carry propagation* or *carry look-ahead.* The longer the operands, the greater the relative gain in speed. Nodal degrees in the tree are limited in practice by the fan-in of available decision elements.

Methods such as these have led designers to arithmetic units that require very few core-memory cycles to complete a floating-point arithmetic operation. (In floating-point arithmetic, incidentally, there are more overhead operations for add than for multiply, and the ratio of multiply time to add time is much smaller than in the fixed-point case.) The tendency is for memory to become a bottleneck unless the design provides overlapping in memory accesses. One way of increasing the effective memory rate is to provide a bank of memory units with interleaved word addresses. With two units, for example, the odd-numbered locations might be assigned to one unit and the even-numbered locations to the other. This leads to a high degree of overlap in accessing programs or vectors.

Clearly, a computer that employs look-ahead and memory-interleaving principles has to be less synchronous than an EDVAC or a 704. In many high-speed computers, effective execution times can be quoted only as averages. The difference in a minimum and maximum execution time may be relatively high, and the performance of the computer for a given mathematical process may be significantly dependent on the organization of the program, the nature of the data, and the kinds of input/output activities that support the computation.

**Input/output overlap.** We saw that the EDVAC, the IBM 702, and the 704 lacked effective means of overlapping computational processes and information transfers between core-memory and magnetic-surface devices. (Whether the surface devices serve input, output, or auxiliary storage functions is irrelevant enough to be subordinated in much of the literature on computers, where *input/output* is often used to designate all traffic with memory.) The UNIVAC input/output scheme was very effective for some applications—sorting provides an example—but it lacked the flexibility and modularity desired of a general solution. The IBM 705, a successor to the IBM 702, likewise provided a scheme of limited utility: A tape read and a tape write could be launched simultaneously, so that the elapsed time required for the two operations was determined by the longer of the pair. However, internal processing ceased during input/output operations.

A general solution was pioneered in the experimental TX-2 computer at Lincoln Laboratories and in the IBM 709, a successor to the IBM 704. In the 709, where input/output blocks can be of arbitrary length, the main computer can delegate the execution of a block read or write to a limited-purpose computer called a *data channel.* A data channel not only has access to the memory, but it is directed by a stored program that requests memory cycles with a higher priority than the main program. In picturesque language, the data channel "steals" memory cycles. The main computer can be designed to mark time indefinitely while waiting for a memory cycle, whereas a magnetic device in motion must be serviced without undue delay.

By providing options for the number of data channels and the numbers and kinds of attachable devices, the data-channel scheme provides the modularity needed to configure a computer system to the needs of a given installation. The scheme has been a popular one, the main design question being how much functional capability to design into the data channel.

## 8.3 Interrupts

Before an instruction can be executed, the instruction must be fetched into an instruction register. The EDVAC, IBM 702, and IBM 704 fetch one instruction at a time and the UNIVAC two at a time. In so-called *one-address* instructions (UNIVAC, IBM 702, IBM 704), a nonbranch instruction typically contains the memory address of one operand, and a special instruction is provided for storing a result. In a *three-address* instruction (EDVAC provides an example), a nonbranch instruction contains addresses for two operands and the result. In a *two-address* machine, the instruction contains the addresses of two operands and the result is returned to the location of one of the operands.

Branch instructions excepted, each instruction in an EDVAC program states explicitly the location of a *next-executable* instruction. In the convention that has come to be typical, however, the next-executable instruction is implicitly assumed to reside in the next-higher memory location. Thus, if a nonbranch instruction occupies location $j$, the succeeding instruction is assumed to occupy location $j + 1$, and instruction succession comes to be implicit in a program counter that is augmented for each instruction. In this convention, a branch instruction in location $j$ contains an explicit address, say $k$. The effect of an unconditional branch is to reset the program counter to $k$; the effect of a conditional branch is to choose between location $j + 1$ (unsuccessful branch) and location $k$ (successful branch).

The events that reset a program counter may be a successful conditional branch, an unconditional (always successful) branch, or an *interrupt.* Because branches are inherent in the idea of a program, we are already very familiar with them. But the objective of an interrupt, as suggested by the term itself, is to seize control from one stored program and pass it to another. Before discussing the potentialities of interrupts, we pause for a few more definitions.

Consider a typical computer (capable of recognizing one instruction at a time) and let it contain $n$ stored programs $P_1, P_2, \ldots, P_n$. From the vantage point of the computer's functional decoding and execution units, arriving instructions constitute a single instruction stream, irrespective of which program may be the source. We say that program $P_i$ is *active* if it yields the instruction currently being recognized. While $P_i$ is active, the other $n - 1$ programs are *passive*. We also say that an active program is *in control* of the computer.

When a successful branch resets the program counter, the action ordinarily takes place within the context of a given active program. Only in unusual cases is a branch used to pass control from an active to a passive program, thereby interchanging the status of the two programs. The main function of an interrupt, on the other hand, is to interchange the status of two programs; the normal result of an interrupt is that an active program becomes passive and a passive program becomes active.

To simplify the problem of interacting programs, typical practice will designate a master program, the *control program*, as the only program that can seize control via interrupts. The control program, which obviously plays a key role in the sequencing function, is held in readiness in memory during normal operation. Because the control program serves a general-purpose function for all other programs, there is ample justification for viewing it as an intrinsic part of the digital computer system.

Although the events ordinarily permitted to cause interrupts are of two kinds—externally imposed and internally generated—the applicable principles are much the same in both cases. Requests are permitted to signify themselves by a *flag* (the ON status, say, of a storage element) in an interrupt mechanism that is scanned each time the program counter is reset. Typically, if one or more interrupt requests exist, the interrupt mechanism will save the content of the program counter and pass control to the control program. The control program may preserve the contents of relevant central registers, determine which request to honor (if more than one flag is ON), and pass control to the appropriate program by branching to a previously agreed-on location. Some convention must be provided whereby a program can branch back to the control program.

Externally imposed requests may be digital signals from analog-digital converters or manually operated terminals. These request the control program to perform a service or to activate a service program. On the other hand, internal requests are generated as a consequence of exceptional circumstances encountered during instruction execution: result overflow, a checking error, a wait or stop instruction, and the like. These are requests to the control program for assistance, temporary deactivation, or termination. Moreover, the functional capabilities of the control program can be extended by timing mechanisms of two kinds: one that interrupts periodically and another that can be preset to interrupt after a specified lapse of time.

The notion of internally generated interrupts was present in primitive form in the overflow mechanisms of the EDVAC design. The use of interrupt for externally imposed requests was pioneered in the ERA 1103, an early scientific computer that was contemporary with the IBM 704. In both instances, the interrupt design was motivated by a "special case"; i.e., the purpose was to extend the functional utility of a single program. Until the concept was generalized in more flexible interrupt mechanisms, the potentialities for switching from program to program were little appreciated. Given a facile interrupt mechanism, the control program becomes the sequencing center of a digital system. The control program can allocate "bursts" in the instruction stream to different programs as required by impinging events and it can assign and reassign physical resources (memory and input/output devices). As a consequence, the control program can attempt to optimize the sequencing of tasks and the allocation of resources.

Jointly, the interrupt mechanism and control program provide one of the greatest challenges to system designers. Conventions need to be established for the handling of different classes of interrupts, of priorities and methods of changing priorities, of interrupts in programs invoked by previous interrupts, and the like. Some of the overall advantages that accrue are discussed in Sec. 8.4, whereas a special application will be mentioned here to round out the discussion of data channels in Sec. 8.2.

After one has invested in one or more data channels that can interpret and direct the execution of input/output instructions issued by the main computer, the problem becomes one of using such channels effectively. The typical input/output transfer persists thousands of times longer than an arithmetic operation, and the program that launched the transfer has no way of predicting the event of completion. On the other hand, the logic of the program usually dictates the earliest point in time, say $t$, at which the next block transfer can be launched. If the program inquires of the data channel at point $t$ and finds the channel busy, at which point should it inquire again? The logic of the program may not provide many points at which it is convenient to treat input/output matters, and these points may be ill-timed in many circumstances. Input/output not only becomes a nuisance at best, but it is highly unlikely that the data channel will be used in an optimal fashion because many transfers may be launched much later than necessary.

A more satisfactory solution has the data channel interrupt the main computer at completion of a transfer. The interrupt can be viewed as a request for more work. If a task awaits the channel, it is launched immediately; if no task awaits, the channel has at least made known that it is ready for another task as soon as one becomes available.

## 8.4 Multiprogramming

In the context of a computer installation, a *job* is a service performed at request. Some jobs will be performed periodically, others at special request. We may assume that system conventions establish the information to be provided by a request: the name of the job, the identity of the requester, essential input data, etc.

Job processing may involve three different phases. First, the request must be recognized and accepted by the system. Second, the request and its attendant information may reside temporarily in a queue. Third, the processing required by the job is initiated and performed. The time lapses associated with these phases are herein called *honor time*, *wait time*, and *service time*, respectively. The sum of honor time and wait time is *reaction time*; the sum of reaction time and service time is *response time*. In the usual system environment, honor, wait, and service times are not job parameters because they depend on the state of the system, the current workload, and relative job priorities. Even after a job is initiated, the system may interrupt the job to pursue another job of higher priority, thus extending the service phase. Let job A be interrupted for job B. Then job A's service time can be further subdivided into busy time and additional wait time.

Associated with any job worth doing is a *response limit*, an upper bound on acceptable response time. For computers that can execute instructions in microseconds and receive requests via communication lines, response limits measured in fractions of a second are not out of the question. On the other hand, most computing centers deal with some low-priority jobs that can wait for hours or even days without impairing the value of the results. In a mixture of computer applications, therefore, jobs may be accompanied by response limits varying all the way from milliseconds to days.

The job is a user-defined unit of work that is useful for accounting purposes and overall control. The instruction is a computer-defined unit of work. Because the job and the instrution differ so widely in motivation and scope, many system designers find it convenient to interpose another category between the two. This category provides for the task, a unit of work defined by the programmers who equip the installation with a program library. Each task is associated with a named program, and the function of the program is to define and direct the task. A job consists of one or more tasks.

The complicated interaction between a computer system and its jobs can be suggested with the aid of another classification that merely recognizes the broad kinds of functional activities that must be carried out by the system. Since the classification to be discussed makes no attempt to isolate functions that can be easily measured, it is strictly meant to be a pedagogical crutch. Consider six classes of activities:

| | | | |
|---|---|---|---|
| UT: | setup time | IT: | input time |
| DT: | setdown time | OT: | output time |
| TT: | terminal time | PT: | processing time |

*Setup time* includes the time required for all make-ready activities needed to prepare the system for the tasks implied by the given job. It may include manual operations such as loading card decks, mounting magnetic surfaces, or inserting plugboards; it includes searching and reading operations that locate needed programs in auxiliary storage and transfer them to memory. Setup time is highly dependent on system design. In a special-purpose airborne computer, designed to exceptional standards of compactness and reliability, setup time may not be an important consideration. For a general-purpose computer, on the other hand, setup time is an important consideration in system design. *Setdown time*, which is somewhat analogous to setup time, includes the time required to interrupt or terminate work that is underway. Examples are removing card decks, dismounting magnetic surfaces, and preserving intermediate results in auxiliary storage.

*Terminal time* is included to recognize the possiblity of direct communication between man and system via switches and displays, keyboards and typewriters, interactive display devices, etc. It is significant because manual operations take place on a dramatically different time scale than computer operations. In the early days of computers, it was not uncommon for programmers to do some of their program debugging at the computer, using the operator's console as a terminal device. This practice was soon discouraged. (Now, the trend is toward greater use of terminals, but in the context of multiple terminals and a high degree of overlapping, as we shall see later.)

*Input time* is the computer time used in reading into memory and *output time* the computer time used in writing out of memory. *Processing time* consists of the time required for the main computer to do the arithmetic, logic, and editing operations required of the job.

One way to utilize a system is to process jobs one at a time and to perform setup, setdown, terminal, input, output, and computation activities serially. In this mode, much of the setup may take place at job outset and setdown at job ending, with the other activities consisting naturally of interspersed operations. The job time $t$ required to perform a job in the serial mode is given by

$$t = \text{UT} + \text{DT} + \text{TT} + \text{IT} + \text{OT} + \text{PT}. \tag{8.1}$$

Suitable mainly for jobs with lenient response limits, the serial mode lends itself best to low-cost systems. Given a sufficient workload, the serial EDVAC-like mode is noncompetitive with more complicated modes.

**Setup and setdown overlap.** By providing faster and faster computers, designers soon forced a careful reexamination of setup and setdown activities. The typical solution has been to provide a marginal reserve in system capacity—

particularly in the number of input/output devices—and to place the setup function under the direction of a memory-resident control program. The control program can analyze the job stream, direct make-ready operations for the next job while the current job is in the execution stage, and direct cleanup operations for the prior job as well.

The discussion of setup has already suggested that we look beyond the individual job. To analyze job scheduling further, our perspective must shift toward a sequence of jobs. First, it should be mentioned that the jobs of a typical batch may differ widely in their requirements. Some jobs will be relatively high in IT or OT and others relatively high in PT.

**Input/output-process overlap.** Assuming that setup and setdown activities can be overlapped, and ignoring terminals for the time being, much can be done to improve system scheduling for a given job. At some marginal cost in extra instructions, channel circuitry, and additional buffer areas in memory, a system can be designed with data channels that permit the input/output tasks to be overlapped in various ways with processing operations. If IOT denotes the input/output time for the available number of channels, then the ideal time required for a job is

$$t = \max(\text{UT}, \text{DT}, \text{IOT}, \text{PT}). \tag{8.2}$$

The ideal expressed by (8.2) may be approximated in some applications. On the other hand, it may be poorly approximated in many applications unless a good deal of planning effort is lavished on the job programs. The problem is that the logic of the job may bunch the input/output tasks in such a way that the channels are overbusy at various points in the job and idle at others. It should be noted that PT is not truly independent of IOT: PT can lengthen to some degree where input/output tasks are stealing memory cycles.

**Concurrent jobs.** If IOT is decidedly out of balance with PT, there is little value in overlapping the two. The only way to achieve a better balance is to concurrently process two or more unbalanced and complementary jobs. This can be done with the aid of an interrupt system and a control program that regulates the instruction stream and allocates bursts of computer time to contending jobs. The objective of the control program is simply to busy the system more effectively with input, output, and computation tasks. If every job is balanced in respect to these tasks, job concurrency cannot be expected to improve system throughput. In fact, however, many jobs are far from attaining a balance.

To illustrate the rationale for concurrent job execution, or *multiprogramming*, as this mode of operation is usually called, consider a small numerical example that ignores setup and setdown. The table in (8.3) contains hypothetical times for two jobs and three categories, IT, OT, and PT:

| | IT | OT | PT | Row Total | Row Maximum |
|---|---|---|---|---|---|
| Job 1 | 20 | 14 | 6 | 40 | 20 |
| Job 2 | 4 | 6 | 30 | 40 | 30 |
| | 24 | 20 | 36 | 80 | 36 |

(8.3)

In a serial mode, the system requires 80 units of time to process the two jobs. If the jobs are executed sequentially, but input and output overlap one another, 18 units of time (viz., 14 + 4) are saved and the total declines to 62. If input, output, and processing are all overlapped but jobs are executed sequentially, the job times reduce to the row maxima in (8.3) and the two jobs occupy 50 units of time. If the two jobs are multiprogrammed, the applicable total time is 36 units, as given by the maximum of the bottom row in (8.3). One can pursue the analysis to permit overlapping within IT and within OT, but this would take more data. To summarize for (8.3), therefore, the ideal times are as follows:

1. Sequential job execution:
   a. Serial mode — 80 units
   b. Concurrent read/write — 62 units — (8.4)
   c. Concurrent read/write/process — 50 units
2. Multiprogramming mode:
   d. Concurrent read/write/process — 36 units

There are three reasons why these ideal times tend to be optimistic. In cases c and d, the channels may delay internal processing by stealing some of the memory cycles requested by the central processing unit. The marginal processing time normally represents a small percentage increase, but it exists and it can be significant where processing time determines elapsed time, as in case d. Second, status switching between two or more concurrent jobs requires attention from a control program at each change of status; as a result, control-program executions add marginally to the processing time in case d. Third, if the logic of the jobs being processed demands a lumpy distribution of input/output tasks with respect to time, the channels may occasionally be a bottleneck that idles the active job (hence, the central processing unit) until a critical input/output task is completed. To sum up, an ideal processing time may be lengthened by (1) memory-cycle stealing, (2) control-program interventions for program-switching purposes, and (3) input/output overloading. If elapsed time is determined by input/output time, it should be noted, factors 1, 2, and 3 may be inconsequential in the determination of elapsed time; the primary consideration is simply one of keeping the channels busy. In one way or another, factor 3 can affect cases b and c in (8.4), and factor 1 can affect case c, but case a is insensitive to all three penalties.

In a sense, multiprogramming is a necessary evil. Were all jobs balanced with respect to input/output and processing, and comparable in priority, multiprogramming would be a nonproductive complication. In practice, of course, the typical installation has a haphazard collection of jobs of widely differing sizes, priorities, and balances. Some jobs consist almost entirely of processing and others almost entirely of input/output. In the face of such diversity, the installation manager is naturally willing to invest some fraction of his resources in multiprogramming as long as the gain in throughput more than rewards the outlay.

Another important motivation for multiprogramming stems from *real-time* jobs with low response limits. Because a low response limit requires that setup time be low, the real-time application program and its files must be held in a suitable degree of readiness. Moreover, to accommodate such an application, system capacity must suffice for the peak loads, even though these peak loads may occur infrequently. Here, the rationale for multiprogramming is obvious: Multiprogramming can be helpful in exploiting remnant system capacity for jobs with more lenient response limits.

We have been ignoring terminal management because it involves all facets of sequencing. First of all, it should be mentioned that every computer includes some form of an "operator's console" that may be looked on as a special-purpose terminal. Such a console is essential in launching the operation of a stored program computer because it permits the operator to direct an idling computer to read and initiate execution of a utility program. This IPL (initial program load) procedure can bring in additional programs that ready the system for operation, usually with the aid of manual setups by the operator. A keyboard and typewriter-like printer at the operator's console can facilitate communication between the system and the operator. No significant sequencing problems are involved.

Genuine sequencing problems do arise, however, where the application environment postulates remotely located terminal devices. At any time, a device at a given terminal may request the attention of the central computer for the performance of a service. Typically, the needed programs exist in a central stored library under computer control; quite likely, related files also reside in the library. Directives of various kinds, and instructions and data not available in the library, must be keyed from the terminal at manual rates. Response limits may vary for different classes of outputs. For example, voluminous listings may be designated for messenger or mail, whereas summary results are printed or displayed at the terminal.

Terminal management may be considered an instance of multiprogramming with *n* overlapping jobs. But note that many factors are at work to aggravate the sequencing problem: *n* may be large (say between 10 and 1000), and the slow input/output rates of terminal devices place exceptional burdens on the data assembly and dispersal functions. A *terminal* typically embraces such functional devices as keyboards, card readers, card punches, slow printers, paper-tape readers or punches, video displays, and the like. For slow devices, it may be most economical for the system to treat each transmitted character piecemeal. As a result, certain setdown and setup activities are taxed, and the system design must emphasize efficient data-channel and program-switching facilities.

From the viewpoint of the system designer, a very significant difference between ordinary multiprogramming and terminal management is that requests for service originate from terminals on an unscheduled basis; the system has no direct control over the sporadic patterns of requests. The system is not only on-line, but it must design for peak loads on the basis of probabilistic assumptions. As in any system configured for peak loads, it is natural to exploit remnant computer capacity by multiprogramming low-priority jobs.

It should be clear by now that a general-purpose computer system designed for multiprogramming must suitably provide for an interrupt mechanism, for data channels, and for a control program. One other functional requirement must be satisfied: the requirement for *memory protection.* In other words, after a program has been allocated a memory area, that allocation must be assured. The need for this becomes obvious when one considers that some of the jobs to be executed will be debugging exercises. To date, the experience of the industry testifies that it is folly to ever assert that a large program is "fully debugged." The number of possible paths through a nontrivial program, considered in the light of differing data possibilities, is so large that many paths will never be traversed during the useful life of the program. To put it another way, "full debugging" of a program library, as we now envision and design such libraries, is a data-processing job that far surpasses the capacity of all computers. Computation is not perfection; the marvel is in the utility of quality controls based on informed debugging.

At present, the most typical technique for memory protection is to have a hardware mechanism monitor the given memory address at each memory access and interrupt to the control program if the given address is outside the range allocated to the active program. The control program itself may be given certain liberties, for example, to branch to the areas of other programs.

**Modes of operation that employ multiprogramming.** With the aid of a control program, an interrupt mechanism, a memory protection mechanism, and data channels, a variety of multiprogramming modes become possible. We shall list the modes that have been most clearly characterized to date.

In *remote job entry*, jobs are communicated to a computer center via a communication line, and some or all of the results are returned in the same way. The response limits are relatively long, and a job is handled on a routine basis. The communication function is eased as much as possible by storing necessary programs and files at the computer center.

In *time sharing*, the basic objective is to reduce turn-around times for the users of a computing center. The individual user, working at his terminal at a human pace, cannot ordinarily make effective continued use of the central computer. To counter this, a number of users are permitted to work concurrently, and each can get a quota of computer time at frequent intervals. Because this mode of operation entails some setup at each interval, it has been little used for accounting applications that involve large files. It is particularly suitable for jobs that can be accommodated in memory and moved intact to random-access auxiliary storage, thus limiting the setdown/setup operations to traffic between the memory and direct-access auxiliary storage.

In *teleprocessing*, the application is typically fixed and its programs and files are held in continual readiness at the computer center. Inputs from remote terminals consist of standardized requests for service that include small quantities of data. The terminal operator expects a reply in a very few seconds, as he may have to query the center for additional information and enter into a short dialogue. At any one time, the central computer may be handling a number of queries at various stages of completion. An airline reservation system exemplifies this mode of operation.

In *process-control* applications, input measurements are periodically processed and "out-of-control" conditions result in exceptional processing aimed at reoptimizing the process. There are wide variations in the extent to which human beings must intervene in the reoptimization phase.

A *command-and-control* application may combine the properties of process control and teleprocessing applications and introduce exceptional degrees of complexity in the terminal devices, the modes of communication, and the nature of the requests to be serviced. Ground-based systems for monitoring and controlling planes, missiles, and satellites provide characteristic examples.

For lack of a more descriptive term, *batch processing* is often used as a comprehensive term for the mode of operation that does not have to contend with remote terminals or sensors. Multiprogramming may be employed to improve equipment utilization (and hence, job throughput) for a mix of jobs. Because other modes of operation tend to configure for peak loads, they are often combined with batch processing. As experience accumulates, the tendency to generalize concepts and to combine various operating modes within one system configuration may be expected to continue. It is probably safe to expect that new modes of operation will spring up at roughly the rate at which old ones are being synthesized.

## 8.5 On Multiprocessing

Multiprogramming is fundamentally a technique for chopping up the instruction stream of a digital computer and assigning each chunk of the stream to one of $n$ contending jobs. It may make the computer appear slower to a given job, but it does not change the properties of the computer. Each contending job sees a general-purpose computer.

*Multiprocessing* is a more elusive concept; the term has been used in several contexts to suggest system resources that permit unusual degrees of task overlapping. We must mention four instances to make the discussion usefully concrete.

First, a few ultra-high-speed computers have been designed with more than one arithmetic unit. The idea has been to accomplish a higher degree of overlap in one instruction stream, i.e., to generalize the look-ahead technique mentioned in Sec. 8.2. As in that case, however, the design is usually intended to simulate a computer with a single program counter. Any application program can be executed correctly, albeit some ways of writing a program may run much faster than others. The design may include two or more arithmetic units or it may specialize the arithmetic units to provide, for example, two add/subtract units and two multiply/divide units.

Second, the data channels of computer system A may be replaced by a full-blown computer system B (with data channels of its own). The problem of synchronizing input/output tasks with the main computer A still exists, but the functional role of B can be generalized beyond that of a data channel to that of any computer. B can then perform, for example, code conversion, generalized editing, formatting, searching, and sorting tasks. Some advantage may be gained from specialization, as by omitting a floating-point arithmetic unit from B. If A is being designed to maximize internal speed in the face of technology barriers, the inclusion of B may be one useful way of enhancing system performance.

Third, in some real-time applications, the requirement that a computer system remain in operable condition very nearly 100 percent of the time is such a critical factor that some throughput capacity is gladly traded for increased reliability. One way is to start with $p$ processing units, $m$ memories, $n$ auxiliary storage units, $d$ data channels, and then design a system that (1) permits communication from each processing unit to each memory, each memory to each data channel, each data channel to each auxiliary storage unit, etc., and (2) permits faulty units to be electrically isolated and "configured out" of the system under program control. The cost of doing all this is, of course, significant, but the probability that the system will be completely inoperative dwindles very dramatically for relatively small degrees of replication, say for $p = m = n = d = 3$. In addition to the extra engineering costs, one should reckon with the extra programming costs involved in making effective use of the system. Let us assume that the application is programmed to (1) work comfortably with three processing units, (2) reduce service and postpone some tasks with two processing units, and (3) limp along on an emergency basis with one processing unit. The analysis and programming effort required to achieve this could possibly exceed the effort required for three uniprocessing applications of complexity comparable to case 1. In a sense, three different applications are being supported and coordinated.

At one time or another, all three of these examples have been called *multiprocessing*. The third is motivated toward improving system reliability. The first and second are primarily ways of extending system performance, and as such, they compete with *array processing*, the fourth and final approach to be mentioned. Experience has shown that many of the computations of mathematical analysis and engineering are based on algorithms that require similar sequences of arithmetic operations at each point in an array. S. H. Unger (1958) directed the interest of computer designers to computations in which each point could be associated with a processing unit capable of communicating with its nearest neighbors in a two-dimensional grid. This scheme leads to a special-purpose system in that only a relatively small class of applications adapt themselves well to such a grid. A noteworthy example of a grid computer system is the ILLIAC IV described by G. Barnes et al, (1968). The system is planned with 256 processing units in addition to a conventional computer.

On the other hand, work on programming languages has convinced many people that vector operations lend themselves naturally and usefully to a wide class of applications. At present, there seems to be growing interest in computer systems with a capability for executing instructions on vector operands. Scalar operands can be treated as vectors of dimension 1. Except where the program refers exclusively to scalars, the system fetches and interprets fewer instructions than a conventional computer. The system must be designed to efficiently process vectors of a given dimension, say $r$, but operands of any dimension $n$ can be subdivided into infixes of dimension $r$ or less. The design may provide for $r$ floating-point arithmetic units, or it may not. One alternative to $r$ units is an arithmetic unit equipped to process several vector components in "pipeline" or "bucket-brigade" fashion; an example of this is discussed by J. F. Ruggiero and D. A. Coryell (1969).

## 8.6 The Control Program

Seen from an abstract management viewpoint, a data system comprises four classes of entities:

1. Physical resources
2. Programs
3. Structurands
4. Jobs in process

An installation with one job, one program, one static set of structurands, and faultless hardware would have little use for a control program. The control functions of *entity accounting*, *resource allocation*, and *task sequencing* would wither away. But computer installations face a nonideal environment, and entity accounting typically involves a myriad of detail, as does any complicated accounting application. Every resource, every program, every structurand, and every in-process job must be systematically described and the description somewhere stored in a record available to the control program. Although a nucleus of the control program must reside permanently in memory, we may presume that much of the information maintained by the control program is held in auxiliary storage.

Of course, entity accounting is not an end in itself; its purpose is to provide enough information so that the control program can do an effective job of allocating hardware and sequencing the instruction stream. At the level of decision-making, the control program can be designed to interact with a human operator, thereby permitting the operator to change priorities or override standard allocation policies at the last instant. This raises a more general question: When are entity records established and where and when does the information contained in them arise?

Although the mechanics of the system must vary from one entity class to another, we can readily list the main junctures at which information arises. These are

1. Control-program generation
2. Source-program documentation
3. Program assembly or compilation
4. Job-request documentation
5. Job-request recognition
6. Job setup (including program loading)
7. Program execution

Assuming that a control program can be tailored to the needs of a given installation, the records that describe physical resources (memory areas, channels, channel-connected devices) can be established at the time the control program is generated, as can the records needed for related systems programs (such as language translators and sorts) or for segments of the control program itself. Of course, the records may have to be updated frequently, even though their life span is long.

We see that information destined for the control program may enter the system via the source program, during compilation of the source program, and via a job request. Provisions may be made for human intervention to modify or fully complete this information at the time a job is initiated or a program is loaded for execution. Obviously, the process as a whole requires a consistent adherence to systematic standards and conventions. These standards and conventions may appear somewhat arbitrary and unmotivated to the casual user of a computer who is not interested in unusual options or operating modes.

From the human-factors standpoint, therefore, it is important that job-request conventions (and high-level languages) be designed in such a way that the user can ignore complications he is not interested in. The system fills out the needed information by default.

In conjunction with its allocation function, the control program carries out—or suitably directs the operator by message—the whole range of setdown/setup activities. It fetches needed programs (i.e., finds them in the library and loads them into memory), locates needed structurands, allocates needed memory area and adjusts the memory-protection mechanism, allocates needed auxiliary storage, allocates input/output devices, and verifies device readiness. Most of these activities occur at the beginning of a job. However, by suitable conventions, a control program can be designed to delay memory allocation for a structurand until the structurand is cited during program execution. Such a method, which is called *dynamic* memory allocation, employs an interrupt whenever a task requires additional area or has area that it can return to the control program. (This is discussed in Chapter 10.)

The control program may also preserve information on an entity we have not mentioned as such: the job request. If a job is requested periodically, it may save time to store the request and employ conventions by which the stored request can be cited and modified at request time.

The sequencing function of the control program is essentially that discussed in Sec. 8.4. If the computer system allows multiprogramming, the control program normally seizes control at interrupts and executes its "scheduling algorithm" to determine which task to activate next. Each time it takes control away from a given program, say $P_j$, it preserves a program-counter value and the internal-register content in a queue; when it returns control to $P_j$, it is obligated to properly restore the program counter and internal registers.

Among the many miscellaneous chores that a control program may be expected to perform are job-by-job accounting of resource time usage and management of checkpoint restart. The purpose of the latter is to periodically record, i.e., *checkpoint*, memory content and program status in auxiliary storage, thereby permitting the control program to *restart* at the most recent checkpoint in the event of system failure. In taking checkpoints, overlapping input/output operations must be permitted to complete if program status is to be correctly interpreted.

The problem of designing a control program for a general-purpose digital system is complicated by several factors. The program must meet the needs of a wide variety of applications, equipment configurations, and operating modes with a suitably low ratio of overhead to user jobs. New applications, new devices, and even new operating modes may emerge during the useful life of the program. A good deal of change can be accommodated by program revision if the conceptual structure that underlies the program is sufficiently general and flexible. However, if this structure must be radically changed, the whole system of conventions that relates the control program to the program library, the data library, and the program may be in jeopardy.

One way to illustrate the decisive relationships between a control program and its users is to mention the topic of memory allocation. A software method of allocating memory in multiprogramming faces the problem of area fragmentation: The area left by a completed job may be either too small or too big for the next job in line, and patches of area soon go unused unless the control program undertakes a complete reallocation of memory. With the help of installation management, this problem can be greatly alleviated by partitioning memory into areas that are given significance in a "design-point" sense. For management purposes, the pretense is that the multiprogrammed computer consists of a set of computers with given memory capacities, say *A*, *B*, *C*, etc. At the time a program is written, a decision is made to optimize the program for a given memory capacity. This decision is actually an allocation decision that will simplify matters for the control program at execution time. (It may also prevent the programmer from agonizing too long over an optional design point—which is not to say that it "simplifies" matters for him.) There are two ways to establish resource allocations. The first relies on the judgment of an informed human being, and the second, the so-called automatic way, relies on the results of a generalized control-program algorithm. In the advancing art of data systems, each new stage of technology tends to bring about a different balance between the decision-making agencies.

## 8.7 Comment

The subject of task sequencing is very broad and this chapter has touched only on high points.

The UNIVAC is described by J. P. Eckert, Jr. (1951), the IAS Computer by G. Estrin (1952), and the IBM 702 by C. J. Bashe et al. (1954). The carry-propagation methods mentioned in Sec. 8.2 are reported by A. Weinberger and J. L. Smith (1956) and O. L. MacSorley (1961). J. Mersel (1956) and F. P. Brooks, Jr. (1957) discuss program interruption. For a discussion of the TX-2 input/output system, see J. W. Forgie (1957).

J. Martin (1965) treats the general considerations involved in remote terminals and P. H. Seaman et al. (1966) analyzes the sequencing activities generated at the central computer by messages from the terminals. P. R. Vance et al. (1957) and G. R. Blackney et al. (1967) have discussed special systems designed for exceptional reliability requirements.

*Chapter 9*

# TRANSLATION TASKS

An executable program must be documented in a program language compatible with execution hardware. The present chapter deals with methods of translating from one language to another.

## 9.1 Instruction Interpretation

In responding to a computer instruction, the circuits of a computer examine the operation code and then faithfully go through the sequence of steps envisioned for that code by the designer. The sequence may include iteration, branches on special cases (a zero multiplier, for example), and operand fetches and stores. Traditionally, the sequences were entirely embedded in electronic circuitry. More recently, however, there has been a trend toward holding some of the required decoding and sequencing information in read-only storage devices. This is one way of reducing the quantity of control circuitry in a computer. The extent to which it is used usually depends on an economic balance between costs and processing rates. Guided by similar considerations, designers have sometimes economized on arithmetic-unit circuitry by employing a series of accesses to protected storage to form results in digit-by-digit arithmetic operations.

In general, the designer endows a computer with one internal sequence for fetching and preparing the next instruction to be executed and with one sequence for each instruction in the computer's instruction repertoire. However, since many instructions can often be grouped into one subclass on the basis of similar properties, one generalized sequence may suffice to execute a whole subclass by judicious provision of entry points and branches. In the literature on the logical design of computer circuits, a distinction is made between *combinational* circuits and *sequential* circuits. A combinational circuit contains no storage elements; as a result, a given vector of inputs completely determines the output vector of the circuit. A sequential circuit permits storage elements. As a result, the circuit may embody conditional branches—which is to say that the output vector is a function of stored content as well as of the given input vector. Since a sequential circuit literally embodies a program, it need not be surprising that designers write of *microinstructions* and *microprograms*, particularly when they are discussing control sequences stored in read-only memory, as in the case of S. G. Tucker (1967). An early discussion of microprogramming was given by M. V. Wilkes and J. B. Stringer (1953).

The physical units in a digital system are often referred to as the *hardware*. To complement this rather useful term, the computer programs in the system are referred to as *software*. To say that the hardware embodies programs is not to say that computer designers and computer programmers have the same job descriptions or face the same practical problems or need the same training. It is to suggest, however, that designers and programmers both have a hand in the overall translation process. And after this circumstance is accepted, it becomes much easier to grasp the arbitrary nature of the line between hardware and software. This line is drawn on the basis of engineering economics, not on the basis of fundamental logical categories.

## 9.2 Addressing

We have been discussing means of decoding the operation code in a computer instruction. Typically, there are one or more memory addresses in the instruction format that also have to be interpreted. The addresses may be modified before they are decoded by the memory unit, and it is the possible modifications that are of interest here.

Let us tentatively assume that the programs and structurands of an entire job can be contained in a random-access memory as one integrated *job table* and that each word of memory can accommodate one table row. These limitations, not always tenable in practice, can be circumvented by techniques to be discussed later.

**Direct addressing.** If its operable programs refer directly to the locations of relevant operands or entry instructions through instruction-contained addresses, a system is said to employ *direct addressing*. For example, the basic EDVAC instruction format provides two ten-bit fields for addressing operands and a similar field for addressing the destination of the result. Each field can contain an address capable of pointing to any location in a memory of 1024 words. Of course, the stored program need not contain explicit addresses for all of the locations be to referred to in the course of program execution, since the program can be written to modify addresses held in its own instructions. The facility to change instruction fields as if they were data was an EDVAC contribution.

Direct addressing can be used with instructions that contain one or two addresses as well as with three addresses. In the two-address format, a first address can designate one operand, and a second can designate the other operand as well as the location of the result. A useful variation of the two-address instruction format assumes $n$ special accumulator registers ($n > 1$); memory is addressed for one operand, whereas one of the accumulators is addressed as the source of the other operand and the destination of the result. If the design makes $n$ small, the accumulator address lends itself to a compact encoding.

**Relative addressing.** In this case, the address or addresses in an instruction are interpreted in light of the location of the instruction. Let $h$ and $k$ denote any two word addresses and consider their difference $\Delta = k - h$. In relative addressing, an instruction stored at location $h$ points to an operand or an entry at location $k$ by an instruction-contained delta. Whenever the instruction at location $h$ is fetched to the instruction register for execution, the desired address $k$ is formed by the relation $k = h + \Delta$. That is, the contents of the instruction counter and an instruction-contained field are added.

One property of relative addressing, clearly, is that the job table can be placed anywhere in memory—addressing become independent of table location. Another property is that the range of $\Delta$ is determined by the dimension of the job table, not by the number of words in memory. These properties offered no striking advantages when computer memories were relatively small and it was necessary or customary to deal with jobs one at a time. Now that memories are larger and multiprogramming is more prevalent, relative addressing has properties that can be very useful.

Let the words in a subroutine be identified by a zero-origin index. In this context, the term "relative address" has also been used to denote the index.

**Implicit addressing.** Where a single accumulator always serves both as operand source and result destination, instructions can have a one-address format. Since it need not be identified by the instruction, the accumulator is said to be designated by *implicit addressing*. In the typical desk calculator, for example, an accumulator is implicit in each arithmetic operation. Likewise, the designs of many digital computers have incorporated an accumulator that is implicit in most operations. Implicit addressing may be employed in different ways for different instructions. For example, some instructions may implicitly address the accumulator, others an auxiliary register, and still others both the auxiliary register and the accumulator.

A stack of registers obeying the LIFO (last in, first out) discipline can embody a generalized form of implicit addressing. In one possible mode, the "top" register is implicit as the location of one of the operands and the result, and memory is directly addressed for the other operand. Another variation employs direct memory addressing only for operand fetches (memory-to-stack transfers) and operand stores (stack-to-memory transfers); arithmetic, editing, and logic instructions then rely completely on implicit addressing. An addition instruction, for example, might be designed to sum the two operands at the top of the stack and return the result to the top of the stack (the net effect being to shorten the stack dimension by one). In fetching from memory, the stack grows (is "pushed down") by LIFO catenation; in processing and storing to memory, the stack dwindles by compression (is "popped up"). Unary operations leave the stack dimension unchanged, whereas binary operations reduce it by one—all in close correspondence to reduction of compound expressions in left-indexed tree form to simple expressions.

An accumulator stack was a feature of the English Electric KDF.9 computer (announced in 1960) and the Burroughs B-5000 computer (announced in 1961).

**Indexed addressing.** Although direct addressing is conceptually simple, some awkwardness attends the need for frequent modification of instruction-contained addresses. The additional instructions required to effect address modifications add to the length of a program, and they substantially increase the effort required for program preparation. Moreover, the extra executions lengthen program running time. To decrease the need for modifying addresses in stored instructions, computer designers have often provided means by which each instruction-contained memory address, just prior to use, can be summed with the contents of an index register to obtain an *effective address*. The indexing addition occurs after the instruction is fetched from memory but before the instruction is executed. Because the indexing operation is elementary in nature and occurs under controlled conditions, the computer designer can easily endow it with exceptional speed.

If only one index register is provided, the index register can be implicitly addressed, but at some inconvenience in that indexing cannot then be avoided without first clearing the index register to zeros. Where automatic indexing is provided, however, several index registers are normally justifiable, and an index register is directly addressed via a short address field in the instruction. In this case, "no indexing" can be indicated by addressing a nonexistent register.

Automatic indexing was introduced (circa 1953) at the University of Manchester in the MADM computer, which provided one index register. Popularized in the IBM 704 (announced in 1954), which embraced three index registers, indexing has been a widely used addressing feature ever since. Indexed addressing is especially advantageous in scanning the elements of an array by a program loop that includes instructions for incrementing (or decrementing) an index, testing index magnitude, and conditionally branching. To facilitate the control of program loops, a computer with automatic indexing must have various instructions for loading, storing, modifying, and testing its index registers.

**Indirect addressing.** Although more economical to implement than automatic indexing, the technique known as *indirect addressing* is also useful in avoiding the need for dynamic modification of instruction-contained addresses. In this mode of addressing, an instruction-contained storage address does not specify the location of an operand; instead, it specifies a location that contains the address of the operand.

The principal cost of indirect addressing is the time required for an extra fetch from memory. The basic advantages of indirect addressing are twofold. First, with the aid of a stored vector of operand addresses, a program can process a given set of tables; then after modification of the vector, it can similarly process a counterpart set residing in another region of memory. Second, if a vector of its entry-statement addresses is stored, a program can be moved from one region of memory to another at the mere cost of adding a constant to each component of the vector.

Indirect addressing was introduced in the IBM 709 computer (announced in 1957).

**Immediate addressing.** Not infrequently, a program needs access to a logical vector or an encoded integer that can be stored in part of a memory word. If the information will fit into an instruction-contained address field, both memory space and memory fetch time can be economized by placing the information within the address field. The information can be obtained, from within the instruction itself, by *immediate addressing*, a mode of addressing that foregoes the usual operand fetch from memory. This is especially useful for instructions that load, increment, or test the contents of index registers; it can also be useful in editing instructions.

Inasmuch as immediate addressing is a special mode of addressing, it requires that the instruction format contain a logical variable that can be flagged in the instructions for which the mode is applicable. Indirect addressing, which is likewise normally employed as a special mode of addressing, can be similarly designated.

**Search addressing.** If each operand, along with a fixed-format name, fits conveniently into one word of a parallel-search memory, then any mention of an operand by name provides a search argument. Thereupon, the parallel-search memory delivers the word containing the name and the desired operand. It is not inappropriate to speak of this event, wherein the operand name automatically leads to a word address, as *search addressing*. Because a search-addressing scheme essentially implements a sweep (see Chapter 4), the rows of different tables can be mingled in memory.

Current technologies put parallel-search memories at a substantial economic disadvantage relative to conventional memories. To aggravate this cost disadvantage, moreover, search addressing requires that every node of a structurand be stored with a name. In the case of arrays, these names take up space that is unnecessary in a conventional memory. As a result of these cost drawbacks, search addressing is now viewed as a technique of limited applicability but one useful in special applications that merit an exceptional degree of flexibility in the allocation and search of small tables.

## 9.3 Program Assembly

The first electronic stored-program computer to be completed was the EDSAC, which went into operation in England at the University of Cambridge in 1949. EDSAC was then a serial, fixed-point, binary computer with a 17-bit word length, a 512-word delay-line memory, paper-tape input/output, and little checking circuitry. It had one address per instruction and its execution sequence was controlled by a program counter. *The Preparation of Programs for an Electronic Digital Computer, with Special Reference to EDSAC and the use of a Library of Subroutines*, by M. V. Wilkes, D. J. Wheeler, and S. Gill, appeared in 1951. This seems to have been the first book published on programming.

In their 1947 and 1948 reports on "Planning and Coding of Problems for an Electronic Computing Instrument," H. H. Goldstine and J. von Neumann wrote of coded sequences of instructions and of subroutines. The EDSAC book distinguishes between the master routine or main program and two classes of functional subroutines. An *open* subroutine is a library routine that is inserted into a main program at the point of use; an open subroutine becomes an indistinguishable part of the main program. A *closed* subroutine, on the other hand, is assigned in use to an area of memory not occupied by the main program. The location of the first word of the closed subroutine is settled before the main program is loaded for execution and is reflected in appropriate address fields. Moreover, the main program and its subroutines are both written in accord with a *linkage* convention. For example, to call a closed subroutine into use, the main program may load the accumulator with a return address and then branch to the subroutine; thereupon, the subroutine sets the address in its exit branch instruction to the number in the accumulator, performs its operational duties, and branches back to the main program. Although conventions may vary in detail, the notion of a linkage convention is inherent in the use of closed subroutines.

The EDSAC library designers also distinguish between *preset parameters* and *program parameters*. The former are fixed at the time a subroutine is read into memory and do not change during program execution. The latter may be respecified during program execution. The subroutine library discussed in the book by Wilkes et al. consisted mainly of subroutines for mathematical functions, operations on complex numbers, and floating-point arithmetic. Subroutines for converting between base 10 and base 2 are also described, as are *assembly* and *interpretive* subroutines. The former aid in the clerical task of inserting correct addresses in a program formed in part from library constituents. The latter are special-purpose closed subroutines that interpret numerical parameters as if they encoded a special command not in the computer's repertoire of instructions (this convention was found convenient in programming complex-number and floating-point arithmetic).

The main purpose of the assembly routine is to assimilate program segments or subroutines witten at different times and possibly by different people into one coherent executable program. A few conventions must be adhered to, but these are a small price to pay for a technique that permits an installation to accrue a library of subroutines and to subdivide big programming efforts conveniently among various programmers. Originally, each subroutine or segment was written as though it existed in a memory area starting from location zero. Later, it was found a convenience to let the programmer use mnemonics in two ways: (1) for operation codes and (2) for program entry and operand addresses. Still later, it was found useful to let the programmer include macroinstructions, which are essentially directives to the assembly routine (also called the assembler) to modify subroutines before they are incorporated into the operable program. A set of conventions for linkages, mnemonics, and the use of macroinstructions is sometimes dignified in the term *assembler language.*

Since an assembler language faithfully includes a counterpart for each instruction of the underlying computer, the programmer can make full use of all of the potentialities of the computer when writing programs in assembler language. Assembler languages still play an important role in programming efforts that stress optimal system performance.

## 9.4 Program Generation

Almost every application program is written with some degree of generality. In other words, the program contains parameters that can be set for different executions of the program. The parameters may govern the basic computational algorithm, structurand dimensions, input/output methods, resource allocations, format options, and various other matters. Since useful generality must be based on intelligent analysis, and since generality ordinarily lengthens a program and, to some extent, increases its execution time, the proper degree of generality for a program is a design decision that must reckon with the anticipated usages of the program.

A distinction is sometimes made between (1) a *general program* that can be specialized for a specific task by setting a certain number of parameters and (2) a *generator program* that goes one step farther and synthesizes the specialized program from a standard set of skeletal routines that serve as "building blocks." Because the latter approach can do more than the former to minimize the memory-area requirement, it substantially extends the useful domain of generalized programs. One way for a computer installation (or a group of installations with tasks somewhat in common) to economize on programmer effort is to employ generator programs for activities like sorting, searching, editing, and input/output device control. In fact, by combining all of these activities and including some way of requesting arithmetic operations, it is possible to design a *report program generator* that can produce tailor-made programs capable of scanning files and producing various classes of reports. Similar approaches can be used for some of the more standardized classes of mathematical computations, such as operations in matrix algebra.

So much is possible with generator programs that a brief discussion of their potentialities must be exceedingly abstract. As a relief to this, the reader may enjoy a concrete discussion by the designer of an early-day generator program. In May 1954, the Office of Naval Research, U. S. Department of the Navy, sponsored a Symposium on Automatic Programming for Digital Computers. Frances E. Holberton, reporting on work done at Remington Rand, discussed a sort generator in a paper entitled "Application of Automatic Coding to Logical Processes." The major parts of her paper are reprinted below. Most of her remarks on analysis are still germane today.

> The generating routine, which I will briefly describe, has been in use for two years. This was my first attempt to program a logical process using automatic coding techniques. The process is one of arranging randomly sequenced data on a tape into an ordered set, better known as "sorting." Because sorting of information is a process to be performed in almost all data handling problems, such a generating routine would be a tremendous time saver for the programmer.
>
> The techniques for sorting information on the computer were developed during the design stages of the UNIVAC System and played an important part in the selection of the size of the buffer storage, the length of the tape, and the desire for the backward read operation.
>
> Sorting is accomplished on the UNIVAC by first passing the randomly sequenced data through the computer, arranging the items in each input group of 720 characters, or one block, into a descending sequence on all the key information by magnitude testing of the data. The ordered blocks are written on two tapes alternately. If the original tape contains 2000 blocks of randomly sequenced items, the first pass through the computer produces 2000 ordered sets. The two partially ordered tapes are read backward into the computer, merging one block from each tape to form sets of two blocks in an ascending sequence

and writing the two-block sets on alternate tapes. This will produce 1000 ordered sets in two-block lengths. For each pass of the data through the computer, always reversing the order of the arrangement from descending to ascending series or vice versa, the number of the sets will be halved and the size of the set doubled, until all the data will be collated into one ascending sequenced set. Alternating the sequence of the data on each pass through the computer and reading it into the computer from a tape moving in the backward direction eliminates the necessity of rewinding tapes after each pass and decreases the computer time for the operation.

This process, called two-way sorting because the length of the ordered sets is increased by powers of two, can be used if only four or five uniservos are available. When more tape mechanisms are available, data can be spread over three or four tapes and the length of the sets built up by powers of three or four, using a three- or four-way comparison merge sequence to reduce the operation time. The number of passes of the data through the computer is a function of the number of items on the tape and the number of tape mechanisms used, and not the number of characters or digits in the key information.

The sorting-generating routine has been devised to produce on the UNIVAC, in less than two minutes, a two-way sorting instruction tape, an edited final report copy of the coding, and a routine to test the sequence of the data operated on by the sorting routine, according to specifications determined by a programmer.

The sorting routine obtained from the generation contains only the coding and the constants required to produce an ascending ordered series determined by a set of parameters. The generating routine can produce sorting routines to handle any one of twelve different item sizes ranging from 24-character items to 320-character items, and various sizes of key information ranging from 1 to 60 characters. The sorting routine produced for a given set of parameters is not a generalized routine modified to fit the criteria, but a custom-built routine designed to produce an efficient sorting procedure for a given set of parameters based upon methods and techniques developed over a four-year period.

The edited copy of the coding produced on the UNIVAC contains a two-page description of the sorting routine and the operating instructions. Each subroutine in the edited copy contains the necessary connector entries, descriptive information, and modified instructions which usually appear in a hand-tailored program. All references are linked to a detailed Flow Chart which is associated with the writeup of the generating routine. The edited copy produced facilitates any modification to the routine a programmer may wish to make.

The sorting-check routine enables the operator to check the sequence of information arranged by the sorting routine. The main purpose of the sorting-check routine was to aid me during the check-out period of the generating routine on the computer, but it has been used to sequence check the sorted data if any manual intervention has occurred during the sorting process. It has also been used as a sequence check on supposedly ordered data obtained from card conversion to determine whether sorting is necessary.

The eighteen parameters supplied to the generating routine specify: the number of uniservos to be used, the input and final output uniservo numbers, the size of the item, the specific digit positions to be used in the key information, the presence or absence of identifying information on the tape, and what is the symbol designating the end of a tape. Many parameters may be used by the generating routine to select one subroutine. The parameters interact to influence the choice of a subroutine or a section of a subroutine in the coding process. Three parameters are required to select one of fifty-two possible subroutines which fabricate instructions to transfer an item from one part of the internal memory to another.

A generalized Flow Chart of the sorting process was first drawn, and from this, each subroutine was coded in relative coding, taking into account the various changes in the subroutine caused by the parameters. From the relative coding, it was determined that 99 specific constants are present in any sorting routine, although about 80 percent of these constants contain variable information stored within them. A maximum of 14 additional constants and a function table of not more than 30 values would also be needed. The fact that so many constants could be located in a fixed position in the sorting routine solved one of the major problems of coding such a generating routine. This meant that over 30 percent of the sorting instructions to be coded could refer to known memory addresses. The remaining addresses associated with instructions must be computed, using the parameter information or the position of the instruction word in relation to the coded sorting routine.

Because the internal memory of the UNIVAC is large enough to hold the completely coded sorting routine for operation for any logical combination of parameters, the routine is generated and held within the computer. One hundred thirty-one blocks, or over 7000 instruction words or constants, are required to generate and edit the specific sorting routine. The generating instructions are inserted into the memory a few blocks at a time, and executed in memory locations which are reserved for data in the final sorting routine. The instructions for the sorting routine are built up in the memory in the actual final operating positions of the routine, which aided in the proving of the generating routine on the computer. Holding the coded instructions in the memory eliminated the necessity for writing partially coded subroutines on tape and processing the tapes for later completion. . . .

The sorting routine is coded on the computer in about 15 seconds and written on tape. The routine contains a maximum of 580 instruction words. The remaining time on the computer is used to edit the coded instruction, supply the write-up for the routine, and produce the check routine. The routine required about six months to prepare, from basic analysis to final report and proven routine.

The ultimate desire of any automatic coding process is to have the computer produce a complete routine which will run correctly on the computer the first time and produce the answers in at least as short a time as a routine hand-tailored by a programmer.

It is highly unlikely that the computer can be made to produce automatically all routines for data-processing problems. But between 50 and 90 percent of the coding involved in a data-processing routine is made up of sections of

> coding or subroutines which the programmer has used in another problem and revamps for the specific use. These operations usually involve multiple input tape control with buffer and auxiliary memory storage, tape alternation, item transfer, matching, selecting, merging, read and write operations, and rerun procedures. It should be possible to have the computer code large sections of data-processing problems. If the computer can be supplied with "what process" it is to produce, how frequently the process is to be performed in a given problem, and the amount of available internal storage, the computer should be able to produce "how" the process should be coded. The "how" it is to be coded can be only as good as the set of subroutines which are available and the pertinent information stored with each subroutine, such as time of operation, amount of space required, and what criteria it will fulfill.
>
> In order to have the computer code a desired process, it will be necessary to break down a process into subprocesses. A subprocess is a section of a process detailed to do a specific job with a given frequency or weight. A subprocess is expressed in a Flow Chart as that part which lies between an entry and an exit point with a given frequency of operation, but which is logically part of a larger concept called a process. For any one subprocess, many subroutines may exist which fulfill the specifications. . . .

The above-described sorting generator was written at a time when each programmer was expected to supply the routines necessary to handle the input/output devices and various "housekeeping" tasks associated with their use. As we shall see in Chapter 10, this problem was later alleviated—with the aid, in part, of generator routines.

Generator routines, large and small, play a very significant role in the whole translation process. The macroinstructions afforded by many assembly languages gain their power from the principle of generation. From simple requests in a nonprocedural language or set of conventions, generators can produce programs for various tasks, a well-known example being that of scanning a file or files and preparing desired reports or summary tabulations.

The essential difference between a general-purpose program and a generator is that the latter includes an optimization phase in advance of program execution. The generator is designed to optimize the number of conditional branches, to reduce the length of the program, and to allocate resources as frugally as is feasible—all in advance of execution of the desired program.

## 9.5 Program Interpretation and Compilation

Let $S$ denote a source program written by human beings in a known programming language and let $T$ denote a translator program that can be executed on computer $t$. The designer of $T$ will normally concentrate on one of two alternatives: (1) He will design $T$ to analyze $S$ and to execute $S$ statement by statement during the course of the analysis, or (2) he will design $T$ to analyze $S$ and produce a *target program*, say $X$, that can be executed on computer $x$. (Usually, computers $x$ and $t$ are identical.) In the first case, $T$ is designed to be an *interpreter*; in the second case, $T$ is designed to be a *compiler*. In the first case, $S$ must be translated by $T$ at each execution of $S$; in the second case, $S$ is translated once and the resulting program $X$ can be run as often as desired without recourse to either $S$ or $T$. If the application task is to be performed once, interpretation should be more efficient than compilation. If it is to be executed as many as ten times, compilation is usually more efficient than interpretation. The break-even point is subject to a great many practical considerations.

Compilation has two possible advantages over interpretation. The first, which was mentioned above, is that it translates $S$ only once. The second is that the raw version of $X$ first emerging from translation can be further analyzed to produce more carefully optimized versions of $X$. Optimization is not an exciting subject because most of the many improvements that can be made in $X$ seem prosaic when considered one by one. Optimization may eliminate logically unnecessary memory accesses, make fuller use of internal registers, replace divide-by-constant operations with equivalent multiply-by-constant operations (multiplication is faster than division), and the like. Optimization is particularly useful for source programs heavily weighted with arithmetic computations; it is less efficacious for programs that deal primarily with table look-up and editing operations.

Since the time required for a compiler to produce an object program $X$ will depend in part on the amount of analysis that the compiler invests in $X$, a user may desire to retain some control over the degree of optimization undertaken by a compiler. For example, consider an instructor who is teaching a high-level language and wants each student to write a source program and examine a compiled version. If pressed for computer time, the instructor may be happy to forego all optimization as a means of accelerating the compilations.

In supplementing a "high-level" programming language, a translator program $T$ must accomplish the functions of an assembler plus (1) scan a string of characters to analyze and tabulate language elements, (2) reduce the compound expressions into simple expressions, and (3) allocate the index registers and memory. Also, if $T$ is a compiler, it will ordinarily contain some provision for optimization of the target program. Moreover, $T$ is usually expected to provide a variety of services for the programmer. Foremost among these is assistance in checking the syntax of the source program $S$; it is a waste of time to attempt to translate $S$ if language rules are mistakenly applied in $S$.

During the 1960's, high-level languages teamed with compilation to surpass assembler languages and assembly as the major method of preparing application programs. A compelling factor in this revolution was the critical shortage of skilled programmers; a pertinent consideration was an expanding technology for languages and compilers. Compilation and interpretation are methods of conserving programmer time at an expenditure of computer time and (for the time being, at least) compilation provides an economic trade-off under a wider set of conditions than does interpretation.

It makes interesting reading to return to some of the discussions heard before languages like FORTRAN and COBOL were developed. For example, at the symposium referred to in Sec. 9.4, John W. Backus and Harlan Herrick of the IBM Corporation presented a paper entitled "IBM 701 Speedcoding and other Automatic-Programming Systems." Speedcoding was an interpretive system with three-address pseudo-commands that provided floating-point (see Sec. 10.5) arithmetic for the fixed-point 701 computer. The system also made address modification (indexing) and input/output operations somewhat more convenient for the programmer. The following remarks are from the conclusion of the paper that consisted mainly of a description of Speedcoding.

> Now let us again return to the subject of automatic programming in general. Up to now the usual purpose of automatic programming systems such as Speedcoding has been to make available to the programmer nonmachine instructions, each of which usually represents a fairly long sequence of machine instructions when translated. Even though the machine automatically expands the instructions of the programmer into the necessary machine operations and thereby saves him considerable labor, the work of the programmer still contains a lot of drudgery. He must still decide what actual or symbolic addresses he will assign to his data and to his instructions and must keep track of these decisions once made. He must still write hundreds or thousands of instructions to specify how the machine is to do his problem. And as he debugs his program he must be intimately familiar with the relationships between all of these assignments and the quantities involved in his equations and between the multitude of instructions and the operations designated by the equations.
>
> Obviously the programmer would like to write "X" instead of some specific address, and if he wants to add X and Y he would like to write "X + Y" instead of, perhaps:
>
> | | |
> |---|---|
> | CLEAR AND ADD | 100 |
> | ADD | 106 |
>
> or some such gibberish. To go a step further he would like to write $\sum a_{ij} \cdot b_{jk}$ instead of the fairly involved set of instructions corresponding to this expression. In fact a programmer might not be considered too unreasonable if he were willing only to produce the formulas for the numerical solution of his problem and perhaps a plan showing how the data was to be moved from one storage hierarchy to another and then demand that the machine produce the results for his problem. No doubt if he were too insistent next week about this sort of thing he would be subject to psychiatric observation. However, next year he might be taken more seriously. . . .

Consider the advantages of being able to state the calculations, decisions, operations on ordered arrays of data, and manipulations of blocks of data necessary for a problem solution in a concise, fairly natural mathematical language.

1. Such a language would mean that there was a close resemblance of the problem statement acceptable to the machine and the original formulation of the problem in a form for numerical solution. Thus, the programmer would be largely relieved of the necessity of making and remembering the extensive translation from the symbols of the original formulation to the addresses and operations of the program.

2. The tremendous increase in conciseness of the problem statement for machine solution and its closer relationship to the original statement will make it possible to check the material presented to the machine much more accurately.

3. Once the concise problem statement has been checked carefully and presented to the machine, debugging might virtually be eliminated.

4. The amount of knowledge the programmer would have to have about the machine and about programming conventions and library programs would be greatly reduced. He would have to know only the rules of the language in which the problem is to be stated and the facts about the memory hierarchy of the machine. This of course would be a tremendous advantage to the open-shop type of computing installation. The programmer would not have to become familiar with dozens of codes, special machine features, timing conditions, addresses of various units, and a host of other facts which are presently necessary to know.

5. Much wasteful duplication of programming effort may eventually be eliminated. In programming many practical problems, programming situations and difficulties are often encountered which require considerable analysis to obtain a good procedure. In a great many instances similar situations have arisen before and a similar analysis has been made. In the rush of completing a problem it is not usually possible to make a good record of the results of such work. Therefore, analysis tends to be repeated again and again and is often never done as well as it could be. Programming techniques which arise in this way could be thoroughly analyzed and incorporated as programming capabilities of an automatic-programming system.

Whether such an elaborate automatic-programming system is possible or feasible has yet to be determined....

Soon after the 1954 symposium, Backus headed a new project in which the objective was to permit any program for solving a mathematical problem involving "calculations, decisions, operations on ordered arrays" to be stated in a "fairly natural mathematical language." The FORTRAN system appeared in 1957 as a language and an attendant compiler; see Backus et al. (1957). The system soon became a widespread tool for programming mathematical computations and has since been generalized in various ways. Dr. Grace M. Hopper, who also contributed to the symposium, was soon to lead a Remington Rand project aimed at designing a compiler that would permit accounting application programs to be expressed in a vocabulary of English words and phrases. Other computer manufacturers eventually took an interest in this work, and urged by groups of computer users, the computer industry standardized on COBOL. More people have probably written programs in COBOL than in any other programming language.

Although dozens of languages have been discussed in the literature, FORTRAN and COBOL are the most widely used languages at this time. These languages gained footholds because they answered to conspicuous needs in straightforward ways. Although they still answer to these needs, FORTRAN and COBOL are coming under increasing pressure because the needs of the industry are changing and it is not clear that they can respond to future enviornments as well as they have to previous environments. For example, COBOL is not a succinct language, and succinctness may become increasingly important if the use of interactive terminals continues to expand. In the long run, it may be desirable for many computer users to have their entire program library documented in one programming language; the considerations related to this are likely to receive a great deal of attention as time goes on. One hastens to add that "language" is the point at which electronic systems intermesh most closely with people. The human race insists on a great many different languages, even though one well-chosen language would appear to offer much in the way of advantage. However, one should further add that the language of numbers and mathematics has enjoyed a high degree of success; perhaps the sponsors of a universal programming language can take heart from mathematics.

The compiler is most advantageous for the programs of repetitive applications with heavy requirements for resources. The interpreter is attractive where a program is typically used once (this is more or less the case in some file-query systems) or where programming is to be made as convenient as possible at an interactive terminal. In the latter case, it is a distinct advantage for a program to be succinct and to exist in one form that can be conveniently examined and changed.

## 9.6 Emulation and Simulation

Let $x$ and $y$ denote two computers of differing designs. Let $T$ denote a translator program written in the machine language of $y$ to interpret programs written in language $S$. If language $S$ is in fact the machine language of $x$, then $T$ is called a *simulator*. (The term is also used, in other contexts, for programs that facilitate digital simulation.) With the aid of $T$, programs written for computer $x$ can be executed on computer $y$. Inasmuch as $T$ must reside in computer $y$ whenever a computer-$x$ program is executed, simulation works most smoothly where $y$ has a larger memory than $x$.

One advantage of simulation is that it offers a means of debugging *y* programs before computer *y* is available. This is the commonplace need that first led to the design of simulators. If an installation has replaced computer *x* by computer *y*, another advantage is that the *x* programs in the library are not made entirely obsolete. It is unlikely that *y* and *T* can simulate an *x* program as cheaply as the program can be executed on *x*, but the extra cost may be justified as long as the available programmers have more rewarding assignments to complete. In other words, simulation can be a means of smoothing out requirements for skilled manpower.

The disadvantage of simulation is that it typically uses the host computer at a fraction of its true potential. A task simulated on *y* may easily take ten times longer than if the task were reprogrammed for *y*. This assumes, of course, that the simulator *T* is embodied entirely as a program, i.e., in software. If *T* executes on computer *y*, and if some of the most significant loops executed in *T* are judiciously embodied in the hardware of *y*, then the efficiency of *T* can be substantially improved. The advent of read-only memories in the early 1960's made this possibility economically attractive. As stated previously, table loop-up in a high-speed special-purpose memory is a means of displacing circuitry for decoding and control tasks. A simulator embodied as a combination of hardware and software is called an *emulator*.

If *y* is a computer that obsoletes *x* on a technology basis, *y* will offer a lower cost/performance ratio than *x* for a typical job. Even though *y* offers a different machine language than *x*, a user may find *y* economically attractive if he can cope with the programming problems implied by the changeover from *x* to *y*. Since emulators are substantially better than simulators in performance, they are widely used today.

Two questions undoubtedly occur to the reader, one concerning high-level languages and another concerning the possibility of a compiler that translates from machine language *x* to machine language *y*. First, if an installation maintains its program library in high-level language, then a changeover from computer *x* to computer *y* can be accomplished by recompiling all of the programs in the library (possibly with some source-program modifications to take advantage of new control-program facilities). Today, however, the typical program library contains many programs that either (1) were not originated in high-level language or (2) have not been maintained at the source-program level. Second, if *X* is a program for machine *x* and *Y* a counterpart program for machine *y*, the problem of translating from *X* to *Y* still lacks a general solution. Although the fundamental difficulties have never been crisply articulated, they are undoubtedly related to the fact that compilation as currently defined is an irreversible process. In other words, after a source program *S* has been compiled to produce a program *X* in machine language *x*, then *S* cannot be reproduced from *X*. Some of the information lost in going from *S* to *X* may be information needed to produce *Y* from *X*.

In the fortuitous special case where computers *x* and *y* are similar in important respects, translation from *X* to *Y* may turn out to be feasible. However, the state of the art rests on empirical rather than theoretical foundations.

## 9.7 Comment

It deserves emphasis that the six processes

1. Assembly
2. Generation
3. Compilation
4. Interpretation
5. Emulation
6. Simulation

may all be encountered in a complex digital system. Clearly, the interpretation process must exist: The system hardware interprets machine instructions. Moreover, the typical system embraces a control program that interprets directives or commands in a so-called *job-control language* that governs allocation and scheduling decisions at execution time. If the system is designed in such a way that input/output instructions cause interrupts, then the control program participates in the interpretation of input/output instructions. Some of the assembly function may be deferred until the program is loaded into memory, at which time the area to be occupied is fully ascertained. During preparation of an application program, the two processes of most concern are generation and compilation.

Despite the advances in high-level languages and optimizing compilers, there are still applications in which it is expedient to program in assembler language (which provides a counterpart for each machine instruction). These are the applications in which memory usage, running time, flexibility, or maintainability pose exceptional requirements and deserve exceptional care from the programmer. Typical examples are control programs, translators, and sorting programs. It is still an open question how well high-level languages and compilers can serve in the design of such programs.

This may be the place to point out that semantic misunderstandings are common enough in the programming field. In 1960, a research mathematician who is exceptionally well versed in programming started his review of a book; "This reviewer holds that programming is a simple art whose fundamentals can be taught in a couple of hours to anyone who needs computers." This may be a defensible view in the context of high-level languages; it is essentially the view we offered in Chapter 6. But the larger truth is that many people make programming their profession; indeed, they correctly view their profession as a new branch of engineering. And bare fundamentals do not go to make the skills and the knowledge necessary for a profession. Misunderstandings can be alleviated in part by a distinction between *systems programmers*, who develop languages, conventions, and general-purpose program libraries, and *application programmers*, who use languages and general-purpose programs to augment libraries. Although the distinction can seem arbitrary in practice, the typical application programmer finds it most rewarding to concentrate on learning application details, whereas the systems programmer is led toward further study of the details of digital computer systems.

The concept of a compiler that prevailed before the development of high-level languages may be judged from R. K. Ridgway (1952) and N. B. Moser (1954). A basis for macroinstruction extensions of assembly languages is reported by M. D. McIlroy (1960). The idea of a generalized assembly system is discussed by G. H. Mealy (1963). Many insights into program optimization are provided by J. Nievergelt (1965) and E. S. Lowry and C. W. Medlock (1969).

# Chapter 10

# TABLE MANAGEMENT

The typical computer installation deals with many different jobs. Each job can be broken down into more tasks, and associated with each task is a program and one or more structurands. Each program and each structurand is represented as a table. This chapter treats of *table management*, the set of activities involved in placing, finding, copying, and searching tables.

## 10.1 Planned Allocation

Where the objective is to introduce the main principles of allocation, a job may be viewed abstractly as a set of encoded tables. For those cases in which all of the tables of a job can be catenated in a fixed order, it is useful to refer collectively to the set of tables as a job table.

To simplify discussion, storage will be assumed to consist of a memory and a much larger auxiliary-storage unit termed the *store*. The store is assumed to be subdivided into homogeneous pages, each page containing the same number of words. Each word of the memory is designated by a word address and each page of the store by a page address.

Tentatively, we assume that each table row fits conveniently into one memory word, i.e., that the number of memory words allocated for a table can equal the number of table rows. For allocation purposes, memory can be arbitrarily subdivided into sections to be called *plats*. Memory takes its simplest form where the memory is devoted to one job and each table of the job is assigned an individual plat. In this case, the entire program is present throughout the job, and the plat for every structurand—including any intermediate structurands that exist briefly during the job—is allocated until the end of the job.

The task of formulating a correct job table can be accomplished in the course of program assembly. The assembly task makes use of a *reference table* that contains one row for each instruction that is branched to and for each structurand that is addressed by the program. With the aid of table dimensions, the assembly procedure completes the reference table by determining the memory locations that should correspond to each reference point. Because assembly precedes the execution phase of a program, and because the addressing information is left explicit in the instruction addresses of a catenated job table, the reference table ordinarily plays no part in the job execution. We mention it only because it crops up again in the context of job tables that are not fully concatenated.

Were not economic considerations and technological limitations always at work, nobody would bother with complicated allocation methods. But a memory layout that provides an individual plat for each table is often wasteful of memory because some tables play a transitory role during execution. The only way to reduce this waste is to use some of the plats over and over again. To resort to analogy, these plats must serve the program as outsized accumulators, much as accumulators serve over and over for different instructions. Thus after the point in execution where table A becomes obsolete, the plat assigned to A can be used to hold a newly generated table B. However, since transitory tables A, B, C, . . . , may exist during different intervals and need plats of differing areas, there may be no feasible way of solving for the optimal allocation of memory. The task of finding a reasonable approximation is then left as a puzzle for the programmer. If the programmer enjoys puzzles, the problem of "squeezing" a job into a memory of given capacity may easily distract him from other programming matters.

The memory is usually implemented by magnetic cores, in current technology, and the store by magnetic surfaces. Economic considerations usually press for a ratio of store capacity to memory capacity in the order of $10^3$ or higher. Moreover, the storage requirements of many files far exceed the capacity of the largest magnetic-core memory. Since the usual strategem is to process the file record by record, it suffices to bring one record of the file into memory at a time. A memory plat reserved for a portion of a table, as, for example, one file record, is called a *buffer*. To facilitate the overlapping of reads and writes, several buffers may be defined. With two input and two output buffers, for instance, the processing operations that yield output from input can be overlapped by (1) a read that fills an input buffer and (2) a write that records the contents of an output buffer. To expedite read/write operations that involve a penalty for each storage gap (as in the case of magnetic tapes), a buffer may be extended in dimension to encompass a block of several records.

Another well-known way to conserve memory is based on the fact that most programs contain some segments that are executed infrequently. If the program is written as a main segment followed by a number of *overlay* segments A, B, C, etc., the main segment, held in memory throughout job execution can lend the necessary degree of control over the overlay segments, only one of which resides in memory at any given time. Assume that segment A is in memory. If the main segment wants to branch to B, it first returns A to the store (if necessary) and then brings B into the area previously occupied by A. If segment A wants to branch to segment B, it must gain assistance from the main segment in order to effect the branch. For the smooth operation of this method, therefore, it is important to minimize the number of branches between overlay segments. The segment traffic between memory and store can be roughly halved if techniques such as indirect and indexed addressing are used to avoid the need for stored-program modification; this done, segments need not be copied back into the store before being overlaid.

Although planned allocation can lead to efficient memory utilization under favorable circumstances, it has serious shortcomings. In addition to the investment in planning required of the programmer, the method lends itself awkwardly to the problems posed by variations in system parameters. The programmer must establish maximums. If the program is widely used for jobs with smaller tables, large areas of memory may well go completely unused in the typical job. Allocation is such a conspicuous problem that multiple programs may be written—each designed to make reasonably efficient use of memory for a particular range of table dimensions. The net effect is that allocation comes to dominate program design.

A related effect is observed for computers with modular memories. A program written for installation A may be useless to installation B because the computer at B has a smaller memory than the computer at A. In the converse, B has a larger memory than A and the program designed for A runs inefficiently on B. A similar effect can occur whenever installation A decides to augment memory capacity.

The need for planned allocation complicates programming in various miscellaneous ways. Where several programmers are working separately on parts of the same job program, coordination is made more difficult by the allocation problem. A program with tightly planned allocation is seldom easy to correct or modify because the logic of the program may be tortured and obscured by memory-saving tricks. Some of the potential of planned allocation must be foregone, moreover, if the programmer is to enjoy the benefits of a high-level programming language. In this case, the programmer cannot predict the length of program segments and to some extent he relinquishes control over the exact sequence in which allocation-dependent events occur.

We have been assuming that allocation decisions are made by the programmer at the time the program is written. If the final step of the assembly phase (which inserts addresses into instructions) can be delayed until the program is loaded into memory, there are advantages to be gained by postponing some of the decisions until load time. In processing arrays, for example, the exact dimensions are usually known at that point. Also, there may be advantages in postponing some of the decisions to the last possible instant during execution. A scheme that defers some of its decisions until execution is usually said to employ dynamic allocation (which is discussed in Sec. 10.2). Dynamic allocation is particularly important in applications where table dimensions are unpredictable: Table A may be huge and table B small at one run, and table B huge and A small at the next run.

## 10.2 Assisted Allocation

**List processing.** The pointer matrix discussed in Sec. 3.3 provides a conceptual basis for one class of software-assisted allocation techniques. Because the pointer matrix can represent structure explicitly with pointers (i.e., addresses), tables containing pointer matrices can be commingled in storage. Assuming that some form of control program intervenes in allocation, the control program can define available memory as a *pool* and allocate memory word by word to the application as needed. Any table can continue to grow and new tables can be established as long as free space remains in the pool.

The application program must be provided with a standardized way of requesting additional space, and it may be provided with a standardized way of relinquishing space to the control program. In the literature, the problem of returning space to the control program is discussed under the name of the garbage-collection problem. The whole body of techniques developed around pointer matrices is referred to as *list processing*. The fundamental advantage of list processing is that it provides a systematic way of allocating memory dynamically for structurands of unpredictable structures and dimensions. One disadvantage is that it usually restricts search to some form of the path search; another is that a format problem arises when different structurands, with strings of differing lengths constituting their nodes, are thrown together. A third disadvantage is that the requisite pointers take up considerable space themselves.

Although list processing provides a convenient and practical way of allocating memory for complicated tree structures with restricted-format nodes, the fact is that most data processing deals with simple structures and nodes that vary in length from table to table. Most software-aided dynamic allocation schemes are designed with less elegant procedures; they assign memory to programs in larger units and use pointers largely for reaching overflow areas.

**Stored reference table.** One way to gain additional flexibility for dynamic allocation is to hold the reference table in memory during execution. For discussion purposes, we assume, not unrealistically, that the reference table contains at most 1024 rows. Hence, if it is stored at the low-address end of memory, and if each of its rows fits into a memory word, the table can be entered with a ten-bit address. Corresponding to each table in the job is a row in the reference table that yields table dimension, table status (is it or is it not present in memory), and a base location in memory (or store, if the table is not in the memory). A ten-bit instruction-contained address can reach any memory-contained table or entry instruction by indirect addressing via the reference table. Indirect addressing can be used in conjunction with indexing to reach elements within arrays. Ten-bit constants can be taken from the instruction stream by immediate addressing, whereas longer constants can be stored in the reference table and addressed directly. Because all tables (except the reference table itself) are location-independent, the control program can move tables and correct for this by changing addresses in the reference table. Given suitable conventions, the program being executed can request and relinquish plats during the course of execution. If A, B, and C are adjacent plats, and A and C have been relinquished, the control program can form a plat D, equal in area to the areas of A and C, by moving the table in plat B and reflecting the change in the reference table.

Such a scheme does not provide a general solution to all allocation problems, but it does offer a useful measure of flexibility for the control program, thereby permitting various degrees of automaticity. The scheme takes its place as a compromise between the two extremes of completely planned and completely automatic allocation. The Burroughs B-5000 (announced in 1960) employed a scheme that used a reference table.

One way to reduce the time required for the indirect addressing is to place the reference table in a memory unit with shorter access time than the remainder of memory. Another possibility is to use indexing to circumvent much of the addressing: In this event, if normal indexing is desired, a double-indexing operation is required and some of the index registers, call them *base registers*, are loaded with base addresses from the reference table. To address a table, its base address must appear in one of the base registers. Assuming that the instruction format still permits "short" addresses (we have been assuming ten bits), any row in a table of dimension less than or equal to 1024 can be addressed by summing a base register and a short address. Additional addressing flexibility can be gained by summing the three quantities from the base register, an index register, and the instruction. Assuming that the summation can be performed fast enough to be effectively overlapped by other operations, the time lost reduces to the time required to load base registers whenever necessary. The required number of such loads is dependent on the number of base registers and the number of different tables being addressed at a given point in a job.

**Paging.** We have glimpsed the main problems that arise in the attempt to make more efficient use of memory. Typically, the memory that is economically justifiable for a job is not large enough to accommodate the job without extensive reuse of some memory plats. If only the memory were 100 or 1000 times larger! If only it were as large, say, as the store!

One way of getting around the memory limitation is to let the programmer employ the fiction that the store is a vast word-addressable memory, and then execute the program via memory by means that are automatic from the programmer's viewpoint. To facilitate discussion, we shall resort to an example involving specific capacities for the memory and the store.

Let a memory of $2^{13}$ words be divided into $2^5$ blocks, each of $2^8$ words, i.e., let a memory of roughly 8000 words be divided into 32 blocks of 256 words each. Similarly, let a store of $2^{20}$ words be divided into $2^{12}$ pages, each of $2^8$ words. The memory is word-addressable and the store is page-addressable; a 13-bit address designates a memory word and a 12-bit address designates a store page.

Since programs are to be assembled as if the store were word-addressable, a 20-bit address field is required of the instruction format. The tables of an assembled job are loaded into the store and, prior to the execution phase, a suitable set of pages is copied into the 32 blocks of memory.

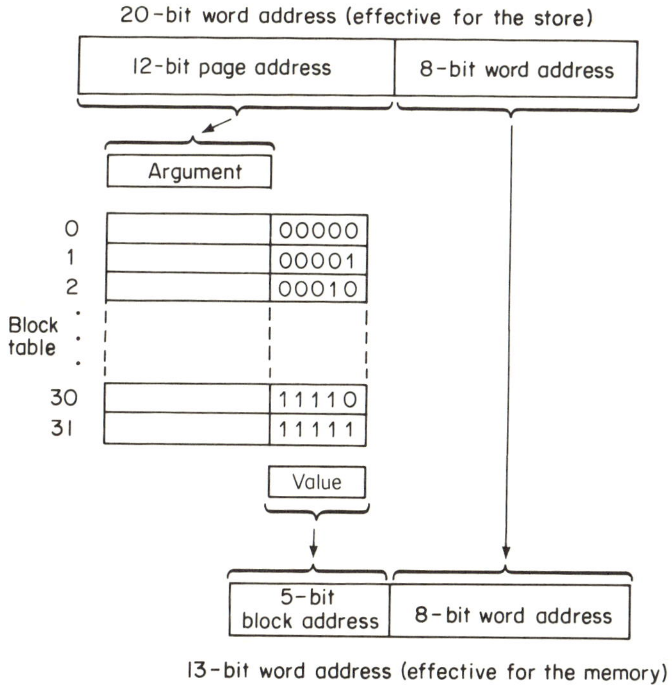


**Fig. 10.1** Schematic of automatic address conversion.

The necessary conversion between effective store and memory addresses, which involves the replacement of a 20-bit store address by a 13-bit memory address, is accomplished by searching a *block table* of 32 rows (one row for each memory block). See the schematic in Fig. 10.1. The search argument is a 12-bit page number and the value obtained is either a 5-bit block number or a *no-match*. Each row of the block table identifies the page that occupies the corresponding block. Because the block table mentions only the pages that are held in memory, a no-match condition implies that the desired page must be *pulled* (fetched) from the store, a task to be performed by a memory-contained control program. Prior to the pull, however, a memory block must be selected to receive the incoming page. If block B corresponds to page P, and if B is selected, then B must be *pushed* (copied) back into P—unless the content of P is known to have gone unchanged during its stay in B. Whenever a page is pulled, the block table is appropriately updated.

Because the time required to perform the block-table search can be made very short by diligent design efforts, the search itself is not a major impediment to this method. Conceivably, the search could be conducted by a chained-scatter algorithm, but search via a parallel-search memory is more appealing because the time requirement is predictable and constant. A more incisive question involves effectiveness in terms of the observed store-to-memory traffic, which in turn involves the question of selecting appropriate blocks to be overlaid. A method that is largely blind to the behavior of a program must occasion some penalty in traffic that would be considered unnecessary by an informed decision maker. Although present evidence is not conclusive on this question, the method is of continuing interest for the convenience it affords.

Moreover, current investigations are showing that the traffic penalty can be substantially reduced by appropriate formulation of applications, such as matrix algebra, that employ systematic algorithms. It may turn out that paging feasibility depends on the programmer. In any case, one disadvantage of paging lies in the unusually long instruction-address fields that are required.

As explained, the paging scheme effectively displaces the programmer's concern with allocation from the memory to the store. In practice, it will not do for every program to assume that the store is private property. Effective use of the computer system naturally demands that programs and structurands of more than one job occupy the store together. This means that a planned or software-aided allocation method is needed for the store. One way to systematize this is to permit programmers to address pages symbolically and have a *page table* of $2^{12}$ rows (one row per page) that identifies the actual location of a symbolically named page. Note that the page table can be held in the store and accessed during searches by paging (like any other table). Only a fraction of the table is of concern to any given job.

The memory-allocation scheme employed in the Ferranti ATLAS (announced in 1958) is similar in many respects to the above-discussed example of automatic allocation. The ATLAS store consists of magnetic drums; its use is reported by J. Fotheringham (1961).

**Compromises.** The three methods thus far discussed (list processing, indirect addressing, and paging) can be viewed as "pure" approaches to memory allocation. However, all three occasion an appreciable penalty in overhead for the service rendered. Where the service rendered is more elegant than needed by a typical user, the dictates of system efficiency may argue for less elegant compromises. A likely compromise permits the user to plan the major aspects of allocation and abets this with a pool of memory that can be dynamically allocated for transitory tables, many of which are typically small. Some of the useful properties of the pure approaches can be exploited where most needed. A control program designed on the basis of compromise may render many valuable services and conveniences to the user. If the compromise involves too many different allocation principles, of course, the system becomes difficult to teach.

## 10.3 Assisted Copying

As the discussions of sequencing and allocation have suggested, the execution of a job usually entails a good deal of traffic between memory and auxiliary storage units. Tables needed in memory have to be copied from magnetic surfaces; tables altered or generated in memory may have to be copied back onto magnetic surfaces. Copying, like allocation, is a chore for the programmer because memories have practical limitations on their capacities. Copying also provides useful answers to the fact that central processing units cannot be completely fault-free. In either case, copying involves a surprising clutter of system details and performance considerations; the typical programmer properly regards these as distractions best relegated to a control program.

Many of the concepts underlying today's control programs were first embodied in the software aids known in the latter half of the 1950's as input/output control systems. These IOCS packages were developed primarily for accounting applications with files stored on magnetic tapes. The typical IOCS made central use of four mnemonic macroinstructions: OPEN, CLOSE, GET, and PUT. If an input file A resided on magnetic tape, the instruction OPEN A verified that the first reel of A was mounted (by examining label information on the tape) and then read in the first data block. If file B was to be written on tape, the instruction OPEN B wrote a standard label at the beginning of the reel provided. OPEN was issued once for each file, at first mention of the file. Thereafter, GET A could be issued to request a record from file A and PUT B to dispose of a record destined for file B. The various services needed for label creation, label checking, blocking, unblocking, reel changing (with a message to the operator), error monitoring, and checkpointing were provided by IOCS. The final reference to each file was to issue a CLOSE macroinstruction.

The general idea at first was that the information needed for central purposes would be provided at the time a program was assembled or compiled. It was soon found useful to delay specification of some of the parameters until job-initiation time; later, some parameters were specified dynamically (at OPEN time); now the general idea is to specify parameters at the latest possible time. This implies, quite correctly, that the control program has steadily intervened more deeply in copying operations.

The milieu in which IOCS was developed gave way, during the 1960's, to a far more complicated one. First, IOCS succeeded so well that it became mandatory for nearly all applications. Second, and more importantly, the direct-access storage device entered on the scene in an important way. These devices have had, and should continue to have, a profound impact on allocation and copying. Not only is device control a complicated matter and performance a function of several variables, but direct access opens up a wider class of useful operating modes. The user can hope to do more and, as a consequence, he looks to the control program for a greater variety of assistance. In particular, he may want more help with searches. Today, the control-program functions that assist a user with allocation, copying, and searching are sometimes collectively referred to as *data management*.

## 10.4 Assisted Searching

In a batch-processing context where processing is typically performed in the course of serial passes over sorted tape files, much of the responsibility for search remains with the user. The most important aid to the user is a general-purpose sorting program. Another convenience may be a utility program that searches through a program-library tape and copies the programs needed by a given job. However, in the context of direct-access storage devices, there is much to be gained by delegating more responsibility to the control program. The user can pass the name of any table to the control program and expect the control program to find the table. The user may then provide the name (i.e., the key) of a record, say R, in the table and expect the control program to find R and copy it in memory. From R, the user may select a pointer and then ask the control program to obtain the record addressed by the pointer.

We see at once that the control program must maintain a catalog of all stored tables. To make this possible, the control program must either control or monitor all aspects of allocation. It must be endowed with the ability to establish new tables and carry through node insertions and deletions in tabled structurands. Essentially, the control program becomes a librarian that is fully enagaged in allocating space and cataloging, finding, copying, and searching tables.

For the sake of convenience and efficiency, the user may want a variety of options for organizing catalogs and tables (a convention for table organization is sometimes called an access method). The control program must maintain information about each storage device, each plat of space, and each table that is currently defined. En masse, this "system catalog" contains a greater variety of information than we normally associate with library catalogs, and all of the information must be stored in tabular form. Since the questions of how to subdivide the system catalog and where to place the segments have a decisive impact on system performance, they receive a great deal of attention in the design of a control program. The solution is likely to be a complicated one, and the first step in learning the structure of a control program is that of learning the structure of the system catalog.

The main catalog, i.e., the portion of the system catalog of most concern to the user, is typically organized in the general form of a tree with alphameric dub tags. This being the case, the control program employs some variation of a path search to find a named table.

Assuming that a system offers the user a variety of options, the ultimate performance of the system must depend heavily on four considerations: (1) library structure, (2) catalog structure, (3) table structure, and (4) setup planning. In an installation with a large number of applications, it is virtually impossible—at least at the current state of the art—to optimize performance for areas 1 and 2 in a mathematically planned sense. There are simply so many variables at work that human judgment must play a role. It is therefore important that the library and the catalog offer enough flexibility that improvements can be made on the basis of installation experience. Much the same is true of area 4, where the goal is to reduce search times by judiciously performing copying tasks in advance of search. Some of the copies may occur at the beginning of a day, others prior to a set of related jobs, and still others at job-initiation time or during the job. The area in which the user can plan most confidently in advance is 3; here the relevant question concerns the searching of a table for a desired record, and the considerations mentioned in Chapters 3 and 4 come to the fore.

Thus far, we have been tacitly assuming that control-program assisted searching was done to retrieve a named table or a named record. However, the potentialities of direct-access storage devices make it worthwhile to consider other possibilities. One such possibility concerns assisted searches for named portions of a record, say groups of fields or individual fields. Another concerns selective searches that examine two or more columns in a table (or even different tables) and select records based on relationships among elements in the columns. Presently, experience with such search programs is accumulating from special-purpose programs of a pioneering nature; for example, see J. H. Bryant and P. Semple, Jr. (1966), R. E. Bleier (1967), and P. J. Dixon and J. Sable (1967).

## 10.5 Representation of Table Elements

Conceptually, there are two distinct steps in the representation of a structurand (and we may consider programs as one class of structurands). The first step creates a matrix that we have been calling a table. The table consists of a matrix that represents the structure of the structurand (see Chapter 3), and adjoined to this matrix is a column of nodes. Because the format of the elements in the table is not directly germane to general discussions of searching, sorting, allocation, and copying, we have avoided the matter as much as possible. The format of the elements is usually referred to as the *representation* of the table.

Representation is a mutual concern of the hardware designer, the software systems programmer, and the application programmer because it has deep implications for performance and convenience. Representation is the practical aspect of data processing that *has* to be considered. It is possible to write books about computers or data processing and discuss little but representation. Most of the reference manuals and training manuals that abound in the industry are predominantly discussions of representation in the system under discussion. From these manuals, the reader is not expected to discern the inherent structure of the system; if the structure is described at all, the description appears in manuals of a more specialized nature. Here our purpose is merely to identify the main considerations involved in representation and mention the solutions currently of greatest importance.

**Text representation.** In many applications, the structurands are elementary in their structures and the nodes consist of alphameric strings of arbitrary or variable lengths. Examples occur in concordance preparation; cryptanalysis; document selection on the basis of titles, abstracts, or key words; computer-aided language translation; message distribution; and text editing and page composition. We mention these applications because of the still-prevalent notion that numbers are intrinsic to computers and data processing. In quite another type of data processing, a far more specialized type, mathematical or logical equations are represented in symbols and processed by formal algorithms appropriate to equations. In these cases the structurands may well have the properties of trees.

Another way that alphameric strings enter into data processing is via assembly languages and high-level languages. The merits of mnemonic aids in programming have previously been discussed. Even after a source program has been translated into machine language, it may embrace alphameric literals, for example, messages to the operator or headings and stubs for printed tables.

A third major source of alphameric strings manifests itself in the identifiers and descriptors that are associated with most accounting and inventory files. Although these strings may contain decimal digits, alphabetic letters, or a combination of both, as the following discussion will show, processing usually makes no distinction between letters and digits. In other words, the digits are treated as characters, not as numbers.

In the normal course of evolution, a natural language comes to provide for ready identification of the classes of objects and events of general interest to society. But as classes to be identified narrow, language becomes increasingly unwieldy for purposes of identification. In the limit, as classes get down to one member, a social language cannot efficiently serve for identification. Ordinary language is inappropriate for identifying the objects and events that must be followed in statistical studies, in public and corporate administration, and in design, production, inventory, and distribution processes. As the success of such activities is dependent on data processing, and data processing in turn on feasible methods of identification, it is necessary to coin identifiers in planning systematic data processes. This minting process is often called *coding*. This use of the term is consonant with the idea of encoding; the *symbols* being encoded are the long phrases that would be needed in the absence of a set of short identifiers.

Because identification is ultimately a form of classification, the principal methods of identification are variants of tree-diagram indexing or dubbing. For example, the interval vector is sometimes referred to as a *sequence code*. In commerce, sequence codes are widely used for identifying checks. Rigidly applied, however, a sequence code leads to problems. For example, if several individuals are writing checks on a joint account, it is often more convenient and informative to assign an infix of an interval vector to each individual; each individual then identifies his checks with sequential numbers from an infix.

A numbering system that uses infixes of an interval vector is often termed a *block code*. Block codes are widely used for check identification. Infixes are usually so chosen that the left-hand digits (or letters) of each check number identify the individual or the accounting center responsible for the check. This done, the block code emulates the names of leaves in a trim of height 2: Root points correspond to accounting centers and each family on the second level to the checks issued by one center. The set of leaf tags so obtained is known, in the general case of $h$ levels, as a *group classification code*, and each level corresponds to a subject classification. Typical examples are provided by numerical codes for states, counties, and cities.

Alphameric group classification codes are widely used for accounting and cataloging purposes. The Library of Congress system for classifying documents is basically a group classification code of three levels. The first two levels use the uppercase Roman alphabet, and the third level uses infixes from 0, 1, 2, . . . , 999. In practice, the third level is followed by a delineator (usually a decimal point) and one or more levels that aid in shelf arrangement and identification of replicate documents. Although originally designed for purposes of legislative reference to a huge collection, the code is widely used by smaller and more specialized libraries.

Another well-known group classification code of three levels is the Standard Industrial Classification Code, which is intended to embrace the whole range of economic activities in the United States. The reporting units to be classified are not legal entities such as corporations but economic units producing goods or services. The first level consists of two decimal digits and the second and third of one decimal digit each. Zero origins are avoided in the numerical labeling alphabets; automatic processing is simplified by employing the zero as a null symbol in the second and third levels. For example, the major group 20 (food and kindred products), optionally written as 200 or 2000, can still be identified as a major group for summation and tabulation purposes. Likewise, 201 (meat products) can be represented as 2010; the first four-digit class under meat products is 2011 (meat-packing plants).

Abbreviations play an important role in many encoding systems. The standard abbreviations for the chemical elements are mnemonic to a useful degree (inspection of an atomic table will reveal some of the problems, as well as some of the advantages, of mnemonic codes). Abbreviations have been widely used for telephone exchanges and, in the automobile licenses of some states, for counties. In the so-called *significant-digit* codes, often used for identifying manufactured items, some or all of the code digits are quantitatively descriptive of the weight, dimension, capacity, production data, retail price, or other characteristics of the item. The knowledgeable reader cannot only recognize an item by its identifier but is informed or reminded of item characteristics as well. Naturally enough, mnemonic or significant-digit codes are often incorporated into group classification codes.

Few other methods of generating identifiers possess direct relevance to the main stream of data processing. In some circumstances, however, phonetic names can be combined with other information to provide more apt identification. (Although phonetic methods are seldom expected to preserve the one-to-one property of a code, they are usually called codes nonetheless.) One phonetic scheme for surnames, which yields a prefix letter followed by three decimal digits, can be characterized by the following rules. The initial letter of a surname or descriptive term is taken as the prefix letter. The letters, A, E, I, O, U, and Y are not encoded, but serve as separators between consonants or consonant groups. The letters W and H are ignored. With exceptions cited below, the first three remaining consonants are encoded as follows:

| *Consonants* | *Encoding* |
|---|---|
| B, F, P, V | 1 |
| C, G, J, K, Q, S, X ,Z | 2 |
| D, T | 3 |
| L | 4 |
| M, N | 5 |
| R | 6 |

When a consonant (possibly the prefix) is followed without separation by a consonant with the same encoding, the latter consonant is ignored. When insufficient consonants exist, zeros are appended to provide three digits in the result. Thus Smoot, Smuth, Smit, Smith, Smithe, Smythe, Schmit, Schmitt, and Schmidt are encoded by S530; Goodwin, Gutwin, and Gotham by G350; and Jeans, James, Janes, Jones, Junius, Jaymek, Joomecks, and Johns by J520.

For example, in a study relating family fertility to the presense or absence of hereditary disease, H. B. Newcombe and his associates (1959) were faced with the problem of linking marriage records, birth records, and a register of handicapped children. The unreliability of identifiers in successive records concerning the same individual or married pair was found to be a major obstacle to the study. Not only were dates and places frequently inconsistent, but many surnames were found either to have been incorrectly recorded or to have undergone spelling changes during the course of time. Phonetic encodings of the husband's surname and of the wife's maiden name proved to be the most satisfactory means of identifying marriages.

The strings that we have been discussing are normally encoded in a six, seven, or eight-bit alphameric code that is a standard (or one of the standards) for a given computer system. Even though great strides have been made in standardizing throughout the computer industry, many computers are designed with the ability to accommodate more than one code at the hardware level.

**Number representation.** Here are six decimal sequences:

1. 01414
2. 0.015625
3. 0.0156
4. 0.3333
5. 1.414214
6. 14.14

These numbers can play a variety of roles, among which are the following: Sequence 1 is an exact representation of the integer 1414; sequence 2 is an exact representation of the fraction $\frac{1}{64}$; sequence 3 is an inexact representation of $\frac{1}{64}$; sequence 4 is an inexact representation of $\frac{1}{3}$; sequence 5 is an inexact representation of $\sqrt{2}$; and sequence 6 is an inexact representation of $\sqrt{200}$. If the term *significant digit* is used to designate digits other than leading zeros, the number of significant digits in sequences 1–6 is 4, 5, 3, 4, 7, and 4. In computation, the number of significant digits in a number representation is a measure of precision; the greater the precision, the narrower the limits implied in numerical operations. High precision is requisite to high accuracy, but it is no guarantee of high accuracy. While more precise than 1.414214, the number 1.4140000 is less accurate as a specification of $\sqrt{2}$. The number 1.414 is an accurate representation of $\sqrt{2}$ and 1.414214 is a more accurate representation, but neither are exact.

In digital computation, integers can be represented exactly. On the other hand, irrationals such as $\pi$ or $\sqrt{2}$ cannot be represented exactly. Rationals (ratios of integers) may or many not be represented exactly, depending on the relationship of the denominator integer to the computational radix. If the prime factors of its denominator are factors of the radix, a rational can be represented exactly—given sufficient precision.

Let us assume, for the sake of discussion, that sequence 2 is represented by sequence 3. An error creeps in, and two helpful ways of reporting the error are the following:

$$\text{Algebraic error} = 0.0156 - 0.015625 = -0.000025 \tag{10.1}$$

$$\text{Relative error} = \frac{0.0156 - 0.015625}{0.015625} = -0.0016. \tag{10.2}$$

In an addition of signed numbers, the algebraic error of the sum is the sum of the algebraic errors in the numbers being added. To the extent that the algebraic errors may be thought to have a random character, this seems to be reassuring. Unfortunately, however, there is no upper limit on the possible increase in the relative errors of addition and subtraction: Two numbers of opposite sign that cancel may provide the denominator of (10.2). On the other hand, if small relative errors are assumed, analysis shows that the relative errors are added in multiplication and subtracted in division. This means that relative error is more stable in multiplication and division than in addition and subtraction.

**VFL computations.** Let the vector of digits used to represent an integer be called a field, and let vector dimension be called field length. In arithmetic operations on integers, the maximum field length of a result is a function of the type of operation and the operand lengths. In multiplication, if a multiplier and multiplicand are represented by fields $x$ and $y$, the product can always be represented by a field of dimension $\rho x + \rho y$. For example, $99 \times 999 = 98{,}901$. In algebraic addition of two operands, the sum can require a field longer than the longest operand by at most one place. In dividing a dividend by a nonzero divisor, the quotient field may equal in length the dividend field ($9999 \div 001 = 9999$) and the remainder field may equal in length the divisor field.

Clearly, if operand ranges are known in an exact integer computation, field lengths for all results can be planned. Three encoding methods suggest themselves. The first is to encode all integers in compatible fields and choose the length that suffices for the largest integer that may be encountered. The second is to represent each operand or result in the longest field that it may require; in this method, field lengths continue to be independent of data values (as long as these data stay within their prescribed ranges). The third method, which avoids leading zeros entirely, encodes each integer in the minimum number of digits; in this case, field lengths are affected by actual data and a computational algorithm must be prepared to handle different field lengths each time it is executed with different input data.

These three methods will be termed the FFL (fixed field length), VFL (variable field length), and MFL (minimum field length) methods, respectively. FFL has the advantage of format simplicity; only one field length is involved. Its disadvantage is that many leading zeros may be required in encoding the integers of a nontrivial computation. VFL reduces the expected number of leading zeros but requires that the lengths of different fields be indicated in some way. MFL avoids all leading zeros but has the disadvantage that the field lengths to be encountered in a given computation cannot be predicted in advance.

The VFL and MFL methods (both have kinships with longhand methods) are most suitable for computers that perform arithmetic operations in a decimal digit-by-digit mode. Field lengths can be indicated by various means. One way is to associate each field with a number in a vector of field lengths. Another is to begin and end each field with a special symbol; in this case, the delineator symbol that marks the end of one field may be used to indicate the beginning of another field. For VFL, field lengths can be instruction-contained. However, the relative merits of VFL and MFL do not hinge entirely on encoding considerations; of the two, VFL has gained the wider acceptance because it is more conducive to efficient search. Where several encoded fields are catenated as one long vector, the position of each infix field is invariant in VFL and data-dependent in MFL. As a consequence, the time required to locate and fetch a MFL field may far exceed the time required to fetch a VFL field.

VFL computations are especially suitable for accounting applications wherein the arithmetic requirements are modest, operand ranges are highly predictable, and special rounding conventions may be desired. A unit price or an interest rate is an exact number, having been made so by fiat. Although a VFL computation is carried through as though it involved integers, it may involve rounding operations, as when mills are rounded up to cents in a penny-accounting operation, or when cents are dropped in the final result of a dollar-accounting operation. At the end of a VFL computation, decimal points are edited into the results in accordance with the planned format.

Integer computations are also widely used in address calculations. In this context, division operations are usually followed by floor or ceiling operations.

**FFL computations.** The computations of engineering and science have little in common with those of accounting. Elaborate mathematical methods may be required, and typically the number of arithmetic operations per solution is high. Seldom are inputs dignified by fiat; the mathematical model, the solution method, the input data—all must be viewed as useful approximations. Moreover, the ranges of the intermediate variables and results may be highly unpredictable; in fact, the main purpose of the computation may be to make an assessment of result ranges. The primary objective in an engineering computation is not to be exact; it is rather to retard the growth of relative error. Secondary objectives concern cost, convenience, and elapsed time.

The currently popular compromise to these objectives combines an FFL representation of base-2 (binary) numbers in a floating-point format. The FFL binary representation is conducive to high-speed execution of arithmetic operations. The floating-point conventions are a convenience to the programmer, accommodate a great range of numbers, and retard relative errors about as well as competitive methods.

A decimal rational number can be expressed in many ways. Consider the following example:

$$9683.426 \times 10^{-1}$$
$$968.3426 \times 10^{0}$$
$$96.83426 \times 10^{1}$$
$$9.683426 \times 10^{2}$$
$$.9683426 \times 10^{3}$$
$$.09683426 \times 10^{4}\,.$$

In this example, the same number is scaled in six different ways. In a floating-point format, a position of the radix point is assumed, once and for all, and any "mistake" made in scaling a number to the format is corrected in an exponent. Let $(f, c)$ denote a decimal floating-point number, where $f$ is a signed ten-digit fraction with an assumed decimal point on the left and $c$ is a signed two-digit exponent. The last two representations of 968.3426 then take these floating-point forms:

$$(+9683426000,\ +\ 03)$$
$$(+0968342600,\ +\ 04)\,.$$

The fields for $f$ and $c$, separately encoded in FFL formats, are normally catenated and moved about as one vector.

A nonzero fraction is said to be *normalized* if it contains no leading zeros, i.e., if the decimal point is followed by a nonzero digit. If two fractions are encoded in fields $x$ and $y$, we know at once that their product can be encoded in a vector $w$, where $\rho w = \rho x + \rho y$. Thus $(.101)^2 = .010201$ and $(.999)^2 = .998001$. Moreover, as this example shows, the product of two normalized fractions may contain at most one leading zero.

To examine division with fractions, let $x$ and $y$, respectively, denote a normalized dividend and a normalized divisor. Then the quotient $q$ will be a normalized fraction if $x < y$. If $x \geq y$, then $q$ is not a fraction but, in the base-$r$ case, a number such that $1 \leq |q| < r$, a condition that is termed *division overflow*. For example, $.101 \div .999 = .101$ (plus a remainder fraction) and $.999 \div .101 = 9.89$ (plus a remainder fraction).

When two normalized fractions of like sign are summed, the sum $s$ is either a normalized fraction or, in the event of *sum overflow*, a number $s$ such that $1 \leq |s| < r$. Thus $.101 + .101 = .202$, and $.999 + .999 = 1.998$. On the other hand, the difference of two normalized fractions of like sign must be a fraction.

An arithmetic operation on floating-point numbers is required to yield a correct exponent as well as a correct fraction. For the sake of discussion, let us assume that the operands are normalized and the result is to be normalized; this is called the *normalized mode* of operation. In obtaining the sum or difference of two normalized operands, the fraction with the lower exponent is preshifted to the right until the exponents match. The sum takes the matching exponent unless an overflow occurs, in which case its fraction is postshifted one place to the right and its exponent increased by 1. A difference takes the matching exponent unless cancellation leads to $k$ leading zeros, in which case the difference fraction is postshifted $k$ places to the left and the tentative exponent is reduced by $k$.

Preshifting is unnecessary for multiplication and division, but a postshift of one place may be required. In multiplication, operand exponents are added to obtain a tentative product exponent. If a leading zero occurs in the product, the product fraction is shifted one place to the left and the tentative exponent is reduced by 1. In division, the divisor exponent is subtracted from the dividend exponent to obtain a tentative quotient exponent. If overflow occurs, the quotient is shifted one place to the right and the tentative exponent is increased by 1.

The maximum precision of a floating-point number system is dictated by its radix and its field length for fractions. On the other hand, the maximum range of a floating-point system is a function of the range of its exponent. A decimal normalized fraction with a two-digit signed exponent has the approximate range $10^{-99}$ to $10^{+99}$.

The automatic rescaling features of normalized floating-point operations preclude overflow in the usual fixed-point sense. Overflow can occur only in summing exponents. Overflow on a positive exponent is termed floating-point overflow and overflow on a negative exponent floating-point underflow. Such overflows indicate that a number is out of range.

One of the advantages of a floating-point system stems from its ability to rescale results individually and at the time they are formed. This rescaling is helpful in controlling the cumulative effects of rounding error. On the other hand, the results of a normalized floating-point computation carry with them no information concerning relative error; unknown to the analyst, the computation may have been ravaged by cancellation error. Did cancellation occur to a serious degree? If so, at what point in the computation? The floating-point results do not provide the answers. It can be argued, therefore, that the best fixed-point computation is better than the best floating-point computation. In a fixed-point computation, the rescaling function is left to the program, rescaling operations are undertaken judiciously, and a whole vector or matrix may be rescaled at one time. A fixed-point program may take more planning than a floating-point program, and may take longer to execute, but it can report on the nature of the rescaling operations that were found necessary, and the information so reported can bolster an interpretation of the computational results. Most floating-point computers are designed with instructions for unnormalized arithmetic; these omit the automatic postshifting function and permit the programmer to intervene in the rescaling function and thereby gather information with a bearing on accuracy. Also, for the cases where additional precision is needed, the unnormalized operations permit the programmer to write programs for *double precision*, *triple precision*, etc. If the ordinary (single-precision) fraction $f$ is represented by $n$ bits, then double-precision arithmetic is fundamentally akin to arithmetic on base-$2^n$ numbers of two digits, triple-precision arithmetic base-$2^n$ numbers of three digits, etc. (Some computers contain special instructions for double-precision floating-point arithmetic.)

The cumulative rounding error in a floating-point computation is dependent in large part on the fraction lengths and the number of rounding operations. For a given rounding method, one can say that cumulative rounding error is decreased by (1) employing longer field lengths and (2) reducing the number of rounding operations. The number of rounding operations can often be reduced significantly by representing products in an unrounded form during the course of a summation. Assume, for example, that the components of two compatible vectors $x$ and $y$ are encoded as FFL fractions. Now consider a statement of the form

$$z = \sum_{i=1}^{\rho x} (x_i \times y_i).$$

If each product $x_i \times y_i$ is rounded prior to summation, execution involves $\rho x$ rounding operations. On the other hand, if unrounded products are accumulated in a double-length register, and if the final sum in this register is rounded to yield $z$, execution involves only one rounding operation.

Apart from the approximations inherent in mathematical models and solution methods, apart from source data accuracy and apart from human blunders and machine failures, we have seen that a computation on FFL fractions is subject to two debilitating factors. The first of these is cumulative rounding error; the second is cancellation. An experienced analyst may be able to estimate rounding error to a useful degree, but the effects of cancellation can be highly unpredictable. And whereas some problems lend themselves to reasonably inexpensive checks on the accuracy of a numerical solution, many do not. For this reason, there has been some interest in representations that start a computation with normalized operands and then rescale overflows automatically but that carefully propagate the leading zeros arising from cancellation. As the leading zeros in a result would then be a measure or index of the digits of accuracy lost through cancellation, such a method will be termed *floating-index* encoding.

Let $k_1$ and $k_2$ be the counts of leading zeros in the fractions of two floating-point numbers, and let $k_3$ be the maximum of $k_1$ and $k_2$. Typically, in floating-index work, a product or quotient formed from given floating-point numbers is represented as a fraction with $k_3$ leading zeros and a consistently chosen exponent. In forming sums or differences, one fraction is preshifted right, if necessary, to provide matching exponents. If a sum overflows, it is corrected as in any floating-point operation, but sums and differences are otherwise never postshifted. Under these rules, cancellation is the only condition that can lead to an increase in leading zeros.

When leading zeros exist, floating-point computations are subject to greater cumulative rounding error than in normalized work. Thus when cancellation occurs, a floating index yields information on cancellation at a penalty in increased rounding error. It has been suggested that the average rounding error can be more carefully controlled by explicitly encoding the number of leading zeros as an integer. Each operand would then be represented in the form $(k, c, f)$, where $k$ denotes the leading-zero index. All fractions could be normalized, inasmuch as leading-zero information would be propagated via $k$. See H. L. Gray and C. Harrison Jr. (1959).

**Radix conversion.** Because one of the objectives of encoding, in the electronic-computer context, is to reduce all operands to a logical representation, the base-2 alphabet ultimately comes into play. For numerical operands, one way of attaining this objective is to convert directly from decimal to binary numbers. At the end of the computation, the binary results can then be converted back into decimal. In discussing radix conversion, however, one might as well treat the general problem of converting between decimal and base-$r$ systems. The conversion of a literal to base-$r$ is best treated in two steps: The first step converts its integral part and the second its fractional part.

To express an integer $x$ in base $r$ is to find coefficients in an equation of the form

$$x = a_n r^n + \cdots + a_1 r^1 + a_0 r^0. \tag{10.3}$$

These coefficients are obtained as remainders when the equation is repeatedly divided by $r$. The first division yields a remainder $a_0$ and a quotient

$$a_n r^{n-1} + \cdots + a_2 r^1 + a_1 r^0$$

of the same form as the original equation. The second division will yield the remainder $a_1$, etc. A zero quotient can signal the end of the conversion.

Example. Convert 155 to five-place octal.

| | | |
|---|---|---|
| 8 | 155 | 3 |
| 8 | 19 | 3 |
| 8 | 2 | 2 |
| 8 | 0 | 0 |
| 8 | 0 | 0 |

The octal result is the vector (0, 0, 2, 3, 3).

Example. Convert 155 to a base-12 number of four places.

| | | |
|---|---|---|
| 12 | 155 | 11 |
| 12 | 12 | 0 |
| 12 | 1 | 1 |
| 12 | 0 | 0 |

The result is the vector (0, 1, 0, 11).

To recover 155 from its base-8 and base-12 encodings, we employ the base value operation. Thus

$$155 = (8, 8, 8, 8, 8) \perp (0, 0, 2, 3, 3) = (12, 12, 12, 12) \perp (0, 1, 0, 11).$$

It is a simple exercise to convert the first eight integers into a binary representation:

| *Integer* | *Binary representation* |
|---|---|
| 0 | 000 |
| 1 | 001 |
| 2 | 010 |
| 3 | 011 |
| 4 | 100 |
| 5 | 101 |
| 6 | 110 |
| 7 | 111 |

(By our usual convention, commas are elided in logical vectors.) Because 8 is a power of 2, one can change an octal number such as (0, 0, 2, 3, 3) to a binary number by mere substitution. Thus the binary representation, say $\boldsymbol{u}$, of octal 00233 is given by (000, 000, 010, 011, 011) or simply 000000010011011. Of course, the base-2 value of $\boldsymbol{u}$ equals 155. Because octal numbers are more easily comprehended than binary numbers, the octal substitution has often been employed to facilitate man-machine communication in binary processes.

To express a fraction $f$ in base $r$ is to find coefficients in an equation of the form

$$f = b_1 r^{-1} + b_2 r^{-2} + \cdots. \tag{10.4}$$

These coefficients will constitute the integral parts of the products obtained in successive multiplication by $r$. The first multiplication yields

$$b_1r^0 + b_2r^{-1} + b_3r^{-2} + \cdots,$$

in which the integral part is $b_1$. If the fractional part is again multiplied by $r$, the coefficient $b_2$ will appear in turn as an integer.

Example. Convert 0.32 to a four-place octal fraction.

| | |
|---|---|
| $8 \times 0.32 = 2.56$ | 2 |
| $8 \times 0.56 = 4.48$ | 4 |
| $8 \times 0.48 = 3.84$ | 3 |
| $8 \times 0.84 = 6.72$ | 6 |

The desired fraction is (2, 4, 3, 6) in a vector representation and the octal point is assumed on the left. Each multiplication yields one octal digit.

In evaluating a base-$r$ fraction of $n$ digits, the appropriate weight vector is given by the series $r^{-1}, r^{-2}, \ldots, r^{-n}$. Thus the weight vector for a four-place octal fraction is (1/8, 1/64, 1/512, 1/4096) and the value of the octal fraction (2, 4, 3, 6) is

$$\frac{2}{8} + \frac{4}{64} + \frac{3}{512} + \frac{6}{4096} = \frac{1310}{4096} = 0.31982421875.$$

**Encoding of decimal digits.** Radix conversion provides one method of reducing a decimal number to logical form. Another method is to treat the number as a string and encode each decimal digit by a logical vector. Most methods of encoding decimal digits as logical vectors employ vectors of fixed dimension. A code of this form can be conveniently displayed as a logical matrix of ten rows; each row encodes one decimal digit. Six of these codes are shown in Table 10.1. In the *fixed-count* codes of matrices $\boldsymbol{A}$, $\boldsymbol{B}$, and $\boldsymbol{C}$, the rows of each matrix possess identical counts.

Matrix $A$, a *one-of-ten* code, is an example of a one-of-$n$ code. Such codes lend themselves well to visual interpretation. Moreover, encoding and decoding can be accomplished by simple means, for example, by devices that relate position to quantity, or that combine counting with vector scanning.

The codes of $\boldsymbol{B}$ and $\boldsymbol{C}$ have fixed counts of two. The *biquinary* code $\boldsymbol{B}$ is formed by combining one-of-two and one-of-five codes in all ten possible ways. The two-of-five code in $\boldsymbol{C}$ exploits the fact that there are exactly ten combinations of five objects taken two at a time.

A code characterized by the logical matrix $\boldsymbol{M}$ is said to be *weighted* if a vector $\boldsymbol{b}$ exists such that for each digit $d$,

$$d = \sum_{i=1}^{\rho \boldsymbol{b}} (\boldsymbol{b}_i \times \boldsymbol{M}_i^d).$$

The one-of-ten code is weighted for $\boldsymbol{b} = (9, 8, 7, 6, 5, 4, 3, 2, 1, 0)$. The biquinary code is also weighted, as inspection will show. The two-of five code in $\boldsymbol{C}$ is a partially weighted code for $\boldsymbol{b} = (6, 3, 2, 1, 0)$, failing only for $d = 0$. Note that the columns of a weighted code may be permuted if the components of the weight vector are similarly permuted.

When the fixed-count restriction is dropped, it becomes possible to generate decimal codes of dimension 4. Three such codes appear as $\boldsymbol{D}$, $\boldsymbol{F}$, and $\boldsymbol{G}$ of

**Table 10.1**

*Six codes for the decimal digits*

| | *One-of-ten* **A** | *Biquinary* **B** |
|---|---|---|
| 0 | 0000000001 | 0100001 |
| 1 | 0000000010 | 0100010 |
| 2 | 0000000100 | 0100100 |
| 3 | 0000001000 | 0101000 |
| 4 | 0000010000 | 0110000 |
| 5 | 0000100000 | 1000001 |
| 6 | 0001000000 | 1000010 |
| 7 | 0010000000 | 1000100 |
| 8 | 0100000000 | 1001000 |
| 9 | 1000000000 | 1010000 |
| *Weights* | 9876543210 | 5043210 |

| | *Two-of-five* **C** | 8-4-2-1 **D** | 2-4-2-1 **F** | *Excess-three* **G** |
|---|---|---|---|---|
| 0 | 00110 | 0000 | 0000 | 0011 |
| 1 | 00011 | 0001 | 0001 | 0100 |
| 2 | 00101 | 0010 | 0010 | 0101 |
| 3 | 01001 | 0011 | 0011 | 0110 |
| 4 | 01010 | 0100 | 0100 | 0111 |
| 5 | 01100 | 0101 | 1011 | 1000 |
| 6 | 10001 | 0110 | 1100 | 1001 |
| 7 | 10010 | 0111 | 1101 | 1010 |
| 8 | 10100 | 1000 | 1110 | 1011 |
| 9 | 11000 | 1001 | 1111 | 1100 |
| *Weights* | | 8421 | 2421 | |

Table 10.1. The first two are weighted codes and are usually referred to by their weight vector. The 8-4-2-1 code encodes decimal digits as base-2 numbers. The 2-4-2-1 code is identical through decimal 4 but assigns 5, 6, 7, 8, and 9 the base-2 encodings of 11, 12, 13, 14, and 15, respectively. The *excess-three* method encodes the digits in $\boldsymbol{\iota}^0(10)$ by base-2 representations of the corresponding integers in $\boldsymbol{\iota}^3(10)$.

Codes $F$ and $G$ of Table 10.1 provide a correspondence between the nine's complement of a decimal digit and the one's complement of its logical encoding vector (see Sec. 7.4). Rows 0 and 9 are therefore related by complementation, as are rows 1 and 8, rows 2 and 7, etc. This property can be useful in implementing decimal subtraction with binary adders. It also follows that an overflow will occur naturally in the binary addition of two rows when the sum of the corresponding decimal digits exceeds 9. In the excess-three addition, the result is not in excess-three code until corrected by $+ 3$ or $- 3$, according to whether overflow has or has not occurred.

The designers of most digital computers have defined a character set comprising the decimal digits; the uppercase Roman letters; punctuation marks; special typewriter symbols such as $\div$, &, \$, $+$, $-$ and $=$; and a number of symbols for intrasystem control. In encoding such alphabets, they usually make a decimal-digit code play a central role. In some systems, each alphameric character is encoded by two decimal digits. In some of these systems, a decimal digit is twice eligible for encoding: It may be encoded as a decimal digit, or it may be encoded as an alphameric. In interpreting a message, it is then necessary to know whether the message is a sequence of decimal digits or a sequence of alphameric characters. Within the computer, the encoding mode may be governed under program control. Messages from an external source must be prefaced by a stipulation of the encoding mode unless, of course, the source employs one mode consistently.

Another popular scheme has been to embed a decimal digit code within an alphameric code. For example, in a six-bit code, which will accommodate an alphabet of 64 characters, a four-bit code for the decimal digits may be a subset. Arithmetic operations can then ignore two of the bits in each character.

Although extensive use has been made of six-bit codes, the development of new applications and the desire for a greater symbol range has also led to seven and eight-bit codes. A seven-bit code is awkward, however; more attractive is an eight-bit code with two modes of operation. In the first mode, the code permits an alphabet of 256 alphameric characters; in the second mode, the code encodes a pair of decimal digits. Such a code permits a practical compromise between a large alphabet and high efficiency in storing and processing arithmetic operands.

In an evolving and competitive industry, nothing is more natural than for different manufacturers to define their own alphameric alphabets and encoding conventions. Moreover, as technology changes, the engineering limitations and economic balances of one day have a tendency to go by the board in the next, generating new incentives for manufacturers to expand alphameric alphabets or to modify encoding methods. In the digital-computer industry, the encoding babel to which these forces led is analogous to a problem of interchangeable parts in the manufacturing industries. Conflicting codes can be an obstacle in efforts to bring many data communication and processing activities into one integrated system. After much work by the American Standards Association and other interested groups, a code called ASCII (American Standard Code for Information Interchange) became an official ASA Standard in June 1963. Although ASCII was not a representative code at the time of adoption, versions of it have since come into wide use.

**Error detection and correction.** In optimizing system performance, an acceptable compromise between system costs and error rates is sought. Encoding methods can play a role in this optimization. No matter how low a machine error rate is driven by engineering practices, random errors will still occur. Encoding principles can be used to detect most of these errors.

An $m$-of-$n$ code obviously lends itself to the detection of errors: If the count of a code vector fails to equal $m$, then one or more errors must have occurred. The one-of-ten and two-of-five codes invite such a count check. Although the biquinary code can be checked as a two-of-seven code, it is even more appropriate to employ selection and separately check the one-of-two and one-of-five portions.

**Table 10.2**

*Error detection and correction codes*

| | | *Odd parity* | *Even parity* | *Hamming code* $H$ |
|---|---|---|---|---|
| | 0 | 1 0 0 0 0 | 0 0 0 0 0 | 0 0 0 0 0 0 0 |
| | 1 | 0 0 0 0 1 | 1 0 0 0 1 | 1 1 0 1 0 0 1 |
| | 2 | 0 0 0 1 0 | 1 0 0 1 0 | 0 1 0 1 0 1 0 |
| | 3 | 1 0 0 1 1 | 0 0 0 1 1 | 1 0 0 0 0 1 1 |
| | 4 | 0 0 1 0 0 | 1 0 1 0 0 | 1 0 0 1 1 0 0 |
| | 5 | 1 0 1 0 1 | 0 0 1 0 1 | 0 1 0 0 1 0 1 |
| | 6 | 1 0 1 1 0 | 0 0 1 1 0 | 1 1 0 0 1 1 0 |
| | 7 | 0 0 1 1 1 | 1 0 1 1 1 | 0 0 0 1 1 1 1 |
| | 8 | 0 1 0 0 0 | 1 1 0 0 0 | 1 1 1 0 0 0 0 |
| | 9 | 1 1 0 0 1 | 0 1 0 0 1 | 0 0 1 1 0 0 1 |
| *Weights* | | 0 8 4 2 1 | 0 8 4 2 1 | 0 0 8 0 4 2 1 |

*Hamming check pattern (one-origin index)*

| *Parity column* | *Column checked* | | | | | | | | | | | | | | | |
|---|---|---|---|---|---|---|---|---|---|---|---|---|---|---|---|---|
| 1 | 1 | | 3 | | 5 | | 7 | | 9 | | 11 | | 13 | | 15 | . . . |
| 2 | | 2 | 3 | | | 6 | 7 | | | 10 | 11 | | | 14 | 15 | . . . |
| 4 | | | | 4 | 5 | 6 | 7 | | | | | 12 | 13 | 14 | 15 | . . . |
| 8 | | | | | | | | 8 | 9 | 10 | 11 | 12 | 13 | 14 | 15 | . . . |
| . | | | | | | | | | | | | | | | | . |
| . | | | | | | | | | | | | | | | | . |
| . | | | | | | | | | | | | | | | | . |

The most likely error affects a single component of a logical vector. If all vector counts are forced to be odd (or forced to be even), such an error is easily detected by a parity check. The count of any logical vector can be forced to desired parity by catenating one component. In Table 10.2 the 8-4-2-1 code for decimal digits is amended to provide codes with odd and even parities. (The parity-bit column is indicated by zero weight.) These simple parity codes illustrate a technique that has been widely employed in alphameric codes for single-error detection.

By extending the parity principle, the single errors may be corrected as well as detected. Code *H* of Table 10.2 is an 8-4-2-1 code modified to afford single-error correction. Codes of this type are named for R. W. Hamming (1950), who first provided a systematic explanation of the error-correcting properties of parity checks. The parity check columns in code *H* are identified by their zero weights. Even parities are used throughout, and one-origin column indexing is assumed. Column 1 provides even parity for columns 1, 3, 5, and 7; column 2 for columns 2, 3, 6, and 7; and column 4 for columns 4, 5, 6, and 7.

To illustrate the error-correction potentialities, suppose that the sixth bit in the code for 5 is erroneously negated to yield (0100111). A parity recheck of this vector shows that the parity components in positions 4, 2, and 1 are incorrect, incorrect, and correct in that order. If *correct* and *incorrect* are encoded by 0 and 1, respectively, the *checking number* obtained is 110, which has a base-2 value of 6. The parity checks therefore signal an error in the sixth position of the vector (0100111) in question. Correct results on all three parity checks are interpreted as "no error." After the sixth component is corrected to give (0100101), a recheck of parities yields a checking number 000, as indeed it should.

To discuss the structure of Hamming codes for single-error detection, let a code matrix contain $p$ parity columns and $n - p$ information columns. We are given $n - p$ and wish to determine $p$ (hence $n$). We also wish to specify the matrix columns to be covered by each of the $p$ parity relations; this can be done with the check pattern shown in Table 10.2. Row 1 of the pattern corresponds to the first relation, row 2 to the second relation, etc. It is evident that the $k$th relation, which starts with column $2^{k-1}$, alternately covers and skips blocks of $2^{k-1}$ columns. The first check starts with column 1 and covers every other column. The second check starts with column 2, covers two columns, skips two, covers two in accordance with the pattern.

Note that each of the columns 1, 2, 4, 8, etc., is covered by one and only one parity relation. Because these columns are independent and cannot influence one another, it is convenient to identify them as parity columns. Because the fourth parity check starts in column 8, a logical vector of dimension 7 requires only three parity columns. Vectors of dimension 9 through 15 will require four parity columns. Powers of 2 are avoided in dimensions; for example, a vector of dimension 8 contains no more information bits than a vector of dimension 7. Ruling out cases of dimension 1, 2, 4, 8, etc., the number $p$ of parity columns for a code matrix of $n$ columns should satisfy the relation

$$2^{p-1} < n < 2^p. \tag{10.5}$$

The Hamming code of Table 10.2 is equal in dimension to the biquinary code. Although the latter code does not correct any errors, it detects more types of errors. However, both are too redundant to be popular as decimal codes. Because the ratio $p/n$ declines as $n$ increases, the Hamming code for single-error correction is most attractive for logical vectors of dimension greater than 7. On the other hand, as $n$ increases, the probability of two errors also increases, and this serves to place an upper limit on a feasible value of $n$.

In practice it may be desirable for all parity columns to prefix the information columns. If columns are reindexed to permit this, checking numbers will be affected by the change. The checking number can still be used, but its interpretation must include a permutation.

The theory of parity checks can be extended to cover multiple-error detection and correction. For example, if an extra parity check over all columns is superimposed on a Hamming code for single-error correction, the faculty for double-error detection becomes available. When there are no errors, all parity checks are satisfied. The extra parity check, if placed in column 0, will reveal a single error and the checking number will specify error location. When there are two errors, the extra parity check is satisfied but a nonzero checking number indicates two errors.

Much work has been done on error-correcting codes since Hamming's paper. Parity codes for single-error detection are widely used; Hamming codes for single-error correction have been used to a limited extent. Although they have had little influence on the design of computers, methods capable of detecting bursts of errors are of great interest in the transmission of digital data over communication lines. The basic idea that underlies one important class of methods called *cyclic codes* can be suggested by examples.

Error detection in a cyclic code employs "logical arithmetic," that is, a pseudo arithmetic in which the basic operation is the *not equal* operation, which is also known as *exclusive-or*. Logical arithmetic does not involve carries, and no distinction is made between addition and subtraction, that is,

$$-1 = 1. \tag{10.6}$$

Rules for addition take the form

$$1 + 1 = 0 + 0 = 0 \tag{10.7}$$

$$1 + 0 = 0 + 1 = 1. \tag{10.8}$$

Addition retains its associative properties, so that $1 + (1 + 1) = (1 + 1) + 1 = 1$. Equations (10.6)–(10.8) apply to logical division, as shown by the following examples:

```
                1 1 0 0 1
1 1 0 1 | 1 0 1 1 0 0 1 0
          1 1 0 1
          -------
            1 1 0 0
            1 1 0 1
            -------
            0 0 0 1 0 1 0
                  1 1 0 1
                  -------
                    1 1 1
```

We assume a divisor, say $P$, that starts with 1. Then $P$ "goes into" any sequence of equal length that starts with 1. Typically, the remainder is nonzero.

Now add the remainder to the dividend

```
1 0 1 1 0 0 1 0
          1 1 1
---------------
1 0 1 1 0 1 0 1
```

and repeat the division on the logical sum:

```
                1 1 0 0 1
1 1 0 1 | 1 0 1 1 0 1 0 1
          1 1 0 1
          -------
            1 1 0 0
            1 1 0 1
            -------
                  1 1 0 1
                  1 1 0 1
                  -------
                        0 .
```

Division of the sum yields a zero remainder.

Let a transmitter divide a message sequence by a fixed sequence $P$ and add the remainder to the message; then let the receiver divide the incoming sequence by $P$. A nonzero remainder will signal that the incoming sequence has been incorrectly transmitted. The only problem is that the process garbles the message and the remainder together. To avoid this, the message sequence and the remainder sequence must be separately transmitted, a condition that is easily satisfied. Note that the remainder cannot be longer than the divisor $P$ and that $P$ is a system parameter known to the receiver as well as to the transmitter. If $P$ contains $c$ bits, the solution is to append $c$ redundant zeros to the message—before the logical division by $P$—and thereby obtain a longer message, say $G$. $G$ is then divided by $P$ to obtain a remainder $R$, this $R$ is added into the zero field $G$, and the encoded sequence for transmission consists of $G + R$.

Cyclic error correction is very suitable for serial transmission of variable-length messages and provides comparable error-detection capability with less redundancy than parity checking. Not only is it superior as a method of detecting bursts of errors, but because its properties lend themselves to mathematical analysis, as shown by W. W. Peterson and D. T. Brown (1961), the divisor $P$ can be chosen to safeguard against likely error patterns.

**Variable-dimension codes.** As suggested by previous examples, the character codes of most interest in system design can be represented as matrices; the encoding vectors are compatible. This makes for systematic formats, a compelling consideration in high-speed computers. In special cases, however, average message lengths can be reduced by relaxing the compatibility requirement. If the symbols in the alphabet being encoded vary widely in frequency of use, it is advantageous to assign the shorter encoding vectors to the symbols of highest frequency.

Inherent in the use of a variable-dimension code is the problem of identifying meaningful infixes in a message string. A delineator symbol provides an acceptable solution if the encoding alphabet has a large radix, in which case the inclusion of an extra symbol has a minor effect on efficiency. But the encoding alphabet is small, and at worst if it consists of only two symbols, the marginal cost of an extra symbol is high. In this case, it is more appropriate to choose a set of code vectors with the property that no vector is the prefix of any other vector. As we have seen, this is a property of index vectors at the leaves of a tree.

As an example, consider the problem of designing an efficient binary code for the decimal digits if their distribution in the message population is estimated to be

| 0 | 1 | 2 | 3 | 4 | 5 | 6 | 7 | 8 | 9 |
|---|---|---|---|---|---|---|---|---|---|
| 0.25 | 0.15 | 0.1 | 0.08 | 0.07 | 0.20 | 0.06 | 0.04 | 0.03 | 0.02. |

With the aid of the method described in Sec. 5.4, a minimal two-way tree can be constructed. As shown in Fig. 10.2, the leaves are specified as relative frequencies, and their zero-origin index vectors constitute a code with the desired properties:

| | | | |
|---|---|---|---|
| 0: | 01 | 5: | 11 |
| 1: | 001 | 6: | 1001 |
| 2: | 101 | 7: | 00001 |
| 3: | 0001 | 8: | 000000 |
| 4: | 1000 | 9: | 000001 |

D. A. Huffman (1952) showed that messages sent in this code will be as short, on the average, as is possible with a binary code. No harm is done if the roles of 0 and 1 are reversed in the code, i.e., if all the encoding vectors are complemented. Moreover, vectors of equal dimensions can be interchanged, e.g., 001 could just as well represent 2, in which event 101 would represent 1.

With the derived code, a message of the form 00532 would appear as

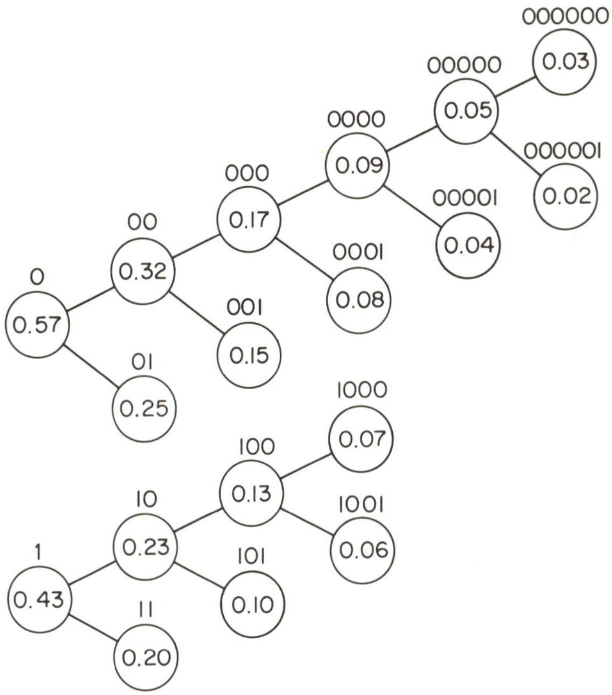


**Fig. 10.2** The tree of a minimum redundancy code.

0101110001101. The only meaningful interpretation permitted by the code will segment the message in the following way:

$$01 - 01 - 11 - 0001 - 101.$$

One disadvantage of such a code is that a single error can invalidate a whole message. The net gain in brevity obtained by the code must therefore take cognizance of any redundancies deemed necessary for error detection and correction functions.

## 10.6 Comment

Because the encoding function spans a wide range of activities, it is rife with possibilities for special techniques. We have therefore confined ourselves to well-known methods that are representative of contemporary electronic digital systems. A computer system that embodied too many encoding methods would lead to chaos. It would be difficult to design, frustrating to learn and use, and costly to implement. Feasibility requires that the designer and user settle for a fairly straightforward compromise. In their efforts to simplify, designers have often tended toward solutions that distinguish clearly between variable-field-length decimal and fixed-field-length binary modes of arithmetic.

*Chapter 11*

# THE DATA SYSTEM

Chapters 1–10 have dwelt on concepts and general information that one needs to begin to appreciate the technology of a data system. The purpose of this final chapter is to bring together the functional components of a system, remark upon one illustrative system, and discuss some of the trade-offs that bear on the design of a system.

## 11.1 Functional Outline

A typical data system embraces

1. A variety of input/output devices
2. A storage hierarchy—from fast-access, low-capacity to slow-access, high-capacity devices—with addressing, formatting, and encoding restrictions
3. Arithmetic and logical units capable of performing a set (say $A$) of *machine-language* operations
4. Built-in programs to control the hardware in performing the tasks of $A$
5. General-purpose control programs capable of directing a large set (say $B$) of resource-allocation, task-sequencing, program-translation, and table-management tasks
6. A data library consisting of a set of structurands represented in the form of encoded tables
7. Special-purpose application programs capable of directing a large set (say $C$) of very complicated tasks
8. A set of job-control conventions by which a user completes the information needed for $B$ tasks at the time that $C$ tasks are executed
9. One or more programming languages with given vocabularies, structurand categories, table conventions, search capabilities, and encoding alphabets, permitting the user to expand $C$

Ten years ago, most discussions of the data system still centered heavily around the arithmetic and logical unit and the machine-language operations in *A*. Since then, attention has been gravitating toward the software control programs and translators in *B*, toward methods for managing the data library, and toward the programming languages the user employs to expand *C*. The importance of *B* has been steadily heightened by developments that permit increasing variety in the input/output devices and the storage hierarchy.

A data system embodies an enormous mass of technical detail. The industry's problem of systematizing this detail is intensified by three circumstances: the technology and the market are expanding rapidly, the users are unusually heterogeneous in their backgrounds and interests, and the software side of the industry has not had time to develop and establish a strong textbook discipline. All of this adds up to an exciting technical challenge for future designers. The same factors, it should be added, tend to frustrate efforts to survey the whole field in a truly balanced and impartial sense. In view of this, an author can do little more than cite examples from representative systems that happen to be conveniently documented.

One rough but useful classification distinguishes among four aspects of a data system: (1) the hardware, (2) the languages and conventions via which the user communicates to the system, (3) the library of general-purpose programs, and (4) the library of application programs. The structure of the data library is restricted, at least in the practical sense, by the capabilities provided in aspects 1, 2, and 3. In today's literature, a planned combination of languages and general-purpose software is termed an *operating system*. Given a hardware configuration and an operating system, the user creates a data library and augments the program library to round out his data system.

To lend the notion of an operating system more concreteness, we briefly survey OS/360, an operating system for medium- to high-performance models in the IBM System/360 family of computers. The typical OS/360 user is expected to program in the FORTRAN, COBOL, or PL/I high-level languages; an assembler language that can be augmented by macroinstructions; or RPG, a report program generator language. Various system macros—such as OPEN, CLOSE, GET, and PUT—provide for interactions between problem programs and the control program. At job time, the user communicates with the control program through a set of parameterized commands known as JCL (job-control language).

The general-purpose program library provides for compilation of FORTRAN, COBOL, and PL/I source programs; report program generation; assembly with macro capabilities; assisted program debugging; and assistance in editing named subroutines and segments to produce an integrated program. Also provided is a many-functioned control program. The control program assists in job queuing and setup, task scheduling, storage allocation, library maintenance and search, record retrieval, and device control. To gain flexibility, the control program supports these functions with a wide variety of options.

Some of the options are frozen at the time the control program is generated, others at the time a control program is loaded, others when a job is recognized and still others during execution. For a concise and informative discussion of the design objectives and planned capabilities of this control program, see the discussions by G. H. Mealy (1966), B. I. Witt (1966), and W. A. Clark (1966).

To supplement OS/360 proper, IBM has developed a program library with dozens of application-oriented programs that provide a measure of generality through options. These programs assume OS/360 and are compatible with it. There are sorting programs, programs for controlling remote terminals, programs for controlling display devices, an extensive set of mathematical subroutines, and other programs for industries and applications too numerous to mention. There are also testing and diagnostic routines for the use of maintenance engineers.

The OS/360 designers distinguish between *reusable* and *reenterable* programs. A reenterable subroutine is a read-only program; any work space required by the subroutine is allocated to the task that calls the subroutine. Since a memory copy of a reenterable subroutine may be treated as a resource that is always available, multiprogrammed tasks can use the resource concurrently. A subroutine is reusable if it terminates by resetting embedded work spaces to initial conditions; a memory copy of a reusable subroutine is a resource that can be allocated to no more than one task at a time. A program that is neither reusable nor reentrant must be fetched from auxiliary storage each time it is invoked.

The OS/360 control program provides a variety of services that assist the user in accomplishing planned program overlays, in dynamically allocating work spaces and buffers, and in regulating the priorities of queued jobs. Modularity in the broadest sense is furthered by defining three versions of the control program for different classes of service: PCP is a primary control program that does not provide multiprogramming, MFT is a control program that provides multiprogramming for a fixed number of tasks, and MVT is a control program that supports multiprogramming for a variable number of tasks. In MFT, the memory area is delineated into $n$ partitions ($n \leq 15$) at the time the control program is loaded. The partition boundaries remain fixed unless the operator elects to combine two adjacent areas at execution time. A partition is assigned to one job at a time and the job is assumed to consist of tasks that can be executed serially. Functionally, MFT operates much as though the system consisted of $n$ separate computers, the relevant property being that each of the $n$ applications is allocated a subset of the system resources. In MVT, on the other hand, memory boundaries can be changed dynamically and an active task can initiate additional tasks. MFT is appropriate for work environments in which resources needed by jobs are relatively stable and predictable and requirements can be met by a simple priority discipline; MVT permits greater flexibility of resource allocation for jobs in which resource requirements can change rapidly.

The System/360 hardware that underlies OS/360 incorporates variable-field-length decimal arithmetic, base-16 fixed-point and floating-point arithmetic with some format options, and binary addressing. An alphameric character is encoded in a *byte* of 8 bits, and provisions are made for encoding two alphameric alphabets (one of them an ASCII convention). To improve performance in decimal tasks, provision is also made for encoding two decimal digits per byte. Sixteen *general registers* are provided as accumulators or index registers. Effective addresses are formed by a three-operand addition that sums two 24-bit memory addresses (from general registers) and a 12-bit *displacement* (from an instruction field). For auxiliary storage, a variety of magnetic-surface devices are provided. Two kinds of data channels are provided, one for high-speed input/output and auxiliary storage devices, the other primarily for large numbers of low-speed terminal devices. A program-interruption system facilitates the control-program functions of task monitoring and sequencing. For protection, memory is divided into 2048-byte blocks. A 4-bit *storage key* associated with each block can be set by the control program. Associated with each task program or data channel operation is a *protection key* that is matched with the storage keys to determine whether memory access is permitted; attempts at unauthorized access are frustrated by interrupts. System/360 decodes about 140 different instructions. One reason this number is large is that several different formats for base-16 operands are provided by the instructions. The design objectives, the general architecture, and the instruction set of System/360 have been described in reports by G. M. Amdahl (1964), G. A. Blaauw and F. P. Brooks, Jr., (1964), A. Padegs (1964), and W. Y. Stevens (1964).

In an expanding and experimenting industry, it may be optimistic to expect that one general-purpose language, or hardware system, or operating system can encompass all applications or market sectors. Hence, it should be added that while the OS/360 and System/360 mentioned here were designed with generality as a foremost objective, IBM supplements them to some extent with other operating systems and computer systems.

## 11.2 Design Considerations

According to the necessity-is-the-mother-of-invention theory, a social want exists, whereupon invention and product development come up with a commodity that gratifies the want. Since the want can be partially gratified by "substitutable" commodities, cost is a critical consideration in the innovation of a commodity. This theory may illuminate many phenomena, but the reason for mentioning it here is that wants—or *needs*, if one prefers—can be somewhat elusive. Today's want may depend on the want gratified yesterday. This is particularly true in the realm of data. If I am a human being engaged in a decision-making process—for example, if I am an editor, engineer, scientist, executive, etc.—every relevant morsel of information educates me, which is tantamount to saying that it changes me. When this happens, I develop a new need for information, and the faster I can obtain and absorb relevant information, the faster I change. At present, it is widely held, most human beings function at a small fraction of their intellectual capacity. Continuing improvements in data-processing technology are often suggested as one way of enlarging this fraction.

Because information can change people, technology levels and user requirements sometimes intertwine in the case of the commodity we call *data system.* The wants for additional data-processing functions may not be insatiable, but they have a way of getting formulated as explicit requirements at approximately the rate at which technology can improve the cost/performance ratio. As a result, the industry is technology-conscious on an extraordinary number of different knowledge fronts. Experimental inquiry goes on at so many different places in so many disciplines at so many different levels of profundity that the observer is easily overwhelmed. The only recourse is to return again and again to first principles and ask which structural elements of the digital system might be simplified (and which might be complicated) as the result of an idea under consideration. We can illustrate the point by examining some familiar *trade-offs*. Obviously, technology has provided decision elements and storage elements that are much faster, smaller, less expensive, and more reliable than those used in EDVAC. The system question is how to exploit this raw potential, and that is where trade-offs come into play.

**Serial versus direct access.** There have been two very significant changes in access technology. The substitution of random-access magnetic-core memories for delay-line memories permitted closer synchronization between accessing and processing and encouraged higher degrees of parallelism and overlapping. The result has contributed substantially to processing potential. In the province of auxiliary storage, the advent of drums and disk units with direct-access properties provided faster access to libraries. Reductions in program setup times have encouraged multiprogramming. In conjunction with on-line terminals, direct access to data libraries has encouraged applications with critical response times, examples being inventory control and aircraft control. Direct access encourages fuller utilization of data than serial access.

On the other hand, the choice between serial and direct search is not entirely a matter of equipment. Accesses that require path searches or search on more than one key entail additional space for indexes or chains of pointers, as discussed in Chapter 4. These indexes and pointers increase the expense of record insertions and deletions. In other words, given direct-access auxiliary storage, programming and operating costs still lead to a trade-off between the complexity of searching a file on many keys or attributes and the simplicity of performing any number of such searches in one serial sweep.

**High-level versus machine language.** The proportion of programs written in high-level language has been on the increase since the introduction of FORTRAN. The advantages of high-level languages relative to assembly languages are that (1) programs can be written more rapidly; (2) programs can contain fewer bugs; (3) programmers can be trained more easily; (4) documentation is improved, i. e., one programmer can follow another's work with less difficulty; (5) the program is more invariant from one hardware design to another; and (6) high-level statements and programs are more appropriate at interactive terminals. On the other side of the coin, translation takes machine time in itself. Moreover, the programmer must in large measure relinquish control over the way in which his task will be executed; this means that he cannot effectively use his special knowledge of the task to minimize memory usage or execution time in critical regions of the program. The trade-offs are exceedingly complicated because they involve not only the programmer but the application languages, software and hardware—all of which may undergo change from time to time. As discussed in Chapter 9, the technology of translation still argues for the use of assembly languages in some cases. Despite these cases, and despite the difficulties of measuring language performance, the high-level language has clearly provided a dramatic impetus to the growth of the computer industry.

**On-line versus off-line input/output.** The on-line principle is one of the most significant data-processing ideas to emerge since EDVAC, although the success of the idea is largely due to improvements in system control, input/output devices, and communication. Some of the potentialities of multiprogramming and on-line terminals at remote locations are now being realized in special-purpose inquiry and inventory transaction applications, as well as in various monitor-and-control applications. The general impact for science, engineering, education, health, government, manufacturing, distribution, etc., appears to be large, but the considerable efforts to date are still at the threshold of potentiality.

This trade-off compels the computer user to reexamine the very fundamentals of his business. Consider a research laboratory. Should each professional have a terminal to a computer that operates in a task-switching mode? Should there be a computing center with programming services and inevitably long response times? Should there be some combination of both? There is no pat answer, but as technology advances, the use of terminals has recommended itself in more and more environments. A related trade-off arises for long lines where transmission capability becomes a costly resource. One way to reduce the quantity of transmitted information is to increase the storage and processing capabilities of the terminal. This is useful as long as transmission costs decrease faster than terminal costs rise.

**General-purpose versus special-purpose systems.** This trade-off has occasioned many a heated discussion. Special-purpose hardware systems for sorting, compiling, and searching have had their advocates but have seldom come to fruition. Over the years, the trend has been toward combining variable-field-length decimal and fixed-format binary capabilities rather than perpetuating them in separate computers. The most convincing case for special-purpose computers arises where computers work on "dedicated" applications that exploit relatively few of the functions provided by a general-purpose digital system. The process-control environment provides examples of this, but the brunt of the trade-off has moved on from hardware to software.

Since the very purpose of every application program is to specialize a general-purpose computer system for a particular class of tasks, a general-versus-special trade-off must be resolved by the programmer in the course of defining the class of potential applications. The programmer may enlarge the class by including more parameters to be specified at execution; however, the degree to which he generalizes will affect his planning, debugging, and documentation investment—and generality is usually accompanied by some penalty in running time and required memory area. The performance loss (particularly in extra memory area) can be minimized by preparing a generator program that tailors a program at task time, but this approach usually costs the most in planning and debugging. The quality of the programmer's decision will depend on the accuracy with which he can predict the usage for the program. In one way or another, every programmer is a product planner; to some extent, he must face the uncertainties of changing markets, conventions, and technologies. This is obvious in the case of the system programmers, but the principle has less conspicuous implications for the application programmer.

**More versus less protection against malfunctions.** Nearly all hardware designs embody redundant checking bits to detect and/or correct errors in copy operations. These bits add to the cost of storage units and data paths. Many software systems have provided checkpoint services, and most applications preserve history files to permit reconstruction in case of disaster. Moreover, multiprogramming systems require memory-protection capabilities. These provisions, and others with less impact on cost, would be superfluous were machines and people fault-free. Suitable amounts and kinds of redundancy depend on the system environment. Real-time control applications, aircraft control, for example, may provide justification for carrying redundancy to unusual lengths.

To put the matter of redundancy in perspective, it is worth recalling that statisticians recommend that manual computations be duplicated—and with some twist to counter the propensity of human beings to make the same mistake twice.

**Hardware versus software.** This trade-off has been widely discussed, but the number of instances in which computer designers have moved software functions into hardware is surprisingly small; the most notable examples being floating-point arithmetic, indexing, indirect addressing, emulation, and some aspects of interruption. As a result, the functional scope of the computer has remained fairly stable, whereas that of general-purpose control programs has expanded greatly. Recently, paging mechanisms that simplify storage allocation have been successful enough to attract increasing attention from system designers.

One advantage of program over circuitry is that it can be modified more readily. A program can be tailored to the needs of a given installation or application; moreover, as experience accumulates, it is usually feasible to improve the program in performance and function. Where a simple, well-established task is involved, a hardware solution performs the task in less time than a software solution. But in the idle state, a library program is a less expensive resource than equivalent function in circuitry.

The traditional distinctions between hardware and software were blurred by the advent of microprograms held in read-only storage devices. These devices offered the hardware designer a trade-off between circuitry and microprograms. If a read/write mode displaces the read-only mode for microprograms, the designers will also be faced with a trade-off between microprograms and machine-language programs.

**Compilation versus interpretation.** Because compilers are a dramatic part of today's operating systems, it is easy to overlook the important role played by interpreters. First, emulation is a form of interpretation, and emulation is widely used today to avoid or postpone reprogramming. Second, much of the communication with a control program is carried on via commands that are interpreted by the control program. Third, on-line applications that consist mostly of tasks of modest size may find interpretation of a high-level language more satisfactory than compilation as a means of obtaining prompt responses.

Of all the trade-offs mentioned, this one balances the most precariously on hardware and software technologies and application environments. It appears that nonnumerical data processing is growing at a faster rate than numerical data processing, that digital simulation—a technique that simulates physical experiments with the aid of flow charts and random numbers—is growing faster than traditional numerical analysis, and that on-line applications heavily weighted with searching and editing tasks are growing faster than batch processing. The effects, if any, of these trends on the compile/interpret trade-off are far from clear.

The language area and the application environment have been changing so rapidly that the literature throws little empirical light on the subject. Questions can be raised, for example, with respect to programs that are seldom executed without changes or with respect to programs in which most of the processing time accrues in a few localized loops. Compiler designers have responded by reducing the cost of recompilation and by permitting programs to be compiled in modules, of which some can be optimized more thoroughly than others. Still another question concerns languages that permit vector operations; unless the operands are of small dimension, the interpretive overhead per component falls dramatically in vector operations.

**Generation versus examination.** To fashion a program that is general for a class of tasks, a program designer must provide for variations in relevant parameters and for options that lend the program utility under a variety of conditions. Assuming that the user specifies parameters and designates options at each execution of the program, there are two ways to design the general-purpose program. The first is to write a generator that can tailor a desired program from prefabricated segments; the generator acts just prior to program execution and then drops out of sight. The alternative is to build an *examiner* that consults parameters and option flags during the course of execution. Relative to an examiner, the generator yields a running program that is more frugal of memory space and execution time, but the generator requires more planning, may be more difficult to debug and document, and entails setup time.

This trade-off is closely akin to that for compilation and interpretation. A generator is a highly specialized compiler; an examiner is an interpreter for one complex operation. In practice, of course, the program designer may find it advantageous to combine both methods in the same design.

**Look-up versus arithmetic.** Most computations can be formulated in various ways, some of which depend more on preestablished tables than others. This permits a trade-off between table space and computation or, from the hardware designer's viewpoint, between memory and processing-unit circuitry. Because memory and circuit technologies have been advancing at fairly compatible rates, this balance has not undergone dramatic change in recent years.

**Space versus speed.** The famed trade-off of space versus speed is a concern in the design of programs for complex tasks. The more tables (programs and/or data) held in memory, the faster the task can be performed. As a result, one cannot simultaneously maximize speed and minimize memory usage. The trade-off takes its most excruciating form in the case of the control program, a nucleus of which resides in memory.

**System performance versus convenience.** By present standards, EDVAC was not convenient to use (although it was far more convenient than ENIAC). Since then, some of the gain in raw hardware speed has been tapped to enhance convenience. The problem with this trade-off is that it eludes crisp analysis. *Convenience* is a subjective term; were it not, it could be treated directly as one of the several variables in system performance. Moreover, system performance is difficult to evaluate in a weighted cost-of-living sense. The value of a digital system depends, at the very least, on convenience, reliability, job throughput, and selected response times—considerations that vary in importance from installation to installation and from job to job. It may also depend heavily on modularity, i.e., the capability to expand or contract as requirements change or technology offers improved system components.

An introduction to trade-offs can hope only to suggest the scope of the technical compromises that must be made in system design. Obviously, trade-off optimums can change over time as hardware and software technologies change and as applications move in new directions. Perhaps more significantly, the trade-offs we have been discussing are not independent. This complicates the design of digital systems because a "best" solution would presumably optimize the total design, and this could move some of the trade-offs away from their individual optimums. On the other hand, design is a discipline for informed decision, not a mathematical exercise. Since a "best" solution would take infinite amounts of effort and time, a state-of-the-art solution is simply one that makes rational use of available data and analytical methods.

## 11.3 Comment

Methods of organizing structurands, translating programs, allocating storage area, searching and sorting tables, sequencing tasks, encoding and decoding fragments of information, and performing arithmetic tasks fall within the scope of both *system design* and *computer science*. The basic difference in the two disciplines arises in their respective emphases and intentions. The system designers, i. e., computer designers, system programmers, and application programmers, are concerned with systems that exist now or may exist in the near future. The computer scientists are fundamentally interested in the digital systems that could conceivably exist at a later date. The system designers are beleaguered by today's algorithms and trade-offs; the computer scientists are charged to develop new methods and to upset old trade-offs.

A computer scientist cannot be an expert in many of the details of a digital system; increasingly, even the system designers have to be specialists. Furthermore, scientists usually elect to cut through detail in an attempt to get at the nub of a problem; they seek to understand simple principles thoroughly before generalizing. At times, computer science appears naive to the system designers. For example, computer scientists sometimes express bewilderment at the large numbers of man-years invested in complex programs, such as compilers or control programs. The experienced systems programmer, who understands the reasons fairly well, is desperately unhappy with the numbers; he would be gratified by more help from the computer scientists in reducing the numbers. Usually, of course, the scientist is not in a position to offer immediate help.

In developing a general-purpose computer or program, the computer designer or system programmer starts with state-of-the-art algorithms in the back of his mind. Because he is usually aware of more algorithms than he can use, he may unconsciously denigrate the significance of algorithms. He is first interested in who will use the system and under what equipment configurations, operating modes, response-time ranges, performance considerations, and language standards. He must combine empiricism and analysis to judge how general the system can be and still yield adequate performance over the assumed range of conditions. He must take pains to assure that the hardware or software will be feasible to debug, maintain, improve, document, teach, and use. Having done this much planning, he can go on to more detailed plans and specifications for functions and options and *interfaces*, i.e., conventions for communicating and coordinating with other units of the system. Well-wrought interfaces, with judicious flexibility for future growth in function, may govern the fate of the system more decisively than the choice of algorithms.

Although the system programmer is a latecomer, his problems are forcing themselves into recognition. The act of writing the program accounts for only a fraction of the cost of a general-purpose system program. Debugging, documentation, field maintenance, follow-on improvements in performance and function, and user education are not only important elements of cost, but they are activities in which the current state of the art leaves much to be desired. The documentation tends to become bulky because manuals are needed for various audiences and at various stages of development. These factors lead to publication and information-retrieval problems closely akin to those being experienced in many other technical fields. Confronted with such problems, the designers of data systems must increasingly turn for assistance to the data systems themselves—and to improved methods for program documentation, publication, information retrieval, computer-aided instruction, and the like.

We started in Chapter 1 with the tree diagram. Although a presentation of the tree diagram may contain some novelty, the underlying notion of structure is an old, old concept that has guided man in his classifications of knowledge. Our implicit thesis has been that a data system is the germ of a classification system that relies on modern methods of exploiting energy. The data system is still rudimentary in its functional scope because it rests on a young, hesitant technology for structuring and searching data, documenting procedures, and sequencing tasks. Nobody should venture to predict where the data system is going beyond a short horizon. But by chapter organization and subject emphasis, we have already betrayed our opinion concerning the disciplines that are likely to gain most rapidly in stature. The disciplines we have in mind are those that deal with the things modestly called tags, tables, and tasks.

*Appendix*

# REFERENCES

Works are listed year by year to highlight turning points in the evolution of the digital system. Within each year, documents are cited alphabetically by author or senior author. Periodical volume numbers are in bold face. Some of the sources are abbreviated as follows:

- *CACM* Communications of the Association for Computing Machinery
- *EJCC* Eastern Joint Computer Conference Proceedings (1951-1961)
- *FJCC* Fall Joint Computer Conference Proceedings (since 1962)
- *IBMJ* IBM Journal of Research and Development
- *IFIPS* Conference Proceedings of the International Federation of Information Processing Societies
- *JACM* Journal of the Association for Computing Machinery
- *MATC* Mathematical Tables and Other Aids to Computation
- *ONRS* Symposium on Automatic Programming, Office of Naval Research
- *PACM* Proceedings of the Annual Convention of the Association for Computing Machinery
- *SJCC* Spring Joint Computer Conference Proceedings (since 1962)
- *WJCC* Western Joint Computer Conference Proceedings (1953-1961)

It should be noted that in 1963 the Institute of Radio Engineers (IRE) and the American Institute of Electrical Engineers (AIEE) merged to become the Institute of Electrical and Electronics Engineers (IEEE). The Institution of Electrical Engineers (IEE) is a professional society in the United Kingdom. Since 1962, the proceedings of the joint computer conferences bear an AFIPS (American Federation of Information Processing Societies) volume number that is sometimes useful in document citation. For the SJCC, the numbers are 1962, 21; 1963, 23; 1964, 25; 1966, 28; 1967, 30; 1968, 32; and 1969, 34. For the FJCC, the numbers are 1962, 22; 1963, 24; 1964, 26; and 1965 through 1969, 27, 29, 31, 33, 35, respectively.

## Before 1945


George Boole, *An Investigation of the Laws of Thought*. London, 1854; Dover Publications, New York, 1951.

W. H. Eccles and F. W. Jordon, "A trigger relay utilising three-electrode thermionic vacuum tubes," *Radio Review* **1** (1919), 143-146.

W. J. Eckert, *Punched Card Methods in Scientific Computation.* The Thomas J. Watson Astronomical Computing Bureau, Columbia University, New York, 1940.

H. Hollerith, "An electric tabulating system," *The Quarterly*, Columbia University School of Mines, **10** (1889), 238-255.

E. V. Huntington, "Sets of independent postulates for the algebra of logic," *Transactions of the American Mathematical Society* **5** (1904), 288-309.

C. E. Shannon, "A symbolic analysis of relay and switching circuits," *Transactions of the AIEE* **57** (1938), 713-723.

1945

J. P. Eckert, Jr., and J. W. Mauchly, "Automatic high speed computing: a progress report on the EDVAC," Moore School of Electrical Engineering, University of Pennsylvania (September).

1946

H. H. Aiken and G. M. Hopper, "The automatic sequence controlled calculator," *Electrical Engineering* **65**, 384-391, 449-454, and 522-528.

A. W. Burks, H. H. Goldstine, and J. von Neumann, "Preliminary discussion of the logical design of an electronic computing instrument," Institute for Advanced Study, Princeton, N. J. (September). An edition is available in JvN's collected works, Volume V (cited under 1963).

H. H. Goldstine and A. Goldstine, "The electronic numerical integrator and computer (ENIAC)," *MTAC* **2**, 97-110.

*The Moore School Lectures.* A four-volume set of lectures on computer principles and technology given at the Moore School of Electrical Engineering, July 8-August 31, 1946. For additional information, see W. W. Youden (cited under 1965).

1947

H. H. Goldstine and J. von Neumann, "Planning and coding of problems for an electronic computing instrument," Part II, Volume 1, Institute for Advanced Study, Princeton, N. J. Available in JvN's collected works (cited under 1963).

S. B. Williams, "A relay computer for general application," *Bell Laboratory Record* **25**, 49-54.

1948

H. H. Goldstine and J. von Neumann, "Planning and coding for an electronic computing instrument," Part II, Volumes 2 and 3, Institute for Advanced Study, Princeton, N. J. Available in JvN's collected works (cited under 1963).

1949

Staff of the Moore School of Electrical Engineering, *Functional Description of the EDVAC.* University of Pennsylvania Research Division Report 50-9 (two volumes).

F. C. Williams and T. Kilburn, "A storage system for use with binary-digital computing machines," *Proceedings of the Institution of Electrical Engineers* **96**, Part 3, 81-100.

B. H. Worsley, "Demonstration of the EDSAC," *Report of a Conference on High Speed Automatic Calculating Machines*, University Mathematical Laboratory, Cambridge, England (June) pp. 12-17.

1950

A. Cohen, "Magnetic drum storage for digital information processing systems," *MTAC* **4**, 31-39.

R. W. Hamming, "Error detecting and error correcting codes," *Bell Systems Technical Journal* **29**, 147-160.

Staff of Engineering Research Associates, Inc., *High Speed Computing Devices.* McGraw-Hill, New York.

1951

J. P. Eckert, Jr., J. R. Weiner, H. F. Welsh, and H. F. Mitchell, "The UNIVAC system," *EJCC*, 6-14.

J.W. Forrester,"Digital information storage in three dimensions using magnetic cores," *Journal of Applied Physics* **22**, 44-48.

W. Keister, A. E. Ritchie, and S. H. Washburn, *The Design of Switching Circuits.* D. van Nostrand, Princeton, N. J.

J. Lukasiewicz, *Aristotle's Syllogistic from the Standpoint of Modern Formal Logic.* Oxford University Press, New York.

Staff of the Computation Laboratory, Harvard University, *Synthesis of Electronic Computing and Control Circuits.* Harvard University Press, Cambridge, Mass.

M. V. Wilkes, D. J. Wheeler, and S. Gill, *The Preparation of Programs for an Electronic Digital Computer.* Addison-Wesley, Reading, Mass.

1952

G. Estrin, "A description of the electronic computer at the Institute for Advanced Studies," *PACM*, 95-109.

D. A. Huffman, "A method for the construction of minimum-redundancy codes," *IRE Proceedings* **40**, 1098-1101.

W. V. O. Quine, "The problem of simplifying truth functions," *American Mathematical Monthly* **59**, 521-531.

R. K. Ridgway, "Compiling routines," *PACM*, 1-5.

Society of Actuaries, *Report of the Committee on New Recording Means and Computing Devices.*

E. W. Veitch, "A chart method for simplifying truth functions," *PACM*, 127–133.

1953

W. Buchholz, "The system design of the IBM Type 701 Computer," *IRE Proceedings* **41**, 1262–1275.

M. E. Davis, "The use of electronic data processing in the life insurance business," *EJCC*, 11–17.

M. Karnaugh, "The map method for synthesis of combinational logic circuits," *AIEE Transactions* **72**, 593–599.

W. N. Papian, "The MIT magnetic-core memory," *EJCC*, 37–42.

N. Rochester, "Symbolic programming," *IRE Transactions* **EC-2**, 10–15.

M. V. Wilkes and J. B. Stringer, "Microprogramming and the design of the control circuits in an electronic digital computer," *Proceedings of the Cambridge Philosophical Society* **49**, Part 2, 230–238.

1954

C. W. Adams and J. H. Laning, Jr., "The M. I. T. systems of automatic coding: Comprehensive, summer session, and algebraic," *ONRS*, 40–68 (May).

J. W. Backus and H. Herrick, "IBM 701 Speedcoding and other automatic-programming systems," *ONRS*, 106–113.

C. J. Bashe, W. Buchholz, and N. Rochester, "The IBM Type 702, an electronic data processing machine for business," *JACM* **1**, 149–169.

A. W. Burks, D. W. Warren, and J. B. Wright, "An analysis of a logical machine using parenthesis-free notation," *MTAC* **8**, 53–57.

F. E. Hamilton and E. C. Kubie, "The IBM Magnetic Drum Calculator Type 650," *JACM* **1**, 13–20.

F. E. Holberton, "Application of automatic coding to logical processes," *ONRS*, 34–39.

H. G. Kahrimanian, "Analytical differentiation by a digital computer," *ONRS*, 6–14.

N. B. Moser, "Compiler method of automatic programming," *ONRS*, 15–21.

1955

B. Gilchrist, J. H. Pomerene, and S. Y. Wong, "Fast carry logic for digital computers," *IRE Transactions* **EC-4**, 133–136.

W. V. O. Quine, "A way to simplify truth functions," *American Mathematical Monthly* **62**, 627–631.

R. K. Richards, *Arithmetic Operations in Digital Computers.* D. Van Nostrand, Princeton, N. J.

1956

E. H. Friend, "Sorting on electronic computer systems," *JACM* 3, 134-168.

R. A. Henle, "High speed transistor computer circuit design," *EJCC*, 64-66.

E. J. McCluskey, Jr., "Minimization of Boolean functions," *Bell System Technical Journal* 35, 1417-1444.

J. Mersel, "Program interruption on the Univac scientific computer," *WJCC*, 52.

G. J. Prom and R. L. Crosby, "Junction transistor switching circuits for high-speed digital computer applications," *IRE Transactions* EC-5, 192-196.

A. Weinberger and J. L. Smith, "A one-microsecond adder using one-megacycle circuitry," *IRE Transactions* EC-5, 65-73.

1957

J. W. Backus, R. J. Beeber, S. Best, R. Goldberg, L. M. Haibt, H. L. Herrick, R. A. Nelson, D. Sayre, P. B. Sheridan, H. Stern, I. Ziller, R. A. Hughes, and R. Nutt, "The FORTRAN automatic coding system," *WJCC*, 188-198.

F. P. Brooks, Jr., "A program-controlled program interruption system," *EJCC*, 128-131.

R. R. Everett, C. A. Zraket, and H. D. Benington, "SAGE, a data-processing system for air defense," *EJCC*, 148-155.

J. W. Forgie, "The Lincoln TX-2 input-output system," *WJCC*, 156-160.

E. D. Foss and R. S. Partridge, "A 32,000-word magnetic-core memory," *IBMJ* 1, 102-109.

D. D. McCracken, *Digital Computer Programming.* Wiley, New York.

A. Newell and J. C. Shaw, "Programming the logic theory machine," *WJCC*, 230-240.

T. Noyes and W. E. Dickinson, "The random-access memory accounting machine: part II, the magnetic-disk random-access memory," *IBMJ* 1, 72-75.

W. W. Peterson, "Addressing for random-access storage," *IBMJ* 1, 130-146.

R. K. Richards, *Digital Computer Components and Circuits.* D. Van Nostrand, Princeton, N. J.

P. R. Vance, L. G. Dooley, and C. E. Diss, "Operation of the SAGE duplex computers," *EJCC*, 160-163.

E. L. Younker, "A transistor-driven magnetic-core memory," *IRE Transactions* EC-6, 14-20.

H. S. Yourke and E. J. Slobodzinski, "Millimicrosecond transistor current switching techniques," *WJCC*, 68-72.

1958

J. V. Blankenbaker, "Logically microprogrammed computers," *IRE Transactions* EC-7, 103-109.

W. H. Burge, "Sorting, trees, and measures of order," *Information and Control* **1**, 181-197.

S. H. Caldwell, *Switching Circuits and Logical Design.* Wiley, New York.

W. P. Heising, "Methods of file organization for efficient use of IBM RAMAC files," *WJCC*, 194-196.

M. Phister, Jr., *Logical Design of Digital Computers.* Wiley, New York.

G. E. Poorte and A. S. Kranzley, "The RCA 501 Electronic Data Processing System," *WJCC*, 66-69.

J. C. Shaw, A. Newell, H. A. Simon, and T. O. Ellis, "A command structure for complex information processing," *WJCC*, 119-127.

S. H. Unger, "A computer oriented toward spatial problems," *WJCC*, 234-238.

1959

G. A. Blaauw, "Indexing and control-word techniques," *IBMJ* **3**, 288-301.

R. de la Briandais, "File searching using variable length keys," *WJCC*, 295-298.

H. L. Gray and C. Harrison, Jr., "Normalized floating-point arithmetic with an index of significance," *EJCC*, 244-248.

P. Hildebrandt and H. Isbitz, "Radix exchange—an internal sorting method for computers," *JACM* **6**, 156-163.

N. Lourie, H. Schrimpf, R. Reach, and W. Kahn, "Arithmetic and control techniques in a multiprogram computer," *EJCC*, 75-81.

H. Nagler, "Amphisbaenic sorting," *JACM* **6**, 459-468.

H. B. Newcombe, J. M. Kennedy, S. J. Axford, and A. P. James, "Automatic linkage of vital records," *Science* **130**, 954-959.

D. L. Shell, "A high speed sorting procedure," *CACM* **2**, 30-32, July.

1960

J. Backus, "The syntax and semantics of the proposed international algebraic language of the Zurich ACM-GAMM conference," *Proceedings of the International Conference on Information Processing*, UNESCO, pp. 125-132. R. Oldenbourgh, Munich; Butterworth, London, (1960).

A. H. Cockayne and E. Hyde, "Prime number coding for information retrieval," *Computer Journal* 3, 21-22.

E. F. Codd, "Multiprogramming scheduling," *CACM* 3, 347-350 and 413-418.

D. E. Ferguson, "Fibonaccian searching," *CACM* 3, 648-649.

R. L. Gilstad, "Polyphase merge sorting—an advanced technique," *EJCC*, 143-148.

A. W. Holt, "Over-all computation control and labelling," *CACM* 3, 614-615.

R. B. Lazarus and R. M. Frank, "A high-speed sorting procedure," *CACM* 3, 20-22.

D. P. Masher, "The design of diode-transistor NOR circuits," *IRE Transactions* EC-**9**, 15–25.

M. D. McIlroy, "Macro instruction extensions of compiler languages," *CACM* **3**, 214–220.

P. Naur (ed.), J. W. Backus, F. L. Bauer, J. Green, C. Katz, J. McCarthy, A. J. Perlis, H. Rutishauser, K. Samelson, B. Vanquois, J. H. Wegstein, A. van Wijngaarden, and M. Woodger, "Report on the algorithmic language ALGOL 60," *CACM* **3**, 299–314.

G. W. Patterson, "What is a code?" *CACM* **3**, 315–318.

A. J. Perlis and C. Thornton, "Symbol manipulation by threaded lists," *CACM* **3**, 195–204.

P. F. Windley, "Trees, forests and rearranging," *Computer Journal* **3**, 84-88.

1961

R. S. Barton, "A new approach to the functional design of a digital computer," *WJCC*, 393–396.

J. Fotheringham, "Dynamic storage allocation in the Atlas computer, including an automatic use of a backing store," *CACM* **4**, 435–436.

W. P. Heising and R. A. Larner, "A semi-automatic storage allocation system at loading time," *CACM* **4**, 446–449.

L. R. Johnson, "An indirect chaining method for addressing on secondary keys," *CACM* **4**, 218–221.

W. Lonergan and P. King, "Design of the B5000 system," *Datamation* **7**, 28–32 (May).

O. L. MacSorley, "High-speed arithmetic in binary computers," *IRE Proceedings* **49**, 67–91.

R. E. Nather, "On the compilation of subscripted variables," *CACM* **4**, 169–171.

W. W. Peterson, *Error Correcting Codes*. Wiley, New York.

W. W. Peterson and D. T. Brown, "Cyclic codes for error detection," *IRE Proceedings* **49**, 228–235.

S. W. Reynolds, "A generalized polyphase merge algorithm," *CACM* **4**, 347–349.

1962

W. Buchholz (ed.), *Planning a Computer System*. McGraw-Hill, New York.

W. C. Carter, "Mathematical analysis of merge sorting techniques," *IFIPS Proceedings*, 62–66.

Y. Chu, *Digital Computer Design Fundamentals*. McGraw-Hill, New York.

A. D. Falkoff, "Algorithms for parallel-search memories," *JACM* **9**, 488–511.

J. C. Gower, "The handling of multiway tables on computers," *Computer Journal* **4**, 280–286.

A. C. D. Haley, "The KDF. 9 computer system," *FJCC*, 108-120.

C. L. Hamblin, "Translation to and from Polish notation," *Computer Journal* **5**, 210-213.

T. N. Hibbard, "Some combinatorial properties of certain trees with applications to searching and sorting," *JACM* **9**, 13-28.

J. K. Iliffe and J. G. Jodeit, "A dynamic storage allocation scheme," *Computer Journal* **5**, 200-209.

K. E. Iverson, *A Programming Language*. Wiley, New York.

K. E. Iverson, "A common language for hardware, software, and applications," *FJCC*, 121-129.

T. Kilburn, D. B. G. Edwards, M. J. Lanigan, and F. H. Sumner, "One-level storage system," *IRE Transactions* **EC-11**, 223-235.

A. G. Mendoza, "A dispersion pass algorithm for the polyphase merge," *CACM* **6**, 502-504.

J. E. Sammet, "Basic elements of COBOL 61," *CACM* **6**, 237-253.

G. Schay, Jr., and W. G. Spruth, "Analysis of a file addressing method," *CACM* **6**, 459-469.

R. R. Seeber and A. B. Lindquist, "Associative memory with ordered retrieval," *IBMJ* **6**, 126-136.

S. Sobel, "Oscillating sort—a new sort merging technique," *JACM* **9**, 372-374.

1963

"American standard code for information exchange," *CACM* **7**, 422-426.

H. J. Bowlden, "A list-type storage technique for alphameric information," *CACM* **6**, 433-434.

F. J. Corbato and V. A. Vyssotsky, "Introduction and overview of the MULTICS system," *FJCC*, 185-197.

H. J. Gray, *Digital Computer Engineering*. Prentice-Hall, Englewood Cliffs, N. J.

D. E. Knuth, "Length of strings for a merge sort," *CACM* **6**, 685-687.

G. A. Maley and J. Earle, *The Logic Design of Transistor Digital Computers*. Prentice-Hall, Englewood Cliffs, N. J.

G. H. Mealy, "A Generalized Assembly System," Memorandum RM-3646-PR, The RAND Corp., Santa Monica, California.

E. H. Sussenguth, Jr., "Use of tree structures for processing files," *CACM* **7**, 272-279.

I. A. Sutherland, "Sketchpad, a man-machine graphical communication system," *SJCC*, 329-346.

*John von Neumann: Collected Works*, Volume V. Macmillan, New York.

1964

G. M. Amdahl, "The structure of System/360, Part III, Processing unit design considerations," *IBM Systems Journal* **3**, 144-164.

J. P. Anderson, "A note on some compiling algorithms," *CACM* **7**, 149-150.

C. W. Bachman and S. B. Williams, "A general purpose programming system for random-access memories," *FJCC*, 411-422.

G. A. Blaauw and F. P. Brooks, Jr., "The structure of System/360, Part I, Outline of the logical structure," *IBM Systems Journal* **3**, 119-135.

H. A. Clampett, Jr., "Randomized binary searching with tree structures," *CACM* **7**, 163-165.

W. T. Comfort, "Multiword list items," *CACM* **7**, 357-372.

E. M. Davis, W. E. Harding, R. S. Schwartz, and J. J. Corning, "Solid logic technology: versatile, high-performance microelectronics," *IBMJ* **8**, 102-114.

A. D. Falkoff, K. E. Iverson, and E. H. Sussenguth, Jr., "A formal description of System/360," *IBM Systems Journal* **3**, 198-262.

D. J. Farber, R. E. Griswold, and I. P. Polansky, "Snobol: a string manipulation language," *JACM* **11**, 21-30.

H. Hellerman, "Experimental personalized array translator system," *CACM* **7**, 433-438.

H. A. Kinslow, "The time-sharing monitor system," *FJCC*, 433-454.

H. S. Miller, "Resolving multiple responses in an associative memory," *IEEE Transactions* **EC-13**, 614-616.

A. Padegs, "The structure of System/360, Part IV, Channel design considerations," *IBM Systems Journal* **3**, 165-180.

C. J. Shaw, "On declaring arbitrarily coded alphabets," *CACM* **7**, 288-290.

W. Y. Stevens, "The structure of System/360, Part II, System implementations," *IBM Systems Journal* **3**, 136-143.

P. Wegner (ed.), *Introduction to System Programming*. Academic Press, New York.

1965

J. P. Anderson, "Program structures for parallel processing," *CACM* **8**, 786-788.

J. B. Dennis, "Segmentation and the design of multiproprammed computer systems," *JACM* **12**, 589-602.

B. J. Dzubak and C. R. Warburton, "The organization of structured files," *CACM* **8**, 446-452.

W. B. Elmore and G. J. Evans, Jr., "Dynamic control of core memory in a real-time system," *IFIPS Proceedings*, Part 1, 261-266.

E. L. Glazer, J. F. Couleur, and G. A. Oliver, "Description of the GE 645," *FJCC*, 197-202.

D. J. Gluck, "A chemical structure storage and search system developed at Du Pont," *Journal of Chemical Documentation* **5**, 43-51.

K. Lock, "Structuring programs for multiprogram time-sharing on-line applications," *FJCC*, 457-472.

J. Martin, *Programming Real Time Systems*. Prentice-Hall, Englewood Cliffs, N. J.

J. Nievergelt, "On the automatic simplification of computer programs," *CACM* **8**, 366-370.

G. Radin and H. P. Rogoway, "NPL: highlights of a new programming language," *CACM* **8**, 9-17.

C. V. Ramamoorthy, "Code structures for protection and manipulation of variable-length items," *CACM* **8**, 35-38.

S. G. Tucker, "Emulation of large systems," *CACM* **8**, 753-761.

V. A. Vyssotsky, F. J. Corbato, and R. M. Graham, "Structure of the Multics supervisor," *FJCC*, 203-212.

W. W. Youden, "Computer literature bibliography, 1946 to 1963." *National Bureau of Standards Miscellaneous Publication* 266. Provides convenient access to over 6100 references (in 463 pages).

1966

J. H. Bryant and P. Semple, Jr., "GIS and file management," *PACM*, 97-107.

W. A. Clark, "The functional structure of OS/360, Part III, Data management," *IBM Systems Journal* **5**, 12-29.

H. Hellerman, "Parallel processing of algebraic expressions," *IEEE Transactions* **EC-15**, 82-91.

F. E. Hohn, *Applied Boolean Algebra, An Elementary Introduction* (2nd edition). Macmillan, New York.

K. E. Iverson, *Elementary Functions: An Algorithmic Treatment*. Science Research Associates, Chicago.

G. H. Mealy, "The functional structure of OS/360, Part I, Introductory survey," *IBM Systems Journal* **5**, 3-11.

J. L. Ryan, R. L. Crandall, and M. C. Medwedeff, "A conversational system for incremental compilation and execution in a time-sharing environment," *FJCC*, 1-21.

G. Salton, "Data manipulation and programming problems in automatic information retrieval," *CACM* **9**, 204-210.

P. H. Seaman, R. A. Lind, and T. L. Wilson, "On teleprocessing system design, Part IV, An analysis of auxiliary storage activity," *IBM Systems Journal* **5**, 158-170.

P. M. Sherman, "FLOWTRACE, a computer program for flowcharting programs," *CACM* **9**, 845-854.

E. B. Van Horn and J. B. Dennis, "Programming semantics for multiprogrammed computations," *CACM* **9**, 143-155.

B. I. Witt, "The functional structure of OS/360, Part II, Job and task management," *IBM Systems Journal* **5**, 12–29.

1967

G. R. Blackney, L. R. Cudney, and C. R. Eickhorn, "An application-oriented multiprocessing system, Part II, design characteristics of the 9020 system," *IBM Systems Journal* **6**, 80–94.

R. E. Bleier, "Treating hierarchical data structures in the SDC time-shared data management system (TDMS)," *PACM*, 41–49.

P. J. Dixon and J. Sable, "DM-1, a generalized data management system," *SJCC*, 185–198.

G. W. Ernst and A. Newell, "Some issues of representation in a general problem solver," *SJCC*, 583–600.

D. C. Evans and J. Y. Leclerc, "Address mapping and the control of access in an interactive computer," *SJCC*, 23–30.

B. J. Gassner, "Sorting by replacement selecting," *CACM* **10**, 358–367.

D. H. Gibson, "Considerations in block-oriented systems design," *SJCC*, 75–80.

H. H. Hellerman, *Digital Computer System Principles*. McGraw-Hill, New York.

B. Higman, *A Comparative Study of Programming Languages*. American Elsevier, New York.

H. W. Lawson, Jr., "PL/I list processing," *CACM* **10**, 358–367.

J. Minker and J. Sable, "File organization and data management," Ch. 5 of C. A. Cuadra (ed.) "*Annual Review of Information Science and Technology*, Vol. 2. Wiley, New York.

M. C. Pease, "Matrix inversion using parallel processing," *JACM* **14**, 757–764.

H. E. Peterson and R. Turn, "System implications of information privacy," *SJCC*, 291–300.

S. Rosen (ed.), *Programming Systems and Languages*. McGraw-Hill, New York.

H. Schorr and W. M. Waite, "An efficient machine-independent procedure for garbage collection in various list structures," *CACM* **10**, 501–506.

G. S. Shedler, "Parallel numerical methods for the solution of equations," *CACM* **10**, 286–291.

D. C. Stenga, "Univac 1108 multiprocessor system," *SJCC*, 67–74.

S. G. Tucker, "Microprogram control for System/360," *IBM Systems Journal* **6**, 222–241.

A. Van Dam and D. Evans, "A compact data structure for storing, retrieving and manipulating line drawings," *SJCC*, 601–610.

1968

ACM Curriculum Committee on Computer Science, "Curriculum 68: recommendations for academic programs in computer science," *CACM* **11**, 151–197. Contains many annotated references.

W. L. Ash and E. H. Sibley, "TRAMP: an interpretive associative processor with deductive capabilities," *PACM*, 143-156.

K. Bandat, "On the formal definition of PL/I," *SJCC*, 363-373.

G. Barnes, R. Brown, M. Kato, D. Kuck, D. Slotnick, and R. Stokes, "The ILLIAC IV computer," *IEEE Transactions* **EC-17**, 758-770.

A. Bayes, "A generalized partial pass block sort," *CACM* **11**, 491-493.

E. W. Dijkstra, "The structure of the 'THE' multiprogramming system," *CACM* **11**, 341-346.

J. Feldman and D. Gries, "Translator writing systems," *CACM* **11**, 77-113.

J. C. Jodeit, "Storage organization in programming systems," *CACM* **11**, 741-746.

D.E. Knuth, *The Art of Computer Programming*, Volume 1, *Fundamental Algorithms*. Addison-Wesley, Reading, Mass.

A. S. Lett and W. L. Konigsford, "TSS/360: a time-shared operating system," *FJCC*, 15-28.

R. Morris, "Scatter storage techniques," *CACM* **11**, 38-43.

R. J. Pankhurst, "Program overlay techniques," *CACM* **11**, 119-125.

B. Randell and C. J. Kuehner, "Dynamic storage allocation systems," *CACM* **11**, 297-306.

P. Wegner, *Programming Languages, Information Structures, and Machine Organization*. McGraw-Hill, New York.

M. V. Wilkes, *Time-Sharing Computing Systems*. American Elsevier, New York.

1969

N. E. Abel, P. P. Budnik, D. J. Kuck, Y. Muraoka, R. S. Northcote, and R. B. Wilhelmson, "TRANQUIL: a language for an array processing computer," *SJCC*, 57-73.

S. R. Arora and W. T. Dent, "Randomized binary search technique," *CACM* **12**, 77-80.

L. W. Cotten, "Maximum-rate pipeline systems," *SJCC*, 581-586.

G. G. Dodd, "Elements of data management systems," *Computing Surveys* **1**, 117-133.

A. G. Frazer, "Integrity of a mass storage filing system," *Computer Journal* **12**, 1-5.

S. P. Ghosh and M. E. Senko, "File organization: on the selection of random access index points for sequential files," *JACM* **16**, 569-579.

M. M. Gold, "Time-sharing and batch processing: an experimental comparison of their values in a problem-solving situation," *CACM* **12**, 249-259.

F. Gruenberger (ed.), *Critical Factors in Data Management*. Prentice-Hall, Englewood Cliffs, N. J.

P. E. Jackson and C. D. Stubbs, "A study of multiaccess computer communications," *SJCC*, 491-504.

H. Katzan, Jr., "Batch, conversational, and incremental compilers," *SJCC*, 47-56.

R. H. Kay, "The management and organization of large scale software development projects," *SJCC*, 425-433.

D. Lefkovitz, *File Structures for On-Line Systems*. Spartan Books, New York.

E. S. Lowry and C. W. Medlock, "Object code optimization," *CACM* **12**, 13-22.

A. C. McKellar and E. G. Coffman, Jr., "Organizing matrices and matrix operations for paged memory systems," *CACM* **12**, 153-165.

J. M. McKinney, "A survey of analytical time-sharing models," *Computing Surveys* **1**, 105-116.

D. L. Parnas, "More on simulation languages and design methodology for computer systems," *SJCC*, 739-743.

Y. N. Patt, "Variable length tree structures having minimum average search time," *CACM* **12**, 72-76.

R. R. Redziejowski, "On arithmetic expressions and trees," *CACM* **12**, 81-84.

J. F. Ruggiero and D. A. Coryell, "An auxiliary processing system for array calculations," *IBM Systems Journal* **8**, 118-135.

J. E. Sammet, *Programming Languages: History and Fundamentals*. Prentice-Hall, Englewood Cliffs, N. J.

J. R. Slagle and J. K. Dixon, "Experiments with some programs that search game trees," *JACM* **16**, 189-207.

L. J. Woodrum, "Internal sorting with minimal comparing," *IBM Systems Journal* **8**, 189-203.

# INDEX

## M



## N



## O

## Y



## Z